# HITLER'S CHILDREN

Gerhard Rempel

# HITLER'S CHILDREN

## The Hitler Youth and the SS

**The University of North Carolina Press**

Chapel Hill and London

The paper in this book meets the guidelines for
permanence and durability of the Committee on
Production Guidelines for Book Longevity of
the Council on Library Resources.

93 92 91 90      5 4 3 2


Library of Congress Cataloging-in-Publication Data

Rempel, Gerhard.
    Hitler's children.

    Bibliography: p.
    Includes index.
    1. Hitlerjugend.   2. Waffen-SS.
3. National-sozialistische Deutsche
Arbeiter-Partei. Schutzstaffel.
I. Title.
DD253.5.R4     1989      943.086      88-28036
ISBN 0-8078-1841-0 (alk. paper)
ISBN 0-8078-4299-0 (pbk.: alk. paper)

For Ann, Hans, and Lise

# Contents

# Tables

# Illustrations

# Preface

This book has been long in the making. Since Professor Robert Koehl first suggested the idea as a dissertation topic, there have been a number of changes. While this has not been a labor of love in any sense of that phrase, it has been a compelling topic in more ways than one. The aftermath of the Third Reich is still very much with us and from time to time surfaces in the attention of the general public, as in the Hitler diary hoax and the Bitburg controversy. A recent visit to the Yad Vashem Memorial in Jerusalem made me keenly aware of how immanent still is the frightful legacy of Hitler and his generation of young disciples. I have attempted to be as objective as it is possible to be, assigning responsibility where evidence clearly indicates it, and avoiding sweeping moralization. Melita Maschmann, Alfons Heck, and Horst Krüger, whose memoirs strike me as particularly authentic, remind us all how easy it was for young people to become entangled in the phenomenon of their time. In that sense I hope this book will serve both sound scholarly purposes and as a cautionary tale against political impetuosity at any age. Simplistic solutions to the problem of socialization, always fraught with emotional and psychological pitfalls, are not the exclusive preserve of the Nazi mentality.

Many individuals have aided and supported my efforts. Robert Koehl, who introduced me to the profession, has been a solid supporter, shrewd advisor, and good friend. I owe him more than he realizes. The late Harold Gordon gave an early version of the book a thorough examination and made many useful suggestions. Professor Theodore S. Hamerow has been more than kind in his advice and support. I should also like to thank Robert Bock, Alan Bosch, Frank Broderick, George Browder, Fred Brown, Albert Carter, Beaumont Herman, Harold Heye, Claudia Koonz, Patricia Miller, Richard Reed, Ronald Smelser, Peter Stachura, Charles Sydnor, Bernd Wegner, James Weingartner, Michael Wells, and Rachel Wilcox, who, in different ways, gave useful advice and needed encouragement. The late Richard Bauer of the Berlin Document Center was most helpful in providing copies of otherwise unavailable documents. Over the years Robert Wolf of the National Archives has never failed to provide assistance.

Without the services of an efficient interlibrary loan system books like this could not be written. The staff of D'Amour Library at Western New England College, especially Suzanne Garber, Olive Lambert, Kay McGrath, and May Stack, went beyond the call of professional duty to respond to my numerous and impatient requests for often esoteric printed sources. My wife Ann and my children Hans and Lise have for years patiently tolerated my preoccupations and deserve as much credit for the conclusion of this project as I do. Finally, I should like to thank the readers and editors, especially Lewis Bateman, Ron Maner, and Margaret Morse, who gave the manuscript painstaking attention and made many helpful suggestions. What errors of fact and judgment remain are of course entirely my own.

Longmeadow, Massachusetts
September 1988

# Abbreviations

The following party and organization abbreviations are used in the text.

AHS    Adolf-Hitler-Schule (Adolf Hitler School)
A-SS    Allgemeine-SS (General SS)
BDM    Bund Deutscher Mädel (Association of German Girls)
DAF    Deutsche Arbeits-Front (German Labor Front)
DJ    Deutsches Jungvolk (German Young Folk)
DRL    Deutscher Reichsbund für Leibesübungen (National Association for Physical Exercise)
DVL    Deutsche Volksliste (German Nationality List)
EWZ    Einwandererzentralstelle (Immigration Center)
FdV    Festigung deutschen Volkstums (Strengthening of Germandom)
Gestapo    Geheime Staats-Polizei (Secret State Police)
HJ    Hitlerjugend (Hitler Youth)
HJD    Hitler Youth Division (12. SS Panzerdivision)
HSSPF    Höhere SS und Polizei Führer (Superior SS and Police Leader)
JM    Jungmädelgruppen (Young Girls Groups)
JV    Jungvolk (Young Folk)
KJVD    Kommunistischer Jugendverband Deutschlands (Communist Youth Association of Germany)
KLV    Kinderlandverschickung (Evacuation of Children)
KPD    Kommunistische Partei Deutschlands (Communist Party of Germany)
KRIPO    Kriminalpolizei (Criminal Police)
LD    Landdienst (Land Service)
LKPA    Landeskriminalpolizeiamt (Prussian Criminal Police Office)
LSSAH    Leibstandarte SS Adolf Hitler (SS Body Guard Adolf Hitler)
NAPOLA    National-Politische Lehranstalt (State Political High School)
NCO    Non-commissioned officer
NSDAP    Nationalsozialistische Deutsche Arbeiterpartei (National Socialist German Workers Party)
NSF    Nationalsozialistische Frauenschaften (Nazi Women's Association)
NSFK    Nationalsozialistischer Flieger-Korps (Nazi Aviation Corps)
NSKK    Nationalsozialistischer Kraftfahrer-Korps (Nazi Motor Corps)
NSS    Nationalsozialistischer Schülerbund (Nazi Pupils League)
NSV    Nationalsozialistische Volkswohlfahrt (Nazi Welfare Organization)
OKH    Oberkommando des Heeres (Supreme Command of the Army)
OKW    Oberkommando der Wehrmacht (Supreme Command of the Armed Forces)
ORPO    Ordnungspolizei (Order Police or regular police)
RAD    Reichsarbeitsdienst (National Labor Service)
RAL    Reichsausbildungslager (National Training Camps)

RJF   Reichsjugendführung (National Youth Directorate)

RKFDV   Reichskommissar für die Festigung Deutschen Volkstums (National Commissariat for the Strengthening of Germandom)

RSHA   Reichssicherheitshaupamt (Central Security Agency)

RuSHA   Rasse- und Siedlungs Hauptamt (Race and Settlement Main Office)

SA   Sturmabteilung (Storm Troops)

SAJ   Verband der Sozialistischen Arbeiterjugend (Association of Socialist Workers Youth)

SD   Sicherheitsdienst (Security Service)

SIPO   Sicherheitspolizei (Security Police)

SPD   Sozialdemokratische Partei Deutschlands (Social Democratic Party of Germany)

SRD   Streifendienst (Patrol Service)

SS   Schutzstaffeln (Elite Echelon)

SSEA   SS-Ergänzungsamt (SS Recruiting Office)

SSHA   SS-Hauptamt (Central SS Office)

SSHK   SS-Helferinnen Korps (SS Female Assistance Corps)

SSTV   SS-Totenkopfverbände (SS Death's Head Units)

SSVT   SS-Verfügungstruppe (SS Special Duty Troops)

TDT   Tank Destroyer Troop of the Hitler Youth

VDA   Verein für das Volkstum im Ausland (Association for Germans Abroad)

VoMi   Volksdeutsche Mittelstelle (Ethnic German Liaison Office)

WBK   Wehrbezirkskommando (Military Recruiting Subdistrict Headquarters)

WEL   Wehrertüchtigungslager (Premilitary Training Camps)

W-SS   Waffen-SS (Combat SS)

For source abbreviations used in the appendix and notes see pages 275–76.

# HITLER'S CHILDREN

# 1 | Introduction

Hitler remained an eternal adolescent:
gauche, sprung from modest circumstances,
never at ease in his polished shoes.
—Saul Friedländer

A whole generation of Germans born in the first third of this century became identified with Adolf Hitler in one way or another. Thousands were absorbed by his dynamic movement before 1933, and millions joined his party after he became chancellor. Additional millions involved themselves to a greater or lesser degree in the multifarious activities of more than two dozen party affiliates, auxiliaries, and more loosely associated organizations. In a broad sense, all Germans were affected by the Nazi movement between 1933 and 1945, even though their thoughts and daily lives may not have been entirely determined by official ideology and policy. Those for whom the latter might have been true were to be found in the inner core of political functionaries and in the prominent party formations. For some 10 million young members of this generation—between the ages of ten and eighteen at the beginning of World War II—Adolf Hitler held a special identity, since the organization to which they belonged had adopted his name as their own. Whether they joined freely or by force of law, whether they believed fully in the Führer's cause or merely said they did because everyone else seemed to say so, whether they actively promoted nazism or actively resisted it, they were all members of the Hitler Youth generation.[1]

From the start of his political career in Munich after World War I to the final bizarre moments in his Berlin bunker, Hitler was obsessed with youth as a political force in history.[2] He expressed it dramatically to Hermann Rauschning in 1933: "I am beginning with the young. We older ones are used up. . . . We are rotten to the marrow. We have no unrestrained instincts left. We are cowardly and sentimental. We are bearing the burden of a humiliating past, and have in our blood the dull recollection of serfdom and servility. But my magnificent youngsters! Are there finer ones any-

1

where in the world? Look at these young men and boys! What material! With them I can make a new world." He went on to draw a stark and primitive picture of "a violently active, dominating, intrepid, brutal youth" from which he rightfully thought the world would "shrink back."[3]

Most of Hitler's boys never reached the "ripe manhood" he thought would result when his inhumane prescriptions were implemented. Millions of Hitler's children learned how to die before they had learned how to live. For the survivors disillusionment, despair, and deprivation became the harvest of a generation. It was expressed poignantly by one member of this generation, Wolfgang Borchert: "We are a generation without adhesion and without depth. Our depth is an abyss. We are the generation without happiness, without home and without farewell. Our sun is small, our love cruel, and our youth is without youth. We are the generation without boundary, without restraint and protection— expelled from the orbit of childhood into a world prepared by those who despise us. They gave us no God who could have captured our hearts when the winds of this world swirled about us. So we are the generation without God, for we are the generation without an anchor, without a past, without recognition."[4]

Few of Borchert's cohorts have told their stories in print.[5] The collective experience of his generation as such has not been written because the sources are sparse and the concept of historical generation lacks precision.[6] Since the Hitlerjugend (HJ) was not an independent organization, it must be understood in the context of national socialism as a movement composed of various functional segments or affiliates. The structural complexity of this movement and the inhuman deeds perpetrated in its name have produced a literature so vast and a diversity of interpretation so diffuse that no consensus is in sight.[7] If there is agreement on any one characteristic, it must be that it was youthful in its origins and remained so, in relative terms, to the end.[8]

The social, political, and military resiliency of the Third Reich is inconceivable without the HJ. It was the incubator that maintained the political system by replenishing the ranks of the dominant party and preventing the growth of mass opposition. It may be impossible to define the influence millions of young people had on parents, teachers, and adults in general, but there can be little doubt that the uniformed army of teenagers had something to do with promoting the myth of Hitler's invincible genius.[9] When the war began, the importance of the HJ as the cradle of an aggressive army became apparent to military leaders and to the creators of the combat wing of the SS.

Hitler and Schirach inspect the HJ at the Nuremberg Party Rally, 1934
(Bundesarchiv Koblenz)

Because the functionary corps tended to ossify after 1933, the party itself
lost influence. Yet millions of politically reliable leaders functioned within
the hierarchical corps of the party and within the affiliates and auxiliaries
through which society was encompassed, if not entirely controlled. Main-
tenance of this ruling elite was dependent on the HJ in a substantial way.
Since the party exercised its power not by instructing the state but by
superseding normal governmental functions, the mobilization, indoctrination, and control of youth became an important factor.[10] It may be true
that the youthful members of the movement were not particularly interested in careers as party functionaries during the middle 1930s.[11] What has
been overlooked, however, is the development of a close relationship
between the HJ and the SS precisely at that time. This collaboration provided the leaders of the HJ with new and more attractive career possibilities. The most dedicated members of the HJ preferred the equally
young and dynamic SS over the party's aging and lethargic political cadre.
The function of the HJ in maintaining Nazi domination did not depend on
transfer to the political cadre, but was exercised in the broader context of
the movement, particularly its association with Himmler's SS, the most
pervasive affiliate in terms of influence and power.

Recent statistical analysis suggests that the age factor was indeed significant. Both members and leaders in the early party were even younger than
had previously been intimated—in their twenties before 1925—and on the
whole younger than the Reich population between 1925 and 1932. There
was a change in the situation after the establishment of the regime, despite
efforts to reverse a familiar institutional phenomenon, which in the case of
national socialism meant the average age rose to the middle and late forties
by 1942–43.[12] This suggests the lack of a consistent pattern of rejuvenation,
and once again points to a different avenue for the expression of youthful
energy. As the fulcrum of power changed to the SS, so did the career drift
of the young and ambitious.

In this context, then, the SS becomes the other crucial factor in the equa-
tion. Organization and indoctrination without systematic terror could
hardly have sufficed to keep the movement in power and the war in being.
It would have succumbed to grumbling, dissent, and opposition.[13] The
regime has been described as a "leadership-state" with an elaborately
mythologized Führer dominating both state and party. The SS in this system functioned as a kind of "Führer's executive," becoming in the process
the "real and essential instrument of the Führer's authority."[14] As a tool of
domination and destruction the SS has long attracted attention. Among
students of the SS, Robert Koehl has now ripped off the "mask of posses-
sion" and revealed a banal and frightening reality in the world of the
"Black Corps." He too was first to note a special relationship between the
HJ and the SS. This generational alliance between key affiliates has been
ignored.[15]

This investigation then seeks to enlarge our picture of the Nazi movement by exploring the institutional and social processes through which the
SS manipulated and exploited the HJ in order to facilitate the supply of
personnel for its numerous programs, tasks, and functions. The histor-
ically significant implications of these structural processes become evident
when the social and psychological effects on the young people involved in
them are incorporated in the analysis. In this way new perspectives can be
gained on national socialist institutions, on Nazi society, and on the interrelationship of generations in the Third Reich. In a highly structured society like that of Germany under Hitler, it is logical to select those programs
and organizational arrangements where this interrelationship can be
exposed in a direct and realistic way, in the mundane contingencies of
everyday life. While recruitment of soldiers was at the heart of the HJ-SS
alliance, I have chosen to concentrate on aspects which involve social control, economic and agrarian policy, demographic engineering, and phys-

ical fitness programs. Ultimately, the intergenerational alliance found its consummation on the battlefield, of course, and most poignantly so on the peculiar field of a "children's crusade" during the twilight of the Third Reich.

Beginning as a movement of youth, the Nazi party after 1933 became all things to all men. In an era of crisis it could pass itself off as a revolutionary movement, but the outcome of its policies and programs was anything but progressive—at least not by calculated intent. Once the NSDAP had attained power, its proclaimed programs were frequently ignored, and even its organizational statutes were repeatedly circumvented. Titles, roles, and jurisdictions were mixed, duplicated, and deliberately confounded. The structure and function of the party changed with the moods of its distant charismatic leader and his self-willed derivative agents. It was more polycratic than monolithic in nature. Retrospectively, one can find evidence of technocratic efficiency and social engineering, utter personal loyalty and pervasive conflict, ancient barbarism and modern social welfare, full productive employment and squandered natural and human resources.[16]

How could any political party contain these diverse elements and channel the various political and ideological objectives? The answers to this question have been debated and discussed for half a century.[17] Now this lengthy discourse has entered a new phase, and a concerted effort is being made to revise the nearly unanimously accepted hypothesis that in terms of its electoral base the NSDAP was a lower-middle-class phenomenon and hence a kind of petit bourgeois revolution. Systematic analysis of leaders and rank-and-file members and sophisticated use of multivariate regression analysis of the social basis of electoral support have fueled the debate about the origins of national socialism. It now appears that the electoral constituency and the class composition of the membership was much broader and more diverse than previously assumed. Some have gone so far as to discount the prominence of youth in the movement before the seizure of power, and some are even tempted in part to bid "farewell to class analysis."[18] This study seeks to demonstrate the utility of the communal ideal as an instrument of social integration in the context of the intergenerational everyday realities of the Third Reich. It carries the revisionist interpretation a step further by showing how the party—newly become regime—sought to turn a much-touted but relatively unstable popular movement into an instrument by which German society could become a genuine *Volksgemeinschaft* transcending class and creed. The preferred agents in this attempted transformation were the HJ and SS.

Although his conclusions about Hitler's "social revolution" have undergone considerable criticism,[19] some of David Schoenbaum's pointed questions still have productive relevance. "How important was a minister, a diplomat, a party functionary, a Labor Front functionary, a Hitler Youth leader, a member of an Ordensburg?" he asked and found no answer. The Third Reich, Schoenbaum believed, "was a world of general perplexity in which, even before the war, 'Nazi' and 'German' merged indistinctly but inseparably, and the *Volksgemeinschaft* of official ideology acquired a bizarre reality."[20] Martin Broszat found evidence of a functioning communal ideal even earlier, as a consequence of World War I. He saw significance in "the socialisation of millions of soldiers from different classes, denominations and provinces within an army under the national flag."[21] More recently Broszat has returned to the theme. Staking out a middle ground in the continuing Schoenbaum debate, he emphasizes the importance of the Nazi appeal to the ideal of a classless community, especially among the young masses of the movement.[22]

In the middle of this debate is the "new" school of *Alltagsgeschichte*.[23] Thus far this kind of scholarship has tended to concentrate on day-to-day experiences, attitudes, and moods of individuals and small groups, largely of the working class. Underlying continuities and persistence of traditional social and moral values have been emphasized.[24] Consequently, the effect of the *Volksgemeinschaft* in bringing about a kind of social revolution—or even the mere perception of one—has tended to be denied, deemphasized, or pictured as a false goal, used merely as a manipulative tool of continuing elitist domination, extending to the persistent class structure of modern industrial society in Germany and other Western countries. Some argue that working-class solidarity was maintained under Hitler,[25] but most contend that there was more dissent, resistance, and opposition on the lowest level of society than had previously been allowed. Potential revolt, so the argument goes, was merely neutralized and postponed by a combination of guile, force, and deceptive image-building, through the propaganda media and dramatic political staging. Two important results flow from this type of social history. One is that a bridge between academically restricted scholarship and the general reading public is being built. The other has to do with the youth factor, particularly the function of the Hitler Youth in the Nazi regime, which is finally receiving the attention it deserves.[26]

The appeal to a "national community," especially for the young, was a factor in the attainment of power and expressed itself particularly well through the party affiliates. The party per se lost influence in major military and political decisions during the war. Army leaders and civil administrators became important elements in the structure, because their expertise was indispensable, and because most of them shared the *Volksgemeinschaft* ideal with the Nazis, if for their own particular social and political reasons.[27] The SA, SS, and HJ, along with other affiliates and auxiliaries, were needed to seize power and to sustain domination. It is particularly in the relationship between the party and its affiliates, and among the affiliates themselves, that fruitful new lines of inquiry into the realities of the system are to be found.

From a purely organizational point of view, fundamental distinctions can be made among three separate elements of the movement, perceived as such. There was, first of all, the political leadership itself, hierarchically structured, beginning with block leaders and capped by the Führer's deputy, but practically administered by the party's organization leader. Some seven affiliates of the party, ranging from the SA and the HJ to the Women's Association (NSF), constituted the second segment. The third element, known as the "annexed formations," was largely the product of political integration effected by the party's monopolistic drive after January 1933. These auxiliaries, including such organizations as the Doctors' Association and the German Labor Front, and the affiliates, especially the SS and the HJ, played important roles in presenting the NSDAP as a socially integrative movement, transcending class and special interest.[28]

The deputy leader, Rudolf Hess, should have had exclusive control over the hierarchical party structure, but the development of some twenty "central offices," loosely grouped together under the designation of "National Leadership," prevented such a monopoly. Since some heads of "central offices" held multiple positions within the party and state ministries, they had the power and found the means to circumvent the deputy's authority. This produced a confusing administrative situation in the party, exacerbated by Hess's lack of ambition and his eccentric personality. These weaknesses were offset partially by the "organization leader," Robert Ley, and the party treasurer, Franz X. Schwarz, whose activities produced at least some element of integration within the administrative machine. His energetic ambition and various posts, in fact, frequently made Ley a worthy rival on almost equal footing with Hess, while Schwarz's recognized expertise gave him virtual control over the finances of the party and its affiliates and auxiliaries throughout the Third Reich.[29]

The party thus had neither a real center of power except Hitler nor any statutory control over the affiliates and their activities. All the party bureaucrats could hope for was cooperation inspired by the common purposes of the movement and the overriding will and charisma of the Führer.[30] That appears to have been enough, since political parties do not exist for their own sake, but for the purpose of gaining and exercising power. The Nazis managed to do that quite successfully, but not with the party apparatus alone. The national leadership was supposed to be a kind of shadow government, duplicating the state bureaucracy and helping to control and transform German society. But the federal bureaucracy was never entirely nazified.[31] The vaunted control of society and the implementation of the communal ideal could not have succeeded to the extent that it did without the assistance of the SS and HJ. Without the exercise of ubiquitous terror in the name of the state and the organization and indoctrination of the younger generation, the shadow government would have been relatively weak. This aspect of the control process suggests at least one reason why the SS and the HJ retained a semiautonomous position in the movement. It also helps to explain why the collaboration between the elites of these two affiliates was particularly intense and continuous. In order to break down social and religious barriers hindering the establishment of a "national community," a combination of terror (by the SS) and indoctrination (of the HJ) was thought to be necessary.

The personalities of Baldur von Schirach and Heinrich Himmler and their relative position within Hitler's entourage clearly had something to do with the development and function of their respective affiliates. Both of them were *Altkämpfer*, having succumbed to the Führer's aura early in their own lives and the life of the movement. Both had personal ties to Hitler throughout their careers, Schirach's being more prosaic than Himmler's, who always maintained a kind of sycophantic distance, while Schirach enjoyed an unusual entree through his wife, the daughter of Hitler's early friend and photographer, Heinrich Hoffmann. While most Nazi leaders fought with each other and frequently despised each other heartily, there is no evidence that Himmler and Schirach ever did so.[32] Schirach's proletarian successor, Artur Axmann, developed especially close ties with Himmler, who had a sentimental fondness for Axmann because he had lost an arm in combat on the Russian front. Goebbels, Speer, Kaltenbrunner, Bormann, Himmler, and Axmann, together with their spheres of activity, survived all the political battles and reached the peak of power at the end of the Third Reich.[33] It can be argued then that the HJ-SS connection and the derivative agents who controlled that alliance helped to keep the system in being.

Yet none of this was apparent in the beginning. The HJ and SS were overshadowed by the prominence of the Stormtroopers (SA) in the early history of the Nazi movement. Until the early 1930s not even Hitler seems to have realized how important it would be for the HJ and SS to be formally and really separated from the paramilitary street fighters. Spreading propaganda, winning voters, and intimidating opponents were the primary activities of all party formations before the acquisition of political office. Once Hitler's charismatic appeal had been effectively used to subdue the periodic factionalism, and once power had been attained, the resentful dissonance of the street fighters became a nuisance. It endangered the process of solidifying the ephemeral grasp on the levers of state power. This was the moment of opportunity for both HJ and SS. The leaders of both affiliates saw this clearly and seized it with alacrity.

The historical origins of the HJ and the SS and their organizational structure are familiar and need not detain us here. In terms of growth Gustav Lenk's and Kurt Gruber's early HJ pointed to the direction in which future success lay. Lenk's experience revealed that right-wing coalition politics was irrelevant under existing conditions, whereas Gruber showed that relative indifference to social class and concentration on generational rebellion promised more in terms of organizational growth, especially if one concentrated on the comparatively large urban youth contingent of the working class. Within two years of his official appointment, he increased the size from 1,000 to 10,000, while in the next year (1928–29) the HJ experienced a 30 percent increase, followed by a 62 percent and 76 percent influx in the next two years respectively. The important breakthrough for the HJ per se and all of its affiliates, except the Pupils League (NSS), came during the last years of the Republic, under Schirach's leadership (Table 1.1). The HJ proper (boys fourteen to eighteen) experienced a 92.2 percent increase during the period stretching from Gruber's resignation in October 1931 to 30 January 1933. This was closely matched by the female branch (BDM), although it suffered from competition with other Nazi youth groups, particularly the rival organizational efforts of the Nazi League of Women. The BDM, JV (boys ten to fourteen), and JM (girls ten to fourteen) were not properly organized until 1931. They were in a fluid state during this period, which accounts for the statistical uncertainty in the available sources. The nearly fortyfold expansion of the JV is hard to fathom, unless the quiet influx from the independent bourgeois associations known as the Bünde and some overlapping memberships account for it. Desertions from the small NSS alone cannot provide the answer. The 13.8 percent decline in NSS membership only amounts to 2,214 pupils, and some of these may have gone elsewhere. From 1 January 1932 to 30 January 1933 the HJ proper had a less impressive influx of 49.6 percent. The overall growth of all Nazi youth groups between 1931 and early 1933 is certainly not inconsiderable, since it exceeds 100 percent. The figure for university students is even higher, although they represented a mere 10 percent of the student population, which in turn was a small minority of their national age-cohorts (Table 1.2).[34]

When these figures are compared with those of its competitors, the HJ emerges as a decided minority in pure statistical terms. The combined youth organizations of the Communist and Socialist parties, including all ages, had over 80,000 members in 1933. The right-wing parties had 253,000, and the Center party youth numbered 35,000. But the KPD and SPD were irretrievably at odds, and the divisions among the youth groups of the Right were so severe that no effective cooperation was possible. The semi-political Bünde, more direct descendants of the classic German Youth Movement, numbered some 70,000, but were also rendered politically impotent by virtue of factional disputes. The most effective socialist youth organization, the SAJ, which was attached to the SPD, should have been the HJ's main challenger, having had 100,000 members already in 1924, but it lost strength in the latter years of the Republic. In 1931–32 the SAJ was able to attract only some 50,000 youngsters to its ranks. The National Commission for Youth Associations, which incorporated all of these groups, as well as very large confessional youth organizations, had a combined membership of over four million.[35]

Only about a quarter of Germany's adolescents remained immune to the appeal of organized youth life in 1933, while the HJ and its affiliates literally exploded, moving from roughly 120,000 members in January to nearly 2.3 million at the end of the year. Between 1933 and 1936, when membership jumped from one to five million, there still was no legal compulsion to join. When the HJ Law of 1936 appeared, making membership compulsory, about one-half of the relevant age group was still outside the HJ. Total HJ membership increased rapidly, after a brief slow-down in 1934–35 and 1937, but failed to reach the goal of total incorporation. Before legal compulsion was implemented, only some 1.6 million young people in the relevant age group of 8.9 million remained aloof to HJ appeals, while nearly 7.3 million (not counting nearly a half million older BDM girls) did respond. Managing to organize some 82 percent of all youngsters in the nation within an official youth organization before legal compulsion was fully applied suggests that Schirach's totalitarian drive was essentially successful (Table 1.3).[36]

The continuing existence of "illegal" Bünde, antisocial cliques, and adamant resisters was a problem only in the unrealistic view of the HJ total-

Hitler greets the BDM, 1939 (postcard; author's collection)

izers. The fact that more than 82 percent of German youth put on the HJ uniform is impressive enough by any standard. That the Nazis managed to ignite a sense of euphoria among Germany's nonacademic youth is patently obvious, even if allowance is made for a large proportion who did no more than submit lethargically. From this perspective a number of important questions arise. Since the HJ gradually evolved as a curious mixture of voluntary and state organizations, an amalgam of mass movement and officially sanctioned institutions, which of these aspects over the course of its development from 1926 to 1939 was most important in the minds of those who joined? Would the organization have disintegrated if legal compulsion had not been applied, or would it have developed into the kind of prestige organization which some party functionaries wanted it to be? More importantly, what would have happened if Himmler had not come in to prop up the National Youth Directorate (RJF) and to strike the alliance that sustained its continued existence as a mass organization?

The size of the SS is another issue, since it never sought to be a mass organization but was always meant to be an elite. The early SS never exceeded the approximate 10 percent of SA strength prescribed for it by Hitler. Shortly after Himmler's arrival in 1929 the SS slightly exceeded this quota, but at the time of the power seizure it was no more than 7 percent of

SA strength and half that of the HJ. In the early 1930s Himmler even expelled some 60,000 members, but at the same time began to build up the armed formations which reached a strength of over 9,000 by the late summer of 1936. The numerical growth of the total SS during the peacetime years was limited, reaching a size of about a quarter million on the eve of war. The question of elitism became problematic after the introduction of foreign personnel into the Waffen-SS (W-SS). By 1944 total SS membership had nearly reached four million, representing roughly 35 percent of the total HJ membership.[37] At that point, it no longer mattered in any respect, since Himmler's future plans for the SS, as a permanent elite replenished from the HJ, could only be realized after a military victory.

Both Schirach and Axmann were twenty-seven when they became national youth leaders. What is more important is the fact that 69 percent of 200 prominent leaders were between twenty-two and thirty-two years old in 1932, with 27 percent of them falling between the ages of twenty-four and twenty-six. Regional leaders were a little over thirty and district leaders were twenty-five on the average. Leaders below that level were only a year or two older than the children under their supervision. No youth group except the communist could match this young leadership.[38] The cadre of professional youth leaders was indeed very young and carried unprecedented responsibility. That a certain nervous dynamic should have prevailed not only at the top but all the way to the local unit is certainly credible by virtue of age alone. Alfons Heck's experience as a young district leader toward the end of the war tends to confirm that judgment. The simple and uniform organizational scheme that Schirach developed clearly appealed to youngsters and could be easily grasped and understood by them.[39] It is a sad commentary on the state of nurture during the Weimar Republic to think that German youth might actually have wanted the kind of structure and direction the HJ provided.[40]

The SS too was much younger than one would have thought for an elite that sought ultimate domination. Himmler's insistence after 1933 that new recruits ought to be under twenty-five was nearly realized during the prewar period. The average age of the SS throughout the Reich on 1 January 1934 was twenty-six years and eight months. While the aging process that occurred in the following years was not surprising, with the average settling at twenty-nine years and four months by 1 September 1937, it was still rather young when one considers the important functions Himmler's order was engaged in by that time. In the case of the Fulda-Werra Region of the Allgemeine-SS (A-SS), which will figure in this study, some 70 percent of all members were under thirty; in fact 39 percent were under twenty-five, and nearly 5 percent were below twenty years of age.[41] Members of the General-SS thus appear to have been even younger than the HJ leadership.

If one looks at the prewar SS officer corps a similar picture develops, making due allowance for more mature individuals in positions of leadership, as in the case of the HJ. The twenty-five to thirty-four age group made up 37.2 percent of the officers from second lieutenant on up, as compared with 29.1 percent of literate adult males, which made up roughly 63.5 percent of the entire population. Those who were between twenty-five and forty-five years of age made up over 80 percent of the prewar leadership in the SS as a whole, the mean age being 37.4 years.[42] Analysis of the W-SS officer corps of 1944 suggests a generational shift, starting at the Standartenführer rank and moving down rapidly to the Sturmbannführer rank, 90.2 percent of whom were forty-one or younger, 37.9 percent of them being between thirty-one and thirty-five years old. Some 13.7 percent of the Sturmbannführer were even younger, falling between the ages of twenty-six and thirty.[43] This latter group could hardly have avoided the experience of the HJ during their teens. The preceding group of thirty-one- to thirty-five-year-old Sturmbannführer most likely contained a large proportion of those HJ leaders who entered the W-SS before the war and performed well enough to get rapid promotion. Since the SS was largely interested in members of the HJ when they reached their eighteenth birthday (between 1933 and 1945), it meant that the HJ age cohort, born between 1914 and 1928, was the most likely active participant in the HJ-SS alliance. The relative youthfulness of the SS rank and file, and especially the prewar officer corps, made the alliance about as natural in terms of age as it could be.

The official claim that 69 percent of the HJ membership in the crucial 1930–33 period consisted of young workers and industrial apprentices on the whole has been confirmed by the research of Peter Stachura.[44] The two-thirds figure is persistent enough to suggest a pattern. Clearly the HJ with its continuing social revolutionary ideology was more attractive to proletarians than the parent party, 26.3 percent of whose rank and file in 1930 and 32.5 percent in 1933 was made up of workers.[45]

The social origin of HJ leaders follows more closely the pattern of the party, rather than that of the HJ membership, being largely middle class in the various levels since at least 1926, but increasingly so after 1931. Only 6.5 percent of 200 prominent early leaders were clearly proletarian in background, whereas 53.5 percent belonged to the social elite, although some of these no doubt should be classified as petit bourgeois. The remaining 40 percent cannot be classified for lack of information. Applying Michael Kater's scheme to the HJ leadership cadre as it had developed by 1939, we

Baldur von Schirach and HJ leaders in conference, 1933 (Bundesarchiv Koblenz)

find that 30.2 percent of some 765,000 leaders (both full-time and part-time) fit the category of an upper-middle-class elite, 27.1 percent could be considered as belonging to the working class, and 42.7 percent fall in the lower-middle-class category (Table 1.4). There is little doubt that the upper ranks of the leadership were occupied by university students and university graduates, with an occasional proletarian like Artur Axmann throwing sand into class-conscious eyes.[46]

The HJ as a whole, however, retained a strong working-class character during the prewar period, even at a time when more than three-quarters of all youth were incorporated in its ranks. The proletarian element at the beginning of 1939, as calculated by methods now in vogue, came within a single percentage point (53.56 vs. 54.56) of matching the percentage calculated for the adult population from the 1933 census. The HJ thus made more substantial inroads into the offspring of workers than has generally been recognized. At the least, it was more heterogeneous than one would have thought, since 21 percent belonged in the elite category made up by university students, secondary school pupils, and teachers, and a mere 25.44 in social categories deemed to belong in the lower middle class (Table 1.5). When this social profile is compared with that of the leadership, we find an interesting but not surprising deviation from the pattern of the rank and file: the number of teachers, university students, and secondary school pupils is down by 6.7 percentage points; white-collar employees by 20.5; those with technical occupations by 5.7; those without any occupation by 7.8. But agricultural occupations are up by 19.6 percent and young blue-collar workers by 21.1 percent. In comparison with the leadership, the much larger percent of blue-collar workers and peasant youth in the HJ as a whole is no surprise. If Peter Stachura is correct in assuming that all of those classified as employed in agriculture were in fact "workers," then the resulting 65 percent working-class segment in the HJ is continued from the pre-1933 period, a possibility Stachura ignores, since he confuses leadership with membership statistics. The equally smaller percent of white-collar employees is arresting. It is also interesting to note that the socially elevated group of teachers, university students, and secondary school pupils is only less prominent in the rank and file by 6.7 percentage points, although age clearly has more to do with this than social class consciousness. Young workers apparently found it just as easy to move from the workplace to the HJ den as students found it to move from the schoolroom to the HJ rendezvous. The leadership was an elite but only in a functional sense, since 20.9 percent of them were young blue-collar workers, and 25.5 percent white-collar employees.[47]

The SS, it has been held, incorporated a large representation of the upper middle class and a notable delegation of the aristocracy in its leadership. Michael Kater found that the more differentiated group of semi-civilians composing the A-SS in 1937 recruited 70 percent of its membership from the lower middle class and 11 percent from the upper middle class. The latter figure is three times that of the employed population and almost twice the percentage of the upper middle class's membership in the party. The number of lawyers and doctors in the A-SS is seven times larger than their numbers in the general population. Lawyers, physicians, and professors had a particular affinity for the Security Service (SD), while the old-line nobility found the medieval pageantry of Himmler's new elite especially attractive. Kater found that 9 percent of all SS leaders from Standartenführer and up were titled aristocrats in 1938, although the average proportion of aristocrats in the total prewar officer corps hovered around 2 percent, according to Wegner. The average income of rank-and-file A-SS members was nearly twice that of the civilian population. The problem of unemployment in 1937 and 1938 no longer existed for SS members, but persisted in the general population and especially in the SA with its hordes of semiskilled and technologically unemployable workers. In creating the SS Himmler had managed to form an enclave for the privileged upper crust, or so it seemed, at least before the war.[48]

A calculation using total SS occupation figures for 1937 and Kater's scheme of vertical occupational categorization yields results that differ somewhat from previous findings. That 28.39 percent should fall within the lower class of unskilled and skilled workers, departing from Kater's 19 percent, may be due to the fact that Kater used a sample only for the A-SS. The 53.01 percent, comprising the lower-middle-class segment, contains heavy representation of lower and intermediate employees, but still deviates from Kater's large proportion because my calculation includes military and office personnel, hence the entire SS. The 18.60 percent in the elite category, with extreme overrepresentation of academic professionals (tenfold), students (fourfold), and higher civil servants (threefold), makes Kater's point even more effectively by using the total membership of the prewar SS. Surprising is the fact that farmers, skilled craft workers, master craftsmen, lower and intermediate civil servants, and nonacademic professionals follow more or less the national trends. Unskilled workers, resulting in 9.85 percent by virtue of this calculation, were underrepresented by more than 27 percent as one would expect (Table 1.6).[49]

Using a modified version of Kater's categories and a large sample that excludes the SD, Herbert F. Ziegler has found the SS officer corps of 1938 to fall into the following social classes: 29 percent in the elite class, 44.8 percent in the lower middle class, and a "surprising" 26.2 percent in the working class. Ziegler's result for the lower-class component, however, is not that unusual when compared with the same figure for the entire SS, deviating a mere 2.19 percent. Aside from the exclusion of the SD, which he considers to be atypical, Ziegler's conclusion cannot be quarreled with. In comparison with the literate adult male population, he suggests that the prewar officer corps had a "respectable" membership measured by "traditional German social standards." It qualified as a social elite, although as such it provided "careers open to talent," giving preference to educated professionals before and after 1939. He argues that the SS was an "open organization both in terms of access and advancement" and that the SS officer corps developed a heterogeneous social structure that was reflected in its general outlook and underlay the decision-making process.[50]

These findings, based on the social categories established by Kater, can be summarized as follows: In the A-SS of 1937 Kater found that 11 percent fell in the elite category, 70 in the lower middle class, and 19 percent in the lower class. My calculations for the total SS of 1937 yield 18.60, 53.01, and 28.39 percent respectively. For the SS officer corps of 1938 Ziegler calculated 29, 44.8, and 26.2 percent for the three class divisions. Together these calculations suggest an even higher representation of the traditional elite than

Kater himself found, and significantly higher representation of the working class in prewar SS ranks than has been generally assumed. Consequently, the lower-middle-class element becomes less pronounced. The SS's claim to be an elite in terms of social class had plausibility before the war, although the SS leadership certainly thought of itself more as a functional and racial or "new" elite than a traditional social and economic elite.[51]

During the war the SS underwent substantial change, although the implications of this change are not entirely clear. One could argue that it became a kind of military elite out of necessity, or that the SD became a specialized elite within the larger context of a multifaceted and heterogeneous structure. Bernd Wegner's analysis of the W-SS officer corps of 1944 suggests that one could characterize the military leadership as a "middle class elite," a term equally applicable to all noncommunist leadership groups. In contrast to Kater, Wegner believes that social mobility and incomplete social change, typical of German society as whole, was also taking place within the wartime SS. In the meticulous pursuit of factors, which determined the "social heterogeneity" Wegner finds in the W-SS officer corps, a picture emerges that defies classification in conventional terms. Changes from the prewar social structure, shifts away from the heavily Protestant orientation of top officers toward religious indifference if not an antireligious ethos, a generational shift toward younger officers with lack of traditional social values, the development of mixed urban-country origins for officers, developing indifference toward party membership, fewer officers with military experience in the old army, all reveal an officer corps that at the end of the war can no longer be characterized as a traditional elite in social and economic terms. Reckless expansion, concentration on military professionalization, and aggressive and unrestrained combat effectiveness became the dominant motifs of the W-SS under the constraints of wartime necessities. A similar change undoubtedly took place in the rest of the Black Corps.[52]

The respective organizational sizes of HJ and SS were a function of aim, personality of leadership, relative autonomy within the movement, and official policy determined by Hitler himself. One sought to be a mass organization, incorporating an entire age-cohort, the other aimed at creating a new elite, replacing the old elite within German society. The professional corps of HJ leaders also can be regarded as a kind of elite, separating it socially and functionally from the rank and file, but it was different from the SS in that its goals were directed toward interests specific to the HJ as a youth movement. It developed a revealing affinity for the SS, which had no mass basis, by virtue of circumstance and the shared goals of the Nazi movement as a whole. The surprisingly high proportion of lower-class elements (27.1 percent) in the HJ leadership corps and the equally arresting working-class element in the SS as a whole (28.4 percent) ought to raise doubts about generalizations regarding their elitist or petit bourgeois character. A notable degree of social diversity and the overwhelming youthfulness of both affiliates made the persistent propaganda about the *Volksgemeinschaft* more plausible and real than has been supposed. The HJ-SS coalition was more than merely an alliance of traditional social elites.[53]

# 2 | The Formation of a Generational Alliance

During his trial at Nuremberg, Baldur von Schirach denied that Heinrich Himmler and the SS had "had any influence over youth organizations and over the education of young people." He accepted responsibility for misleading German youth, but his memory failed him when it came to a connection with the SS, a connection he fostered and his successor solidified. It was a tie so strong that even the party secretariat resented it. Just two years earlier, during a conference of leaders representing the party chancellery and the National Youth Directorate (RJF), one of Martin Bormann's protégés protested bitterly: "All affiliates of the movement adhere to party regulations, except the SS and the HJ. It is even sadder that both of them march in closely synchronized cadence."[1]

Certainly there was little indication before 1933 that such a relationship was in the cards. Both HJ and SS were totally involved in the consuming effort to create viable political organizations. They grew up side by side within the larger confines of the raucous SA in the scattered cities, towns, and rural regions of Germany.[2] It was during the critical period of the Nazi takeover when SS and HJ emerged as important affiliates, severing their tenuous ties to the SA. Himmler's operators served Hitler as assassination squads to rid the regime of a potential threat and were repaid by a grant of relative independence. Schirach and his minions judiciously withdrew into temporary oblivion, probably at the suggestion of Hitler, who knew that there was sympathy for the SA in the HJ and that Schirach himself might have been in danger during the SA purge of 1934. The social revolutionary elements within the HJ were closer in spirit to the SA than the SS at that time. When Schirach emerged from hiding, he began a not too circumspect campaign of denunciation against the Stormtroopers, his title as SA-Gruppenführer notwithstanding.[3]

## HJ, Party Affiliates, and State Ministries

Intermittent attempts by the new SA to gain influence in the HJ after the "blood purge" were effectively blunted, usually with the aid of Himmler and Hess. In 1935 Schirach and SA Chief Victor Lutze agreed to transfer doctors to the HJ, since the HJ was as short of medical assistants as of most other technical personnel, in a period of relatively rapid expansion. Schirach made sure, however, that permanent assignment meant complete detachment from the SA, now in swift decline. The possibility of transfer at eighteen still existed. In 1938 the RJF ordered that "standing communication" with SA regiments be maintained to facilitate these transfers, but few HJ graduates availed themselves of this opportunity in the late 1930s. The army, in the person of Erwin Rommel, began to take special interest in the HJ as early as 1937, which Schirach at first encouraged and then regretted. Rommel's attraction to the youngsters was not only deflecting SA overtures, but threatening to outshine Schirach's standing with his boys.[4]

Lutze's recruiters employed desperate means to flesh out the special military regiment Feldherrnhalle, a feeble attempt to counter the growing renown of the SS-Verfügungstruppe (SSVT). In 1938 Himmler himself objected vigorously to the SA's habit of offering monetary inducements and accused them of defaming the SS. SA recruiters had alleged that the SSVT were being enlarged "unnecessarily," since they were "merely a parading unit" and could not provide an alternative to obligatory military service. Himmler complained that recruitment was difficult enough without such venal competition. There was, of course, much more involved here than a single instance of resentment. The SA tried repeatedly and unsuccessfully to recover some role in the effort to remilitarize Germany.[5]

Hitler assuaged SA resentments by allowing them to engage in pre- and postmilitary training, a vague formulation bound to confuse. The SA was to begin this training with seventeen-year-old boys and carry it out under HJ auspices. At the end, HJ youngsters were to receive SA Defense Medals, hardly coveted symbols in 1939. Those eighteen or older were to be trained under SA control, unless other affiliates of the party were involved, a limitation which gave Lutze little room to maneuver. Schirach took advantage of this situation and soon eliminated the SA from all interference with premilitary training in the HJ, but not without some effort. In the fall of 1939 reports came to the RJF that the SA was trying to incorporate seventeen-year-olds. Lutze clearly had decided that the HJ was ripe for some political poaching. This led to a minor crisis among rival agents for military training on the eve of war.[6]

While the relationship with the SA until 1934 and with the SS thereafter was the most important from the standpoint of the RJF, the latter maintained working agreements with other affiliates and the party under Hess and Bormann, always trying to keep its youthful affiliate under control and hardly ever succeeding.[7] In matters of finance the situation was different. Early on Schirach tried to get an independent budget from the Finance Ministry under Schwerin-Krosigk, but Party Treasurer Schwarz would have none of it, and the RJF had to contend with the tight-fisted Schwarz for the duration. Whatever extraordinary state funds Schirach acquired had to be extracted through Schwarz from the general monies allocated for the party by the finance minister.[8]

Collaboration with the Reichsarbeitsdienst (RAD) was close, if not always congenial.[9] Robert Ley, the tsar of the Labor Front, remained a strangely incongruous friend to Schirach, but the relationship between Konstantin Hierl's Ministry of Labor and the RJF was more problematical, due to competition for leadership talent, increasingly scarce during the war. The importance of the RAD connection is underscored by the fact that many RJF officials were doing double duty for the Labor Service or the Food Ministry.[10] Between Richard Walter Darré and Herbert Backe of the Agricultural Ministry and the Food Estate, respectively, collaboration was constant and generally harmonious, because of mutual interest in the HJ Land Service.[11]

The RJF made a variety of agreements with the Nazi Welfare Organization (NSV), which regulated HJ and BDM participation in such ameliorative measures as Winter Relief, designed to assuage discontent and maintain popular support. These sorts of activities and the experiences of the labor service figure prominently in memoirs of former members of the BDM, usually couched in positive terms. Especially during the war, BDM girls seem to have proudly taken the place of adults in a host of welfare activities and health care jobs, so that one gets the impression the HJ had taken over most of these functions.[12] The relationship between the Women's Organization and the HJ was never a happy one. It began with a struggle over the control of the JM and certain BDM age groups in the 1930s and reached crisis proportions in 1939 and 1940. Schirach's creation of the "Faith and Beauty" program in 1938, for BDM girls up to the age of twenty-one, was designed to keep young women under RJF control, away from the cantankerous matrons of the Frauenschaft (NSF).[13]

Since the 1920s the HJ conducted a "foreign policy" of its own. The Foreign Office of the RJF sought to exert influence and stimulate organization of youth in foreign and occupied countries of Europe or wherever German minorities were found. This led to extensive relationships with the Association for Germans Abroad, Ribbentrop's Foreign Office, and Rosenberg's Ministry for Occupied Eastern Territories. Endless jurisdictional and ideological squabbles with Rosenberg invited SS interference in support of the RJF.[14]

Working agreements with the army played a role after the introduction of conscription, but collaboration was ridden with conflict because of competition from the SS. The special formations of the HJ engaged in some type of premilitary training, but most served as feeder organizations for party affiliates, not the armed forces. The Motor-HJ fed personnel first into the NSKK and only later into armored units or the W-SS. The Air-HJ fed into the NSFK first and then the air force; the Marine-HJ fed into the Marine-SA; only the Signal-HJ fed directly into the signal corps of the air force and army. The HJ Patrol Service (SRD) and the attached Fire-Fighting Squads provided recruits for the A-SS, the police, the SD, and the W-SS. Belatedly the HJ also created a conduit for entertainment units of the RAD and the army through so-called *Spieleinheiten*. All of this activity led to lengthy negotiations with Göring's air ministry and Goebbels's propaganda ministry.[15]

The crucial relationship was with Bernhard Rust's Ministry of Education. The struggle here was continuous and bitter, because Schirach never gave up his ambition to replace Rust and become a kind of education tsar. Even after his appointment as Gauleiter in Vienna, when gossips dubbed him "the crown prince," he still retained vague responsibility for youth and used every opportunity to weaken Rust's position. There were constant negotiations and numerous agreements, punctuated by broken promises and renegotiations, particularly over control of the Adolf Hitler Schools, the Land Year, and the Child Evacuation Program. Here, as in all other competitive situations, the SS never failed to come to the aid of the RJF. The special ties between HJ and SS were reaffirmed in the process.[16]

**Evolution of the HJ-SS Alliance**

After 1934 the SS faced two important problems. One was the onslaught of opportunists, solved by mass expulsions, constant reorganization, and shifting relationships within the hierarchy. Developing methods for the recruitment of reliable manpower, however, involved a direct challenge to the armed forces. Resolution could only come if Hitler amended his promise to retain the army as the "sole bearer of arms." The issue was joined soon after the formation of the SSVT at the end of 1934 and was not settled until Himmler became chief of the Replacement Army ten years later. It is questionable whether differences could have been composed in any event, since they grew out of Hitler's dependence on both to carry out his aims. It was not unreasonable to envisage a mass army as the tool of an aggressive foreign policy and the SS as an instrument of domestic control. In the beginning this was precisely what Hitler and Himmler had in mind. This functional synthesis soon gave way, however, to crass anomalies. Driven by the imperatives of power and racial mystique, Himmler insisted on expanding the SS beyond reason. The SSVT, at first merely an adjunct police force, gradually became the cadre for a "parallel army." Hitler never rescinded his promise to maintain the exclusivity of the armed forces, but events and political intrigue led him to make significant amendments in favor of what was to become the W-SS.[17]

When Defense Minister Werner von Blomberg announced the formation of the SSVT in September 1934 he allowed Himmler to recruit personnel from the "number of those liable [sic] to military service." Army reserve authorities would relinquish volunteers for the SSVT only if "pressing army needs" did not prevent it. Legally SS recruits were considered as deferred from army service, although SS service counted as regular military duty. Since Himmler was eager to expand and Hitler was unwilling to antagonize army leaders, no SS division was formed until after the Polish campaign. In this peculiar fashion Hitler and Blomberg created the conditions for a struggle between SS and army with the young men of the HJ in the middle. The "defense law" that followed reintroduction of conscription preserved the functional exclusivity of the Wehrmacht, but ignored the armed formations of the SS and the SA. Legally the SSVT never became part of the armed forces, despite several de facto equalizations.[18]

Within this nebulous framework Himmler eventually built a "parallel army." A series of instructions issued in the fall of 1935 laid the groundwork for mutual accommodation between army reserve authorities (WBKs) and recruiters for the SSVT.[19] These complex rules grew out of conscription and the anomalous position of the SSVT. They did not apply to the SS Death's Head Formations (SSTV), founded earlier to guard concentration camps, since service in these did not release a man from military duty. But they did hold for Hitler's Body Guard, since that was considered to be part of the SSVT. In fact the *Leibstandarte* is an interesting illustration of another anomaly within the SS. Initially formed to guard the Reich Chancellery, it eventually became the showpiece division of the W-SS.

The Recruiting Office, created in January 1935, accompanied a general bureaucratic expansion and a shift of SS offices from Munich to Berlin. Proliferation did not mean growth in numerical terms, however. Overall membership increased comparatively little between 1934 and 1938, rising from 221,000 to 238,159 men. The largest influx had occurred in the year of the power seizure, when the entire SS organization literally exploded from 52,000 to 209,000 members. The middle 1930s were years of consolidation and elitist refinement.[20] This effort clearly pointed to the HJ. In the fall of 1935 August Heissmeyer, the new chief of the Central SS Office, issued a message to all units: "In order to initiate and preserve good relationships with the segments of the HJ, the Reichsführer-SS wishes that all superior leaders of the HJ should be handled in a proper and comradely fashion during ceremonial occasions." This meant that invitations from the HJ should be accepted by high SS leaders, who were obliged to show "lively interest" in HJ activities.[21] While it had always been assumed that eighteen-year-olds would transfer to party formations, including the SS, systematic recruiting in the HJ was not discussed until 1935. Hartmann Lauterbacher, representing Schirach, stipulated that SS and HJ regional leaders should arrange details independently. Some local SS leaders soon interpreted this consent to mean that the SS was the preferred destination of the best HJ graduates. The RJF balked at this turn of events and was forced to temporize. Yet misunderstandings continued to plague local leaders on this score, and the more important question of general party membership being postponed by the early entrance of Hitler youths into the SS. SS candidates from the HJ were finally informed that joining the SS was equivalent to party membership, a finessing of existing regulations that did not please party bureaucrats.[22]

The year 1936 was a turning point in the HJ-SS relationship, as it was for both the HJ and the SS. In June Hitler confirmed Himmler's unprecedented police powers by making him national police chief, and in December Hitler issued the "HJ Law" making membership theoretically compulsory. In fact, the HJ seems to have become a major focus of SS activity in that crucial year. With a degree of self-conscious pride, Himmler noted in a speech to SS-Gruppenführer in November that he had given more speeches to HJ audiences during the year than to the SS. Schirach and his leaders responded to this concerted overture. A common summer solstice ceremony, so important to Himmler's view of the emerging SS "order," was conducted on top of the Zugspitze, Germany's highest mountain. The most important of Himmler's speeches, however, was the one he gave in May. Schirach assembled a group of HJ leaders on the Brocken mountain in the Harz, famed site of Goethe's *Walpurgisnacht*, to hear a remarkable exposition of Himmler's plans for the Black Order.[23]

Because the initial exigencies of political struggle had been overcome, Himmler thought it was time to retrench for the future. This meant a yearly influx of 25,000 to 30,000 young recruits, about 10 percent of draftable

Hitler greets his youth at an SS installation, 1930s (Bundesarchiv Koblenz)

youths in Germany. In Himmler's view this was about all one could expect until the planned "sterilization laws" and "biological measures" took effect. He spoke of rigorous physical training, which would protect SS men from bureaucratic calcification, and he explained how spartan racial qualifications, requiring proof of Aryan heritage back to 1650, would guarantee elitist effectiveness. He thought that institutional rotation, enhancing understanding and experience of the entire organization, would create loyalty and esprit de corps. Beginning with service in the SSVT at eighteen, future leaders would be carefully selected for the cadet schools at Braunschweig and Bad Tölz, where practical achievement rather than educational attainment would further separate stronger leaders from weaker followers. Several months of service in each of the various SS agencies would follow. The last step was to be a stint in the A-SS, which George Stein has called the "backbone and spiritual fountainhead of the prewar SS." Here practical principles of leadership would be inculcated, since every leader would learn to win the hearts of his subordinates, which to Himmler was the "most significant thought in leadership training" inaugurated by the SS. It is interesting that he placed particular emphasis on the police, every officer candidate having to spend at least a year in some aspect of police work before moving to commanding positions in the A-SS or armed formations. In Himmler's mind the SS was still principally a militarized police force, but one with broad social, racial, and political responsibilities.[24]

Earlier Himmler had cleared the way for a firmer connection by reducing the probationary period in the SS for those who had been in the HJ before 1933. He also made it possible for SS leaders to become part-time leaders in the HJ, and Heissmeyer began to provide sports "trainers" for HJ units. Reports indicate that local SS leaders frankly admitted they wanted to be "in a position to exert influence on the HJ." In June, Paul Hausser, the inspector of the SSVT, ordered his troops to provide the HJ with training and advice similar to that ordered by Heissmeyer for the A-SS. Meanwhile Schirach arranged to allow HJ leaders serving in the army to attend HJ leadership conferences and camps. Hausser and Himmler followed suit for HJ leaders serving in the SSVT. The RJF also managed to get special dispensation for HJ leaders who wanted to fulfill their military obligations in the SSVT by having the height requirement reduced. But the attempt to have HJ service counted in partial fulfillment of four-year service obligations in the SSVT was rejected by the SS. All Himmler would agree to was "special leaves," after one year of service, in order to avoid "unnecessary hardships" for "HJ veterans."[25]

Among the remote aspects of Himmler's Brocken fantasies lay a practical demand: the need for manpower. This called for immediate action, particularly since the SSVT had only 9,000 men in 1936 and the A-SS contained mostly political veterans.[26] But the army prohibited general recruiting. So Heissmeyer leaped to the attack by ordering that "connecting links" be established with HJ District Directorates and other party agencies. He demanded an immediate contingent of 800 suitable men to be furnished by October and expected 100 volunteers before examination from each of fourteen A-SS Main Sectors.[27] Undoubtedly it was the racial selectivity that forced Heissmeyer to anticipate only 800 suitable recruits from 1,400 volunteers. While recruits were expected to secure a physician's certificate of fitness before examination, the emphasis on youth and barring of army veterans further inhibited success. Early in September Himmler sought to expedite matters by suggesting that SS aspirants commence searching for evidence of Aryan ancestry one year before transfer. The "race specialists" of the SS Mustering Commissions were to make this clear during the examination for suitability. Since much of the SS mustering of seventeen-year-olds at this time was done surreptitiously, it is difficult to understand how this suggestion could have been followed systematically.[28]

While these factors contributed to the limited success of the first recruiting drive, the most prohibitive obstacle was the prerequisite for SS membership. Outright rejection followed discovery of criminal records, except for sentences incurred in "the struggle for the movement." Enlistees were expected to be ethnically, spiritually, physically, and racially irreproachable, ideologically within the camp, and temperamentally inclined toward the soldierly profession. They were to be fit for service in the infantry, as well as in the specialties for which they volunteered, which included 5'9" minimum height for the SSVT and 5'10" for the Body Guard. Most of the early volunteers had to be veterans of the RAD, although some exceptions were made if they had been members of the Student Association or served with the pre-Nazi voluntary labor service. Wearers of corrective glasses and those with dental deficiencies were barred. All applications had to be accompanied by personal histories and "police certificates of good conduct," as well as statements from previous employers and the RAD. Volunteers had to attest their freedom from debts and produce written permission for enlistment from parents if under age. Most difficult of all, however, was the production of an Ancestral Chart, demonstrating Aryan ancestry back to 1800. It demanded prodigious research in church and community archives, a task beyond most recruits. Originally Himmler had set the target date at 1650, which got changed rather quickly to 1800, and finally to the "Small Ancestral Chart," requiring proof of racial purity only for the preceding two generations.[29]

Lack of desired success stimulated new arrangements. Late in 1936 Himmler reached an agreement with Blomberg permitting the Body Guard to recruit volunteers throughout Germany, while the rest of the SSVT was limited to prescribed military districts. This left the earlier 800-man contingent unaffected. That campaign was conducted nationwide, but only within party organizations, mainly the HJ.[30] Localization of recruitment may explain Himmler's motive for increasing the command prerogatives of regional A-SS leaders. SD and Race and Settlement (RuS) personnel, i.e. Heydrich's and Darré's men, hitherto independent, were subordinated to the Main Sector leaders' authority. Recruiters subordinate to the Recruiting Office were installed in the staffs of Main Sectors, Sectors, and Regiments. These new officers were to secure reinforcements for the entire SS. Moreover, they were enjoined to foster a spirit of belonging among youthful newcomers, thus performing indoctrination tasks simultaneously. Assuming responsibility for general policy and all major activities of the SS within their geographic areas, the Main Sector leaders received a considerable increment in power. Himmler warned them against temptations to use that leverage for divisive empire-building. His intent clearly was to integrate his growing interests, but he was too sanguine if he thought these measures would "serve the goal of creating within the SS a living National Socialist Order."[31]

Until now recruitment had been the task of local A-SS staff members.[32] When certain men were designated specifically as recruiters by Berlin, recruiting policy had a greater chance of success.[33] Most of these early efforts were made on behalf of the militarized formations. Personnel for other SS agencies were channeled through the SSVT and SSTV. Standards of enlistment for the latter two were dissimilar and determined by their diverse functions. The SSTV took newcomers in April and October of each year; the SSTV accepted recruits at any time. Service in the SSVT entailed a four-year commitment including three months of probation; service in the SSTV was only for one year with a similar period of probation. NCOs in both formations enlisted for a period of twelve years. Members of the SSVT received the same pay as soldiers in the armed forces, but only for the two years when they fulfilled their general military duty; pay for the remaining two years remained unspecified, although the normal fringe benefits enjoyed by army personnel also applied to the SSVT. Members of the SSTV received the usual uniforms, board, room, and pay according to the SS salary scale. The SSTV was on the state budget. The SSTV differed from the SSVT in one other respect: it was willing to accept shorter and younger men, those who were at least slightly over 5'5" tall and had completed their sixteenth year.[34]

By making the term of service in the Death's Head Formations short and by accepting very young recruits, Himmler involved hundreds of young men in the dehumanizing experience of concentration camp duty at a tender and malleable age. Probably few boys realized in 1936 that volunteering for the SSTV would involve them in genocide, but the fatuous claim made by postwar SS apologists that the W-SS had no connection to the concentration camp guards has long since been disproved. It is true that these units went through a relatively autonomous historical evolution beside the SSVT and the A-SS, but exchanges of personnel occurred regularly, and recruiting for both units was carried out jointly from at least 1936.[35]

About a week after Hitler issued the "HJ Law," while Schirach was still busy explaining what his new "national authority" meant, the RJF moved to solidify the established connection to the SS. Undoubtedly at Schirach's behest, the RJF worked out an agreement with the SS Recruiting Office that involved both party affiliates in a systematic recruiting effort. Setting a goal of forty volunteers within the area of each A-SS regiment, the RJF ordered its district leaders to cooperate fully and to conduct "preliminary musterings" in order to avoid unnecessary delays. Organization leaders of HJ regions were made responsible for the success of the venture. The SS Recruiting Office believed optimistically that this agreement finally would clear the way for the securing of adequate replacements from the HJ. Friedrich Hauser, apparently impressed with Schirach's new official status, informed his recruiters that a "mere reference to the RJF order would remove all difficulties."[36]

As he made clear in his Brocken speech, Himmler was interested in something more than mere recruiting arrangements and positive image-building. He wanted to make sure the racial worldview of the SS was conveyed to the younger generation even before they entered the Black Corps by ordering the SS to furnish meeting rooms for the HJ and contributing to the RJF campaign for the building of HJ Homes. March and April of 1937 were proclaimed as "special months of cooperation." "Reciprocal under-standing" and lasting "friendly connections" were to be established by a series of joint activities, including "educational evenings," musical jam sessions, common courses, outings and camps, and exchange of films.[37]

If scattered pieces of evidence suggest a general trend, then these ar-rangements were implemented, but with mixed results. In the city of Weimar, the SS was prepared to provide three field kitchens and two cooks requested by HJ Jungbann 37 in Troschkau, but the HJ was expected to pay for fuel and salaries, and therefore performed the task itself. A BDM re-gional leader in Hessen-Nassau managed to get SS help for an encamp-ment of 1,000 girls through the intercession of the party's provincial chief. A local medical company of the SS erected and dismantled tents, sanitary facilities, and field kitchens. Since the men had remained for the duration of the camp, the BDM leader expressed her gratitude for the "neat, com-panionable assistance" of the SS.[38] In Frankfurt am Main the SS "race expert" staged common solstice rites with the HJ and produced a play entitled "The Last Farmer." He boasted that his lectures had produced the "assumption that church weddings were now out of the question." He arranged to hold SS ceremonies, inducting new couples into the "kinship-community," concurrently with civil ceremonies in the Town Hall.[39]

Early in 1937 recruitment still fell below expectations. Only a few A-SS regiments provided the required contingent of forty volunteers, and some did not produce any. Heissmeyer assumed that the fault lay in "false measures and insufficient preparation," but clearly more than individual initiative was needed.[40] To accelerate the process, vita folders were routed to the Recruiting Office directly, instead of to Darré's RuSHA. Darré's star was in decline. Within a year Himmler would force him out of office because he failed to meet bureaucratic expectations and was too critical of Himmler's rather instrumental interest in the peasantry. Confusion about responsibilities led Heissmeyer to explain that the recruiting work of the A-SS regiments was limited to the districts of the HJ and only supplementary to efforts made by the SSVT and SSTV "mustering commissions," apparently random groups of SS officers, race "specialists," and physicians attached to these units. Because of their aggressive approach, the latter had been much more successful than A-SS recruiters.[41]

Despite additional expedients and agreements,[42] regional and local implementation was difficult. Within SS Main Sector Fulda-Werra, for instance, the request for forty recruits from each A-SS regiment, issued in December 1936, was filled only by one. The chief was displeased and ordered new contacts with HJ district leaders and RAD camps. In 1937 the RJF received complaints from HJ Region Hessen-Nassau, within Fulda-Werra, that the SS was mustering boys of seventeen under the pretext of an order from Himmler. Since Schirach had forbidden premature transfers, a conflict developed between his district leaders and SS recruiters. Heissmeyer thereupon demanded strict adherence to existing agreements, and Fulda-Werra was instructed to distinguish between actual mustering and "quiet observation" of boys who were sixteen and seventeen. HJ District Leader Lettmar, however, took his complaints about "so-called musterings" directly to Prince Waldeck-Pyrmont, the SS chief of Fulda-Werra, declaring his readiness to arrange musterings for SS armed formations, but protesting against irregular recruiters who were "hunting for prospects for the A-SS among his Gefolgschaften." In Taunus certain mustered boys had even been "commanded to perform SS duty." The prince reprimanded his zealous recruiters and assisted several HJ leaders by assigning SS men to duties in HJ headquarters.[43]

During 1938 the situation in Fulda-Werra improved. After observing a mustering commission for the SSVT at work, the race specialist reported that tactful approaches had been utilized. The Body Guard also made a recruiting expedition, the propriety of which was questioned by the RuSHA man, who had the volunteers transferred to the SSVT. The A-SS strength of Fulda-Werra in January stood at 10,523 men. This respectable figure was deemed to fall short by 7,206. If one assumed a yearly attrition rate of about 11 percent and another 30 percent for eliminations due to physical inadequacies, the HJ would have to produce 5,218 volunteers in two years. While this was rather optimistic, Waldeck-Pyrmont banked his hopes on improved relations with the HJ. In August new "recruiting leaders" were installed in the regimental staffs, but it was too late to affect the quota. Results fell short by 959 men.[44]

If we turn to the local level we find that the HJ-SS relationship was not yet on firm ground, at least not in Frankfurt am Main, the largest city in Fulda-Werra, with a population of 555,857 (1933). Frankfurt had a Protestant majority of 57.2 percent at that time, a Catholic population of 33.1 percent, and the largest Jewish community of any German city (4.7 percent). The liberal *Frankfurter Zeitung* had taken a consistent anti-Nazi position throughout the Weimar period. Beginning with slight success in 1928, the Nazi vote exceeded the national average in 1930 and 1932, amounting to 38.7 percent in the July 1932 Reichstag election. Nazi support seems to have been strong in the upper bourgeois districts, rather than in the petit bourgeois inner city.[45] The HJ, like the party itself, did not do well in Western Germany during the early 1930s. Rhineland-Ruhr and Westphalia had a mere 1,700 HJ members in 1932, largely because of Catholic opposition and strong left-wing organizations. In the Rhineland-Palatinate and in Hesse-Nassau, including Frankfurt, the HJ did better, largely because of strong *völkisch* traditions and anti-Semitism in the peasantry. Saxony, the best area for the HJ, had 3,888 members in April 1932.[46] Frankfurt, furthermore, experienced consistent opposition to the HJ throughout the 1930s. Early in 1938 there were about 10,000 members in the Frankfurt HJ.[47]

It is no surprise, therefore, that the A-SS Regiment in Frankfurt was unsuccessful in its recruiting efforts during the spring of 1937. Since 75 percent of some 300 prospects, mostly from the HJ, had turned out to be unsuitable, the whole campaign was in doubt. The SS charged the HJ was offering them bad "human material," while keeping the "best racial and physical types" for its own administration.[48] In the fall of 1937, Walter Moreth, commander of the Frankfurt SS, persuaded HJ leaders to organize a mustering session for boys of seventeen and eighteen. This affair took ten days, because the SS camouflaged its efforts by calling them "health examinations." Only two HJ leaders knew the identity of the examining committee. SS examiners, however, nearly sabotaged the affair by making injudicious remarks, requiring the intervention of higher officials. The outcome shocked the SS. Although 1,280 youths were called up, a mere 603 actually appeared and only 50 percent of these qualified for service in the SS. Considering its peculiar racial standards, this was not an unexpected outcome, yet the HJ was blamed for inadequate organization and lack of discipline. SS examiners then went on to make a grim assessment of conditions in the Frankfurt HJ.

Within the inner city they found evidence of malnutrition, rachitis, and other "signs of degeneration." They discovered evidence of "racial mixing," with "non-European" and "alpine" types predominating. HJ doctors, it seems, had not examined most of the recruits before, and they as well as HJ leaders "were repeatedly amazed to find obvious physical and other deficiencies." What appalled SS examiners most was the "feminine elements" that made their appearance in many groups: "broad pelvis, narrow shoulders, secondary female sexual characteristics, fatty tissue, thin bones, feminine movements." Some "even had their hair cut in a feminine style," while others were "heavily perfumed." The authorities in Frankfurt were upbraided for their indifference to Article 175 of the Criminal Code, which dealt with sexual abnormalities. HJ and SS leaders agreed that the "feminine types" were unsoldierly, unfriendly, and fit only for "aesthetic functions" like leading discussion groups. Any kind of achievement could not be expected from these "living cripples," but worse yet was the fact of their presence among the healthy. The SS would have to introduce HJ doctors and leaders to the "racial-biological" concepts of the SS, although it is unclear how this would change the physical condition of youth in the inner city. The SS in Frankfurt appears to have been unaware that many HJ leaders did not share the inherent elitism of the SS and thought of the HJ as an egalitarian mass movement. The examiners blithely went on to recommend expansion of HJ-SS contacts by including "kinship evenings," common educational sessions, and visits to cultural functions.[49]

The SS had no better luck with the HJ in 1938. Within Fulda-Werra only Frankfurt failed to produce a single candidate by the February deadline. Other areas overcame difficulties with the HJ, but not without airing excuses. The HJ leader in Bad Homburg complained that terms of service were too long (12 years in the SSTV!), that the lack of military service equivalence in the SSTV was unattractive, that jobs in business were more promising. The leader of the Frankfurt HJ, Hermann Lindenburger, meanwhile gave Moreth a realistic appraisal of the situation when he explained that 2,000 of the 10,000 members in Frankfurt belonged to the special formations of the HJ. This clearly indicated their preference for the regular army. To assuage Moreth's anticipated wrath, Lindenburger resorted to the standard excuse that Frankfurt was not one of "the best racial districts."[50]

Moreth's superiors then sent him to a conference of HJ leaders at Wiesbaden to discuss prevailing problems. He emerged with nothing more than additional evidence of indifference and organizational ineptitude among HJ leaders. Moreth learned, however, that the HJ planned a national "health campaign" and suggested that the SS utilize this opportunity to muster boys between sixteen and eighteen. A question about recruiting boys who had been mustered by the army got no specific answer. Regulations forbade devious tactics like these, at least before the advent of Gottlob Berger. While Moreth was allowed to use the "health campaign" gambit, he had little luck. Specific dates were frequently postponed or canceled by the HJ without the SS being informed, with the result that only eight prospects were found in Frankfurt.[51]

A-SS units in other cities of Fulda-Werra were more successful, although they also confronted youthful indifference even if HJ leaders were on the whole friendly and cooperative. At Meiningen the ancestral chart appeared to be the greatest stumbling block, further complicated by the averred refusal of peasant boys to respond to any kind of appeal, even "official orders." This reaction should have given alert SS recruiters pause, since they were repeatedly told the best "human material" was to be found among country folk. Leaders of HJ districts generally promised much but delivered little, being eager to discuss but slow in the necessary paper work, a not unfamiliar complaint about young people. In Erfurt the SS succeeded in netting 20 recruits from 175 promised by the seven HJ districts in the area. Some district leaders insisted that a very small percentage of eligible boys could actually meet the requirements of the SSVT. Others seemed to be totally ignorant of any agreement between Himmler and Schirach, while many neglected to inform subordinate units about such a pact. The HJ in Kassel was more responsive, and the Meiningen HJ, which was the only one meeting its 1938 quota of 360 volunteers, must have overcome general reluctance to join the Black Corps.[52]

### Confirmation of the HJ-SS Alliance

Friedrich Hauser, chief of the SS Recruiting Office, came to regret his policies. They led to independent forays among the HJ by the armed formations. These tactless drives produced critical reaction from the public and prospective recruits. Nevertheless, since the RJF cooperated, the operation had been properly initiated. After all, he reminded Heissmeyer, the A-SS recruiters had managed to round up some 4,260 volunteers for the SSVT and SSTV during the first ten months of 1937. He saw little reason to doubt that he could produce 11,375 volunteers during the coming year.

Local recruiters were not so optimistic. The regional recruiting center in Hamburg, for instance, showed meager results at the end of 1937. Of 1,492 candidates gathered by the A-SS, only 308 were found to be fit for active service. SSTV and SSVT mustering commissions, it seems, had been steered by the A-SS toward small towns and the countryside, where the quality of "human material" had not met SS standards. A-SS leaders were also misleading potential recruits about service prerequisites. Some were told that the SSTV was part of the regular army, others were led to believe falsely that service with the SSVT did not fulfill military duty and that every SSVT veteran had to join the police force. While the latter was clearly Himmler's intention, it was not considered advisable to publicize the fact. What bothered Berlin most was the fact that some A-SS leaders were still advertising in the local press, a practice explicitly forbidden.[53]

Clearly Himmler was eager to prevent the army from discovering the extent of his recruiting. This clandestine policy was also the cause for the subterfuges used by the A-SS, the "ignorance" of some A-SS recruiters about existing regulations, and the hesitant cooperation given by regional and local HJ leaders. Schirach's orders to them appear not to have been widely distributed, but passed on only through semiconfidential journals like the *Reichsbefehl* and *Amtliches Nachrichtenblatt*. SS complaints about the incompetence of HJ leaders may therefore have been quite baseless or at least exaggerated. In any case, the involvement of the SSTV, SSVT, and SD in the Austrian *Anschluss* and the Czech crisis, with the connivance of army authorities and the explicit approval of Hitler, made Himmler much bolder and led to a major change in SS recruitment policy and practice.[54]

Hauser continued to make procedural adjustments, but his repeated declarations that each new arrangement settled the matter had become irrelevant. He was about to be replaced and the Central SS Office entered another period of reorganization. In May 1938 Himmler transformed the old recruiting office into a new registration office, incorporating and centralizing SS registration and statistical activities. A new recruiting office, established in July, received the task of "securing adequate and suitable recruits" for the entire SS organization. Himmler envisaged these activities on a much broader scale than previous practice suggested, since statistical surveys revealing qualitative racial distinctions were to become the basis of effective recruitment. As a central agency the new office became responsible for organizing and supervising the various mustering commissions. Friedrich Hauser moved over to the Registration Office and Gottlob Berger became Himmler's recruiting tsar.[55]

Himmler's selection of Berger turned out to be a judicious decision. One of eight children born to a Swabian sawmill owner, this World War I volunteer, heavily wounded and decorated, embarked on a career fairly typical for many SS bureaucrats. An assault-squad leader during the war, he became embroiled almost immediately in the postwar activities of the notorious Free Corps. He also prepared himself for a more prosaic career as physical education instructor and actually served as gymnastics coach, grade school teacher, and principal in the 1920s. When the SA emerged as a paramilitary successor to the Free Corps, Berger led an SA group in Württemberg between 1930 and 1933. He headed the Provincial Gymnastics Institute in Stuttgart, was "correspondent for the physical education of youth" in the Culture Ministry of Württemberg, and a secondary school headmaster. For a short time he was an advisor for physical training to the Nazi Teachers Association. Berger's budding career in the SA was shattered in 1933 because of disagreements with other SA leaders, who denounced his overweening ambition, "big mouth," and "lack of self-criticism and soldierly discretion." After Röhm's murder, he was a subordinate to the SA training chief, Friedrich Wilhelm Krüger, whose recommendation to the SS could not have done Berger much good, since Krüger was himself suspected of playing a double role during the abortive SA putsch. Although derided by his former associates, Berger managed to ingratiate himself with Himmler and finally joined the SS in 1935, holding several different staff positions in Württemberg and Berlin.[56] His checkered background reveals a man who was unscrupulous, blunt, and inelegant in manner and expression, yet also full of genial loquacity and racy humor. One observer has attributed to him a mixture of oriental intrigue, peasant cunning, and candor. Berger's skill as a bureaucratic manipulator, a trait Himmler could appreciate, bordered on making him an SS prototype.[57]

Himmler had fretted for years over the problems of recruitment. With a single stroke, he now sought to guarantee that the "most valuable German people" would enter his racial community and at the same time eliminate the divisive competition among his satraps. Only a dominant center with a strong boss could implement these purposes. It meant that the leaders of the armed formations were excluded from recruiting. Himmler was particularly eager to remove this form of independence from Theodor Eicke, the head of the Death's Head Formations and the concentration camps, because his men frequently chose to do their military service in the army. Even the SSVT occasionally revealed disdain for the A-SS, whereas Himmler regarded the civilian SS as a "nuclear troop," without which the SSVT would become merely a "black-coated division of the army." Berger was expected to "incite" the A-SS to "find individually valuable young men" and incorporate them in the "blood-aristocracy of the SS." This required that recruiters be knowledgeable about the towns and villages in their territories. Mustering commissions had to be selected and trained with care. The SS would thus be able to pinpoint recruitment productively and exercise "exceeding tactfulness."[58]

Tact was a rare commodity among SS examiners. Heissmeyer had to remind them on several occasions that they were dealing with volunteers, not conscripts. Gruff treatment could mean adverse reaction, especially in the HJ, as recent experience had shown. Heissmeyer, furthermore, thought that fallen arches or bad teeth ought not to keep good men out of the SS, particularly if proven "leadership-personalities" were involved. Himmler, too, admitted standards had been too high. The health of the current generation had been affected by a childhood spent in the hunger and misery of the postwar years. Fewer than six cavities were not grounds for rejection, nor were bad posture or faulty "connective tissue," in the estimate of Heissmeyer, who seems to have read the Frankfurt recruiting report. Glasses for minor correction of sight were now allowed, and height requirements were scaled down.[59]

Berger soon found cause to replace the old recruiters with "recruiting leaders" and to expand their duties. This occurred in July 1938, two months after his appointment. It anticipated a permanent agreement Berger was then negotiating with the RJF. This was to make members of the SRD automatic candidates for the SS, thus strengthening the "requisition" of recruits by A-SS leaders. A firmer HJ-SS relationship was bound to develop, since the recruiting leaders began to supply the HJ systematically with sport trainers and lecturers. The search for young men now also included secondary schools and agricultural and vocational institutions.[60]

The agreement that Berger negotiated and to which Himmler and Schirach signed their names on 26 August 1938 was to become a political tie which bound the fate of thousands of young boys in the SRD and with them the entire HJ organization to the misfortunes and misdeeds of the SS. It made SRD leaders responsible for the enrollment of its members in the SS and required that constant communication and collaboration be maintained with "all SS leaders and officers." The HJ agreed to give SS leaders the opportunity "to instruct" every member of the SRD "in the duties and history of the SS." Schirach thus provided potentially far-reaching access to the younger generation for systematic indoctrination by mystical racial ideologues and criminal practitioners of unlimited police power. While this was to be done in the context of the conventional SRD training program, it was the SS that now supplied the trainers and the training materials.

Almost as an afterthought, the agreement stipulated that SS officers were to be given a free hand to recruit soldiers for the SS armed formations. The various police branches were not mentioned, but institutional rotation took place from the start. Also left unsaid was the fact that the SRD by definition had a determinative role as the instrument of discipline and control for the entire HJ, as well as in the initiation of younger members from the Jungvolk (JV). The SS received a broad institutional base for the exertion of its influence over the organized younger generation. In order to secure this pact, Himmler apparently had to do no more than satisfy the political ambitions of HJ leaders by offering them more or less equivalent ranks in the A-SS and the SD, should they decide to follow their charges into the Black Corps, as most of them did.[61]

Gottlob Berger, whose blustery manner seems to have won the day in the RJF, was clearly the man who engineered this agreement. His aims, disingenuous as always, had the immediate purpose of building up Himmler's emerging "army." In late October he gathered his recruiting leaders for a high-level conference in the House of Youth in Berlin-Neukölln. While no minutes of the conference have survived, it is clear from the agenda that Berger was interested in establishing his position in the hierarchy of the SS and about to push for expansion across the board. There were speeches and discussions, incongruous visits to the local theater and Sachsenhausen concentration camp, and a tour of Lichterfelde Barracks, the home of the Hitler's renowned Body Guard. The inspector of the SSVT, Paul Hausser; the chief of the SD, Reinhard Heydrich; and August Heissmeyer, Berger's superior as head of the Central SS Office, discussed all aspects of SS activity and doctrine. There is no evidence that representatives of the RJF were present, although it would have been strange indeed if they had been excluded.[62]

Two important developments in 1938 made Berger's task easier. A scandal involving Blomberg and trumped-up charges of homosexuality against Werner von Fritsch, the commander in chief of the army, allowed Hitler, in the course of the crisis, to assume personal command of the armed forces. As supreme commander he created the Oberkommando der Wehrmacht (OKW) early in February. The smoldering opposition of army officers to SS expansion was thus effectively dampened. Once in control, Hitler found courage to end the anomalous position of the SS armed formations. A secret decree defined the police duties of the SS and its wartime rela-

tionship to the army. The A-SS remained unarmed, but the military formations, including cadet schools and Death's Head reserve units, were to be
trained and armed for service with the regular army. Himmler retained
command in peacetime, but wartime operations would put the army in
charge. Formation of new units were left to Hitler's discretion, meaning
that recruitment would be determined by negotiations with the OKW.
Himmler, who had a hand in changing early drafts of the decree, finally
found legitimization for his troops, which was bound to embolden Berger's
recruiting among the HJ. The decree specifically stated that "reinforcements for the SSVT in case of mobilization" would come from "volunteers
of the younger . . . classes." Since the SSVT did not have its own reserve
units, "police reinforcements" could be used for this purpose. This particular provision subsequently allowed Berger to transfer large numbers
from the SSTV and party auxiliaries to the SSVT, thus sealing the unholy
tie between concentration camp guards and W-SS. Simultaneously, Berger
found a "loophole" that allowed him to mount recruiting campaigns to
replenish the ranks of the denuded SSTV.[63]

While the HJ avoided tight control by party bureaucrats, it moved with
naive alacrity toward an alliance with the SS, potentially a more dominant
patron than the PO, SA, RAD, or other affiliates of the movement. The
gradual evolution of this alliance was confirmed in 1938, when two agreements, signed by Schirach and Himmler, made the SRD and the LD (Landdienst) "feeder organizations" for the SS. The latter called for "close cooperation to achieve results" in mutual efforts to halt the exodus from the
land, to build a "new community of peasants," to bring the "best part of
our people into a new relationship with the home soil." Himmler and
Schirach agreed that similarity of educational goals made the LD especially
well suited to provide recruits for all SS projects. Since the LD had favored
boys with the kind of prerequisites cherished by the SS, LD boys were now
destined to become "defense farmers" under SS aegis. Some 50,000 youngsters had filtered through the LD by 1938, and 80 percent of that year's
contingent of 18,000 was sixteen or younger. There was an opportunity
here for recruitment and the exertion of influence that Himmler and Berger
could hardly resist.[64]

Berger became the key figure in the development of the HJ-SS alliance
and the creation of the W-SS. The national recruiting apparatus created
when the war was fully underway became the instrument of his will to
power. It functioned through seventeen recruiting stations with bound-
aries identical to A-SS Main Sectors and Army Military Areas. Located
within the Main Sector headquarters, each station operated indepen-

dently. As chief of the Recruiting Office Berger had direct control over the stations and received full autonomy except in "fundamental questions," which required consultation with Heissmeyer. This was an unnecessary precaution, since Berger soon became chief of the Central SS Office himself. Once there he meddled in every detail of recruitment far beyond policy issues. Although station staffs incorporated representatives from various SS agencies, Berger and station managers retained power of command over them. For at least four months each year every officer was seconded to a W-SS unit in order to refresh his knowledge of active military leadership. NCOs and privates remained with the system until discharged, when they served as trainers for W-SS reservists. Being responsible for recruiting procedure as well as relations with the armed forces and other agencies of the state led Berger to expand. In 1939 the Berlin headquarters employed 51 persons, and the whole system some 612 officers, NCOs, and civilians.[65]

When Berger's meticulously created apparatus began to function, he was not unprepared for opposition inside and outside the SS, but the sly Swabian repeatedly availed himself of easy access to Himmler. He explained that the recruiting stations had been modeled on medium-sized WBKs. Superficial comparison with the obviously greater needs of the armed forces might raise eyebrows, but not if the difficult task of the SS were understood properly. SS recruiting stations had to concern themselves with the planning of recruitment, physical examination, releases from the WBKs, and processing of military passes—an altogether more complex task than that of the military draft, which had a total national staff of 33,287.[66]

Berger did not always win his underhanded games with army authorities, which began in 1939, but the rapid erection of a national recruiting network, paralleling and duplicating that of the army, was no mean feat. Opposition from A-SS leaders and Superior SS and Police leaders (HSSPF) he crushed quite easily. His friends, Karl Wolff and Rudolf Brandt, on Himmler's personal staff, became important conveyors of Himmler's support.[67] Berger thus managed to establish himself as chief recruiter for the SS. Basic techniques and the general political context within which SS recruiting policy was implemented were largely determined by him throughout the war. In fact, he became the real founder and expander of the Waffen-SS. Within eight months of his appointment he brought in 32,500 recruits, and the SSVT had its prescribed number of reinforcements for the first time since 1934. Berger ascribed this success to four factors: the personal efforts of Himmler; a number of "higher SS leaders," who had made special efforts; the recruiting leaders, whom he himself had installed in the regiments of the A-SS; and, most importantly, a "warm working relationship with the RJF." Berger believed that the "personal note which had characterized recruiting from the beginning," had much to do with it as well. Hundreds of young volunteers had expressed "the feeling that in Berlin there was a place which really cared about them."[68]

It was not coincidence that the HJ-SS alliance should have been consummated by the establishment of a pseudo-religious common practice known as the solstice festival. The first time it seems to have occurred was in the winter of 1935 on the Brocken, sponsored by the SS, followed in the summer of 1936 on the Zugspitze, sponsored by the HJ. Thereafter SS and HJ took turns in conducting this cycle of ceremonies on various mountain tops or in wooded glens with different detachments of both affiliates participating, but with the general staging pretty much the same, in order to create a kind of sacerdotal tradition.

On 21 June 1939, for instance, Berger's Central SS Office arranged a joint ceremony with the staff of RJF, held in the Kiesgrube near Pichelswerder. It began at ten in the evening and lasted two hours, every detail carefully planned as Himmler had ordered. Three SS torchbearers and one HJ leader, who lit his own torch by those of the SS, marched to the place of the fire. Other staff members with their families followed, their voices ringing in song. Arcane recitation specifically prescribed by Himmler himself, speech making, torch passing, and finally dancing by specially trained BDM girls, followed in due course. The rite was then concluded by games and more dancing in the local pub. Much more than a pleasant little company picnic celebrating a successful merger, the solstice festivals expressed Himmler's deepest concern and obsessive effort to create an emotionally satisfying substitute for the Christian cult festivals he sought to eradicate in his own order and the younger generation as a whole. It was part of the "ancestor worship" he saw in the pre-Christian Germanic past now to be restored via his *Ahnenerbe* projects, his marriage code, clan-book registration, Wevelsburg ceremonials, the distribution of winter solstice and birthday candleholders, and other paraphernalia. Eager to promote what he called *Gebärfreudigkeit*, or "happiness in producing offspring," he was building a racially pure "chain of generations" of which each member of the order was merely a link, but, nevertheless, a self-conscious link in a kind superior future "gene pool" preserving Germandom for all time.[69]

## Maintaining an Independent Youth Organization

Hartmann Lauterbacher, Schirach's deputy, had been an honorary member of the SS with the rank of "general" for some time. Gottlob Berger managed to establish a productive relationship with Lauterbacher during those important negotiations of 1938. He was not hesitant, therefore, in ordering HJ district leaders to work closely with the SS in order to secure reinforcements "under all circumstances," making sure that they were "the best young men" available. Since OKW had explicitly accepted Berger's recruiting apparatus and ordered its regional corps commanders to cooperate, they seem not to have felt the need for special agreements, assuming, no doubt, that most youths would go into the army automatically. Premilitary training was another matter. The WBKs had HJ liaison officers, who had provided advisors for HJ war sports since 1935. Although Schirach's experiments with the charismatic Rommel in 1937 had proved to be a fiasco, General Wilhelm Keitel, the pliable chief of OKW, was more acceptable. In January 1939 Schirach concluded a pact with Keitel to engage "the entire leadership in all areas of premilitary training." Courses were set up in order to have a uniform program meeting army specifications, emphasizing target practice and terrain maneuvers. Schirach, always hesitant to surrender control to the military, made sure that trainers were former members of the HJ and that each course was headed by a current HJ leader.[70]

The Schirach-Keitel pact stimulated a triangular rivalry involving OKW, SA, and SS with the object of their contention being as always the HJ. Immediately at issue was premilitary training, but control over the entire organization and the independence of the RJF hovered in the background. Misinterpreting Hitler's decree for premilitary training, the SA put an oar into troubled waters. Regional SA commanders disseminated rumors implying that the last two age-cohorts of the HJ were about to be subordinated to it. HJ leaders hastened to alert Schirach, who demanded the immediate intervention of Rudolf Hess. The latter assured a nervous Schirach that his authority was not in question and that eighteen-year-olds would remain under his control. Keitel too assured Schirach he would hold to the limited agreement of January. The High Command of the Army (OKH), nevertheless, had a project in hand that envisaged comprehensive "postmilitary training" in direct conflict with tasks allotted to the SA. Himmler had expressed opposition to this scheme, obviously fearing that the SS would be left out of the picture entirely. Schirach also felt uneasy about the OKH project, but Keitel assured him that he would be involved in all deliberations and that liaison officers would be assigned to the RJF. This promise had been requested by Hess, who also asked that the SS be involved. Himmler, no doubt, had already been informed when Schirach sent him a note on 2 February describing these events, but it is significant that he felt it necessary to inform the Reichsführer-SS. In doing so he felt more secure and expressed the hope that he and Himmler would be spared "surprises" of a similar nature in the future. He concluded his letter to Himmler as follows: "Since the . . . Führer . . . has given . . . his assent to the implementation orders of the HJ Law, we have the right to hope that the ambiguity produced by the SA decree will be removed. Since the implementation decrees are long overdue, order can once more be restored in the area of premilitary training, without in the least depriving the SA of any authority."[71]

Himmler, apparently on the periphery of these events, had been simply waiting for the right moment to get Schirach's signature on the LD pact negotiated during the preceding December. He moved quickly to exploit Schirach's vulnerable position by naming liaison officers for major SS branches. All of them were appointed in June 1939 and reported to Gebietsführer Heinrich Lüer, chief of the Surveillance Bureau, and Obergebietsführer Heinz Hugo John, who headed the Personnel Office of the RJF. In August Schirach appointed the section chief in the Personnel Office, Bannführer Fritz Rubach, to be the RJF liaison to the Personnel Office of the SS, where he again became section chief and received the rank of SS-Hauptsturmführer. In this manner the SS outmaneuvered both SA and OKW.[72]

SA and OKW made renewed attempts to gain control over the HJ, but by then Gottlob Berger had concluded his reorganization of the SS recruiting system and found ways to influence OKW or else subvert its policies. Late in October 1939 Berger was negotiating with the RJF over expansion of the SRD. During the discussions he observed a "deep sense of depression," stemming from internal dissension and the palling effects of the war. Schirach had told his leaders, according to Berger, that he expected all of them to be in the front line when the war came. He would be the first to go, being temporarily replaced by Lauterbacher. In rotation, at least half of the leadership would always serve with the troops. Once the war began, however, Schirach did not volunteer, and Lauterbacher was denied service with the air force on Schirach's order. At OKW Berger picked up intimations which suggested "new leadership for youth." OKW officers believed that "fine work" was being done in the special formations, where "experienced soldiers had guided training," but the rest of the HJ was ill prepared.

Berger thought OKW was testing SS reaction to a possible army takeover of the HJ. To counter this threatened coup, Berger suggested that Himmler assign A-SS men and wounded SSTV and SSVT men to the HJ as trainers. At the same time, SRD units should be kept at full strength. Himmler replied that any change in the leadership of the HJ was "out of the question," but the bravado lost some of its punch when he agreed to adopt the proposed training scheme.[73]

Beginning to feel the pinch of the draft, the RJF feared that too many leaders would volunteer for the SS armed formations and thus endanger the whole organization. So Lauterbacher ordered that all SSVT and SSTV volunteers should first secure the assent of their superiors in the HJ so as "to maintain adequate leadership under all circumstances." Yet, according to Berger, "efforts were afoot to draft the entire leadership corps of the HJ and students of the Adolf Hitler Schools" as well. He believed Hitler had agreed to this "without considering the consequences." The "reinforcement program" of the SS would thus be jeopardized. Problems of leadership in the HJ were already acute, expressed in the undeniable "degeneration of youth." One could see this in the "formation of cliques led by asocial personalities, as yet unpunished or unnoticed by the police." So Berger detected a conspiracy to use the war as pretext for a "destruction of the RJF." Even the SA was more or less openly expressing intentions "to seize power over youth." This was done, he thought, in collusion with "certain circles in the army." During current musterings of SA men for the SS Death's Head Regiments, many SA leaders had "emphasized" that the SA would soon "take the entire youth in hand in order to train it for military service."[74]

As usual, Berger had a countervailing ploy for Himmler. A list should be compiled of A-SS officers and men who had not yet been inducted into the Death's Head Regiments and who were prepared to assume part-time leadership in the SRD and other HJ units. He suggested a preliminary quota of thirty men from each A-SS regiment. Lauterbacher, meanwhile, agreed to compile his own list of HJ leaders who were to be mustered for the SSVT and "Police Reinforcements," the key facet of Himmler's expansionary scheme. Those who could be replaced by A-SS men or wounded veterans would then be sent to the front. That was not all. The SRD units were now being filled by direct transfers from the JV. While this would produce significant SRD growth, Berger wanted the actual strength of SRD units kept secret in order to avoid "jealous reaction by other party formations." If the war lasted longer than expected and the HJ actually collapsed, the SRD should remain intact, becoming a kind of "nuclear HJ, collecting all racially pure blood." Boys suitable for the SS should be kept within their units until ready for induction. Premature transfer to the A-SS would be unwise. Since there was no more limitation on terms of military service, it was possible to get all of them for the SS and provide the RJF with needed leaders at the same time.[75]

It was a neat scheme, and Himmler saw it as such. He ordered Heissmeyer to implement the plan immediately. All available A-SS personnel were ordered to put themselves at the disposal of the HJ Regional Directorates, while the RJF struggled to get enough deferments to man the most important national posts. Despite these frantic efforts, most draftable HJ leaders went to the Wehrmacht and a goodly share of them to the armed SS during the first month of war. The RJF was forced to reorganize itself into a lean and trim format, consisting of three "command stations" and five independent offices, drastically reducing its top-heavy officialdom, but it remained intact. In fact, the RJF soon began to involve the HJ in a host of auxiliary war activities. Berger's fears about the intentions of the SA and OKW did not materialize, perhaps because of his and Himmler's manipulations. Thus Himmler's desire for determining influence in the youth organization became a fateful reality.[76]

In January 1940 a succession squabble developed within the RJF, involving Himmler's special interest. Hartmann Lauterbacher and Artur Axmann, the main candidates for Schirach's post, were not equally liked by the SS. While tension between the youth leader and deputy had existed for some time, the former resented the latter mostly because he had managed to establish "close ties" with Himmler. Between January and June, when Schirach put in a stint in an elite unit of the army and Lauterbacher served as his plenipotentiary, these uneasy relations deteriorated rapidly, exacerbated by interference from Schirach's wife. Lauterbacher, who soon found his succession barred, quickly joined the SS Body Guard, arranged by Berger. In July the ambitious and bitter deputy wrote to Himmler asking for his assistance in acquiring a satisfactory appointment. Shortly thereafter Schirach became state governor of Vienna. Axmann succeeded, and Lauterbacher received a post as provincial leader in Hanover. Himmler's role in bringing about this turn of events cannot be documented, but is most likely.[77] Axmann, in turn, seems to have realized how awkward his position was and wasted no time in offering "friendly cooperation" to Himmler. A week after his accession, Axmann told Himmler he believed the SS to be "the organization with which the HJ enjoyed the happiest relationship." Both promised mutual support and the desire to maintain the independence of the HJ.[78]

Artur Axmann, national youth leader (Bundesarchiv Koblenz)

The diffuse character of Himmler's empire should have logically reduced its power and diluted its appeal to upwardly mobile young men in the HJ, but quite the reverse was true. Stringent conditions for joining this self-declared new elite created an aura of preferment that made it relatively easy to attract and foster loyalty and dedication. All SS men had to enter through the doors of the Recruiting Office and were legitimized as full-fledged members by its complicated procedures. Institutional rotation, beginning with the armed formations, further contributed to the special sense of belonging to an innovative corporate body that had important political and military roles to play. Himmler and Berger expertly used recruiting policies to develop controls over a diverse group of organized activities that evolved into the wartime "SS state," the cutting edge of which was the Waffen-SS. The HJ-SS alliance that evolved in this process helped him to create that "state." The SRD combined with the LD was to be the institutional connection on which the HJ-SS alliance hinged for the duration of the Third Reich. SS involvement in the premilitary training of the HJ, to be embodied subsequently in the premilitary training program (WEL), and the HJ participation in the population and settlement policies of the SS, to be expressed in the RKFDV, was to further cement this symbiotic relationship between two Nazi generations. Symbolic of this relationship was a significant number of prominent early HJ leaders who transferred to the SS and the 800 leaders who left for the W-SS in 1939–40, setting a pattern for younger men and women in their charge to follow during the course of the war.[79]

# 3 | Unifiers, Delinquents, Enforcers

Maintaining a reasonable degree of order in any society surely depends not so much on an efficient police force as it does on a sense of shared values, without total harmony being attained or desired. The police can help to preserve social comity by containing violent eruptions, but they cannot create communal unity. In Nazi Germany, however, the political police claimed the right to determine the nature of social relationships. Any initiative, independent thought, lack of enthusiasm, or suspicion of opposition was cause for police intervention. In the United States during the interwar period police professionalism moved in the direction of crime control, rather than concern with crime prevention. Public pressure to mount a war on crime reached such a pitch that plans were developed to militarize state police forces, and suggestions were even made to shoot criminals on sight and make jails unbearable. In Germany, where ordinary crime was frequently diverted into political acts against the Republic and the police were less immune to politicizing, crime prevention and social control were primary and led to new conceptions of police power that laid the basis for the police state.[1]

The politically determinative power of the police, characteristic of all modern authoritarian states, inspired not only the men of the Gestapo and Criminal Police, but was eagerly imbibed from them by the leaders of the HJ. They tried to apply it through the Streifendienst (SRD), a kind of junior Gestapo, detective bureau, and morals squad rolled into one. The slightest deviation among young people became treasonable departure from the inflated "moral code of the youth movement." It was no longer a question of shared values, as in the traditional German youth movement, which allowed for individual cultural, social, and sexual expressions, but rather a matter of uniform organization, official ideology, and prescribed activity.[2]

## Vagrancy, Sex, and Social Control

The SRD was a response to the particular situation the HJ faced in 1933. It was a time of opportunities and problems. The ambitious young political

**47**

warriors, who had gathered around Baldur von Schirach during the early 1930s, had helped Hitler come to power and were now eager to establish domination over youth. This totalitarian imperative was the motive force behind all HJ activities in the period of the youthful "synchronization" and turned all competing youth associations into deadly enemies. While the HJ was loudly proclaimed to be voluntary, it was officially sponsored, and pressure to join soon degenerated into coercion backed by police, government, and party. From the first day of Nazi power such methods of intimidation, subterfuge, and terror bred groups of resisters. This fact has produced disagreement about the extent and significance of youth opposition in the Third Reich. Most scholars have dismissed it by ignoring it, a few references to the "White Rose" serving as a kind of alibi. Some have argued implausibly that opposition to the HJ was massive, determined by social class allegiance and clearly defined goals. Others insist it was aimless and without practical effect. The time has come to bring this issue into focus, in this case, by exploring the instrument of repression.[3]

The process of coordination amounted to a campaign of conquest. Communist and socialist youth groups were outlawed along with the sponsoring parties after the Reichstag fire. On the strength of a Decree for the Protection of People and State, youth groups associated with other political parties or private organizations were also disbanded. After Schirach seized the headquarters of the National Commission for Youth Associations and the National Association for German Youth Hostels, the associations within them were disbanded and individual members pressured to join the HJ, as thousands did. The Bünde were outlawed after Schirach became national youth leader in June 1933, even though many had banded together for the first time and were prepared to join the HJ collectively if some independence could be maintained. Evangelical youth coalesced with a similar aim, but were outmaneuvered by Schirach and newly appointed Reichsbischop Ludwig Müller of the nazified German Christians. Sports organizations and youth groups attached to the Labor Front and the Food Estate were incorporated subsequently. This left Catholic organizations to provide the most serious problem for the totalizers in the RJF.[4]

Secret government and police reports suggest that a war of nerves between HJ and Catholic youth groups, supported by priests and parents, brewed in strongly Catholic regions of the West and South. During negotiations for the Concordat with the Vatican this tension receded, but thereafter the clergy encouraged Catholic youngsters to boycott the HJ. They were aided by HJ leaders, whose tactics were rude and provocative, and by the fact that Catholic youth groups provided better facilities and more organized activities. The moderator of the Aachen diocese told a government official in February 1934 that the "HJ could have had us a long time ago if a more tactful approach had been used, particularly if HJ leaders had not turned the problem of transfer into a small war, which hurt the pride of our boys and unified them." The expanding HJ, wedded to the principle that youth should be led by youth, suffered from a lack of qualified leaders. This raised fears among Catholic parents, who were used to adults and priests as leaders of their youth. Such fears were reinforced when a minor riot broke out in Aachen, stimulated by Schirach's dismissal of a district leader for "offenses against discipline."[5]

The RJF set up schools to train new leaders, but it took time before this program could take effect. In the Aachen district the "undisciplined behavior in the HJ," the "de-railing of certain leaders," and frequent changes in leadership, as well as the low salaries of full-time leaders and meager budgets of HJ offices, kept the HJ in a state of uncertainty throughout the 1930s. The replacement of younger leaders with older ones was greeted with optimism in party circles, but the discovery of homosexuality among JV leaders presented new problems. Priests warned parents that heathenism was promoted within the HJ. Promotion of the HJ by government officials was greeted with some optimism, but calls for more experienced HJ leaders continued. Some advised the HJ to avoid making martyrs out of priests, since the clergy were particularly antipathetic to Alfred Rosenberg and especially to Schirach, whose remark, "the way of Rosenberg was the way of German youth," was regarded by the clergy as a declaration of war on religion.[6]

In 1935 tension between HJ and Catholic youth groups throughout the country was on the increase, and in the Aachen district many Catholic youngsters appeared in public wearing traditional apparel. The struggle even crossed over into Belgium, where a committee "for the protection of children" was formed to warn parents in Eupen-Malmédy not to expose their children to dangers that faced them by contact with the SA, SS, and HJ. Priests recruited for Catholic youth organizations during religious instruction, which was prohibited by the Concordat. In July, Gestapo chief Heinz Seetzen reported that the Aachen HJ was making progress, although within some units indifference prevailed and made it seem as if "what the HJ had to offer was not quite satisfactory." In many instances, especially within the BDM, youngsters resorted to double membership, and party rallies were well attended by the HJ, who used them to recruit new members.[7]

The problem of leadership within the HJ was particularly acute in the JV, the junior division for boys ten to fourteen, since many former leaders of the illegal Bünde decided to join with their groups intact in order to bore from within by maintaining the old styles of youth work and sowing discord. These infiltrators, denounced as "social revolutionaries" by Schirach's coterie, spread rumors about SA dissidence and corruption among high HJ officials. The attempt at subversion failed. Probably influenced by the Röhm purge, the RJF began its campaign against these disguised "enemies" in the summer of 1934, and this led to "JV rebellions" in several large cities during the winter of 1934–35. In one city the HJ home and administrative headquarters were demolished, and papers and furniture were thrown out of the windows. The police, SS, and SRD were brought in to suppress the rebels, whereupon several police cars were overturned and destroyed. Over a hundred JV boys were arrested and beaten in the police barracks, but subsequently released. The HJ then moved its headquarters to another city; the Marine-HJ unit, where some of the trouble seems to have started, was dissolved; and the former leaders of the Bünde in the JV and HJ were quickly transferred or expelled.[8]

Synchronization itself created leadership problems, since the outlawing of competing associations and the annexation of others, as well as a bandwagon psychology that brought in thousands of formerly unorganized youngsters, gave the HJ a membership of over 3.5 million by the end of 1934. This enormous influx, illustrating the magnetic appeal of the HJ well described by Inge Scholl and Melita Maschmann, should caution us against exaggerating the significance of early resistance. At the same time the unanticipated growth, which led to a temporary membership ban, points up the difficult organizational task the overwhelmed RJF faced and the need for discipline and order that now arose.[9]

Sexual morality was another problem to which the HJ was especially sensitive. Certain segments of the despised old youth movement, which always shied away from including girls in their groups, had been known to have a homosexual problem, and the early HJ was widely suspected of similar tendencies. Schirach believed he had cured the problem by bringing boys and girls into harmless contact, but his confidence was misplaced. Article 175 of the Criminal Code became as well known as Article 231 of the Versailles Treaty in earlier years. The Weimar law was extended by the Hitler regime to a maximum penalty of ten years penal servitude if threat of bodily harm occurred, superior rank or position was used, persons over twenty-one misled persons under that age, or financial blackmail accompanied an act of fornication between males. The Nazis also raised the penalty for major offenses and made "unconsummated lascivious relationships between men" subject to penalty.[10]

A regime based on racial fecundity and the propagation of a "dominant race" could not tolerate sexual deviation. Yet the SS was a closed male club, the HJ maintained separate organizational structures for boys and girls, and the army in subsequent years deprived millions of German males of normal social contact with the opposite sex. These conditions were peculiar to the HJ generation and should be kept in mind when considering the problem of sexual irregularity. How serious then was the problem within HJ ranks? In Aachen, for instance, forty cases of suspected homosexual activity during the course of 1934 were reported to the Gestapo. Other cases within the JV came into the open the following spring. A twelve-year-old girl was disciplined for passing a song with immoral content around her JM group. Older HJ boys and BDM girls established liaisons that could not be kept under cover and gave parents the impression that "a certain degeneration" existed within the HJ, ascribed largely to immature leaders not qualified for the positions they held. In another instance, sixteen members of the HJ stayed overnight in a remote public shelter and engaged in collective masturbation, regarded by the police as a serious "moral lapse."[11]

The situation in Aachen was not atypical. There were highly publicized legal prosecutions of moral offenders during this time. The Land Year camps were a particular bone of contention, since parents feared their children were subjected to moral dangers and ideological corruption. The HJ got its revenge when one camper in Wiesbaden accused a Catholic priest of having used religion classes to recruit boys for homosexual activity between 1931 and 1934. The prosecutor accused the priest of turning the parsonage into a bordello while sending flowers to the unsuspecting mothers of the boys. A BDM leader in another city reported numerous teenage pregnancies and deplored the fact that "everywhere there is talk about the BDM." "It really hurts," she went on, "because we are getting the same reputation as the earlier Socialist Worker Youth." An HJ-Bannführer serving as youth specialist in the Propaganda Ministry asked one of Schirach's top assistants, a retired army captain, to stop HJ and BDM leaders from signing their real names on hotel registers. The assistant replied, "what else are BDM girls for except to take them to bed. It is necessary since otherwise they might become lesbians." Teenage pregnancies and promiscuity in the HJ was more prevalent than officials admitted. Homosexuality, meanwhile, continued on into the war years when HJ boys frequently became victims of molestation at the hands of their SS tutors;

Himmler consistently took a hard line against it publicly but was quite willing to mitigate his penalties privately and keep every incident as secret as possible.[12]

Detected cases of homosexuality and moral offenses in general among youth were rising substantially after 1933, according to the National Statistical Office. The RJF could not deny this, although they tried to improve their image by insisting that homosexual activity before 1933 had been much more intense than after but had remained hidden because prosecutions and penalties had been less severe. Given the unreliable nature of all criminal statistics, there may be some truth to that, but the fact still remains that moral offenses were second on the list of crimes increasing during the 1930s, closely followed by the specific crimes of incest, child molestation, and rape, all ahead of murder and extortion. Since the first item on the list was perjury, it can be said that "immorality" as defined by the Nazis was one of the more intractable problems facing the HJ before the war. Himmler's view was that Germany had then about twenty million "sexually capable" men and probably one to two million homosexuals—an intolerable situation that had to be corrected if the nation was to survive. Within the SS he ordered degradation, expulsion, legal prosecution, consignment to concentration camps, and finally "shooting while trying to escape," if all else failed to cure the offenders.[13]

After the Röhm purge, when Hitler himself exposed the homoeroticism within the SA, the RJF and the Criminal Police (KRIPO) went on the offensive. In July 1934 Schirach established the Streifendienst to combat juvenile crime, delinquency, and undisciplined behavior within the HJ. Training and supervision was handed to the Police Liaison Bureau, organized earlier within the Personnel Office of the RJF. In charge of the Bureau Schirach had put his trusted spokesman and adjutant, twenty-year-old Heinrich Lüer. He had joined the party in 1930, served in the Nazi Student Association, and become Schirach's factotum in 1933. Rapid promotion followed. In July 1935 Schirach put Lüer, already Gebietsführer in rank, in charge of the Bureau for Youth Associations as well. As head of these important offices, Lüer had responsibility for all youth organizations other than the HJ, confessional questions, and the crucial relationships with the Gestapo and the Security Service (SD). As head of the SRD he was subordinate to the chief of the Personnel Office, Heinz Hugo John, his senior by a mere two years, who was an early honorary member of the SS and subsequent SS-Obersturmführer.[14] The SRD link to the police and SS was thus established right from the start. It is also clear that the struggle against illegal youth associations was combined with the war on crime and homosexuality, and with discipline and social control.[15]

The SRD worked closely with the police, since these junior policemen could not make arrests, conduct investigations, or give orders that had the force of law. While local and district SRD groups were being organized, Lüer and John at the end of 1934 got the assistance of the Prussian Criminal Police (LKPA) on two matters vitally important to the RJF: vagrancy and homosexuality. The LKPA became the national headquarters of the KRIPO as Himmler moved to integrate the police in Germany. It was associated with the Gestapo and incorporated by Himmler and his political police expert Reinhard Heydrich after the Röhm affair. The KRIPO was interested in using "preventive measures" as a way of suppressing crime. Special sections were soon created to deal with homosexuality and related sexual offenses. In this instance the LKPA agreed to aid the RJF in apprehending youths who wandered about the countryside in HJ uniforms. They were sent home or put in protective custody if immoral tendencies were suspected. The RJF was informed so that it could apply its own disciplinary measures.

The RJF was particularly anxious for KRIPO support in the campaign against homosexuals and agreed to inform KRIPO offices of every suspected case, so that investigations could be set in motion and legal actions taken. Lüer and John began to compile semisecret lists of missing youths and of "criminal elements" within the HJ. They were used to cleanse individual units of undesirables. Regional and district HJ directorates were ordered to report every suspicion of immorality, "after checking its accuracy," to the relevant KRIPO office. With the latter, "personal relationships" were to be established in order to avoid unwarranted "damage to individuals and the organization" through the resulting investigations. Every HJ member who "wandered off" without knowledge of parents or superiors was to be reported to the police and the Liaison Bureau. The police were thus drawn into the effort of getting a disciplinary grip on the HJ and moving it toward uniformity and control.[16]

Each HJ region got its own SRD leader, who reported directly to the Gebietsführer and the RJF. He supervised the district SRD units, evaluated their reports, and gathered information from leaders, including those of the BDM. Within the district, or Bann, a maximum of seventy boys made up the SRD group, strengths varying according to population and landscape, since areas where camping and hiking occurred required more surveillance. Local SRD leaders headed the actual patrols, varying in size according to need. They took their orders from district SRD or local HJ leaders. Patrol leaders could initiate actions if they had the approval of superiors. This rigid system left little room for maneuver, despite RJF insistence that local patrols "should be flexible." It was not a matter of reaching strength immediately, but rather to "grow organically by the careful selection of reliable boys." They were picked from regular HJ formations and temporarily excused for patrol duty. On their lower left arm they wore a blue-black stripe with the yellow inscription, "HJ-Streifendienst," a conscious imitation of Heydrich's SD. They had the right to intervene when any type of irregularity occurred within the HJ, JV, BDM, or JM. Their effectiveness, as we shall see, depended on the skill and initiative of patrol leaders.[17]

Lüer and John were eager to test their instrument and have it accepted within the HJ. They also wanted to impress police and public with the fact that the HJ could discipline itself. Since the RJF had already declared its disapproval of "wild wandering and idle tramping," it was decided to mobilize the SRD for its first national action during Whitsuntide 1935. For three days thoroughfares, camp grounds, and youth hostels were watched by patrols of half a dozen boys in three shifts. The planning had been thorough and secret. Control points were established with telephone connections to headquarters and the RJF in Berlin. Messengers on bicycles and motorcycles carried orders and reports. The identity, size, age, origin, and destination of wandering groups were recorded by direct inquiries or indirect means. The behavior of every group was assessed and recorded. If resistance was encountered, the local police was called in to assist the SRD. Arrangements with youth hostel elders provided the SRD with information about their guests. At district headquarters reports were gathered and analyzed and summaries prepared for the RJF. Berlin wanted to know who was responsible for undisciplined behavior, how widespread it was, and what further regulations were necessary to rid the HJ of its bad reputation. The RJF also was extremely eager to get information on competing youth groups. Results were conveyed to state officials, police chiefs, and "top party circles."[18]

A few days before the operation Lüer had elaborated the functions of the SRD in order to avoid ambitious actions that could have compromised his purposes. There were four basic goals: surveillance of youth outside service hours; enforcement of RJF regulations, especially those relating to uniforms, passes, curfew, outings, camps, and marching; confiscation of uniforms and passes of those who had been expelled or were not members of the HJ; and observation and identification of non-Nazi youth groups. Usually the SRD merely observed and reported, but in cases where the reputation of the NSDAP was endangered, they could intervene directly. Lüer insisted the SRD was not "a police, not even an auxiliary police." When it became necessary, policemen were to be called in to apply appropriate measures. Yet Lüer demanded SRD leaders be trained by the police. In Ruhr–Lower Rhine courses had already been held for this purpose, and Lüer suggested they be used as a model in the rest of the country. They included physical exercises and practice with pistols (despite the fact that SRD members were forbidden to carry weapons without permits). Force could only be used if suspects refused an order to come along to the local police station. Such incidents usually had to do with the surrender of passes and uniforms by youths who were not members of the HJ or had been expelled.[19]

This concern with proper apparel is not hard to understand, since the uniform was to be the outward evidence of a uniformity of outlook transcending class and religion. Confiscation of illegal uniforms, insignia, and passes was based on the "law against malicious gossip" designed to protect state and party from damaging slander. At times confiscations created hardships, since former members altered uniforms and substituted them for needed apparel. Whether uniforms, which usually appeal to children anyway, were visible proof of a *Volksgemeinschaft*, or a demonstration of the totalitarian urge to regiment all citizens—including adolescents—depended on where the observer stood. Youth leaders and millions of youngsters accepted the former view and only subsequently came to see it as regimentation.[20]

The general effect of the Whitsuntide operation is difficult to determine. The RJF was satisfied and Lüer called it a success. The Gestapo seems to have approved. In one known instance, however, the action was stillborn. The administrator of the Aachen district, Eggert Reeder, heard about the plans from the Gestapo, feared that conflicts with non-HJ groups would have been unavoidable, persuaded the *Landräte* of this, and then managed to have the administrator of the Rhine Province prohibit the operation in his jurisdiction. A month before, during an Easter outing, thousands of HJ and BDM youngsters had behaved so badly that the police and party had to be called in to restore order. This incident, and the fact that thousands of foreign visitors were enjoying the glorious holiday weather in the region, may have influenced Reeder's intervention. Whether the Whitsuntide operation as a whole dampened the celebrated *Wanderlust* of German youth is hard to say, but it certainly gave the RJF a pile of useful information and thousands of SRD boys a romanticized taste for police work. It put the SRD on the map.[21]

Some specific results revealed themselves in due course. The prevalence of begging in large cities and camp grounds by youth in HJ uniforms was one of them. The SRD paid particular attention to this clever form of mendicancy, confiscated passes and uniforms, and had the police send the beggars home. Some SRD leaders had exercised a bit too much freedom with regard to sexual irregularities, forcing the RJF to demand that investigations of homosexuality be left to the KRIPO and Gestapo. The surfacing of illegal youth, however, was the most shocking revelation. So the operation was repeated in 1936, with "fewer wild groups" being discovered. For the moment Lüer intensified SRD activity in pursuit of these determined opponents. He did not want the SRD to be lulled into a "leisurely winter's nap" just because discipline had improved. A token of growing SRD status was the agreement Lüer concluded with Bernhard Rust, which gave the SRD surveillance rights over participants in the Land Year program. For the long run more drastic measures were already underway, including legislation, police action, and a new code of discipline. Social conformity was to be enforced by every available means.[22]

### Dissidence, Delinquency, and Discipline

The existence of the SRD in itself was proof that German youth was not yet unified. The totalitarian imperative was still more of a quest than a reality. While the HJ continued to grow, the six-month membership ban being lifted in January 1935, it soon became apparent that all teenagers were not going to flock into the organization voluntarily. The draft and compulsory labor service made it easier for the regime to control young people over eighteen, and led youth leaders to contemplate sterner methods to regiment younger ones as well.[23]

All youth associations except Catholic ones were prohibited, and the tempo of repression against the latter increased. In July the Prussian police, soon followed by other provinces, forbade Catholic youth to wear identifying apparel, go on outings, publish periodicals, or engage in any but purely religious activity. Two years later the organizations were banned completely. Yet illegal activity continued. Some Catholic youths formed new associations, and old ones grew in size. To a lesser extent Protestant groups also continued to exist. The Bünde and autonomous youth associations, many of whom had been generally sympathetic to the nationalist element in national socialism, were quixotic about resistance.

The most clearly political early resistance came from left-wing youth groups, although smaller, independent groups like "d.j.1.11." appear to have been more adamant than those associated earlier with Socialist and Communist parties, while working-class youth were active among wartime rebels.[24]

Existing evidence indicates that the motivations of opponents remained vague and diffuse, except for the attitude all of them shared: an elementary urge to avoid the regimentation of the HJ. Perhaps not much more could be expected from young people in a police state, when the great majority of adults did precious little except resort to "internal migration." Daniel Horn, who first raised this issue after Arno Klönne's pioneering work, insists that "the greatest opposition to the HJ and its system of 'dominance' came from lower-class boys," although his limited evidence, largely based on wartime incidents, came mostly from nonproletarian youth. Detlev Peukert too has focused on proletarian dissidents and suggests that one could speak of the development of distinct youthful subcultures, the most important of which were those revealing a working-class ethos. Heinrich Muth has taken a broader view by arguing that the diffuse and incoherent nature of the youthful rebellion, greatly overestimated by the RJF and the police, ought to be viewed from the perspective of the juvenile rebellions in the imperial and Weimar periods. Based on more elaborate empirical foundations than Klönne's work, he argues that the claims for a new kind of proletarian youth subculture made by Peukert could apply to the youthful rebellion as a whole without reference to social class.[25]

It is evident that non-Nazi youth associations did not realize the danger they were in until their independent existence was threatened, and then it was too late to resist effectively. Small groups and defiant individuals were in constant conflict with the SRD and provided the RJF with perpetual irritation, which they blew up into a serious political threat. RJF spokesman, Gottfried Neesse, for instance, denied that the "continued existence of Catholic youth organizations was a special problem." The HJ was strong enough to overwhelm them, but what he called the "bündische Jugend," by which he meant all resisters, was quite another thing. Even in 1936, he admitted, dissident groups had not been suppressed, revealing a surprisingly strong "anarchistic" tendency, ascribed to communist and "national bolshevist" influence. In fact, some left-wing youth joined Catholic and *bündisch* resistance groups and members of the Bünde joined Catholic groups, but few of the Bünde revealed any left-wing sympathies. The *Kittelsbachpiraten* of Düsseldorf and the Leipzig-based *Meuten* did have left-wing elements in them. Although Schirach was getting worried and requested special funds from the German Gemeindetag in 1937 to help finance the SRD, the latter was slow to come to grips with the problem, despite arrests, prosecutions, and repetition of the prohibition against *bündisch* youth well into 1939.[26]

Early resistance expressed itself in delinquency rather than politically conscious opposition. In 1934 thirty JV boys from Duisburg avoided a party demonstration by sneaking out of town "in mufti," spending the night in a mountain retreat, singing old Bünde songs, and returning early in the morning, "so that the SRD could not get wind" of their excursion. Another group operated "in the wild" by going on hikes and setting up a clandestine den. SRD patrols forced them to be "very careful." They were frequently "written up" by the SRD, who made "the situation in the streets unbearable." The group then resorted to paddling in collapsible boats on remote streams, but by 1937, when their leader was in jail, the band disintegrated. Many arrests were due to SRD spade-work and Gestapo follow-through. The letters of suspects were scrutinized by the SRD, as one resister found out during interrogation in the Frankfurt Gestapo headquarters. In a remote village of the Taunus a "strawberry festival" served as camouflage for a group of boys to gather and sing forbidden songs. On their return trip they ran into conflict with SRD patrols. Shortly thereafter the Gestapo raided a riverfront hangout and arrested 150 dissidents. Twenty were charged with illegal activity, although the evidence against them was flimsy—a guitar became corpus delicti.[27]

Some members of the Christian Boy Scouts did not cease work after the HJ incorporated them in 1934. Despite house searches, interrogations, and SRD surveillance, they managed to take trips to the Saar in 1935 and Finland in 1936. The so-called Black Band existed from 1934 to 1945. It took the SRD a year to determine their identity, but then they were blamed for every incident deemed unfavorable to the HJ image. The "Black Band" was accused of filching flags from HJ camps and offering physical resistance when ambushed by the SRD and arrested by the police. Composed of working-class boys from left-wing youth associations, they took a strong position against tyranny and fascism in general, although their actions were no more effective than those of less ideological groups. All of them attacked the SRD whenever the opportunity arose. Some youth leaders who had emigrated maintained contact with their followers in Germany. Pamphlets, songbooks, and opposition periodicals were printed abroad and smuggled into the country. The Günther Wolff Verlag in Plauen continued to publish slightly disguised literature of the Bünde until 1936. The

Prussian minister of the interior ordered confiscation of illegal material and gave SRD sleuths a rich new field of operation. Wolff himself was beaten and imprisoned.[28]

Continuing opposition despite increased SRD surveillance and police intervention, decreasing HJ growth with membership losses in certain areas despite collective induction of ten-year-old boys into the JV, continuing leadership problems noted and reported by the SD despite systematic training programs, and the disquieting level of delinquent and criminal activity among youth within and outside the HJ—all pointed to sterner methods of social control. The HJ Law released in December 1936 gave legal recognition to its exclusive claim for all youth work outside of home and school. It gave the RJF authority similar to that of a state ministry. The HJ Disciplinary Code, also issued in 1936, gave the RJF a rational means of enforcement, and enhanced SRD authority by turning the SRD into a juvenile police force backed by state authority.[29]

Every offense against discipline and order made members subject to legal prosecution, involving the assistance of state authorities. The HJ legal system became necessary, since nonmembership could create serious disadvantages. Party membership required four years of service in the HJ; those expelled from the HJ could not join other affiliates; and most vocations, particularly civil careers, required previous HJ membership. The Disciplinary Code, issued with the approval of the Party Court, the Reich Chancellery, and the Ministry of Justice, was thought to make the HJ unique among historic youth movements. That this move was to some degree a response to continuing opposition is indicated by reference to the "need for cleanliness and justice" in the organization. Until 1940, when the Code was revised to include stiffer penalties, a variety of relatively innocuous measures could be used to enforce acceptable behavior. In ascending order they included warning, censure, forced leave, demotion, temporary exclusion, and finally, expulsion. Multiple-member regional "courts" and a "superior court," with a single judge appointed by the youth leader, heard cases and applied penalties. The hearings were confidential, no lawyers were allowed, and appeals had to be made within fourteen days. While department heads and parents could attend hearings, judges decided verdicts and penalties.[30]

Hitler assumed from the start that youth would have "their own state" in his empire. The HJ Law, disciplinary and legal procedures, and their enforcement by the SRD, were part of the attempt to implement Hitler's dictum. There was to be no significant life for young people outside the HJ. That is why Schirach made camps the prevailing form of experience for teenagers. There were camps for everything because they lent themselves to supervision and control. Weekend outings and small hikes, to which dissidents were forced to resort, were too improvised to suit the authoritarians in the RJF. The great majority of young people were misled by "the romantic facade of tents and open air cooking, field sports and camp fires, which camouflaged the military nature of life under canvas," as Hans Peter Bleuel has put it. But a certain degree of romanticism was also involved in the clandestine activities of the dissidents, and there were many hardy souls who escaped from the mainstream of youthful existence.[31]

In 1936 a Frankfurt group of dissidents built a "country den" in a remote corner of the Taunus, where boys pursued by the SRD were hidden. While the Frankfurt SRD and police "were on the heels" of *bündisch* delinquents more than ever, the den remained undetected. In the Rhine-Ruhr area dissidents from the Socialist Worker Youth, Red Falcons, Bünde, and Catholic groups coalesced and called themselves *"Nerother"* or "Kittelsbach Pirates." Their organization was "very loosely structured," but they managed to stage outings with increasing frequency, so that the HJ became "virtually defunct" in certain localities. The SRD and Gestapo regularly mounted "large raids," one of which resulted in 2,000 arrests. It was in response to such incidents that the Gestapo decided to set up a special bureau in 1936–37 to deal with so-called intrigues *(Bündische Umtriebe).*[32]

In Berlin, close to Gestapo headquarters, the SRD appears to have been unusually effective. The HJ magazine reported that the junior sleuths were well trained, organized, and informed. Displays of confiscated apparel, insignia, pennants, and literature of illegal groups were used to aid detection. A telephone call from any HJ leader was enough to set them in motion via motorcycles or automobiles. Small flags on large wall maps indicated the location of police stations. The result of investigations was submitted to personnel sections of HJ districts where interrogations were conducted. Serious cases were submitted to the HJ courts. Morale was extraordinarily high. They especially enjoyed patrolling billiard halls and amusement parks, where "a lot of light-shy rabble hung around." On one occasion they "grabbed an Obergebietsführer" who was not even a member of the HJ. These youngsters of seventeen and eighteen clearly enjoyed playing policemen, and regarded dissident youths who languished in jails or experienced the brutal nature of Gestapo interrogations as enemies of the state who deserved what they got.[33]

The opponents were forced to break up into small groups because of increasing SRD surveillance. Excursions outside of Germany declined sharply in 1937, although it was still possible to outwit SRD patrols by wearing official uniforms and singing HJ songs. Inevitably such tactics diminished the political impact of resistance. One dissident youth reported after the war that the fact of illegality had caused the "political foundations" to be weakened. So, he went on, "we simply made our youthful spirit of resistance known in our own way. . . . It was a healthy rejection of the prison organization forced upon youth." Another resister reported that the SRD and Gestapo "became disturbed" because the distribution of resistance pamphlets increased. While periodicals from Czechoslovakia, presumably the exile headquarters of the SPD, could no longer be smuggled in, hand-copied and mimeographed sheets circulated in enough profusion "to cause the Gestapo to scratch its heads." On one occasion a group had a regular street battle with the SRD, who, appearing in civilian clothes, had ambushed them. During the melee they extracted one of their friends from SRD clutches, but some of their compatriots subsequently became the object of SRD revenge.[34]

In recognition of legal status and the established collaboration with KRIPO and Gestapo, Lauterbacher changed the name of the Police Liaison Bureau to the Surveillance Bureau and enlarged it to include regional offices. Its duties were broadened to encompass "all political and criminal activities among German youth." The SRD could now bring charges against offenders before HJ courts and convey relevant information to regular civil courts. This was heady wine. Schirach's success in getting extraordinary funds turned older SRD leaders into salaried full-time specialists and allowed the SRD to conduct regular patrols. The connection to the KRIPO was reaffirmed, and the BDM began to furnish recruits for the female branch of the KRIPO. The latter had primary responsibility for "preventing juvenile crime." As such it served as an intermediary between police and youth welfare agencies and frequently took "criminally and sexually endangered" children under protective custody. It was also engaged in fighting an increasing traffic in pornography. In pursuit of these tasks the Female KRIPO regularly patrolled railroad stations, amusement parks, army depots, warehouses, and port facilities. By local arrangement the SRD increasingly participated in these hunts.[35]

A sign of maturing stature, Lüer and John issued new guidelines in 1938. Freely admitting that the SRD had become a type of auxiliary police, they made no more distinctions between HJ members and other youths. All boys from ten to eighteen and girls from ten to twenty-one were subject to SRD observation, but only the Surveillance Bureau had jurisdiction over RJF staff members, Land Year camps, and NAPOLAs. Smoking, drinking, improper saluting, tramping, curfew violations, singing of prohibited songs, disorderly conduct in billiard halls and dance halls, and similar aberrations from the puritanical Nazi code of conduct were subjected to SRD intervention. Illegal users of uniforms were not to be forced to "disrobe in the street," and only passes of illegal organizations could be confiscated. While Lüer and John lauded the SRDs socially valuable function in helping the police to stamp out vagrancy and purposeless "bumming around," they were conspicuously and understandably silent about the fact that teenagers were learning the techniques of intimidation and repression.[36]

Lüer and John gave special directions on ways to handle "extraordinary cases," mostly sexual misconduct. Girls were to be treated carefully to avoid physical injuries and dealt with only if serious misbehavior occurred. "Wild inns" known to be lax about cohabitation were to be patrolled only in conjunction with the police. The SRD was allowed to patrol "red light districts" in mufti, but searching of brothels was left to the police. Private homes were not to be searched, although bars and public houses could be kept under observation, while underage drinkers were to be removed by SA patrols. Any activity of illegal youth groups was, of course, considered "treasonous" and had to be reported to the police. These "traitors" could be detected by their bizarre apparel and disorderly grooming. Members of church groups were to be watched to make sure their activities were purely religious and did not degenerate into political acts.[37]

The ink was hardly dry when Himmler moved in to adopt the SRD as a "feeder organization" for the SS, soon followed by the HJ Land Service. In both instances the RJF accepted SS patronage without a murmur about its freedom from adult direction. Schirach was confident enough of his influence with Hitler not to worry about SS poaching. He was at the height of his power and eager to accept a further boost in prestige from Himmler. The SS too was enjoying a reputation as the elite guard of the movement with enormous power centered in the nationalized police apparatus. It was the culmination of a calculated policy on Himmler's part. From the beginning the SRD had worked closely with the Gestapo in hounding illegal youth groups. The Criminal Police had actively aided the SRD in controlling vagrancy and sexual aberration. The third branch of the SS, the SD, which was more purely SS in origin than the Gestapo and KRIPO, had been slower to collaborate with the SRD because its function before 1936 was primarily one of domestic espionage and because it was busy establishing itself alongside the more powerful Gestapo. In 1936, in fact, the SD became concerned about rumors that Lüer was trying to develop the SRD into an "independent information service." The SD also resented the support the SRD was getting from the Gestapo and KRIPO, not to mention the fact that some SRD units were copying the SD practice of using secret informers. Himmler believed the time had come to establish a more direct and permanent connection with the HJ.[38]

### The Establishment of SS Patronage

In anticipation of the important changes about to occur, the SRD was reorganized. Schirach was not hesitant to state that the tasks of the SRD within the HJ were the same as those of the SS within the Nazi movement, by which he meant racial indoctrination and suppression of dissent, disloyalty, and deviance—in short, social control. So the SRD became a special formation, superficially akin to the status of the more obviously premilitary segments of the organization. But the Marine, Signal, Motor, and Air divisions of the HJ proper, which contained some 18 percent of the membership in 1938–39, had a fairly technical orientation and seem to have attracted less ideologically inclined youngsters. Because of its function as a juvenile political police and its association with the SS, the SRD was to have a much more potent influence within the HJ.[39]

Evidence of this was the fact that Schirach soon appointed liaison men to supervise close cooperation between HJ and SS on all levels. SRD leaders were upgraded to Regional SRD Inspectors, and their responsibilities were increased to include collaboration between SRD units and the HJ as a whole with A-SS Main Sectors. Since the territorial segmentation of the HJ and the SS did not coincide, Schirach appointed special liaison men in some areas. Friedrich Hengst was made responsible for SS Main Sector West, Otto Heinrich Braun for SS Main Sector Southwest, and Gerhard Butscheck for SS Main Sectors Donau and Alpenland. The liaison in the Central SS Office was Fritz Topeters. All of them were appointed in June 1939 and reported to Heinrich Lüer, as chief of the Surveillance Bureau, and Heinz Hugo John, still chief of the Personnel Office. In August Schirach named the section chief in the Personnel Office, Fritz Rubach, to be the RJF liaison to the Personnel Office of the SS, where he again became section chief and received the rank of SS-Hauptsturmführer.[40]

Orderly expansion was introduced at the behest of the SS. Each October and November fifteen-year-old SRD candidates were examined for physical health by HJ and SS doctors. Then between November and April the SS conducted musterings to select from the "healthy" those deemed suitable for the SRD and the SS. Himmler's intent to use the SRD as a wedge into the HJ became evident when Lüer instructed SRD leaders to include HJ members who were not in the SRD but indicated a desire to join the SS on the SRD mustering and membership lists, which were regularly submitted to the SS. Aside from stiff physical requirements and the lack of any previous connection to the bedeviling Bünde, admission into the SRD depended on four years of membership in the HJ with some leadership experience and anticipated height of 5'6" at the age of twenty-one. Traits like calmness, dependability, self-confidence, and "nimble perceptivity" were especially sought after. Local SRD leaders were to be at least seventeen with one year of SRD experience, while district chiefs had to be at least twenty with two years of experience. Schirach projected a total strength of 80,980 young men by April 1940. The SRD fell short of that goal, because of organizational problems, the strong competition for wartime manpower, and the racial standards raised to satisfy the SS. There were 50,000 members in November 1940.[41]

The implementation of top level agreements is not automatic, even in a police state. But it is clear that the SS established an institutional foothold within the HJ through its patronage of the SRD. This becomes evident when we examine the changing relationship between HJ and SS after the Himmler-Schirach pact within SS Main Sector Fulda-Werra.

A situation survey, initiated by Gottlob Berger early in 1939, suggests that the SS-HJ alliance was assuming new importance. Preliminary examinations and subsequent musterings by mixed SS-HJ commissions were carried out by all but one of seven A-SS regiments in Fulda-Werra by the middle of June. Cooperation was satisfactory, although some organizational sloppiness and deliberate obstruction on the part of HJ leaders still prevailed in larger cities. At Jena many boys, apparently coached by antipathetic leaders, refused to enroll in the SRD, since it implied lengthy careers in the police and SS of which they wanted no part. SRD leaders were more cooperative than other HJ leaders, who sought to keep the best boys out of the SRD. This was particularly true at Erfurt and Meiningen. RuSHA examiners and A-SS recruiters noted that SRD units did not always have "the best material" and looked with envy at the fine prospects in other HJ special formations or the regular HJ. This was the case in Frankfurt, where SS examiners were given family and professional reasons for rejecting the SRD and the SS. But the quality of personnel in the SRD on the whole was deemed satisfactory.[42]

The situation in the countryside was less pleasing. There was less opportunity for contact with the SS; and the HJ organization itself was less secure in rural areas. The boost that the HJ Land Service received from the SS at this time and more systematic use of Darré's farmers' organization promised to improve prospects for the SS-SRD. In the rural areas around Erfurt some twelve SRD-Gefolgschaften (approximately 120 boys) already existed and others were being formed. More publicity was in order here if Schirach's plan to have a Gefolgschaft of 150 SRD boys in every district was to be realized.[43]

A promising beginning had also been made in transferring SS men to the HJ for the purpose of leading SRD groups. At the time of the survey nine SS men had been assigned to this task. Little material assistance had been given, and most SS regiments had not yet received duplicate SRD membership lists. Some SS leaders thought financial assistance other than transportation costs should be supplied by national SS sources. But in the Kassel area the SS was quite successful in conducting indoctrination sessions and order drills. Two SRD units (approximately 250 boys) had been used to help the SS control crowds at a veterans' day celebration. Because Kassel had SS men leading the SRD, it was becoming a visible element of HJ life and beginning to contribute to the orderly behavior of young people.[44]

During the first eight months of 1939 RuSHA officers in Fulda-Werra examined a total of 5,585 potential SS recruits, including the SRD, which comprised 31 percent of the total. Some 27 percent of the SRD boys examined were rejected as unsuitable, while 29 percent of other examinees were so designated. After a housecleaning, the SRD was left with 1,256 members in the territory, averaging thirty-three boys per HJ District and falling short of Schirach's goal. But some 240 boys still remained to be examined, and there was every indication that the SRD would come close to reaching prescribed strength by the end of the year. That the recruiting situation had been affected by the Schirach-Himmler pact is clear, since a total of 4,003 new members were taken into the SS during the first eight months, compared with 1,589 during all of 1938. This does not take into consideration that SS influence within the HJ extended beyond the SRD, since many boys were quite prepared to join the SS without enrolling in the SRD. At Frankfurt, for instance, 105 HJ members remained in the regular HJ but committed themselves to the SS and were found to be suitable. At Kassel 560 boys were deemed to be good SS material but a much smaller number served in the SRD. These SS aspirants were a kind of fifth column in the HJ and could be depended on to defend and promote the interests and the spirit of the SS.[45]

Gottlob Berger was a major force behind the expansion of the SRD. At the end of 1939, when the RJF was in danger of being dismantled by OKW or its independence destroyed by the SA, he skillfully used the Schirach-Himmler pact to strengthen the alliance. He knew that SS expansion could only be achieved through recruitment in the HJ and that the lode of potential SS warriors would erode unless SS influence was increased. He negotiated feverishly with OKW and the RJF, where he insisted that Schirach's aim of putting over 80,000 boys into the SRD was too modest. Berger wanted 150,000 as soon as possible. It appears that Berger was not alone in fearing that OKW was about to take over the RJF by simply putting its numerous reserve officers at the disposal of the HJ for premilitary training, as we have seen. Lauterbacher and other friends of the SS in the RJF feared the same thing. Himmler soon relieved these fears by putting the entire leadership of the SRD into the hands of SS men.[46]

Early in December Berger had a long discussion with Lauterbacher from which he emerged with several important conclusions. It appears that OKW had managed to persuade Hitler that every HJ leader between the ages of eighteen and twenty-nine should be drafted forthwith, which would, of course, have denuded the HJ of experienced leaders and jeopardized the continued independent existence of the organization itself. There was already a shortage of leaders which, in Berger's opinion, accounted for a patently obvious demoralization among youth, symbolized by the development of "cliques led by asocial degenerates." The SA was collaborating with OKW in the effort to "destroy the RJF." Berger, therefore, wanted Himmler to assign at least thirty A-SS men in each Main Sector to the HJ-SRD. Berger had no objection to HJ leaders performing military duty, but he wanted them to do so in the SS, not the army. He had already persuaded Lauterbacher to give him a list of all HJ leaders not yet drafted, and both agreed to have them all mustered for the SSVT and the "Police Reinforcements" by the end of January. Those who could not be replaced by young recuperated veterans of the W-SS could then be inducted by the SS.[47]

Lauterbacher also bowed to Berger's request that boys fourteen years old at the time of their transfer from JV to HJ be put directly into the SRD, thus obviating preliminary examinations. Furthermore, Berger asked the RJF not to publicize the number of such transfers so as to keep the strength of SRD units secret and avoid jealous reactions from other party affiliates. In the event of a long war and the possible disintegration of the HJ organization, Berger wanted at all costs to save the SRD-Gefolgschaften by gathering into them the "racially purest blood," thus making them into a "Nuclear HJ." Berger had one further scheme in this connection. The normal transfer of eighteen-year-old SRD members into the A-SS, scheduled for 1 April 1940, was to be canceled. He wanted all SRD members to stay in the HJ until they could be inducted by the W-SS, which would give the HJ needed leaders and at the same time prevent possible seepage to the regular army. Himmler agreed with all of Berger's recommendations and ordered that they be put into effect.[48]

We know that the HJ had 765,000 male and female leaders in May 1939. Among these, 8,017 were full-time professionals occupying major salaried positions. A sizable number of the latter either volunteered or were drafted by OKW in the first few months of the war, excluding approximately 800 SRD leaders (10 percent), who went to the W-SS. Berger's scheme, worked out with Lauterbacher and heartily endorsed by Himmler, meant that OKW's draft of HJ leaders was slowed down and that many of the remaining leaders were replaced by wounded veterans or undraftable A-SS men. This helped to maintain the leadership of the HJ and at the same time— along with other parts of the scheme—significantly increased the opportunity for SS influence within the HJ. In October 1940, Axmann, who had replaced Schirach and blocked Lauterbacher, stated that 95 percent of the leadership corps had either served at the front or was currently in military uniform. Yet, all HJ activities had been maintained, which indicates that army and SS veterans were doing the job and that many HJ leaders served only a short time and then returned to their HJ duties, being able to say that they too had served. All of this confirms that Berger's scheme was implemented.[49]

While there was no need for the SRD to become a "Nuclear HJ," it did become an effective conduit for SS recruitment. Lauterbacher made this clear when he stressed the security functions of the SS, its need for "carefully-chosen reinforcements," and urged the "preparation and early training" of recruits from the HJ.[50] There is no direct evidence that Himmler's adoption of the SRD helped Hitler decide to make the HJ fully compulsory, but Himmler's confidence in SRD boys may have persuaded Hitler that wartime control of youth could be achieved by formal decree and SS coercion. At any rate, in March 1939 Hitler issued the long-delayed implementation decree to the HJ Law of 1936, the so-called youth service obligation. This decree gave youth leaders legal power to dispose of teenagers' time and energies normally free from institutional interference.[51]

HJ leaders believed they were acting not in loco parentis but on behalf of the mystically conceived *Volk*. In doing this, Germany was supposed to have advanced over the democracies, where "calcified plutocrats filtered aged wisdom into the heads of young people who naturally resisted this type of authority since they perceived great new priorities alien to the older generation." The "youth service obligation" was not thought of as a tiresome additional burden, but as equalization of demands made by schools and professions, thus awakening youthful energies not otherwise expended usefully. Four specific kinds of conventional HJ activity were now considered obligatory: physical training, political indoctrination, cultural work, and social guidance.

Physical training was the most important, since it prepared teenagers for inevitable military combat. Much of this occurred in the special formations, which contained boys over fourteen who were headed for the armed forces, whereas the SRD had more than military objectives, was the exclusive preserve of the SS, and was intended to contain about 20 percent of HJ boys over fourteen. Boys in the fire-fighting groups, a part of the SRD, and girls in the BDM, particularly the older group (nineteen to twenty-one) under the "Faith and Beauty" rubric, were also obligated to participate in physical training. Indoctrination occurred formally during the "home-evening," now obligatory under state law, as were all those activities referred to as "cultural work," which included singing, storytelling, playing, and craft activity. By official coercion boys and girls were to be driven to "overcome reserve and shyness," obviously asocial in the context of Nazi society. Under the category of "social guidance" the HJ now made participation in the Land Service, the National Vocational Competition, legal aid services, and living in youth homes obligatory. One HJ leader boasted that "no youth organization in the world had involved youth itself in decisions determining their own social environment more responsibly or comprehensively than had the HJ." It was certainly comprehensive. How responsible it was the war would reveal.[52]

The service decree made avoidance of the HJ difficult. The police could force enrollment in the organization and demand compliance with special orders of the youth leader. Among the latter were harvest assistance, aid to government offices, the post office, railroad stations, the army, and various collection drives. While the RJF encouraged leaders to use persuasion, enticements, and peer-group pressure to gain compliance, it did not hesitate to threaten legal action. Failure to register a ten-year-old child could result in a fine of 150 RM or imprisonment for parents, while anyone who willfully sought to keep a youngster from performing HJ duty could be punished with up to five years imprisonment and a maximum fine of 10,000 RM.[53]

The public life of young people was severely restricted. The entire generation aged ten to eighteen was now subject to HJ discipline and party control. Children were inducted systematically into the JV and JM upon reaching the age of ten, and a uniform ceremony marked the swearing-in of fourteen-year-olds. The latter became a substitute for "change of life" ceremonies earlier conducted by the party and confirmations held by churches. While school commencements were not abolished, the party clearly intended that all significant social events for teenagers should occur within the HJ.[54]

The Disciplinary Code had to be revised because expulsion no longer made much sense. The new Code, drafted by Heinrich Lüer, retained a single judge and used "investigators" on the regional and district levels. The latter positions were filled largely by the "legal experts" who had been introduced in 1934 and on the whole were well qualified, with 67 percent of them being jurists. The investigators were assisted by aides. In criminal cases the aides were SRD leaders, who gathered evidence against the accused. When social circumstances appeared to contribute to an offense, the head of the relevant Social Office became an aide. In matters of pure discipline the unit leader became an aide. Since the investigators and their aides worked under the auspices of the political leaders, there was no question of any kind of objectivity that might have benefited the offender, particularly since the chief HJ judge, Heinz Otto John, was also chief of the Personnel Office. While the accused had a right to see records and reports of witnesses relating to technical facts, political assessments were kept from him. The latter were collected by SRD leaders from various sources, including HJ superiors, school teachers and officials, party people, army personnel, and SD and Gestapo officials.[55]

The new rules prohibited exclusion or removal of rank by capricious leaders. Permanent expulsion under the circumstances was not only illogical but might contribute to the general demoralization of those who were thus virtually excluded from society. Public reprimand and censure in the presence of the units to which the offenders belonged was the preferred disciplinary means for relatively minor cases. Appeal of decisions by district leaders to regional superiors was possible, but it had to be done within two weeks, and the appellate decision was final. For most full-time leaders disciplinary matters were decided by the youth leader, his deputy, or the superior HJ judge. Expulsion was now a serious matter, since such individuals could never again become HJ leaders, join the party, embark on academic careers, or become military officers. The parents of expelled youths lost the child support dispensed by the Ministry of Finance. These sanctions did not eliminate expulsions. Some 2,701 youths were expelled from the HJ between July 1939 and August 1941. One percent expellees in a compulsory organization of some 10 million suggests that at least formal control had been asserted over Germany's younger generation.[56]

Ever stricter discipline alone does not account for the effectiveness of control. The state played an increasingly important role in containing criminal activity among the young. State juvenile courts were overloaded during the war. The KRIPO created a special bureau in 1939 (*Reichzentrale zur Bekämpfung der Jugendkriminalität*) to combat juvenile crime. The Gestapo's C-5 Bureau, dealing with *Bündische Umtriebe*, was even more active in the 1940s, handling many youthful offenses not normally considered to be political. While the *Reichzentrale* worked closely with the provincial youth offices, juvenile courts and the Youth Aid Bureau of the Nazi Welfare Organization (*NSV-Jugendhilfe*), as well as the Female KRIPO, to rehabilitate delinquents, the employees of the Gestapo's C-5 Bureau made few attempts at such constructive efforts to reform youth who strayed from prescribed paths of behavior. To deal with serious social rebellion and actual crime among teenagers, the Criminal Police organized protective detention camps, which were something less than concentration camps and certainly more than conventional reform schools.[57]

The A-SS officers—soon to be replaced by W-SS veterans—who had assumed direction of most SRD units, were instrumental in another major effort to control aberrant social behavior: the "Police Order for the Protection of Youth" issued in June 1940 by Himmler in the name of the Ministry of the Interior. Police orders in the Nazi state, of course, had the same effect as certified law. This one was more than a curfew to keep young people under eighteen off the streets and out of restaurants, inns, and bars, and those under sixteen out of motion picture theaters, variety shows, and cabarets after 9:00 P.M. It prohibited the consumption of alcoholic beverages and tobacco by teenagers under sixteen as well. Violators could be imprisoned for three weeks and fined 50 RM, while adult accessories could be fined 150 RM and incarcerated for six weeks.[58]

Lüer self-consciously denied that the Police Order was an attempt to "suppress youthful vigor" or "lust for adventure," and justified this departure from self-discipline on grounds of protecting HJ members from corruption by defectors. It revealed, nevertheless, how far a fascist regime is prepared to go to restrict individual freedom in the name of protecting youth from harmful practices, which in the circumstances take on the nature of treason against an ideal social order. The SS involved young people themselves in repression, since some 50,000 SRD members were used to help the ordinary police enforce the Order. This claim that the Order was effectively enforced is supported by complaints from youth who resented being considered old enough to be soldiers but not old enough to drink, smoke, and see adult films. The RJF admitted that there were cleverly devised evasions of the Order, sometimes supported by parents who thought it was too restrictive. Yet, various places of amusement were diligently patrolled by the police and the SRD, drinking and smoking by teenagers was constantly reported and probably reduced. Movie theaters were checked regularly, and many underage patrons prevented from seeing restricted films. In the process the SRD boys became enmeshed in regular policing functions. Many assumed duties within police stations, since the Police Order required that the SRD write regular reports on asocial gang behavior, sexual molestations, and anti-Nazi political activity.[59]

A final logical measure was the "youth service arrest," a form of detention more severe than that of the schools, but less stringent than incarceration by police or courts. Introduced in September 1940, this means of discipline was more appropriate to a compulsory organization necessarily reluctant to resort to expulsion. It allowed HJ leaders to order detention for boys between fourteen and eighteen for up to ten days. To emphasize the deterrent aim, "service arrests" were to be made after rapid hearings and within twenty days of incidents provoking them. Culprits sentenced to weekend detentions had to exist on bread and water, but longer periods entitled them to full meals.[60]

While Lüer and Axmann claimed credit for the idea, touted as "the most modern means of Nazi education," it was clearly Himmler who suggested it, and his police stations provided the facilities for its implementation. When some areas made little use of it, Himmler became disturbed and put pressure on reluctant youth leaders, some of whom, nevertheless, continued to prefer money penalties to detentions, particularly toward the end of the war. Part of the problem was that the Justice Ministry had its own form of "youth arrest." This measure designed to deal with delinquency was adjudicated by youth judges, implemented by the police, and involved a maximum sentence of four weeks. Double sentences were avoided by negotiation between HJ leaders and local police officials. While the two types of detentions were never merged, Axmann and Himmler agreed in 1942 to have both supervised by the Ministry of Justice. This meant that HJ leaders now had to communicate with states' attorneys as well as police officials in order to apply youth service arrests.[61] Youth service arrest was an effective way of enforcing discipline and served as a deterrent, which helps to explain why no mass rebellion occurred within the HJ. Toward the end of the war it was frequently used to enforce HJ service obligations and aid recruitment for the Waffen-SS.[62]

# 4 | Policeboys, Informers, Rebels

During the 1939 party rally 800 selected Streifendienst leaders in resplendent new uniforms were put on public display.[1] The event bespoke the new status the SRD had attained as a client of the SS and served as a harbinger of the important role it was to play in maintaining discipline among Germany's wartime youth. It was no coincidence that official recognition camouflaged more sinister clandestine ventures upon which the SRD was about to embark. Reinhard Heydrich realized soon after the war began what a marvelous opportunity the SRD presented for the incubation of secret agents. It was important to select them before their minds were cluttered with information irrelevant to the cold-blooded conduct of domestic espionage. The KRIPO and Gestapo, together known as the Security Police (SIPO), had collaborated with the SRD from the start. Heydrich's personal creation, the Security Service (SD) of the party, had assisted the SRD since 1936. These police forces, together with the Order Police (ORPO), were combined into the Central Security Agency (RSHA) under Heydrich's command and Himmler's titular leadership. This done, Heydrich began to hunt for new recruits from the HJ.

## Young Spies and Informers

Heinrich Lüer was eager to cooperate. In fact, SD officials thought that SRD enthusiasts were too eager to get explosive SD information and advised caution. Lüer toured the country in the spring of 1939 and spoke at SRD conferences about new vistas for the HJ police. Richard Hildebrandt, a Superior SS and Police leader, and Lüer together addressed joint SRD and SD meetings designed to foster cooperation. During the summer the SD hit upon the idea of holding workshops for SRD leaders, where indoctrination could be conducted under controlled conditions and where potential recruits could be more easily spotted. The SD was eager to acquaint SRD leaders with its current functions, the status of various outlawed religious youth organizations, and the means of detecting im-

72

Reinhard Heydrich, chief of the Central Security Agency (Bundesarchiv Koblenz)

moral and homosexual practices. The path was cleared for a permanent arrangement between RSHA and SRD.[2]

In September Heydrich and Lüer agreed to utilize adolescents in a variety of police activities, including those of the Gestapo, KRIPO, and SD. If insufficient SRD members were available, qualified boys of the regular HJ could be used, and even BDM girls were not excluded. Young agents could work in offices or in the field, conduct research, serve as drivers and dispatchers, and function in that characteristic métier of the SD, "confidential observation." Although Heydrich warned about using the SRD in field work not "appropriate to youthful informers," he insisted that they be recruited for SIPO careers by using "personal influence." This kind of persuasion was effective with youngsters fascinated by spying under government auspices. Lüer was so thrilled by Heydrich's overture that he ordered subordinates to make every possible SRD boy available to the RSHA, even if they had to dip into the Motor-HJ and Signal-HJ for recruits. Releases from school were secured by giving "auxiliary police work" as the reason, while the project as a whole was wrapped in secrecy. Participants received lectures about the seriousness of their task: "This is no romantic escapade; do not count on playing policemen in any fashion, but expect your work to be simple and sober!"[3]

When it was decided to use teenage spies, RSHA lost no time in arranging training for them. At a frontier police school in Pretzsch on the Elbe instruction began almost immediately. Because of their age Pretzsch recruits had to be released from school and apprenticeships by cumbersome negotiations involving local police and SD officials, regional HJ leaders, school administrators, and employers. Permission had to be secured from parents, many of whom were reluctant. Heydrich considered all recruits to be SIPO and SD candidates, but he camouflaged their callup for Pretzsch to avoid the draft and to mislead quizzical parents. They were designated as "reinforcement personnel" for a mysterious "Project Tannenberg" or as replacements for the army's Secret Field Police (Abwehr).[4] While the latter was not yet a part of the SIPO, Heydrich and Wilhelm Canaris, the chief of the Abwehr, had a working agreement which allowed for this subterfuge. Recruiting under disguise was certainly more innocuous than telling the public that teenage Gestapo, KRIPO, and SD agents were being sought. In any case, the campaign was successful. Within two months over 200 youths between seventeen and twenty-one were recruited from across the country.[5]

This school for secret agents became a SIPO school for junior commanders and moved to Fürstenberg in 1941. Scattered evidence suggests that it continued to operate throughout the war and that large numbers of the SRD were filtered through it into the Gestapo, KRIPO, and SD.[6] Cautious officials tended to push graduates into noncovert jobs, a practice that these eager young snoopers resented. They must have complained, because the RSHA was soon compelled to order that graduates be used in "duties which prepared them for their future careers" and not merely as guards and messengers.[7] Continuous recruitment remained difficult, since school authorities raised bureaucratic obstacles, some of which were overcome by an agreement between the RSHA and the Ministry of Education, providing for early leaving certificates. This was done in the name of "wartime emergency," a favorite device of the SS. Efforts to gain releases from labor service were largely unsuccessful.[8]

The Pretzsch-Fürstenberg School and the Police Order for the Protection of Youth enmeshed the SRD in all policing functions of the SS. Regional Inspectors, almost all SS men after 1939, made groups of SRD boys available for day-long operations of the adult police. Arrangements with school officials released them from classes. Large numbers of the SRD were employed as aides in police stations. Many of them acted as assistants to police chiefs, and some even assumed executive positions in the municipal police or ORPO. The SIPO even began to use BDM girls, although mostly in office work. This was strong medicine for teenagers and led HJ officials to warn that such "sober tasks" should not be treated as "romantic adventures."[9]

With experienced HJ leaders away on front-line duty, the churches tried to reassert their influence over young people. Secret SD reports return to this theme repeatedly. To combat these efforts the SD decided to use the SRD in the clandestine surveillance of religious services. Beginning to experience manpower shortages and plagued by operational instability in its field offices, the SD found a partial solution in the SRD.[10] In Koblenz, for instance, extensive preparations were made as early as the winter of 1940. Test runs with SRD monitors gathering evidence on how the churches affected the population, what methods they used, and the kind of political positions they took turned up such interesting results that the Koblenz SD church specialist and the regional SRD inspector laid out detailed plans for intermittent surveillance. The boys who were used for this type of snooping were carefully selected. The SD instructed them on important ideological points. Their background was scrutinized to make sure they would be immune to influence by the clergy. Any previous or current connection to the churches automatically disqualified a potential monitor. It was a clever way of keeping tabs on the clergy without entailing the risks of adult observers, who might have aroused more suspicion than young strangers showing interest in religion.[11]

The SRD as a whole was now trained by the SS. Within individual units monthly training schedules provided for indoctrination during "home evenings," physical exercises, jujitsu and other personal defense techniques, combat training, and technical SRD instruction. This was supposed to foster a sense of "self-confidence in moments of danger." For seventeen- and eighteen-year-old leaders national courses were set up in special camps. The directors of these were experienced HJ leaders, but actual training was conducted by W-SS NCOs and A-SS men. The program as a whole was jointly administered by Heinrich Lüer and Gottlob Berger. The HJ aspect of the program involved indoctrination, internal orderliness, terrain familiarization, and parade drill, whereas the SS concentrated on specialized terrain exercises, target shooting, special weapons, and military engineering. The national courses lasted three weeks, with tight schedules running from 6:00 A.M. to 9:30 P.M. Each day began with a newsreel, followed by the various types of training, and ended with lectures, discussions, and homework. On Sunday mornings an ideological program was substituted for church services, and Sunday nights were set aside for motion pictures.[12]

Primarily ideological in emphasis, the training dealt with surveillance functions, laws and regulations affecting youth, and the roles of the SS within Nazi society. At the core of this process stood the "home evening," a euphemism for relatively freewheeling discussions. These sessions were designed to become a "source of faith," a kind of political experience that would give participants "strength for the day."[13] Whether these controlled "bull sessions" actually did that depended on the individuals involved. All forms of indoctrination are difficult to assess. It is fashionable to dismiss ideological "schooling" in the SS as largely irrelevant, since former SS men have themselves said they endured it pro forma and ignored it when the bizarre lectures were over. It is doubtful, however, that impressionable SRD boys were quite that cavalier about it. Like the drill masters in the schools, the SRD indoctrinators could count on being heard and obeyed. Ideological repetition, like attrition warfare and saturation bombing, does have its intended effect. So, one can only judge the effect of SRD indoctrination by the outcome, i.e., the SRD continued to function and expand, even under the constraints of wartime Germany. There certainly is no question about the positive effect of SRD indoctrination on SS recruitment within the HJ.[14]

SRD Expansion and Functional Division

By the winter of 1941 the SRD had acquired public status, significant influence, and power within the HJ. It was an important source of manpower for Germany's varied police forces. Much of this was due to Himmler's patronage, assiduously exploited by Gottlob Berger, and the skills of Heinrich Lüer and Heinz Hugo John. The latter were wary of Berger's single-minded pursuit of cannon fodder. Because of association with Lauterbacher and Schirach, who graduated to gauleiterships, both Lüer and John were on their way out. After a stint in the army, John continued to run the Organization Office of the RJF, a wartime consolidation, while remaining chief HJ judge, liaison to the party court, and ministerial counselor. In 1944 he joined the new SS division made up of Hitler youths and fell during the Normandy campaign. John appears to have been shunted aside to minor roles by Axmann's new men. That was not the fate of Heinrich Lüer, the father of the Streifendienst. In May 1940 Berger reported to Himmler that Lüer wanted to be transferred to the W-SS. But in October Axmann was compelled to tolerate Lüer's presence as Schirach's representative. This made him chief of a liaison group created after the issuance of the HJ Law. In 1942 Lüer became Axmann's representative with Alfred Rosenberg's Reich Commission Ostland, heading a new Youth Bureau in Riga. For more than two years Lüer was busy building native youth organizations in the Baltic region.[15]

Lüer was hard to replace. At first "Etsch" Heuser took up the reins. He began by streamlining the working rules and the organizational structure of the SRD. Within the Personnel Office of the RJF two separate departments were created, one dealing with the SRD and the other with surveillance. This was done to separate the order function, mainly the task of general SRD members who were fifteen and sixteen, from espionage roles reserved for older boys. SRD inspectors, working within regional personnel departments, were still responsible for district SRD leaders, who in turn had one or more SRD-Gefolgschaften under them with maximum strengths of 150 and minimums of 100. These in turn were divided into SRD-Scharen, and now even SRD-Kameradschaften of six to twelve boys.[16] The main thrust shifted from surveillance to "positive tasks," maintaining orderly public behavior and discipline within units. Unlike Lüer, Heuser was a W-SS veteran and more susceptible to SS pressure. When enough JV boys could not be found to put into the SRD, the SS pushed to have older boys from the general HJ incorporated in the SRD to meet contingent requirements set for each region by Berlin. While the danger that the SRD would become primarily an SS recruiting instrument was already quite evident, the RJF appears not to have been concerned.[17]

At a 1941 conference of HJ leaders and RJF officials in Munich, it became clear that the SRD as an instrument of SS influence within the HJ was a fait accompli. Helmut Möckel, who had replaced Lauterbacher, invited one of Gottlob Berger's men as an observer. The latter used the occasion to promote SS interests among the forty-two regional leaders, most of whom were well disposed toward the SS and nearly a third of whom were prepared to switch over to the W-SS from their reserve status with the army. Party Treasurer Franz X. Schwarz and Reichsleiter Karl Fiehler both referred to the SRD as a most important organization. The minister of the interior, Wilhelm Frick, praised the SRD for keeping juvenile crime "within normal bounds." Ernst Schlünder, the premilitary training chief of the RJF, revealed his plan to replace most of the army trainers in the national training camps with SS and police trainers, since army trainers were trying to exert undesirable political influence. Schlünder asked for more SS trainers, and Möckel told regional leaders not to assign SS men working with the SRD to any other duties. Axmann, who resumed his duties as youth leader on 7 December, highlighted SS support for the HJ Land Service and the SRD. While army and SA were sharply criticized— the former privately, the latter publicly—the SS was lauded and courted by all.[18]

With such a friendly attitude working in its favor, the SS quickly moved to expand the SRD. At each SS Recruiting Station, Heinrich Jürs (who had replaced Berger as chief of the SS Recruiting Office when the latter took over the Central SS Office) installed a new replacement leader (Abteilungsleiter Nachwuchs), whose duty it was to maintain smooth working relationships with the regional SRD inspector and keep the flow of recruits from the SRD and the HJ active. The replacement leaders became chief liaison officers to the HJ Regional Directorates and supervised district liaison men appointed in 1938. The various liaisons were obliged to visit SRD units at least once a week, provide facilities for SRD activities, furnish speakers for meetings, supply magazines and books, and lend sports equipment. In short, the SS replacement leader became a kind of political and spiritual godfather to the boys of the Streifendienst.[19]

Efficient extraction of recruits put the stability of the SRD, in its broader aspect of a juvenile police, in jeopardy. Since the oldest and best were periodically skimmed off, forcing new enlistments of fourteen-year-olds, the membership underwent nearly intolerable fluctuations. This becomes evident when monthly reports of one SRD inspector are examined. In this case, Ernst Bingger, W-SS sergeant and regional SRD inspector in Swabia, may serve to illustrate the point. Bingger had a difficult time maintaining stable membership roles and conducting systematic training, much less continuous patrolling, since the replacement leader in Munich constantly demanded new recruits. Starting with 2,000 potentials, monthly figures between September 1941 and January 1942 varied between 1,334 and 1,477, including all fourteen HJ districts, the average per district after examination being less than the required minimum of one hundred. By June 1942 only Augsburg, the largest city in the region, had met the minimal quota, probably by poaching on other special formations.[20]

In his early twenties, Bingger believed in the intrinsic value of the SRD. He deplored changes in leadership caused by SS recruitment and challenged his subordinates to keep SRD-Gefolgschaften functioning as originally intended. His remarkable career in both HJ and SS was not atypical of most young men who bridged the HJ-SS generation gap. Born in Lindau, the son of a railroad employee, he graduated from the *Realschule*, spoke English, and joined the Hitler Youth in 1933 at the age of fourteen. Handsome, articulate, and reliable, he moved up rapidly, earning all the important medals. In 1937 he volunteered for the SS Body Guard and participated in the victorious march into Austria, the Sudetenland, and Czechoslovakia. During the invasion of Poland he had an accident that made him ineligible for further duty on the front. He then made a desk career for himself in the SS. In 1941 he became SRD regional inspector for Swabia and for a time also served in the Munich Recruiting Station. In 1942, at the age of twenty-three, he was promoted to wartime leader of HJ Bann Memmingen. His promotion in the SS was also more than routine, reaching the rank of Untersturmführer by 1944. In 1942 he was one of the select few chosen to attend the Academy for Youth Leadership in Braunschweig.[21]

Since Swabia was a small HJ region, it may have had atypical problems in meeting Berlin's recruitment quotas and fulfilling the intrinsic aims of the SRD. HJ Region Westmark, with headquarters in Koblenz, had 1,200 mustered SRD members and an SRD-Gefolgschaft in every district as early as June 1940. Westmark had an energetic SRD inspector in Heinrich Ebert, who worked particularly well with the SD in drawing his boys into surveillance activities and providing SIPO candidates for Pretzsch. But Ebert was not lax in building SRD membership to a maximum. He also claimed to have recruited some 8,000 youngsters for the W-SS since the beginning of the war, although only half survived mustering. Nevertheless, Ebert was proud to be first in the country in terms of SS recruitment.[22]

By comparing Swabia and Westmark, at different time periods, it becomes clear that Berger's goal of maintaining a membership of 150,000 never materialized and that Axmann's more modest promise to Himmler of 80,000 probably was exceeded. There were nearly 1,000 HJ districts in 1943. If each had an SRD unit at minimal strength of 100, Germany had at least 100,000 SRD boys at that time. Had this force been used exclusively to contain social deviancy and enforce discipline, it might have reduced the amount and seriousness of rebellion within the Hitler Youth. When Heuser became SRD chief in 1941, he seems to have thought that the organization could continue as an instrument of discipline and also provide recruits for the SS. As the W-SS expanded to some ten divisions by the spring of 1943, the SS Recruiting Office put tremendous pressure on SRD inspectors for ever-increasing numbers of recruits. Heuser and his inspectors therefore found themselves in the difficult situation of serving two masters with conflicting priorities.

An incident occurred at the Munich Recruiting Station that illustrates this dilemma. Ernst Bingger, his colleague from HJ Region Hochland, and one of his district leaders were ordered to appear at the Station. When they did so, SS-Obersturmführer Willy Beck, Jürs's adjutant in the SS Recruiting Office in Berlin and official liaison to the RJF, and the chief of the Munich Station, SS-Obersturmbannführer Hans Büchl, berated them for not producing enough recruits. Beck's low rank would not have given him much power except that he represented Jürs and Berger, who used Beck to exert pressure on the RJF to turn the SRD into a recruiting corral, thus jeopardizing surveillance and disciplinary functions. Beck had begun his pressure campaign at a conference of SRD inspectors in the fall of 1942. Now he blatantly told Bingger that he was not interested in what happened to the Hitler Youth, only in the maximum numbers of volunteers for the W-SS. Bingger was incensed, confidentially informed Heuser of the incident, and begged him to take some action to preserve SRD independence. This was a difficult time for the SRD. Two new SS divisions were being organized, and Berger had to transfer older SRD members to the W-SS to flesh out the new units.[23]

External pressure forced Heuser to contemplate a change in SRD functions. At an SRD conference in Hallein, Heuser, Beck, and the forty-two SRD inspectors debated the issues, with Beck leading the charge and running roughshod over HJ sensibilities. Heuser then asked his friend and veteran SRD inspector of Franconia, Karl Schweizer, to comment on his proposed redefinition of the SRD's wartime role. Schweizer did so and also involved two fellow inspectors, Willi Adam of Bayreuth and Ernst Bingger of Swabia. Schweizer disagreed with Heuser's draft proposal, which still tried to retain the surveillance function and the role in recruitment for the SS. Schweizer, in effect, adopted Beck's position and inferred that most inspectors agreed with him. This meant that the RJF would have to agree that the SRD would be primarily a recruiting device. Since the RJF had already shifted the SRD Department from the Personnel Office to the Office for Premilitary Training shortly before the Hallein conference, it seemed as if the new priority for the SRD had already been established. So Schweizer suggested that the SRD stop playing policeman and adopt a combat insignia to identify its members as the future fighting elite of the W-SS. Such "external paraphernalia," Schweizer felt, would be a reasonably adequate substitute for the romantic appeal of covert activity.[24]

In the RJF, as well as in Adam's and Bingger's offices, strong reaction to Schweizer's ideas set in immediately. Heuser smelled an SS invasion of HJ prerogatives and wanted to retain SRD independence. Beck, speaking for Jürs and Berger, put strong pressure on Axmann and Möckel to adopt Schweizer's suggestion. Bingger and Adam supported Heuser. Bingger insisted SRD inspectors had to fulfill their "leadership duties to the boys and could not be SS recruiters exclusively" if they did not want "to cease being HJ leaders." While the dual role of inspectors was admittedly "a mongrelism," Bingger thought it was possible to be effective SRD leaders without degenerating into "willing instruments of SS recruitment."[25]

Heuser and Bingger were fighting a lost cause. The SS prevailed. In August 1943 the RJF officially announced that preparation for combat in the SS was the principal task of the SRD. Surveillance, reduced in scale and scope, became the exclusive duty of the remaining surveillance sections in the Personnel Office of the RJF and the regional personnel departments. On the district level "specialists for surveillance," usually the existing "legal experts" or "investigators," assumed the task. Covert activity and pursuit of opponents and antisocial cliques thus became an irregular function of the regional and district staffs. In effect, surveillance was handed back to the KRIPO, Gestapo, and SD, at whose headquarters "deputies for youth questions" were appointed at the request of Axmann.[26]

HJ patrols, led by a "surveillance expert" and staff members chosen by him, were still used to enforce the Police Order and watch all illegal and immoral activity within the HJ and outside of it. But these patrols were now conducted in collaboration with the police, especially when theaters, bars, and inns were involved. Himmler ordered his police officials to make use of HJ patrols, especially when their knowledge of juvenile behavior could aid in the apprehension of culprits. HJ district offices, meanwhile, were informed by the police when youth were involved in any illegal activity, and the names of sexual offenders, in particular, were duly reported to HJ headquarters.[27]

Heuser was uncomfortable under the guidance of Ernst Schlünder and lasted only until January 1944, when he requested transfer to the HJ Division of the W-SS. In July he fell during the battle of Caen. The choice of his successor, Herbert König, reflected the surrender of the RJF to the SS. König had been Beck's subordinate in the Recruiting Office and was completely committed to the ideological fanaticism and aggressive style of Berger's pied pipers. He was on active duty during 1943 and wrote his former colleagues in Berlin from the battlefield of Kharkov, denouncing the defeatism he saw in the regular army and asserting his faith in ideology as the decisive factor in the war. He believed that racial ideas, assiduously propagated at home and at the front, would bring eventual victory. When he returned from the East to assume direction of the SRD in February 1944, his enthusiasm for the W-SS as the savior of Germany had not abated.[28] But the SRD had lost its raison d'être. At the conference of inspectors at Weimar new directions were discussed at length. The RJF had rejected Schweizer's idea of introducing combat insignia, knowing that it could not replace the romantic appeals of spying, and pushed instead for renewed emphasis on fighting fires and aiding the police in emergencies brought on by bombing. By this time Heuser had clearly given up on the SRD, while his successor König tried to find some new, appropriate name for the SRD which would express its primary function as a catch-basin for future SS soldiers. None was found. But neither the SS nor the HJ would let the SRD die.[29]

Another conference, held at Eipel near Prague in May 1944, even called for SRD expansion, but mainly by adumbrating fire fighting and police assistance. SRD units could also be used for sentry duty and protection of gas works. Many SRD leaders by this time had been seconded from the regular police, and further transfers from the ORPO were suggested. Since municipal police officers were now frequently used to compel volunteering for the W-SS, it made sense to have patrolmen themselves assume leadership of SRD units. The contingents of transfers from the JV into the SRD were actually raised. Thus, in HJ Region Swabia the RJF ordered that 700 boys of fourteen be committed to the SRD, as compared to 660 for the Motor-HJ, 500 for the Signal-HJ, and 200 for the Marine-HJ. But in Swabia as elsewhere these directives were very hard to follow. Teenage manpower was getting scarce and the SRD was used during 1944 mostly as a mechanism for SS recruitment from the HJ as a whole. Its intrinsic functions had largely disappeared.[30]

At the end of 1944 König, who had tried to turn SRD headquarters into a kind of field station of the SS Recruiting Office, was replaced by Axmann with a veteran HJ leader who had never been in the SS. This belated reassertion of HJ independence flew in the face of reality. During the last six months of the war SRD units became mere extensions of SS Recruiting Stations. SRD inspectors, now largely members of the Order Police, spent more time pressing seventeen-year-old boys to volunteer for the Police Division of the W-SS than training them to fight juvenile crime and social rebellion.[31]

### Crime, Rebellion, and Suppression

Turning now to social conditions within the HJ, we are confronted by a curious phenomenon, the presence of exactly those elements of antisocial behavior that the SS was trying to eradicate from German society and the SRD was designed to prevent from developing among future citizens. Criminal statistics are notoriously unreliable, but they are the only measure available to us. The scope and degree of deviancy, particularly in the realm of sexual morality, is also problematical. Yet there is general agreement that the recorded rate of crime has been increasing in the last half century in most industrial societies. It is now apparent that police-ridden societies, like Nazi Germany, did not escape from this trend. Brutal efforts were made there to contain crime and to cast all nonconformist social behavior as political crime, stemming from a self-serving definition of deviancy as racial disease.[32]

While juvenile crime usually reflects the strength of the adult moral fiber, it can be said that the existence of the HJ and its SRD, along with the repressive SS state, played a role in reducing the rate of teenage crime during peacetime. The overall rate declined, but criminality became more prevalent among the lower teens, which HJ leaders attributed to earlier puberty. In this group what became particularly notable was perjury, "general moral offenses," incest, child molestation, rape, murder, manslaughter, child murder, negligent bodily injury, and extortion. Among older youths, homosexuality, that very special Nazi "crime," became a prominent feature of the criminal landscape, mostly because the HJ and SS, by no means immune from this supposed flaw, mobilized a "sharpened fight" to eradicate it.[33]

The war brought with it, as it did in other countries, a drastic increase in juvenile delinquency. The RJF itself estimated that this increase during 1940 alone amounted to between 17 and 18 percent as compared to the favorable peacetime rate of 1938. A postwar author has noted that adjudicated cases of juvenile delinquency in 1941 were twice the number of 1937, the most favorable prewar year. It is important, however, to keep in mind that the increase was mostly in the area of victimless crimes—moral offenses and the like—rather than statutory violations or serious crimes like assault or burglary.[34]

According to a top secret RJF report, based on all available statistics, including monthly reports of SRD inspectors and the files of the Surveillance Section, 17,173 incidents of juvenile crime came to light during the first six months of 1940. More than a third of these crimes (6,216) were committed by youths who were not members of the HJ, leaving the obviously desired impression that nonmembership made young people much more susceptible to crime. Among the 10,958 crimes committed by Hitler youths, the most common were theft (5,985), homosexuality (901), "moral offenses" including lesbian activity (829), and embezzlement and fraud (758). Twenty murders were perpetrated by Hitler youths during this period, while fifteen professional HJ leaders committed crimes ranging from murder to homosexual acts and theft (Table 4.1).[35]

These figures still leave a blurred picture of juvenile crime, which can be focused by comparing another set of statistics derived from HJ expellees. On 25 September 1941 the HJ Court issued a complete list of all young people expelled from the organization between 1 July 1939 and 1 August 1941. Of 2,701 youths who were expelled or separated (a less severe form of condemnation), 1,989 were males and 712 were females. Twenty-two were members of the RJF staff at the time of expulsion and twelve were members of HJ organizations in occupied foreign lands. Six different types of offenses were given for the court's decisions, with offenses against property (49 percent) leading the list, followed by general morals charges (23 percent), homosexuality (11 percent), deleterious attitude (14 percent); and far less significant numerically were violent acts (2 percent) and abortion (1 percent) (Table 4.2). Interestingly enough, two males were thrown out of the HJ for causing females to have abortions, and lesbian offenses were either too embarrassing or too insignificant to be categorized, and were therefore buried in the general "moral offenses" figure.[36]

At first glance it would seem that thievery and "immorality," with the former by far the more serious problem, were primary reasons for the court's understandably reluctant decision to expel youngsters from a compulsory organization. Culpability in the matter of property crimes, was, of course, much easier to determine than the elusive acts of sexual "immorality." Since the RJF Report listed 900 cases of homosexual crimes during a six-month period alone, and only a third of that number were expelled during a twenty-five-month period by court action, it suggests that the RJF was more hesitant to uphold Article 175 of the Criminal Code than its official propaganda would have had the public believe. Either that is the case, or the wheels of justice in the HJ ground exceedingly slow indeed. Similar discrepancies obtain between the two sets of figures for the other types of crimes as well. Tentative as our conclusions might therefore have to be, it is clear that respect for communal property and moral rectitude were seriously blemished virtues within the HJ. Yet these problems were no more serious than in German society as a whole, which had an estimated 1.5 million homosexuals in 1929, and West Germany alone is believed to have 2 million homosexuals today. Larceny is a more serious problem in West Germany today than it is in the United States (Table 4.3).[37] The crime rate among juveniles in Germany in the 1930s and 1940s was a third that of the United States then and now, and less severe than Japan and Israel in the 1960s.[38]

While the juvenile crime rate, particularly its increase during wartime, embarrassed the RJF, youth leaders produced ephemeral explanations. Blaming most juvenile crime on children from single-child families or saying that juvenile crime was no more than a mirror of criminality in the adult population was about all that youth leaders could do to justify a bad record. The SS, in the person of Paul Werner, the chief of the Juvenile Crime Bureau at Criminal Police Headquarters, not surprisingly, favored genetic theories and derived the increase of serious crimes and greater incidence of crime among younger adolescents from "antisocial kinships." Werner also tended to equate rebellious delinquent behavior and sexual aberrations with serious crime, finding biological reasons for all.[39]

Juvenile court officials were more realistic. One such court in Munich in 1942 cited the following reasons for the shocking erosion of wartime moral standards among the young: limited parental supervision, evening parades of the HJ, minimally qualified HJ leaders, youth camps and employment of teenagers, increased circulation of pornography, and relaxation of police patrols for juveniles. The latter was hardly the case until after 1943, but the other reasons are all plausible and were generally recognized as such even by some of the youth leaders. Courts, lawyers, and juridical officials had a difficult time trying to apply principles of justice to this situation, attempting to uphold some semblance of reason in the face of irrational demands for drastic action by SS and HJ fanatics.[40] In confounding victimless crimes, political dissidence, and prankish behavior with crimes against property and persons, officials left the impression that the younger generation found itself in serious criminal jeopardy, when, in fact, most offenses were in the nature of moral deviations and petty larceny. The increase in wartime delinquency in itself was a response to police and SRD efforts at disciplining the young. The extent and scope of juvenile crime in Nazi Germany was less serious than it is in many postwar free societies, where delinquency can be a function of affluence or deprivation of economic and professional opportunities.[41]

A regimented society contends with less crime while it surrenders political and social liberties. The young, accustomed to the regimentation of schools, army, and parents, appear to be more willing to make this sacrifice than are adults. The simplistic maxims of totalitarianism always appeal more to the young than their more experienced progenitors. Wars release sexual inhibitions, since they reduce normal social contact between the sexes, especially among age groups whose sexual awareness is usually at a peak. The sexual promiscuity and irregularity of top Nazi leaders has been well documented. What is not quite as well known is the prevalence of sexual experimentation among the very young, who had not yet been exposed to the male environment of army life, but for whom the sexual separation in the structured Hitler Youth provided an equivalent to military conditions. A few examples will suffice to illustrate the point.

The juvenile welfare department of Frankfurt recorded these crimes of indecency in 1939. Some girls of fourteen and fifteen were lured into an attic by five HJ boys, also fourteen and fifteen, three of whom restrained the girls while the other two raped them. In two other cases young girls paid several visits to nearby barracks to satisfy a thirst for sexual experience. They were only thirteen and fourteen, having barely reached puberty. By 1941 the courts were so "swamped by a rising tide of juvenile immorality," that the whole educational system was brought into question. The juvenile court in Munich recorded some telling examples. Group sex was practiced by three boys and three girls who regularly met for that purpose, and two other boys, aged thirteen and sixteen, procured three girls barely nine years old for similar reasons. The fine art of sexual technique and use of contraceptives was explained by a girl in primary school to her attentive classmates. A group of fifteen- and sixteen-year-old girls engaged in sexual intercourse with French prisoners of war in order to test their theory that Frenchmen "could do it far better than Germans." Antiaircraft gunners found themselves the beneficiaries of two fifteen-year-old girls who spent several nights with them practicing various positions. Other girls were so oblivious to monetary gain that they sold their favors for small change. A sixteen-year-old boy, not to be outdone by the girls, hired himself out as a male prostitute, forecasting a social phenomenon of the contemporary urban street scene. Some of these young deviants justified their behavior in most ingenious ways. A fifteen-year-old girl who was scolded by her mother for constantly associating with SS men and soldiers replied that she was only fulfilling the Führer's ideal of German motherhood, should her cavorting result in pregnancy.[42]

Hitler, Himmler, and Axmann were themselves poor models of moral rectitude. Not only was the Führer's kept mistress a matter of public knowledge, but more privately his behavior was even less exemplary. He had a passionate affair with his seventeen-year-old niece, who was rumored to be pregnant, undoubtedly contributing to her suicide, and he pathetically and clumsily tried at one point to seduce the seventeen-year-old daughter of Heinrich Hoffmann and future wife of Baldur von Schirach. Himmler warned his men to protect the purity of young German women by reminding them "how incensed they would be if their underage daughters or sisters were ruined" for life. Yet, Himmler's racial fanaticism also led him to suggest in a barely veiled way that good SS soldiers should father some good German children before they went off to a war that might curtail their procreative opportunities. He encouraged promiscuity among his men by organizing a lying-in hospital for unwed mothers impregnated by them. He also maintained a mistress and two illegitimate children in reasonably comfortable style with covert party funds provided by the sympathetic and notoriously promiscuous Martin Bormann.[43]

Artur Axmann, less strait-laced than Baldur von Schirach, was no paragon of moral virtue. At a conference of HJ leaders Axmann piously promised "to bring the relationship between boys and girls unto a basis which reflected a knightly, clean and clear form," thereby admitting that sexual irregularities in the HJ were more than idle and malicious rumor. The camps of the HJ gave ample room for sexual trafficking, and no degree of control could eliminate experimentation in that environment. Toward the end of the war Axmann and his closest colleagues stole away frequently to a plush villa where empty-headed movie starlets and fatuous BDM leaders provided sexual entertainment for the HJ elite. Melita Maschmann, herself accosted by the Jugendführer, has given a graphic description of these clandestine debaucheries during the fading months of the Third Reich.[44]

In 1939 the rate of moral offenses charged against young people between ten and eighteen amounted to 27.3 per 100,000. In the first six months of

1940, 1,259 of 17,173 adjudicated crimes in the HJ were of a moral nature, and nearly one quarter of 2,701 youngsters expelled from the HJ between July 1939 and August 1941 were thus punished for offenses against sexual standards. These statistical indicators, while they are merely that, suggest a degree of immorality within the HJ that totally contradicts the puritanical ethics so assiduously propagated by the leadership, itself not immune from practices they condemned. Forty-nine of the 1,259 youths convicted of immorality in the first half of 1940 were leaders. By today's standards this degree of sexual license may not appear as serious as it did then, but misdemeanor and crime in any society must be measured against the standards of its own time and place.[45]

For the HJ and SS homosexuality was a bête noire. By placing so much emphasis on it, they brought more of it to light. Hitler, of course, tolerated notoriously widespread homoeroticism within the SA until he found it could serve as a convenient excuse for eliminating Röhm's threat to his policy. He used it more shabbily against Fritsch, but he tolerated other known homosexuals, like Walter Funk, the minister of economics. Himmler developed his policy gradually, although he was aware of the prevalence of homosexuality in the SS, since at least one case a month was reported to him in 1937. Once culprits had been dealt with by the courts, Himmler sent them to concentration camps, where they were "shot while trying to escape" if all else failed. In 1941 Hitler issued a decree prescribing the death penalty for homosexuality within the SS. In 1942 the Ministry of Justice prescribed death when castration proved to be insufficient. In the 1920s sociologist Robert Michels and sex researcher Magnus Hirschfeld had estimated that Germany had had 1.2 million homosexuals. Himmler and the editors of *Das Schwarze Korps* inflated the figure to 2 million. Thus 10 percent of German males were thought to be infected with this "frightful legacy from the liberal period." Homosexuals were branded not only as enemies of the state, but as offenders against racial hygiene and the desired maximum population growth.[46]

Homosexuality was a sensitive subject in the HJ. The despised youth movement had had homoerotic proclivities, and the HJ never escaped from continuing rumors about uncontrolled homosexuality in its ranks. Even Schirach, who surrounded himself with a guard of handsome young men, was wrongly suspected of bisexual leanings. A primary feature of the early collaboration between KRIPO and SRD had to do with the phenomenon, and the 1940 guidelines placed heavy emphasis on the detection of homosexual offenses. These directives forbade entrapping suspected homosexuals by having SRD boys offer their sexual services in order to secure evidence. Such tactics were forbidden on pain of expulsion, because they ran the risk of corrupting inexperienced baiters. A major campaign was launched to quash the traffic in explicit erotic literature.[47] While statistics indicated a decline in known homosexual offenses, the following examples illustrate its continuing prevalence. In Mannheim sixteen HJ members were denounced for violation of Article 175, and a thirty-year-old flying instructor from the NSFK was sentenced to three years and three months penal servitude for seducing ten student pilots from the HJ. The district court in Mainz sentenced a student teacher and a student to a total of four years and seven months penal servitude. Together these district youth leaders had engaged some twenty boys of the HJ and JV in homosexual acts while they attended camps for candidates of the Adolf Hitler Schools.[48]

According to the National Statistical Office, the rate of sentenced juvenile homosexuals declined from 20.9 per 100,000 in 1937 to 20.3 in 1938 and 8.4 in 1940. Statistics gathered by the RJF told a different story, showing a rate of 60.1 per 100,000 in 1939. In terms of actual numbers, the RJF also revealed a decrease from 3,079 in the first half of 1939 to 2,269 in the second half and 1,467 during the first six months of 1940. The latter figure represented 9 percent of all recorded criminal offenses in that period. The expulsion record between July 1939 and August 1941 shows that 15 percent of expellees were separated for violation of Article 175.[49]

All indicators reveal that sexual immorality was a serious problem within the Hitler Youth. The rate of sexual offenses for 1939 amounted to 87.4 per 100,000, while 16 percent of all criminal offenses in the first six months of 1940 were sexual in nature. The most suggestive indication comes from the expulsion record, since 922 out of 2,701, or more than one third of all those expelled from the HJ between July 1939 and August 1941, suffered this mixed blessing for reasons of sexual deviancy. The RJF was eager to rid the HJ of this moral incubus, while the method of punishment remained less severe than that of the SS. Many who developed homosexual tendencies as adolescents in the HJ later suffered the fate of castration and execution prescribed by the SS and the Ministry of Justice.[50]

Criminality, social rebellion, and political opposition were closely associated in the police-state mentality of the SS and the HJ. It is in this context that the proliferation of "wild cliques" can be examined most usefully. None other than Reinhard Heydrich informed the RJF in 1939 that a number of illegal youth bands existed. He believed they endangered the HJ because they contained former members of Marxist, communist, and bourgeois youth organizations. Many were exmembers of the HJ who had "lost interest" and camouflaged their opposition by joining relatively innocuous Nazi associations like "Strength through Joy," a popular vacation program of the Labor Front. Heydrich claimed that homosexuality was a distinctive characteristic of many rebels and did not hesitate to prescribe five-to-eight-year penitentiary sentences. He asked the SRD to cooperate with the Gestapo and SD in bringing these delinquents to justice. The RJF, more aware of these groups than Heydrich realized, obliged him by issuing detailed directions to the SRD. The RJF alleged that the rebels used girls as bait to entice HJ members into desertion. "Flying patrols" mounted on bicycles were organized to keep typical gathering places under surveillance. In youth hostels special rooms were reserved for standing SRD patrols. Theaters, bars, and inns were watched regularly.[51]

The combined actions of the Gestapo, KRIPO, SD, and SRD appear to have kept the wild gangs within certain bounds, at least until 1943, although they were never able to suppress them entirely. In western Germany, as before the war, cliques of one kind or another kept the Gestapo and SRD on their toes. As many as 200 boys and girls would gather clandestinely, partially protected by sympathetic older youths who sat in bars and restaurants keeping an eye on police activity. According to Gestapo reports these rebellious gangs attacked HJ members and SRD patrols after dark. The SRD was able to grab many of them and bring them to Gestapo headquarters to be arrested, but at least one SRD inspector in the West reported that "the activity of wild groups was on the increase." In April 1940 twenty-five youths from a *bündisch* clique were transferred to a special court in Berlin; in October twenty youths from another western city were apprehended after the SRD gathered literary evidence of a *bündisch* character; and a combined patrol of SRD and KRIPO agents corralled sixteen rebels in a ravine.[52]

Juvenile gangs of one type or another were to be found throughout the country during the war, mostly in larger cities and in industrial areas. Many of them adopted the garb, demeanor, and manners seen in American films or British magazines. There were "Harlem Clubs," "OK Gangs," "Charlie Gangs," "Bush Wolves," "Loafers," and "Swingers." As a rule their names were quite inventive: in Kassel they called themselves "Bear Gangs," in Düsseldorf it was the "Club of the Golden Horde" and "Shambeko Band," in Ahlfeld the "Snake Club." Proud of deceiving the authorities, a group of rebels in Wismar called themselves "The Blue Miasma," in Braunschweig there were the "Dreadful Stones," in Danzig the "Dusters" obscured the vision of police officials, and Chemnitz had the cleverest group of all, the "Municipal Bath Broth." What all of them had in common was a desire to associate independently of the HJ and in defiance of laws and regulations. There was crime and immorality in their midst, as there was defiance of authority and distaste for the meager cultural offerings of the regime. The RJF tended to see political opposition, whereas the SS saw antisocial behavior, interpreted as a factor in the increasing rate of real juvenile crime. It is unfair to dismiss all of this as sheer hooliganism. It is also inaccurate to characterize it as concerted resistance.[53]

These groups were amorphous in their structure, goals, and composition, illustrated most clearly by the Kittelsbach Pirates. Organized in 1934, they took the name from a brook that flows between Duisburg and Düsseldorf. At first friendly to the Nazis, they changed when the "good element" joined the HJ, leaving a nucleus of diverse, disgruntled youngsters. The Gestapo noted ominous infiltration by working-class teenagers and members of communist youth groups. At the beginning of the war, when the police became concerned with a host of new delinquent hordes, the Kittelsbach Pirates were joined by former members of the Bünde, by socialist elements, and even by youths from former confessional associations. They took on a kind of generic character now, since semicriminal elements were detected among them.[54] In 1940 the Gestapo charged them with harboring HJ renegades. They began to attack HJ leaders in the streets, provoking calls for police intervention. A series of raids in 1941 brought arrests and warnings, but street brawls continued and HJ leaders were beaten up in the streets of Duisburg. Confused with the "Edelweiss Pirates" in SD reports, they did not merge with them until 1943. This event spread the influence of the group beyond regional borders and gave them an attractive symbol of freedom. Congregating in large numbers during air raids, they made a nuisance of themselves and painted slogans on ruined walls: "Down with Hitler!" "The High Command Lies!" "Medals and Awards for the Great Murderer!" "Down with the Nazi Beast!"[55]

At a time when the SRD lost most of its surveillance function, the Kittelsbach and Edelweiss Pirates were roaming the streets of Duisburg in groups of sixty to seventy, armed with instruments of gang warfare like brass knuckles. The Gestapo reported from Wuppertal in March 1944 that they were proliferating and systematically agitating against the HJ. Press reports from England in 1945 suggested that the Edelweiss Pirates represented a substantial movement of political opposition among German youth. As in the case of the well-known "White Rose" movement, significant transformation of the group and resort to important action came only after the changed public mood following the disaster at Stalingrad.[56]

For Danzig the novelist Günter Grass has drawn a sardonic picture of the "Dusters." Formed in 1944, they were a random collection of a few dozen teenagers. Sporting assorted stolen apparel, their leader the son of the police chief, they had their hideaway in the basement of an aristocratic general's suburban villa. They were bent on mischief and intimidation. Grass calls them "hoodlums," "scamps," and "adolescent Romantics." A handful went AWOL from their duties as air force auxiliaries. They returned to the 88s, however, when attacks materialized, in part to camouflage their nocturnal raids on government and party installations. They collected an assortment of deadly weapons, but never used anything more than brass knuckles to rough up SRD members. While collaborating with another group made up of working-class apprentices led by a self-styled communist, the bourgeois branch of the Dusters rejected political activity and fiercely denied any part in the arson that burned a training submarine in the harbor. With the aid of the choirboys among them, they stole religious symbols from local churches and decorated their basement storehouse with them, mixing death's heads and unicorns with pictures of saints. They were caught one midnight while dismantling holy statuary. Given a summary trial, with the girl in their midst testifying against the boys, they were hung from trees as the Russian troops approached the city.[57]

Another case in point: the "Swingers" of Hamburg. Early in the winter of 1939–40 several hundred Hamburg youths who had met in an ice-skating rink formed "Loafer Clubs" and "Gangster Cliques." Later the term "Swing Youth" was applied to them because of their predilection for American music and English apparel. They were almost all from well-to-do families, and their activity consisted of aberrant jam sessions akin to the antics of contemporary "punk rock" groups. During one session in the Hotel Kaiserhof 408 were arrested. All but two were under twenty-one. In October sixty-three so-called ringleaders were rounded up by the police, ranging in age from fourteen to twenty-one. Fifteen were members of the HJ and BDM, twenty-one had been expelled, and the remaining twenty-seven had never belonged to any youth organization. Only one came from a working-class family, four were children of artisans, and the rest came from upper-middle-class homes.[58]

Their resistance to the HJ was motivated more by a taste for a life of leisure, a sense of jaded cultural superiority, and distaste for Nazi mediocrity than by a clear recognition of political oppression. Most were habitués of coffee houses, seaside resorts, and bars; showed no interest in politics or the exploits of the army; and rejected the HJ as an invader of privacy and individual freedom. They regarded the Labor Service as "evil chicanery," condemned the war, and rejected the army on grounds of the uncivilized life one had to lead within it. They considered dissolute and indolent behavior, coupled with English-American manners, clothes, and music, worthy of imitation. Revealing the pronounced Anglophilia always present in Hamburg, the "Swingers" looked on England and its citizens as models of civilized liberty. While they welcomed so-called *Mischlinge*, there is no evidence that the "Swingers" were motivated by revulsion against the persecution of the Jews or that they were even aware of genocide. According to SD and RJF reports, "strong criminal elements" were present. Their life style required money obtained by break-ins and prostitution. So-called "hot festivals" in the homes of absent parents became drinking bouts and sexual orgies. On his trip home one inebriated youngster assaulted a woman, and when she cried out for help, he proceeded to masturbate in the street. Bed-hopping with multiple partners occurred fairly regularly. Some of the parents of the arrested "Swing" leaders were shocked to hear police revelations, but claimed there was nothing they could do with their children. Lack of parental supervision was blamed for most of this type of behavior, and much was made of the fact that one-third of those arrested came from broken homes and that the fathers of most of the rest were away on military duties.[59]

Very similar to the "Swingers" were two groups in Frankfurt am Main, the "Harlem Club" and "OK Gang," made up of fourteen- to twenty-year-old students of secondary schools and lyceums. Both organized in 1939, the first found its impetus in a love of Negro music, and the second was formed by a group of BDM girls helping to bring in the harvest. Altogether, eighty-eight girls and seventy-two boys were involved, according to the police, who dissolved the clubs, although they reemerged later. Once again, theft and embezzlement were used to accumulate money, while English and American hit songs were the common element of their social rebellion. Sex parties in the villa of one of the parents and in a ski hut on the Oberreifenberg were frequented by members of the clubs. One precocious sixteen-year-old girl engaged in sex with five boys at the same time. Girls as young as thirteen proudly confessed to police interrogators that they had been deflowered and that sexual liaisons had been consummated in dark corners of restaurants.[60]

The Hamburg "Swingers," meanwhile, continued to bedevil the authorities. Between 1940 and 1942 the school administration dismissed or transferred some fourteen students because of suspected "Swing" activity, while the director of a secondary school reported attacks on HJ members. Records of forbidden swing music continued to circulate, and amateur swing bands sprang up in various quarters. In August 1941 one wild jam session in the Alsterpavillon was attended by 300 youngsters, who "were degenerate and criminally inclined" according to the SD. Even worse, in the eyes of the SD, was the fact that some of them were of "mixed blood." The SD and Goebbels considered the "Swingers" to be "reactionary," "disruptive," and "treasonable," and recommended drastic action by the Gestapo. Goebbels was understandably incensed since the "Swingers" loved to sing the English song, "We will hang our wash on the Siegfried Line." Bormann got involved, too, when the ranks of the "Swingers" grew to some 500 or 600 youths five months later.[61]

The SRD, a favorite target of the "Swingers," was unable to control them, which finally forced Axmann to request Himmler's assistance. The youth leader thought "the sharpest" means were necessary to deal with "these dangerous Anglophiles," by which he meant consignment to work camps. Himmler decided sterner penalties were called for and ordered Heydrich "to eradicate the entire evil" in a "brutal" and "thorough" way. Heydrich then sent the ringleaders to concentration camps, where they were subjected to thrashings and hard labor. One "Swingjunge," Hasso Schützendorff, had his hair shorn, was beaten with an iron bar, and then compelled to push heavily-laden trolleys uphill for two weeks. Some parents and teachers, who had condoned such wanton rebellion, were deprived of property and dispatched to concentration camps. While these drastic steps seemed final enough, the "Swingers" re-emerged a few months latter and spread to other cities: Berlin, Saarbrücken, Hanover, Dresden, and Vienna. Music was for all of them a way of defying the regime and protesting an unbearably restrictive life within the Hitler Youth. Conditions imposed by war had a way of leveling people that these patrician youngsters found unpalatable. Their defiance fell short of explicit resistance, exemplified by the "White Rose" in Munich and other cities, including Hamburg.[62]

The "Mutineers" in Leipzig attracted larger numbers and stimulated considerable juridical activity. As early as 1937 groups of boys between the ages of sixteen and twenty-one began to gather in "hangouts" of the city, taking from each locale a characteristic name. They made themselves conspicuous by their bizarre but uniform apparel, leading some foreign visitors to the Leipzig Fair to mistake them for the "state youth organization," a fact the HJ found most embarrassing and the Mutineers must also have resented, since their activity was directed against the HJ and the SRD. The latter's effort to corral them united the separate groups, so that authorities estimated that some 1,500 dissidents existed by 1938. Frequently violent clashes with the HJ involved a hundred or more. No overt political motives emerged except among small groups within the larger mass who had been former members of the "Red Falcons" and the KJVD. In 1938 the Peoples Court in Leipzig staged two show trials of certain "ring leaders," some of whom were in fact communist, and falsely conveyed the notion that they had attempted to influence the whole group to commit treason. These legal efforts had little effect on the apolitical rowdies as a whole. In smaller numbers the Mutineers continued to bedevil the HJ and the courts well into the war, when restrained actions were taken against them. Between November 1942 and January 1943, 157 Mutineers were imprisoned, 338 put under "youth arrest," and 236 condemned to weekend arrest.[63]

Despite brutal police intervention and increased watchfulness, the cliques did not disappear. There is little to suggest that dissent became a national movement or that systematic contact among the various groups was established, but it has become increasingly evident that numerous cities, large and small, experienced some form of spontaneous and inchoate youthful rebellion. Toward the end of the war the gangs became more overtly resistant, engaging in physical attacks on the SRD and HJ, breaking into various party offices, sometimes even resorting to genuine sabotage. According to police reports, some dissidents made irregular contact with resistance cells among conscripted foreign workers, although the BBC and other foreign media exaggerated the frequency and importance of these contacts. It is likely that the rebellion involved no more than 5 percent of teenagers in the country at any one time. Yet it was serious enough to concern the patently surprised officials of the RJF, the Justice Ministry, and Himmler's police.[64]

Adapting ideas promoted by English sociologists of contemporary working-class youth, Detlev Peukert has advocated the concept of "subculture" to encompass rebellion by youth in the Third Reich. He has concentrated on the Edelweiss Pirates of the Ruhr and has sought to demonstrate a new form of youthful proletarian solidarity, largely oblivious to SPD and KPD tradition. In effect Peukert continues the implausible argument Daniel Horn made earlier. Horn insisted that "the greatest opposition to the HJ and its system of 'dominance' came from lower-class boys." In Horn's view, working-class youth "did not respond well to any system of authority," and hence it "was they who provided the overwhelming majority of youthful opponents." Horn's empirical base is weaker than Peukert's, since most of his examples come from nonproletarian youth, and Peukert's ill-defined "subculture" idea has been challenged. Heinrich Muth suggests that the diffuse and incoherent nature of the youthful rebellion, greatly overestimated by the RJF and the police, ought to be viewed from the perspective of the juvenile rebellions in the imperial and Weimar periods. Muth's argument, that the claim for new forms of generation-specific and class-specific subcultures made by Peukert could apply to the youthful rebellion as a whole, and in broad historical perspective, without reference to social class, seems eminently reasonable. In response to such criticism, Peukert has extended his thesis to encompass the pre-Nazi period, but the concept of subculture remains obscure.[65]

While definitive explanations may have to wait because basic issues are in dispute, there is no disagreement over the hysterical reaction of Nazi officialdom.[66] Minister of Justice Otto Thierack, Axmann, and Himmler agreed on a united front in 1944. Thierack informed judges and prosecutors that "the constantly increasing number of cliques gave rise to the danger that the political and moral unity of youth might be seriously undermined." He suggested strong measures against ringleaders and active participants, involving assignment to penal work camps and protective custody camps, operated by the police. In milder cases "youth arrest" and unlimited imprisonment while under investigation might be sufficient. If collective hearings in juvenile courts ran the risk of encouraging defiance, the culprits were to be brought before the courts in smaller groups or as individuals. Legal grounds for prosecution were vague, since Hindenburg's Decree for the Protection of People and State (1933) and Himmler's last proscription of the Bünde (1939) was considered adequate. It was unnecessary to demonstrate explicit political motives; intent "to disturb the work of the HJ" was reason enough.

Speaking for Himmler, RSHA chief Ernst Kaltenbrunner issued orders to the relevant agencies. He defined "cliques" as "collections of young people outside the HJ" who rejected Nazi ideology, had "no interest in fulfilling their duties to the community," and were "particularly indifferent to the demands of war." They appeared in various disguises, but common to most were the symbols of the Edelweiss, death's head rings, and colored pins. He believed they were loosely organized, although some connections among various groups had been detected.[67] Kaltenbrunner sorted the groups according to the danger they presented to society. First, there were groups of a criminal and antisocial nature, whose acts were characterized by deeds of nuisance, brawling, violations of police orders, collective thievery, and immorality—especially homosexuality. Second, there were those who revealed attitudes of political opposition, although not always with a definite resistance program. These groups rejected the HJ and the aims of the war, attacked HJ members, listened to foreign broadcasts, spread treasonable rumors, and nurtured traditional songs and habits of the Bünde; frequently these opponents successfully infiltrated party organizations. Third came those who exhibited liberal and individualistic predilections, exemplified by pro-English ideals, love of jazz and "hot" music, swing dances, and a pronounced taste for sexual amusements. Kaltenbrunner also made distinctions among ringleaders, participants, and fellow travelers. Some of the ringleaders were thought to be adults or leaders in the HJ who disguised themselves by blameless public conduct. Many of the participants and fellow travelers had criminal records, according to Kaltenbrunner, and came from "disorderly family environments and antisocial kinships." All groups exhibited common apparel, hair style, and behavior.[68]

The Gestapo and KRIPO received primary responsibility for the suppression of cliques, but since suppression was a "war-related necessity," all agencies had to be involved, especially the HJ. Once the existence of a clique was discovered, the SD was expected to use covert observation and stealthy infiltration, thus preparing the ground for massive raids and arrests. To prevent further proliferation, Kaltenbrunner ordered systematic patrolling by police officers assisted by HJ leaders, party men, youth office workers, and NSV employees. In special cases experienced HJ leaders were to be used as detectives. The SRD had lost its surveillance rights in 1943 and therefore was not mentioned by Kaltenbrunner. The proliferation of cliques and concerted RSHA action may be directly related. By converting the SRD into an incubator for soldiers, the SS opened the door to demoralization, since it reduced the degree of surveillance to which teenagers were subjected in the normal course of events.[69]

Appalled by the eruption of juvenile rebellion and the impudence and defiance it implied, officials resorted to extreme measures. Himmler was minister of the interior by 1944, his police had the nation in a tight grip, all military recruitment was controlled by him, and his influence with the RJF was predominant—in fact, there were few government and party activities free from SS influence. In this situation the proliferating rebellious behavior among the young was indeed a dangerous phenomenon, particularly to those who thought that it was the duty of the political police to root out the slightest sign of disloyalty. Himmler, therefore, resorted to increasing use of protective custody camps. These had existed since 1940, when, in the course of discussions leading to the Police Order for the Protection of Youth, Göring suggested that they be established. The SS—more specifically the KRIPO Office—was given the task of organizing and running the camps, even though the police had no legal right to do so and the promised "custody law" never materialized. Yet the Justice Ministry participated in the venture from the start, while juvenile court judges and social welfare officials saw it as a significant prophylactic against juvenile crime for those immune to milder forms of correction.[70]

The first camp at Moringen, in the Solling hills northwest of Göttingen, was reserved for boys and had some 150 inmates in 1940. At that time the first reports by visiting penal officials and public prosecutors began to arrive on Thierack's desk, raising serious questions about prevailing practices. It seems juvenile offenders were transferred to the camp right after release from prison and without committing any new offenses, while some young delinquents belonged more properly in welfare facilities. Most jailers were police officers, supported by soldiers who had been ordered to perform a duty about which they knew nothing, and a number of freshly recruited HJ leaders. In fact, Heydrich specifically asked the RJF to provide "educational leaders" and assistants for Moringen. Disciplinary measures were harsh: hour-long compulsory physical exercises accompanied by denial of evening meals, corporal punishment applied with hazel switches, and solitary confinement up to twenty-one days.[71]

By 1942 there were 620 inmates at Moringen. Since the opening of the camp only 124 had been released. Among the latter, forty-seven had been sent to the army, twenty-five to a halfway house in Bavaria, eighteen to insane asylums, ten were sent home to parents, and ten had been sent to concentration camps. Three had been returned to Moringen, one from the army and two from the halfway house. The remaining fourteen probably died in the camp, although the HJ writer who cited these figures did not mention it. In June the KRIPO also set up a camp for girls in Uckermark and filled it with 200 inmates within two months.[72]

The HJ and the SS regarded detention of unspecified duration at Moringen and Uckermark as a normal way of dealing with incorrigible offenders and troublemakers. Kaltenbrunner suggested that any adolescent detained by the police longer than three weeks should be sent to the camps. A new criminal law for youth, issued in 1943, specifically instructed juvenile judges and penal officials to hand offenders over to the police for unlimited detention in the camps if there appeared to be little hope of rehabilitation. When rebellious cliques proliferated, Thierack and Himmler issued directives designed to increase the use of protective custody. Juvenile offenders were handed over to the police by the courts and the welfare agencies, without consulting parents and legal guardians, solely on the authority of Himmler. While the HJ was consulted and discussions among welfare agencies and juvenile court officials occurred, in the final analysis, the KRIPO Office in Berlin decided who belonged in a protective custody camp and who did not. The KRIPO had preempted all other agencies responsible for the welfare of troubled youth in German society. Himmler even instructed provincial youth offices, responsible for social welfare of juveniles, to search through state-run homes in order to find youngsters over sixteen who were likely candidates for the camps.[73]

In April 1944 Himmler stipulated that all inmates should be examined and classified by the Criminal-Biological Institute of the SIPO. Those who were capable of rehabilitation, a small minority, were to be sent to the army or the Labor Service at some unspecified future date. Those who were not were eventually transferred to asylums, hospitals, supervised semiopen facilities, and concentration camps. Their physical labor was to be fully exploited. In order to allow the psychologists to do their work, all inmates were kept in an observation block for an initial period of six months. After that they were separated into so-called "positive" and "negative" blocks, depending on the outcome of the examinations, a procedure that justifiably has been labeled as a particularly insidious form of "social racism" by Gisela Bock and Detlev Peukert.[74]

A report by a judicial official from Heilbronn reveals the stark reality of life in the camps. A total of 674 offenders, mostly between sixteen and twenty-one, were held at Moringen in 1943. Forty were classified as unfit, feebleminded, and braindamaged, most of them ultimately destined for insane asylums. Nearly fifty were considered to be *Störer*, mentally weak, mischiefmakers, and "high-grade degenerates," all prime candidates for concentration camps. Eighty had been psychoanalyzed as *Dauerversager*, or "permanent failures," charged with every conceivable crime, and basically "inclined to go astray; some of these were headed for halfway houses but most of them were bound for concentration camps. Another eighty were classified as *Gelegenheitsversager*, lightheaded, subject to recidivism, and mostly destined for a permanently supervised facility known as the *SS-Heimathof.* Youths in this category were all candidates for sterilization. At the time some twenty-two inmates had already been sterilized. Some twenty-six deaths had occurred in the camps, twenty-one "natural deaths," two by accident, one by suicide, and one inmate was simply shot while trying to escape. The escape record is most revealing indeed: thirty-one youths had attempted to escape, ninety-nine had been temporarily successful in escaping, and five escapees were still at large at the time. A 20 percent rate of attempted escape underlines the unbearable conditions, further aggravated by shameless exploitation of inmate labor. While inmates were supposed to be paid ten Pfennig a day, the value of forced toil by 674 inmates at Moringen amounted to 27,000 RM for May, 22,000 RM for April, and 25,000 RM for March, giving new meaning to child labor in the Third Reich.[75]

The number of deaths among inmates, sterilization, and corporal punishment made the protective custody camps a pale reflection of concentration camps, for which probably a third of the inmates were headed. A conservative estimate is that more than 2,000 young people with greatly varying degrees of criminal and felonious culpability—perhaps even mere social rebellion and nonconformity—were "protected" by the police in these camps between 1940 and 1945. This figure includes the Jugendverwahrlager Litzmannstadt set up in 1942 for Polish delinquents. It is doubtful that many of these troubled youngsters survived this form of SS protection.[76]

### The SRD Role in the Control of Social Deviancy

A final assessment of the role the SRD played in controlling social deviancy rests in part on how opposition, rebellion, and delinquency are viewed. Effective political resistance to Hitler on the part of youth did not exist. The Scholl's and their "White Rose" circle is the exception that proves the rule. While various groups, like Berlin's "d.j.1.11.," distributed anti-Nazi leaflets and broke into HJ Homes to steal uniforms and passes, their discussions of tyrannicide and plans for sabotage never materialized. The Hamburg "White Rose" made vague plans to blow up bridges, but never actually did so before they were arrested and some thirty members executed.[77]

There is no doubt, however, that considerable opposition to the HJ existed, both within and outside the organization. Most opposition had its source in personal resentment against regimentation inherent in the organizational structure and ideological uniformity of the HJ. Because unified resistance was literally impossible, overt acts of dissatisfaction were frequently diverted into a form that turned out to be largely apolitical social rebellion, delinquency, and semicriminal aberration. This worked to the advantage of the law enforcement agencies and made the SRD more effective than it otherwise would have been. The HJ, like the SS, built its coercive system on a moral code that harked back to a preindustrial era. This antiquated code held that anything alien to one's own beliefs and mores, anything forbidden by superiors or authoritative leaders, must be abnormal or criminal. The SRD thus found itself on the side of morality and right, while their antagonists were cast into the shadows of immorality and wrong. The sterile environment of the HJ home and hostel stood in stark contrast to the degenerate milieu of the clique, the smoke-filled tavern, the jaded Swing jazz festival, and the occasional sexual orgy.

We can begin to understand how well the SRD functioned when we examine its successes and failures in three significant respects: spying out religious influence, detecting immoral conduct, and preventing violations of police regulations and the proliferation of rebellious cliques. Most of the illustrative incidents come from HJ Region Swabia, which happens to be the only area from which a sizable number of monthly SRD reports have survived. Swabia may not be typical, but comparison with SS reports on SRD effectiveness in Fulda-Werra suggests that Swabia was not atypical. According to these reports, all HJ Districts had more or less active SRD units, conducting more or less regular weekly patrols throughout the war. To a lesser degree the SRD maintained surveillance of religious groups and institutions and kept a close eye on moral irregularities.[78]

From their point of view, these juvenile policemen, working without precedent, achieved more than might have been expected. The model collaboration between SD and SRD in Koblenz suggests that widespread surveillance of the churches by SRD monitors was a common practice, yielding valuable information to those who made church policy. Numerous other examples could be cited. In August 1939, SRD leaders in Augsburg persuaded the police to close down several Evangelical Bible camps, because the youngsters attending them were antipathetic to the HJ. The Augsburg BDM, at first resentful of male interference in their work, came to depend on the SRD and at one point requested SRD assistance in stopping covert recruiting for illegal Catholic girls' groups in the *Maria Theresianschule* and several *Mittelschulen*. An illegal Catholic group, known as *Neudeutschland*, in a western city, discovered that the streets and railway stations, particularly on Sundays, were heavily patrolled by the SRD, together with the Gestapo. Many a youngster did not return from a weekend excursion until Tuesday or Wednesday, having been caught by the SRD and imprisoned by the Gestapo. In Memmingen, a small city in Swabia, the SRD kept an Evangelical group under surveillance because their pastor, a veteran of the Eastern Front, utilized history lessons and seemingly innocuous stories to "win converts" away from the HJ.[79]

In the small village of Stottwang, another Evangelical pastor was denounced by the SS and then constantly watched by the SRD, because he had delivered a sympathetic eulogy at the funeral of a Polish worker. The Kempten SRD kept local churches under surveillance because HJ officials suspected covert ideological activity against the regime. In Lindau the SRD harassed several clergymen who influenced youth to avoid HJ and party service. During September 1940, at Neu-Ulm, a program of education for girls in the Catholic church was disrupted when the BDM leader scheduled HJ activities simultaneously, at the instigation of the SRD. The chaplain, Alfred Müller, who had arranged these meetings secretly, protested SRD interference, but subsequently was "advised" by party officials to announce his classes from the chancel, if they were indeed purely religious in nature. A resourceful SRD leader in Nördlingen recruited two seminary students as spies who regularly reported on seminary teachers and officials. In 1941 and 1942 the SRD in Augsburg paid particular attention to renewed religious interests among young people. They kept the churches in their sights, being encouraged to do so by the SD, but could do little to prevent Catholic teenagers in the countryside from attending mass instead of HJ meetings on Sundays.[80]

Detecting and reporting sexual misconduct was one of the SRD's earliest, most difficult, and most persistent tasks. Much of the evidence for the RJF statistics on immorality came from the monthly reports of SRD inspectors. These reports suggest that the SRD as a junior morals squad performed its duty well. While most enjoyed this kind of snooping, for some at least it must have been difficult to report sexual experimentation by cohorts, when the snoopers themselves were confronting the impatient demands of maturing libidos. Certain voyeuristic tendencies among the SRD spies are indicated by occasional admonishments from superiors to be discreet.

In Pfronten, a small village on the Wertach River, two fifteen-year-old girls were caught by the SRD loitering in the streets with soldiers at 1:00 A.M. While this was "terrible enough," district leaders made the "general observation that girls cavorted with soldiers during even later hours." In Kempten the SRD described the "moral situation" in the spring of 1940 as uniformly bad. One HJ leader was dismissed after the SRD found him in a "morally compromising" situation, and another member of the HJ was harassed for dating a Polish girl. Homosexuality in the district was "on the increase," according to the SRD, who held a sexually prolific local puppet show employee responsible for it. Police and army officers were brought in by the SRD to break up "relationships" between young girls and soldiers quartered in their homes. In the District of Günzburg the SRD found a sixteen-year-old boy engaging in sexual intercourse with a thirteen-year-old girl.[81]

The Lech District SRD contended with a problem prevalent elsewhere. A young delinquent with a record of minor thefts, for which he had spent eight weeks in jail, was not expelled from the HJ. In September 1940 the SRD surprised him and several prison workers in a wild homosexual orgy in broad daylight on a roadside. With sensational evidence like this in hand, the SRD leader then sought to have the culprit penalized more heavily and finally expelled from the HJ. But it took some time before this occurred, suggesting that the enforcement of Article 175 was lax. The SRD, like all police forces, frequently complained that its assiduous detective work did not always result in appropriate punishment. In the regional capital of Augsburg, KRIPO Chief Steindle was at first (1940) reluctant to release men for joint patrols with the SRD, telling them to "do it alone." But independent SRD patrols were frequently ignored or mishandled by soldiers in the company of young girls. Steindle, in fact, advised the SRD "not to take their jobs so seriously where girls of seventeen and eighteen were concerned." His lack of support was no isolated case, since the Regierungspräsident subsequently ordered police officials to cooperate by referring to a Himmler decree that made joint patrols mandatory. After that, SRD-police collaboration in Bavaria improved noticeably.[82]

Controlling expressions of disorderly conduct and social rebellion had its origin in the Police Order for the Protection of Youth. Detecting religious influence and sexual misconduct was one thing, but actually maintaining orderly behavior and preventing violations of police regulations was quite another. Success in this area was more modest, because the objective was more demanding, even though the behavioral modification the SRD was attempting to bring about was certainly ephemeral and hence less accessible. A few examples will suffice to illustrate the point.

At the request of the RJF, the Swabian SRD inspector organized patrols to retrieve unauthorized campers from the countryside, because they infringed the hospitality of farmers during the harvest season. An incident along the same bucolic lines occurred in a small town. SRD observers noticed that disaffected youngsters from various localities, sporting the bizarre apparel of the former Bünde, were using a "goose pen" for a rallying point. The SRD unit prepared an ambush and rounded up a number of rebels. Mass raids in conjunction with the police, particularly when wild gangs of delinquents became troublesome, were a recurring feature of SRD activity. Dresden was the scene of a major SRD-KRIPO raid in May 1940, which rounded up 1,715 youthful offenders against public order, more than half of whom were members of the HJ. In Mainz the SRD seized 400 delinquents and found that 19 percent were HJ members. A major raid in Cologne netted 600 "Navajos." One hundred ringleaders were shipped off to reform institutions. Two years latter the Edelweiss Pirates failed to execute their plan to attack HJ Homes because the SRD was too strong.[83]

A former rebellious HJ leader reported after the war that illegal excursions into the countryside were extremely hazardous, because SRD patrols watched all the major thoroughfares, gathering points, and forest paths. In April 1944 a group of Swing rebels east of Lübeck armed themselves with pistols to ward off intruding SRD patrols. A shooting incident also occurred in Augsburg. Günther Grass, the novelist, reports that SRD patrols were attacked in the streets of Danzig by gangs who tied up two of their dreaded leaders and then drowned them in a lake. The SRD may have lost surveillance rights per se after 1943, but clearly it was still quite active in fighting disorderly behavior—with varying degrees of success. In Kiel, Klaus Granzow reports, one anemic SRD patrol was prevented from disturbing a clandestine jazz session simply by being pounded with drum sticks and hardwood *Querflöten*.[84]

At times entire SRD units invaded restaurants and coffee shops looking for curfew violators and underage drinkers and smokers. The owners naturally criticized the HJ for interfering with business, and SRD inspectors frequently had to admonish local SRD leaders to patrol public establishments only with police escorts. How frequently patrols were conducted is difficult to determine. In Swabia SRD Inspector Ernst Bingger insisted that a theater patrol and a restaurant patrol be carried out at least once a week in every city and larger town. Street patrols were conducted several times a week and all violations of the Police Order had to be reported immediately.[85]

In Memmingen, a city of some 30,000, twenty-four youths were stopped by the SRD for breaking curfew, smoking, and other offenses. A convivial "Cork Club" of underage drinkers and smokers in Kaufbeuren was dissolved by the SRD. At Immenstadt the SRD harassed a local theater owner who admitted underage patrons to forbidden films free of charge. He did this to defy SRD patrols who were hurting business. HJ authorities had to be called in to "educate" the irate owner and convince him to allow SRD patrols in the lobby. In Lindau SRD leaders arranged with theater owners a mutually acceptable way of keeping teenagers from seeing restricted films. An SRD member sat in the ticket booth and identified underage patrons. Their tickets were then confiscated and the money was given to the Winter Aid fund. If youths refused to surrender tickets they were reported to the police. This method "cleared youngsters out of the theaters." During a single month the Günzburg SRD reported twenty-four curfew violations, eight arrests in restaurants and bars, six in movie houses, and twelve cases of public smoking. Eight additional violations were under investigation. In some districts SRD reports of violations went unnoticed by the police. In Augsburg the SRD failed to prevent the formation of anti-HJ cliques in 1940, despite regular patrolling. Two years later, when the SRD in the city had ninety members, rebellious gangs even fired on the SRD. Increasing violations of the Police Order kept the juvenile officers of the law perpetually busy.[86]

The SRD failed to prevent a revival of religious interest toward the end of the war. It could not substantially reduce immorality or cleanse the HJ of homosexuality. Most conspicuous of its failures was the inability to keep antisocial cliques from intimidating loyal members of the HJ and from creating a certain degree of public disorder. Unwarranted fears among party and police officials that social rebellion might endanger the fighting potential of the troops increased.

In the fall of 1944 a group of youths, thirteen and older, were pressed into service digging tank traps. The HJ-Bannführer who supervised their encampment utilized the SRD to draw a tight ring of security about the camp, allowing the youngsters to enter and exit only in long columns accompanied by an SRD patrol of forty boys, described by one participant as a "select bunch of oppressors." The result was that an "opposition front" developed to resist the planned induction of the group into the W-SS. In a similar situation an entire HJ Bann was mobilized to dig tank traps for several months and did so without any disciplinary problems, in fact with pride and gusto. The SRD could not replace the informal controls inherent in social consensus and organizational comity.[87]

The totalitarian imperative of the HJ was not and could not be achieved. As in the adult party, there was explicit and implicit resistance, policy diversion, and failure to implement policy decisions through political and personal rivalries, ineptitude, or deliberate obstruction. Yet a degree of control existed that few societies have been able to impose on their young, much less generate among the young themselves in the form of cohort self-discipline. How can the commitment on the part of youth until the bitter end be explained, when most adults had surrendered to despair and accepted defeat, except by the notion that their experience in the self-contained Hitler Youth had created a common faith in the rightness of their cause and engendered a loyalty and conformity which brooked relatively little deviation? The SRD was not able to eliminate juvenile crime and delinquency or prevent social rebellion. If it had been able to do so, it would have been most unique indeed. On the other hand, the SRD was an unusual way of dealing with rebellion among rambunctious teenagers, and as such it played an important role in keeping the degree of disorder and deviation within limits. As Marlis Steinert concluded, "only a small fraction of the teenagers developed a political consciousness: the vast majority blindly obeyed the commands and regulations of the Hitler Youth or took refuge in a youth league romanticism."[88]

The most important result of SRD activity was that it had a disruptive impact on family life. One young opponent, after describing the ingenious and carefully planned ways by which he and his friends avoided the ever-present SRD patrols, gave expression to an ethos that must have prevailed among many dissidents who gathered in secret hideaways: "We felt as if we had been transported by Aladdin's magic carpet into a past where freedom still existed, or on some alien planet where there were no SRD patrols, no gendarmerie, no promotion-seeking teachers. . . . Our parents suspected what was happening . . . and added to our external difficulties by creating internal conflicts. We became quieter and talked less and less at home about the things that moved us. Many of us had brothers and sisters who participated enthusiastically in HJ activities and from whom we had to protect ourselves. The situation ruptured our families and our hearts." Steinert found that HJ informants constantly reported what was going on in schools, in clubs, at work, and in religious groups. Many private conversations were no longer private. No one was sure that his words were not being passed on to the police. "Caution and silence replaced candor and guidance as the twin commandments of family life."[89]

# 5 | Peasants, Farmers, Warriors

"Blood and soil" was a key slogan of Nazi propaganda. Promoted by the Third Reich's peasant ideologist, Richard Walther Darré, this call for a racially pure agrarian aristocracy found resounding echoes within the ranks of the HJ. Along with the law entailing small estates, price and market controls, and the National Food Estate, the HJ Land Service took its appropriate place as a youthful contribution to the Nazi program. One of the more permanent preoccupations of the party, agrarian policy was designed to alleviate the effects of industrialization, urbanization, and recurring agricultural crises. Many youth leaders, building on *völkisch* predecessors, believed that systematic efforts to keep the sons and daughters of farmers on the land and returning city youths to the depleting countryside could bring a halt to the universally deplored "flight from the land." As an early associate of Himmler and the party's farm leader, Darré was in a position to help facilitate the transfer of these aims to the younger generation.

### From Artamanen to HJ Land Service

Himmler and Darré met in 1930 while both played minor roles in the right-wing youth movement known as the Artamanen,[1] the former as short-time regional leader in Bavaria and the latter as member of a sponsoring group. When Himmler became head of the SS and Darré created the Agrarian Apparatus of the party, their ideological interdependence grew into mutually beneficial association. Darré soon joined the SS and became chief of a newly founded SS Race and Settlement Office. He reaped the political support of farmers for the party through the Agrarian Apparatus, which infiltrated the organizations of German farmers and landowners. In 1933 this important achievement earned him appointment as national farm leader and minister of food and agriculture. The Artamanen reflected Himmler's and Darré's agrarian-racist theories.[2]

The Nazi love affair with authentic peasants, like anti-Semitism, re-

**107**

mained a consistent element of their political vocabulary. It was part of the antimodern, anticapitalist, antisocialist, antiurban ambience of the resentful failures who made up a large segment of the leadership. Himmler discovered early in life that the peasant was the source of all that was good, pure, strong, and beautiful. Ignoring structural changes in agriculture, he envisaged a neo-feudal empire, inspired by the "noble peasant of his people," Henry the Fowler, king of Saxony and conqueror of the Slavs. For a time Himmler even tried his hand at farming. His activities in the Artamanen stemmed from the same fantastic imagination, which saw migrating Slavs and urbanized Jews as deadly enemies of German culture. Darré provided a respectable facade for these half-baked notions. He saw the wellspring of the Nordic race in the combat-ready peasant settlers of the pre-Christian past, who had maintained pure bloodlines and thus provided the essential elements of European culture. The creative peasant was held up as an ideal model, in denigrating distinction to the destructive and parasitic nomad. By careful racial selection and large-scale return to the land these pristine values, Darré believed, could be recovered and the land "denomadized." The artificial and dehumanizing character of urban life thus could be contained and Nordic superiority restored.[3]

The Artamanen sought to give these ideas practical meaning through actual physical labor on landed estates and through pioneer settlements in the eastern border lands. The group made a modest beginning in the summer of 1924 as small groups of dedicated young men volunteered for collective work on various landed estates, mostly in northern and eastern Germany. One of their motives was the displacement of migrant Polish farm workers. By 1929, when 2,000 of them worked on 300 different estates, an extensive literature and complex organization made the Artamanen a recognizable element in the *völkisch* youth movement of the Weimar Republic. The settlement schemes, however, remained largely unrealized. Factional strife, fostered by the intrusion of Nazi politics, brought about gradual disintegration. A significant element transferred to the SS, where some former Artamanen became prominent among Himmler's functionaries. The black uniform, one-man rule, sponsoring organization, biological selection, marriage code, elitism, and "order" concept were all characteristic features of the SS inherited from the agrarian pioneers.[4]

At the suggestion of Himmler, Darré attempted to incorporate the Artamanen in his Agrarian Apparatus. The party rejected the idea as politically inexpedient. In June 1931 Albert Wojirsch created a new faction that styled itself "Association of Artamanen, Voluntary National Socialist Labor Service of the Land." Almost all members belonged to the SA. They soon won the support of a provincial bureaucrat by the name of Walther Granzow, and by the spring of 1932 their numbers reached 200. They deemphasized vague hopes of future settlements and regarded agricultural work as a form of political action. At a convention in July 1933 in Güstrow, 400 of Wojirsch's black-clad Artamanen marched through Nazi-dominated streets and were addressed by Granzow. A month later several leaders of the Artamanen in East Prussia aligned themselves with the "East Prussian LD," a group attached to the local HJ, but in September 1934 other factions were subordinated to Darré's Food Estate for a time.[5]

The turning point came on 7 October 1934, at Güstrow. A festive ceremony, crowded with masses of Hitler youths, sealed the acceptance of Wojirsch's Artamanen into the ranks of the HJ as official Landdienst (LD). Artur Axmann, then head of the Social Office of the RJF, had persuaded Baldur von Schirach to take this step. Schirach made it seem as if several hundred followers of Wojirsch were the entire Artamanen movement and as if it had always been a part of national socialism by inner conviction and resolute purpose. In reality only one segment had been nazified, although the movement as a whole with its *völkisch* predilections certainly was sympathetic to many Nazi ideas.[6]

For several years Albert Wojirsch provided a transitional tie between Artamanen and Landdienst. In February 1935 he still called himself "Leader of the Artamanen," but by the fall of 1936 he had become an HJ-Bannführer and "chief expert for the LD." Most former Artamanen assumed leadership of new LD groups, which each spring descended on farms in increasing numbers, many of them escaping unemployment. The National Labor Exchange, an autonomous body supervised by the minister of labor, paid each young man 9 RM per month to defray living costs and help maintain communal camps, attached to local HJ units. The LD grew from 500 participants in 1934 to more than 6,600 by the end of 1936, an impressive increase, unthinkable without the support of state and party.[7]

In the fall, when harvesting was done, LD groups broke up into various parts. Some stayed in the villages to work through the winter, the best were sent to leadership schools or agrarian institutes, and the rest coalesced into amateur theatrical companies. The latter traveled from village to village, entertaining and propagating the blood and soil ideology. They also held evening meetings in towns and cities, where they recounted experiences on the farms, "preached the nobility of agrarian labor," put on plays that contained "healthy rustic humor," and recruited new members. Taking a cue from Schirach, who portrayed the LD as "illustrative socialism," Wojirsch tried to build the LD into a "school for national socialist communalism." Since participants' lives were locked into the rhythm of the countryside, desirable character could be forged by "severe discipline, simple lifestyle, hard work, and daily duties." In this sense the LD was supposed to achieve social as well as economic goals. In practical terms it meant that the LD extracted healthy youths from congested urban areas and put them at the disposal of farmers. But there was more at stake than momentary relief of unemployment and temporary supply of needed farm labor. City youths who discovered a natural way of life in the country were expected to stay on the land, found families there, and help to increase the rural population.[8]

## Battle against Unemployment and Land Flight

Eager to carve a niche in agrarian policies, youth leaders entered the battle against "flight from the land" with gusto. They latched on to Hitler's simplistic slogan which predicted inevitable decline unless Germany once more became an "empire of peasants."[9] This goal was to be realized by restoring pride in hard work and creating respected occupations out of agricultural toil. Because farm families had a tendency to die out within three generations, as one writer averred, a kind of biological renewal had to be fostered. Food Estate officials believed that the "spiritual strengthening" of the rural population had to fall on the shoulders of youth. Legislative measures to reclaim wastelands and provide public lands for homesteading and new settlements were held up to sons of peasants as enticements against the prevailing urban urge. The fact that the percent of Germans engaged in agriculture had declined from 63.9 in 1871 to 36.1 in 1933 was not encouraging, but realistic demographic reasoning was not a conspicuous trait of blood and soil enthusiasts.[10]

During the early years the LD was only one of several rural projects. In cooperation with the Labor Service, teenagers were filtered to agriculture through training camps supervised by personnel from the RJF Social Office. The National Labor Exchange initiated a project known as "Agricultural Assistance" and gave the HJ responsibility for the welfare of youths within its ranks. Acting as intermediaries between farmers and local labor exchanges, HJ leaders helped to steer some 200,000 young people into temporary farm work by the end of 1934, contributing to the relief of unemployment and indirectly to the establishment of HJ organizations in country villages. The most important of these projects was the Land Year. Instigated by the Prussian minister of culture in 1934, it was later adopted by the National Ministry of Education and peripherally involved

the RJF from the start. Submitting selected boys and girls to a year of agricultural work in field and household after the completion of the eighth year
of schooling, Land Year organizers forced participants to wear HJ uniforms and drew them into the social and political activities of regional and
local HJ organizations. Initially many of them came from impoverished
mining families in Upper Silesia; later they came from cities all over Germany.[11]

Demand for female workers in agriculture and unemployment among
urban girls led youth leaders to direct females toward the farm. In response to a request from the national labor exchange, the RJF set up eight-
week "reeducation camps" to help urban girls adjust to farming tasks.
Some 10,000 of them, seventeen and older, went through these BDM
camps, attached to landed estates or large farms, during the first two
years. When 900 females were brought into the LD in 1936, a natural pro-
gression from reeducation camp to LD membership was established.
Leaders were trained at a BDM school for camp directors in Diedersdorf
near Berlin. In collaboration with regional labor exchanges and farmers'
organizations, the BDM also provided "harvest assistance." Nearly 30,000
girls moved into the potato and grain fields during 1936.[12]

The LD clearly benefited from these related projects as it did from being
part of a broad campaign to organize rural youth. Darré facilitated the
effort. Particularly close relationships evolved between the RJF Social
Office, headed by Axmann, and the National Food Estate, created by
Darré to "reagrarianize" Germany and secure her agricultural self-sufficiency. This special affinity resulted in the dissolution of all competing
agrarian youth organizations and the official incorporation of its members
in the rapidly expanding HJ. An agreement between Axmann and the
Food Estate, concluded in 1935, created local posts with the archaic title of
"youth wardens," who became responsible for the social welfare and
occupational training of rural youngsters. They were recruited from local
HJ and BDM leaders, especially from the "ideal types" found in the LD.
Since the HJ sought to ignore social distinctions between children of agricultural laborers and landholding farmers, symbolically expressed in convivial village gatherings, common youth centers, and gymnastic facilities,
a kind of social leveling did occur. The youth wardens were the agents of
this process.[13]

Hans Bofinger, who directed the Youth Office of the Food Estate and a
related post in the Social Office of the RJF, tried to turn the youth wardens
into apostles of agrarian rejuvenation. Denouncing "cabbage nobles" and
abjuring "class socialism," Bofinger lauded the corporate ideal of the Food

Estate as genuinely socialistic. This ideal was to be propagated among rural youth and underlay the collaborative work of the Food Estate and the RJF. Four tasks were thought to be crucial: the creation of a communal sense, a clearly perceived racial ideology based on primitive naturalness, promotion of rural culture through the preservation of healthy customs, and the furthering of a life within the context of the folk community.[14]

To encompass rural youth the HJ attacked deplorable conditions. They had good ammunition. Infant mortality in small towns and rural villages far exceeded the national average, and deaths during childbirth among farm women (2.34 percent) were almost three times as frequent as among employed wives in cities (0.74 percent). Current surveys revealed that many rural children had deformed backs and faulty feet. Scaldings, burnings, drownings, and vehicular accidents victimized them disproportionately. A shortage of teachers and classrooms meant that rural children spent only eleven to thirteen hours per week in school, while larger schools provided sixteen to eighteen hours of instruction. Excessive use of child labor produced passive behavior in class. The HJ promised to help improve conditions. Faulty physical development was to be prevented through physical exercise. Stimulated by HJ health officials, the authorities began to construct showers in agricultural schools. Regular physical examinations were organized, and dental care was vigorously promoted. Alcohol consumption and smoking were discouraged. One HJ doctor suggested that rural public health could be maintained if "genetically healthy" young peasants found equally spotless marriage partners, thus creating a pure new generation of farmers.[15]

The regime's autarchic policies and rearmament plans led to the promotion of agricultural self-sufficiency. This could be achieved if the young were harnessed to the plow and sufficient numbers of them were trained for agrarian occupations. Attempting to raise the status of agricultural toil, the Food Estate tried to equalize it to urban-industrial occupations by formalizing training, providing educational facilities, and granting financial assistance to youths attending agricultural schools. Eligibility for aid depended on HJ or BDM membership and participation in the National Vocational Contest. This project of the peacetime years pitted millions of teenagers against each other in spirited competition to achieve proficiency in numerous specific vocational pursuits. It was inaugurated and directed by Artur Axmann in cooperation with Labor Front leader Robert Ley. A category for agriculture was included. In 1936, 250,000 rural youngsters competed in eleven different categories, furnishing twice as many participants as any of the other sixteen vocational groups.[16] Their projects, staged in 5,185 villages, were judged by 32,127 farmers. On the whole those with some specific occupational training performed noticeably better than those without it. The lack of training was most apparent in the eastern areas of Germany, the region of large landed estates, where only 11 to 15 percent had had formal training, and the southern regions, with 8 to 9 percent. In central and northern Germany 30 to 35 percent of the contestants had been given vocational education. This fact helps to explain why the LD was promoted so vigorously in the East and South.[17]

Formal agricultural education was introduced by Darré in 1936. It specified a four-year training period, with two devoted to full-time training under a qualified farmer, followed by two years as an apprentice. Those who avoided the program were not regarded as "career agrarian workers" but merely seasonal, migrant, or occasional agricultural employees. The Food Estate recognized service in the LD as equivalent to the required training time, as long as that time was spent within prescribed LD groups in rural villages. This venture in social politics could not compete with established agricultural schools granting diplomas. It was intended to create professional solidarity among the diverse and socially disreputable groups of farm laborers. Labor contracts were concluded with HJ officials. The LD group leader, who assumed responsibility for the circumstances of LD service, was regarded as a trustee of the HJ. His role was more demanding in village groups than estate groups, where the estate manager had more influence and where LD service was not yet recognized as equivalent to professional agricultural training. This explains why the early tendency to send most LD groups to larger estates was gradually changed to increasing use of village groups, which could be controlled more easily by the HJ.[18]

The HJ came to look upon itself as an exclusive instrument of indoctrination for agrarian youth. They insisted that participants live collectively in HJ Homes, rather than with individual farmers. These temporary facilities were primitive at first and led to a vigorous campaign to build LD Homes that reflected order, cleanliness, and social togetherness, in the spirit of the egalitarian folk community. Efforts to achieve parity in salaries with other agricultural workers and protection from overwork for youngsters under sixteen bore some fruit by 1937, thanks to Darré's intervention. There was a conscious attempt to mix urban and rural youth within LD groups, to prevent the latter from deserting the land and acquaint urban youngsters with the problems of the country. Farmers and estate owners were warned repeatedly not to regard the LD volunteers as cheap labor but as future farmers. All LD members had to make contributions to a savings fund to be used for future agrarian settlements on newly cultivated or reclaimed land. Believing that social relationships, salaries, working hours, and housing conditions were the elementary causes of land flight, the HJ sought to improve them. Darré's dream of an independent class of peasants could be realized only if the HJ did its part.[19]

It was estimated in 1937 that Germany needed approximately 200,000 new entrants in agriculture to meet the goals of self-sufficiency, about half of whom would have to begin training each year. Half of the latter, some 50,000, were to be sons of independent peasants and larger farmers, who were expected to fulfill their training obligations on their own family farm, while the other 50,000 were to be sons of landless agricultural workers. Only the latter were incorporated in the training program during the first year. For them 41,595 learning places were arranged in the spring, meeting the goals quite closely. But only 6,782 youngsters availed themselves of the opportunity. Even if we add the 14,880 youths committed to the LD, which was theoretically equivalent to formal training, reaching a figure of 21,670, less than half of the target for landless workers was reached during the first year. The HJ's own estimate was that only a third of LD members were serving in conditions that met training criteria. The actual number of trainees may have been closer to 15,000. The HJ blamed parents, who objected to their children embarking on unpromising agrarian careers, and asked school teachers to counteract parental pressure.[20]

References slipped into the literature almost surreptitiously make it clear that resistance by parents to the HJ as a whole and the LD in particular was developing. The expansion of the HJ Patrol Service, the HJ Law of 1936, and the gradual intrusion of the SS into HJ affairs on various levels and at various points were likely responses to this resistance. It remained to be seen how successful the Food Estate and HJ would be in establishing comprehensive agricultural training.

The HJ received a boost when the National Labor Exchange recognized the LD as the exclusive agency for all forms of group agrarian assistance and stopped financial support for individual agricultural helpers. BDM girls, who had been obligated to spend at least a year in the LD following four weeks in reeducation camps, had their LD service reduced to nine months. In cases where female LD groups had been requested by local labor exchanges or Food Estate officers, the National Labor Exchange assumed financial costs. These measures, too, were designed to overcome parental reluctance to submit young daughters to the difficult environment of rural work. Meanwhile, thousands of HJ and BDM youngsters, more than 100,000 in Württemberg alone, were made available to bring in the 1937 harvest without receiving salaries. They underscored the HJ commitment to agrarian renewal and helped to legitimize the LD in the eyes of peasants and farmers.[21]

After four years of concerted effort, the LD managed to establish itself as a recognizable institutional arrangement within the field of agrarian politics. The support of the Labor Exchange and the Food Estate and general measures to reduce unemployment and relieve the shortage of agricultural laborers aided the development of the LD. The HJ, with a membership of 5.5 million, had received the partial imprimatur of the state in 1936. This gave such suborganizations as the LD, which was essentially voluntary, an aura of legitimacy, reinforced by the Food Estate's organization of the farm population. The inauguration of the Four Year Plan and a policy of economic autarchy helped the LD in its self-conscious efforts to become an institution of long-range significance for agriculture. This depended, of course, on its ability to impede the exodus from the land and make agrarian labor an attractive occupation for youth. Ignoring unwelcome circumstances, such as a major war, the HJ leadership was sanguine.[22]

In the light of long-range demographic objectives, the most salient feature of the LD was the presence of females. They constituted 14 percent of volunteers in 1936, grew to 23 percent in 1937, jumped to 36 percent in 1938, and overtook the males in the war year of 1939 with 55 percent. This social fact made the LD a much more promising experiment than the Artamanen movement. It therefore needs to be evaluated in a broader context. The attempt at full utilization of females, as distinguished from genuine equality, was a prominent feature of Nazi socioeconomic policy. The BDM helped to implement this goal through participation in the Land Year, the NSV, harvest assistance, the LD, and two additional projects: the Home Economics Year and the Female Duty Year.[23]

The Home Economics Year had been introduced in the spring of 1934 as a joint effort of the RJF, the Labor Exchange, and the Nazi Organization for Women to find employment for school-leaving girls. It was a voluntary means of relieving female pressure on the labor market, since girls served for a year in a household without pay. While it was initially a device to stimulate full employment, the BDM and RJF sought to use it to turn a significant number of participants toward permanent domestic professions, especially in the country. By 1938 the military necessity of female employment, particularly in agriculture, which needed some 240,000 workers, led to the Female Duty Year. It obligated all unmarried women under twenty-five to show proof of having spent one year in agriculture or domestic service before being gainfully employed. The LD benefited from this, since the Duty Year obligation could be satisfied by participation in the LD. The LD was clearly perceived as the lesser of two evils, probably because of the organizational efficiency of the RJF and the concept of mutuality promoted within the HJ.[24]

In March Axmann enlarged the female contingent of the LD. A radio campaign was launched to recruit female group leaders, and girls who volunteered for the LD with a distinct liking for agricultural work, home economics, or welfare professions received preference. In localities where sufficient BDM members volunteered for the LD, nonmembers were expelled, as were those over eighteen. Among the 44,000 girls who served under the aegis of the Duty Year in 1938–39, some 1,900 did so within the LD. The rest were distributed among the Home Economics Year (12,000), the Labor Service (1,600), the Land Year (1,600), in Food Estate apprenticeships (400), and finally a substantial number in free labor contracts with wages and social insurance benefits (26,500). After the initial year the numbers of participants in the Duty Year increased sharply, but the obligation remained extremely unpopular, as did that of the Labor Service, which became compulsory for women over eighteen in 1939. The voluntary nature and racial selectivity of the LD gave it an advantage in terms of the aims it sought to achieve, that of making permanent agrarian occupations attractive to teenage girls.[25]

With Darré's influence on the wane, the LD embarked on a new phase in 1938. In his address to the HJ at the Party Rally in September, Göring asked German youth to decide on careers that were most significant for the state and the people. Baldur von Schirach followed suit by ordering systematic career counseling, and his staff chief, Hartmann Lauterbacher, placed particular emphasis on recruitment for the LD. In anticipation of change, Walter Wojirsch announced that future LD groups would be sent only to "healthy areas," and only to villages where the housing question had been solved in advance. It appeared as if the LD was to become a more pliant instrument of state policy, when in reality the doors were opened to the SS by awakening Himmler's interest.[26]

### Formal Alliance with Himmler's SS

Bavaria played a special role in the history of the LD. There was no LD there or any training for agrarian workers until 1937, when Wojirsch created an "LD Inspectorate South" with twenty-five-year-old Adalbert Schindlmayr as its chief. His feverish activity soon gave Bavaria a unique place in the LD. Mobilizing the support of reluctant HJ leaders, officials of the farmers' organization, the Labor Front, and the Economics Ministry, Schindlmayr began to recruit. Near Hindelang he set up a leaders' school, while appeals appeared in the press and on the radio. Food Estate officers provided instructional materials. The Red Cross and health offices offered medical assistance. In June he began to publish his own newsletter. The Food Estate's youth wardens provided basic training. By August the Bavarian LD had established forty-six camps with 470 volunteers. Farm Leader Hermann Deininger provided money to hold a leaders' conference and offered Schindlmayr space for his headquarters. In March 1938 Himmler donated 1,000 RM to furnish two LD homes, reminding Schindlmayr, who had requested help, of his own long-standing commitment to reagrarianization. It was the beginning of Himmler's patronage, crucial for Schindlmayr's budding career and the progress and orientation of the LD.[27]

Born the son of an *Oberlehrer* in Augsburg, "Bertl" Schindlmayr received his diploma from the *Realgymnasium* in 1931. He worked a while for various rural concerns and studied agriculture at the Technical College in Munich. In 1934 the HJ and Labor Front employed him as a counselor for young agrarian workers. He attended an NSV school and in 1936 headed the Youth Welfare Bureau of the NSV in Augsburg and Munich until Wojirsch gave him the difficult task of getting the Bavarian LD off the ground. As a boy of sixteen he had begun to make monthly financial contributions to the NSDAP and joined the party when he became eligible. Between 1928 and 1931 he had served in the Augsburg SA and in 1931 joined the SS as well, although he does not appear to have been very active until Himmler's patronage became important to him. He was more active in the Augsburg HJ, which he joined in 1934 and which he served for a time as press chief. Schindlmayr's SS commander praised his "unchangeable loyalty and discretion," and the president of the Augsburg city council testified that he had "performed his duties knowledgeably and in an exemplary manner." His racial pedigree was impeccable, his enthusiasm contagious, and his commitment to national socialism beyond question. Schindlmayr was the kind of young man Himmler could use.[28]

Darré's interest in the HJ did not flag, although Himmler grew impatient with his theorizing and dismissed him from the RuSHA in 1938. During the Farmers' Rally in Goslar, Darré praised the achievements of the LD extensively, asked reluctant farmers to accept these young idealists with open arms, and boldly asserted that the LD represented the regime's most "positive contribution to the struggle against the flight from the land." Himmler may have grown tired of Darré, but he clearly shared the latter's view of the practical possibilities the LD provided for implementing the SS fascination with farming and the settlement of properly indoctrinated young peasants on Germany's frontiers. Since roughly 50,000 youngsters had filtered through the LD by 1938, and since 80 percent of that year's contingent of 18,000 was sixteen or younger, there was an opportunity for recruitment that Himmler could not ignore.[29]

The support of the SS gave HJ leaders recognition and bolstered their position vis-à-vis resisting parents and skeptical farmers. The gradual warming of relations between SS and HJ came to a decisive turning point in 1938 when the SRD pact was signed in August, followed by the agreement to make the LD an SS feeder organization in December.[30]

Asserting that the LD had favored boys with the kind of physical features, character, and attitude that the SS cherished, Himmler and Schirach determined that those boys who were willing to become "defense-peasants" would be actively "directed" into the LD. The idea of defense-peasants, a kind of agrarian militia, was derived from late Roman and more recent Austrian experiments on the Turkish border.[31] There is no evidence that the HJ showed much interest in the scheme before this time, and even Darré appears to have thought Himmler's ideas impractical.[32] It is ironic that Himmler dismissed Darré for being too theoretical and then tried to lay an institutional basis for a scheme that would settle LD and SS veterans on defense-peasant homesteads. There was further irony in the reservation that such settlement would occur at the discretion of the Reichsführer, and "in cooperation with the . . . National Farm Leader," namely Darré. So far it was all promise, however, since settlement would occur "continuously as these new farmsteads became available," that is land to be conquered in the East.[33]

From the vantage point of the HJ, the agreement inaugurated a "new epoch" for the LD. A distinction was made between boys who were judged to be potential defense-peasants and the rest who were to be trained as agrarian workers, a class difference contradicting the previous LD aims now surrendered to the elitist SS. Beginning in the spring of 1939, LD groups were made up of youngsters who had just left school. They were withdrawn from the care of school officials and parents and totally embraced by the HJ. The work contracts became uniform. A fifty-four-hour week was stipulated, extended to sixty hours during the harvest. One afternoon each week was set aside for vocational training and HJ service, without reduction in pay, now determined not only by age but according to length of service and successful completion of the agrarian workers' examination. Systematic training as defined by the Food Estate was required of all participants, so that each entrant at fourteen knew exactly what steps he had to take to arrive at the ultimate goal of becoming an independent peasant or trained agrarian worker. Newly appointed LD-Gefolgschafts-führer, responsible for six to fifteen groups, became overseers of vocational training. They were enjoined to place LD members in agricultural schools, to foster specialized training, and to counsel future settlers on SS frontier farms.[34]

For those who qualified as SS frontier settlers an "LD Settler Association" was created, to which they continued to belong while they served in the SS armed formations. Since they entered the SS after their eighteenth birthday, this meant that most of them would not have become eligible for settlement until they were at least twenty-four years old. While they were in the SS, the "settler applicants" were subjected to constant indoctrination by the officials of RuSHA, which gradually began to emerge from the disgraceful cloud cast over it by Darré's departure and began to acquire a new field of activity in Himmler's population policies.[35]

Gottlob Berger seized upon the opportunity provided by the LD pact. In a confidential memorandum to SS leaders he analyzed the significance of the LD for the SS. Citing well-known causes for the land flight, Berger feared that the exodus of agrarian workers would soon also lead to an urban migration of peasants. That the rural population had to be the focus of a comprehensive "racial and demographic policy of renewal" was beyond question in his view. The rural population had to be made aware that large, hereditarily healthy families, provisions for the building of a native agrarian corps of leaders, and creation of possibilities for vocational advancement were of primary concern. The main goal of the LD was the return of a portion of urban youth to the soil and represented the obverse side of mutually dependent measures. Still one could not appeal to urban youth on the basis of material or vocational advantages, but rather to its idealism. Teaching youth to commit themselves voluntarily to a rising "vanguard of pioneers" was dictated by "unavoidable historic necessity." This task, Berger believed, now had been invested with "overriding political importance."[36]

It was now possible to use more stringent selective criteria. A weeding out of undesirables began even before the pact was signed and continued once the SS was involved directly. Female LD groups exhibited better racial quality on the whole than male groups, according to Berger, mainly because the obligations of the Home Economics Year could be satisfied by LD service and had provided a larger pool for selection. More qualified LD group leaders could now be chosen, since the SS raised their expectation of eventual land ownership. It was a crude bait, but Berger had no reservations about its effectiveness, because the SS had achieved sufficient prestige and stimulated enough fear to dampen inconvenient questions posed by astute LD volunteers or their parents. Berger backed the practice of preferring village groups, who helped small and medium-sized farmers, to groups engaged by larger estates or individuals hired by single peasants. Village groups who lived in their own HJ Home could be controlled by peer-group pressure. The LD Home was becoming the center of life for the youth of the entire village, thus contributing to the nazification of the rural population.[37]

Berger was especially concerned with the financing of the LD, hitherto a troublesome matter. The RJF had been able to raise salaries, but there were still considerable regional variations. Monthly pay ranged from 12 to 45 RM for LD members. Group leaders received a maximum of 45 RM and a "leader bonus" of 25 to 50 RM, furnished by estate owners or village farmers, who also paid the salaries of the Gefolgschaftsführer, which amounted to a maximum of 150 RM per month. The Labor Exchange provided 7.50 RM monthly for each new volunteer and the estate managers and farmers gave an average of 15 RM yearly to defray organizational costs. These resources were inadequate. A request for 1,704,310 RM directed to the minister of finance in March 1938 to build LD Homes remained unanswered a year later. Berger estimated that a minimum of 8 million RM would be needed yearly to relieve poor peasants of the organizational costs, of leader bonuses and Gefolgschaftsführer salaries. An additional 10 million RM would be needed to provide the requisite number of decent LD Homes for a projected 34,000 volunteers.[38]

Berger compared these costs with the budget of the Land Year, financed by the Ministry of Education, which then also included about 34,000 youngsters between the ages of fourteen and fifteen, and amounted to 15 million RM. Land Year participants worked only half the number of hours of LD members, many of whom remained permanently on the land, an estimated one-third in 1938. The comparison is revealing, but Berger had more in mind than putting the LD in a favorable light. While he gave faint praise to the objectives of Bernhard Rust's Education Ministry, he strongly implied that the LD pact made the competing program obsolete. Rust's bureaucrats must have gotten wind of SS intentions to displace the Land Year, for a secret memorandum signed by F. C. Schiffer of the Central Institute of Education made an elaborate justification for the Land Year. The two programs could have been complimentary if an overlap in ages had been avoided and if the political warfare had been less intense. The

Land Year continued its competition, even in the eastern occupied areas, which Himmler came to regard as his special preserve.[39]

With SS support the LD moved forward rapidly. Plans were drawn up for an extensive home-building program, and existing homes were refurbished with a grant from agricultural credit associations (Raiffeisen e.V.). By the middle of 1939 over 25,000 youngsters had volunteered, and a brief campaign for group leaders brought more applications than the RJF could handle. LD group leader became a full-time career. More young people now seemed to be willing to embark on permanent agricultural occupations, probably hoping they could defer the draft. Nearly 5,500 young people made that decision at the end of 1938. These, along with thousands of earlier volunteers, were taken into the SS Settler Association.[40]

SS leaders began to lend their personal prestige by attending LD functions. At a conference of LD leaders in February 1939 Himmler appealed to their idealism by assuring them that he "was not ashamed" to say that he himself had been a farmhand (*Bauernknecht*) and was "deeply grateful" for that experience. He went on: "You must first serve and learn! Then come the years of being a peasant and a boss! Thus once more we shall become a people with many children of good blood and through your strength, your willpower, your abilities, the flight from the land will be stopped; instead there will be a conscious movement of the best youth from the city to the countryside, to a new way of life."[41] In rural areas agreements were interpreted liberally by SS leaders, who tried to incorporate older HJ members in SS units with the help of sympathetic government officials (*Landräte*). In Swabia and Bavaria it stirred up quite a controversy, promoted by irate HJ leaders who saw their own independent political existence threatened. In some cases young men who had refused to join the HJ now suddenly joined the SS and appeared before faithful HJ members in coveted black uniforms, an intolerable situation for veteran HJ leaders. After all, one had to follow the normal course of advancement, through the SRD and LD into the SS.[42]

### Adaptation to Wartime Conditions

As war clouds gathered, *Wille und Macht* dedicated an entire issue to the peasant question. Friedrich Schmidt, former Artamanen leader and then head of the party's Education Office, called for a new agrarian social order by declaring war on the city, on progress, on modernity. He believed the LD was in the vanguard of a much larger task which required that the HJ become the cultural and communal regenerator of society. Perpetuation depended on the "recreation of a genuine racial social order with characteristics native to the peasantry." Walter Gross, head of the Office of Racial Politics, bemoaned the decline in peasant fecundity and saw the LD as a way of freeing peasant wives from demanding physical labor in order to devote themselves to childbearing. Matthias Haidn, a Food Estate official, attacked the "urbanization" and "proletarianization" of the countryside and called for the reinstatement of agrarian values, the "cultural world" of the peasant, even the transfer of the "yearning for blood and soil" to the city itself. Rudolf Proksch contributed a nostalgic account of the Artamanen. The editors appended a final collection of quotations from classical writers dealing with the decline of independent farmers in antiquity. Reading this issue one could get the idea the Nazis were about to launch a peasant war on urban Germany, rather than contemplate the invasion of Poland.[43]

There was danger that the draft or SS recruitment might rob the LD of its leaders. At the end of August Hartmann Lauterbacher demanded all LD groups be kept intact, since the LD was "one of the most essential tasks of the HJ." Nevertheless, when the war came, most HJ leaders soon found themselves in uniforms and 95 percent of all LD leaders were compelled to perform military service, mostly in the W-SS. Younger men and women had to be pressed into leading positions and the number of LD volunteers itself declined from 26,000 in 1939 to 16,475 in 1940.[44]

Expedients were quickly introduced to tide the organization over the temporary recession in personnel. The city defense commissioner in Berlin, for instance, allowed the HJ, in September 1939 to recruit youngsters from public and private intermediate and secondary schools for temporary service in the LD. Within eight days trains filled with youngsters began to roll into the villages of the Kurmark. Recruitment for more permanent LD service continued throughout the country during the fall and winter of 1939–40. In Bavaria, Bertl Schindlmayr, himself temporarily on the quiescent "Westfront" as soldier, reminded agrarian officials of Himmler's interest and demanded full cooperation. In the RJF an *Arbeitsgemeinschaft Bauerntum* was created to coordinate village HJ units and bolster the LD.[45]

The LD did not collapse. Himmler's interest had seen to that. In March 1939 Hitler was finally persuaded to issue two implementation orders to the HJ Law of 1936, which put the HJ under the authority of the party treasurer in financial matters, defined the respective authority of the youth leader and the minister of education, and made HJ service compulsory. The function of the HJ with regard to the Land Year was left explicitly for subsequent resolution, which meant that competition with the LD would continue, but the introduction of compulsory HJ service had the effect of making the LD a state concern. This was confirmed when the minister of labor, Franz Seldte, issued regulations on the utilization of LD groups. They were to be used wherever agricultural workers were especially needed, and those who had not yet decided on a vocation were to be preferred. Age limits were set for girls (fourteen to twenty-one) and boys (fourteen to eighteen). Agrarian youth were to be taken into the LD only to the degree they were needed to help acquaint urban youth with the agricultural environment, and their number was not to exceed 30 percent of any one group. The salaries of volunteers became equal to that of farmhands, supplemented by pocket money. The RJF received a yearly allocation from the party treasury to cover the costs of housing, medical services, clothing, administration, recreation, and transportation. All aspects of LD activity were regulated, a by-product of putting the institution on secure financial ground and submitting it to budgetary control.[46]

Between the conquest of Poland and the invasion of Norway, while the RJF was undergoing internal change, Darré quietly moved to solidify his long-standing support of the LD. He signed an agreement with Lauterbacher that delimited respective responsibilities. The HJ retained control over indoctrination, as well as over recruitment, selection, and the communal environment, whereas the Food Estate assumed responsibility for creating a receptive attitude among farmers, took care of economic arrangements, and supervised the occupational training of participants. Distinctions were made between diplomas for agrarian workers and agricultural economics certificates. LD members, who remained in the service longer than a year, received preferential treatment and could take the former at sixteen, the latter at eighteen.[47] The Ministry of Agriculture encouraged settlement officials to make use of the LD wherever possible, and the Food Estate set up special courses to train members in agrarian occupations.[48]

Lauterbacher streamlined the LD by organizing members into manageable LD-Scharen of ten to forty-five boys and girls, submitting them to HJ and BDM leaders in matters of discipline, medical observation, camp supervision, and personnel contingencies. Two or more Scharen in turn became Gefolgschaften or Gruppen, the leaders of which were incorporated in Regional HJ Directorates. Each Region received an LD Agent, who served as specialist in the Social Section of the Directorate. In this way the LD became a regular part of the HJ organization. As such the full resources of the HJ were used to recruit for the LD within the HJ and the schools. By accepting mostly youngsters who had decided on agrarian occupation, who wanted to become settlers or defense-peasants, the LD became more susceptible to SS purposes. Selection committees carried out regular musterings based on four criteria: physical fitness, SS suitability, completion of the *Volksschule* or a higher school, and a certificate of good conduct for boys under sixteen. Similar prerequisites applied to girls, including a degree of "racial fitness" akin to SS suitability. With these guidelines established, a recruiting campaign began in February 1940. Efforts were made to bring volunteers into a training situation where LD service would count for part of the required apprenticeship.[49]

LD homes received renewed emphasis and became subject to approval before a work contract could be signed. The earlier campaign to build some 50,000 HJ Homes, strongly supported by a Hitler decree that obligated local communities to commit money, while hampered by the outbreak of war, continued in 1940. For the LD, prefabricated wooden structures on cement foundations were used with increasing frequency. Financial support from the Raiffeisen cooperatives and party and state sources kept the home-building effort from being curtailed.[50]

In the RJF the *Arbeitsgemeinschaft Bauerntum* was absorbed by a major new Office for Farming and Eastern Lands. An accomplished farmer, Food Estate official, and SS-Oberführer, Rudolf Peukert, was appointed to head the bureau. While the LD remained under the organizational control of the Social Office, its LD section chief, SS-Hauptsturmführer Ernst Schulz, was subordinated to Peukert in order to maintain "unified action with regard to the anticipated eastern settlement activities." Within a month part of the section in the Social Office dealing with "agricultural youth work" was transferred to Peukert's domain, followed by appropriate changes on the regional and district levels. Lauterbacher, who competed with Axmann for Schirach's mantle, was not prepared to challenge the Social Office chief directly by extracting the long-cherished LD entirely from his jurisdiction. Axmann, who did succeed Schirach, however, held no brief against Peukert at this time and lauded his practical experience in agricultural matters.[51]

Rudolf Peukert was a good choice for the LD, hampered for lack of a dominant figure since Wojirsch's demise, a slack taken up by permanent staffers like Schulz. The unmarried Peukert was thirty-two, had joined the party in 1928, and served as provincial farm leader in Thuringia. He was a protégé of Gauleiter Fritz Sauckel, who became Hitler's plenipotentiary for foreign laborers. Peukert was also associated with Darré, whom he served as "deputy for youth work" in the Food Estate. The latter probably was influenced by Peukert's earlier connection to Sauckel, since Polish farm laborers were already becoming a problem, perceived as unfair and racially damaging competition.[52] Peukert proceeded to appoint regional and district Farm Agents, mainly Youth Wardens of the Food Estate. They functioned as political liaison in a complex system.[53]

In the fall of 1939 the 26,016 boys and girls, divided into 1,753 LD-Scharen, stood practically without leaders, of whom 90 percent had been drafted or recruited by the SS. Leadership was thrust on younger members—on average, nineteen-year-olds—who had spent less than two years in the LD. Three-fourths of them remained for several years, providing some continuity. After financing had been taken over by the party, funds became available to restructure the organization, provide uniforms, and secure decent camp facilities. The first few months of war were used for this purpose. Then, on 1 April 1940, 1,063 newly furnished camps were opened with considerable fanfare, although the number of volunteers had been reduced to 18,400, with girls in the clear majority for the first time.[54]

This relatively high number was diminished during the course of the year by sickness, assumption of apprenticeships, and 165 expulsions. Two-thirds of the remaining 16,475 members were fourteen or fifteen. It was a drastic lowering in age, which put the LD in direct competition with the Land Year. The RJF insisted, however, that the quality of the LD was better than ever, since most of them were better educated. Keeping LD participants permanently on the land was as difficult as before the war. The opening up of agricultural land in the East created a new situation, however, to which the volunteers responded decisively. Some 40 percent of the recruits wanted to serve in eastern LD camps, although their parents were reluctant to allow them to go that far away from home. In the end only 6 percent of the boys and 4 percent of the girls went east, mostly into the Warthegau, where conditions were quite a bit more primitive and the work more challenging than at home.[55]

Female labor became crucial in Nazi Germany, particularly in agriculture. For unmarried young women and teenage girls two agencies played significant roles: the Labor Service for older girls and the LD for younger ones. While compulsory female labor ran into serious difficulty, especially in agriculture, the inclusion of females in the voluntary LD was more successful. There were certain advantages to volunteering. Under the pressure of war and in response to requests from the RJF, the Reich farm leader allowed LD girls who wanted to embark on agrarian home economics training after their initial year in the LD to take the home economics examination. After passing that, these trainees would normally have had to undergo a three-year apprenticeship, but Darré gave female LD leaders the right to substitute at least one year of LD experience for this *Praktikum*. Qualified LD girls could also become domestic nurses and home economics teachers. For these purposes places were opened to them in agrarian women's schools and the female sections of agricultural schools.[56]

To halt female desertion of the land, Erna Pranz, the specialist in the RJF and the Labor Front, believed the HJ was "putting girls back into the community of the people" by strengthening their "ethical, cultural, political, and physical education." Her faith was based on the fact that most of the "Compulsory Year" girls were meeting that obligation in the countryside, and that the total number of girls having served at least one year in the LD during the peacetime years of the Reich amounted to 21,664. More important was the fact that some 10 percent of these girls had married farmers and remained in the country. Now when women and girls were doing most of the work on the farms, one could be more selective and thus enhance the role of the LD as a pioneering racial elite in the countryside.[57]

While the female LD was expanded, with even small regions like Swabia running thirteen camps with 174 participants, recruitment continued unabated. The military conquests of 1940 spread euphoria about the land that was reflected in the attitude of HJ leaders. To them the LD achieved new significance now that the acquisition of "living space" was attaining reality in the East, and an aristocracy of blood and soil would be needed to fully exploit the won ground. One writer saw significance in the findings of an academic researcher who calculated that nearly half of some 10,000 leading public figures of the past, like Scharnhorst, Moltke, Arndt, and Fichte, had had rustic origins. Whether the LD would produce figures of similar stature was doubtful, but clearly the HJ-SS agreement was seen as the "crowning" event of a long struggle. Collaboration with the SS in seeding the eastern marches with culturally superior agrarian-military enclaves was an exciting new imperial prospect.[58]

Artur Axmann was understandably optimistic about achieving the aims of the intrepid Artamanen, whose "declaration of war on a liberal world" had now received a "much wider and broader base in the LD." At an LD conference in October 1940, surrounded by his old friends and colleagues, he took credit for this achievement. Despite the loss of experienced leaders, all the old activities of the HJ had been maintained. Virtue had grown out of necessity, and "so out of the HJ leaders who fulfilled their duty in the field and out of the new leaders who proved themselves at home, an iron ring had been forged around youth," which made the future a rosy prospect in Axmann's eyes.[59] The old bureau once again got changed, to the Office for Farming and Land Service, and all agrarian activities were concentrated under Rudolf Peukert's direction. Axmann, meanwhile, went to see Himmler to reaffirm the HJ-SS relationship, since the youth leader had defeated Himmler's protégé, Lauterbacher, for the post. In the course of their friendly discussion Axmann committed himself to the development of the LD. Himmler was grateful and in turn promised ample financial support.[60]

In April 1941, 19,595 volunteers left for camps in the countryside, 3,000 of them in the newly annexed areas, where some 80 percent of the 1940 contingent had chosen to stay. It was a relatively small increase from the previous year, and more than half of them were girls. The boys as in 1940 were very young.[61] By this time nearly 100,000 youngsters had filtered through the LD, an institutional experience that could be capitalized on. With adaptation to wartime conditions concluded, Peukert and his staff concerned themselves with recruitment.[62] The *Schulungsdienst der HJ*, which published monthly indoctrination pamphlets, carried numerous interpretive essays and personal stories about the work and life of LD participants.[63] Beautifully produced and illustrated booklets were issued with regularity, always highlighting the wishes of the Führer, the support of Party Treasurer Schwarz, the Food Estate's Darré, the Ministry of Labor, and most of all Himmler's unflagging zeal regarding reagrarianization. Various ideal sketches of farmsteads and *Wehrbauern* establishments were reproduced from SS sources. The orderly simplicity and pastoral appeal of these imaginative drawings must have made an impact on the youthful mind, saturated with bucolic propaganda as it was. Otto Stolle, a key staffer in the Office for Farming and Land Service, was firmly persuaded that the LD was well on its way of becoming "the farmer's school for German youth."[64]

## Complete SS Takeover Aborted

Adalbert Schindlmayr, appointed inspector for Bavaria by Wojirsch, early established contact with Himmler and played a significantly role in the conclusion of the LD pact of 1938. He continued to maneuver behind the scenes. While drafted by the army in August 1939 and shipped to the Western Front, he found time during the *Sitzkrieg* to pursue his LD interests through correspondence. While a mere private in the army, he got himself promoted to HJ-Oberstammführer and SS-Hauptsturmführer, got married, and obtained a "new farmer certificate." In the spring of 1940 he corresponded with the German Resettlement Trust, a part of Himmler's

RKFDV system created to look after settler property interests. He wanted to make sure he could get a state-subsidized homestead as an SS defense-peasant after the war.[65]

Himmler's interest in Schindlmayr as a potential instrument for the complete absorption of the LD was thus stimulated. While on furlough, Himmler called him to Berlin and instructed him "to activate" the shaky LD in Bavaria as an SS project by "gradually forging connections" between individual SS offices and the RJF and by establishing LD camps on farms owned by the SS. Himmler also discussed the matter with Oswald Pohl, chief of the SS Administrative and Economics Office, and tried to get Schindlmayr released from army service. Upon his return to Bavaria Schindlmayr proceeded to cultivate influential SS leaders with brash abandon. He established contact with Otto Hofmann, who had replaced Darré as chief of RuSHA, not only to satisfy Himmler's order, but also to please Rudolf Peukert's desire to use him as liaison between the RJF and RuSHA. Hofmann arranged a series of meetings where they discussed plans, supplied Schindlmayr with ideological materials, and spoke at LD leadership conferences in Bavaria. RuSHA's extraordinary interest soon created jealous reactions among HJ leaders and landed Schindlmayr in hot water with the RJF.[66]

Schindlmayr's troubles with the HJ began in July 1941, when Heinrich Emsters of Region Mainfranken sent an angry letter to Ernst Schulz. Resentful of Schindlmayr's SS rank and influence, Emsters attacked his irregular procedures and questioned his sexual identity. Emsters must have known that Schulz himself held the rank of SS captain, although he was clearly unaware of the latter's friendship with Schindlmayr and Schindlmayr's proximity to Peukert. Emsters and a number of other HJ leaders relied on the new RJF chief of staff, Helmut Möckel, to resist SS incursions. Peukert soon called Schindlmayr to task in order to avoid a bruising power struggle. Uncowed, Schindlmayr with one of Pohl's subordinates toured SS farms with the idea of turning them into model establishments for the LD. Peukert appealed to Hofmann to help arrange a meeting with Himmler, ostensibly to get Himmler's support for a "national cultural conference" in Weimar, but the real intent was to secure his own job as chief of the LD should it become an SS appendage. When no meeting materialized, Peukert decided to contact Himmler directly. He had a good pretext, or so he thought.[67]

Walther Darré, himself struggling to retain his offices, had declared his intention to reactivate the Agrarian Apparatus and named Rudolf Peukert as his deputy in the *Reichsleitung*. Fritz Sauckel had already agreed that

Peukert could retain his post as farm leader, and Axmann had requested that Peukert also continue to head the LD. Now Peukert wanted to talk with Himmler and Axmann together about further development of the LD. Peukert intended to name Schindlmayr liaison between his LD Office and Hofmann's RuSHA. The stage was set for an SS takeover. But Himmler kept his own counsel and refused to move, probably because he feared reaction from OKW, already resentful of the close relationship between HJ and SS. In any case, Schindlmayr was redrafted by OKW at the request of the RJF, although at the last minute Himmler's personal staff had the order rescinded and Schindlmayr remained at his post as LD inspector for Bavaria. Schindlmayr quickly tried to placate Emsters, denying one-sided preoccupation with SS interests, and kept Hofmann informed of developments. The latter continued to support him and tried once again to establish communication between Peukert and Himmler.[68]

Never hesitant when it came to promoting his own career, Schindlmayr tracked down Rudolf Brandt, chief of Himmler's personal staff, at the Führer's headquarters. Brandt put him off by talking about two Russian boys who had been put in Schindlmayr's care by Himmler with the idea of turning them into "useful workers" through Germanization in LD camps. These victims of SS experimentation, Constantin and Paul Gerelick (eleven and sixteen), were housed at LD Camp Höfen in Upper Bavaria, where, as Schindlmayr put it, they were supposed to learn "the difference between Bolshevik dirt and decent camp education, an attempt thus being made to turn racially halfway good Russian youths into usable fellows within a proper environment." Brandt informed Schindlmayr that Himmler intended to send him additional Russian children. When Schindlmayr raised questions, Brandt told him these Russian guinea pigs need not receive salaries, and other incidental costs would be picked up by RKFDV. When they got around to discussing Schindlmayr's problems with HJ leaders, Brandt suggested that he consult Gottlob Berger, who "would undoubtedly remove these difficulties." To encourage him further he was given permission to hire a secretary at RKFDV expense.[69]

Schindlmayr's maneuvering did not go unnoticed. When he returned to Munich he found a letter from the RJF, demanding he decide whether to remain an HJ leader or become a full-time SS officer. Disturbed, he immediately sought Schulz's help in retaining his post, reminding him that Axmann had agreed to his assumption of Himmler's charge to construct model LD farms under SS auspices. Schindlmayr then informed Berger, Pohl, and Hofmann that concerted attacks were afoot "on the part of the HJ against the work of the SS." At a recent conference of Bavarian LD leaders,

Hofmann and a W-SS recruiter had elicited good response, but HJ leaders, particularly Bannführer Loos of HJ Region Franken, complained that "nothing positive" had resulted because few participants had been interested in "how to become W-SS men or defense-peasants." More serious was Loos's charge that the Bavarian LD had become "a kind of Young SS." Schindlmayr went on to charge that the RJF had refused to accept Himmler's offer of 2 million RM for LD expansion with the remark that "the HJ could not be bought by the SS." Furthermore, Schindlmayr's release from the army, engineered by Himmler, had been countered by RJF intervention with OKW on the excuse that Schindlmayr was working mostly for the SS and was of little use to the HJ. When Schulz requested Schindlmayr's promotion, he was informed it was impossible because double membership in the HJ and SS, a conventional practice for years, was undesirable. Schindlmayr assumed these attacks were not entirely personal and revealed a developing anti-SS attitude in the RJF, so he begged Berger to take appropriate action.[70]

Schindlmayr also wrote to Himmler, pledging his unfailing loyalty, and assured him that his main concern was the members of the LD who had been recruited with difficulty and awaited future careers as defense-peasants—one could not disappoint them now. Himmler "was the man on whom they pinned their hopes for the future." In a letter to Schulz, Schindlmayr informed him that agents of the RKFDV and RuSHA were eager to pursue the LD ploy. Hofmann told him that he and Peukert, whom Hofmann had formally attached to his own staff at RuSHA headquarters, considered Schindlmayr in effect the liaison between LD and RuSHA. But all that was wishful thinking. Concerted resistance to increasing SS pressure was maturing in the RJF.[71]

While Schindlmayr's moves brought about lengthy separate conferences with Helmut Möckel on the parts of Berger, Schindlmayr, and Himmler himself, the result was not what Schindlmayr expected. Schulz was supposed to be shipped off to the front at Peukert's request, a sacrificial lamb to the latter's political ambition. The LD Inspectorate South was dissolved, and Schindlmayr lost his status as an employee of the RJF. He was incorporated in the staff of HJ Region Hochland and received the meaningless title of LD Deputy for Bavaria, a mere sop to his pride. His old periodical, *Struggle for the Soil*, was prohibited, as was the wearing of his SS uniform and any simultaneous recruiting for W-SS and LD. He was forbidden to conduct any negotiations with RuSHA or other SS agencies. In case Schindlmayr did not get the message, his paychecks were withheld. The tasks Himmler had given him in October 1940 now became practically impossible. Hofmann then arranged a discussion between Peukert and Himmler, and told Schindlmayr to wait for Himmler's decision. Without waiting, Schindlmayr asked Hofmann to put him in charge of the RuSHA office in Bavaria, which obviously would have kept him closer to the goal of getting an SS defense-farm after the war, his ultimate aspiration.[72]

It turned out that Himmler was not prepared to give up the idea of using model LD farms on SS properties as a way of infusing the whole institution with SS objectives and spirit. Brandt wrote Schindlmayr in December demanding to know what progress had been made in setting up LD model farms. Schindlmayr had not been idle in this matter. At two former nursing homes taken over by the SS near Stralsund and Lauenburg in Pomerania, LD groups composed of second-year volunteers who were firmly committed to becoming farmers were to begin training on 1 April 1942. Similar arrangements for LD girls were made at Partschendorf in the Sudetengau in a former Jewish-owned "castle" confiscated by Himmler's Well of Life Society (Lebensborn e.V.), and at Bretsteintal in Styria, where a prefabricated house was to be used for girls serving the surrounding farms. All the business arrangements with Pohl and the RJF had been made, with the SS picking up the entire cost.[73]

Peukert's attempt to save himself at the expense of Schulz backfired. Axmann simply announced Peukert's resignation on 10 February 1942 and appointed Simon Winter in his place. This thirty-two-year-old merchant's assistant had joined the party in 1933, served in the Labor Front, attended several party schools, and made a career in the HJ without any noticeable distinction. At the time he was a youth warden, but he had been an organizer of the Vocational Contest, which explains why Axmann selected him. Axmann had a tendency to depend on old associates, and Peukert, after all, had been chosen by Lauterbacher. The fact that Peukert was closely associated with Darré had something to do with it as well. Shortly before his departure from the Ministry of Agriculture, Darré could not resist making a resentful stab at the RJF and the SS by forbidding transfer of four Food Estate instructional farms to the LD, an arrangement Himmler had personally negotiated. Simon Winter was an unknown quantity. His neutrality may have appealed to Axmann, who may not have wanted the SS to completely take over the LD, but who was also not prepared to surrender SS financial support. Within a month Axmann created an LD Inspectorate for the East at Seebruck. Symbolic of a compromise with the SS, Ernst Schulz became its chief and remained in the RJF.[74]

Schindlmayr now saw a chance for employment by Pohl's office. He felt, apparently, that Himmler was prepared to start a competitive LD. Since Himmler was indecisive, Schindlmayr sent him a letter, appending his farewell message to LD members in Bavaria, with numerous romantic and nostalgic references to the work of the LD.[75] The controversy flared up again when Schindlmayr tried to publish a book entitled "Plow and Sword," with a foreword by none other than Himmler. Simon Winter led the attack. Schindlmayr was accused of trying "to disturb the good relationship between HJ and SS by spreading false rumors." The Nordland Verlag, an SS subsidiary, which was prepared to publish the work, was nonplussed by these developments. Brandt tried to get the RJF to change its mind in view of "today's situation" and Schindlmayr's "decent intentions." The party's censorship commission took the side of the RJF. The matter was not concluded until September 1942, when the HJ Court decided merely to censure Schindlmayr. He had no choice but to resign from the HJ. Himmler still wanted Schindlmayr to continue as overseer of SS-LD model farms. Schindlmayr then reminded Brandt that his resignation made it impossible to carry out Himmler's assignment, since it required a man who was a member of both organizations.[76]

Himmler was thus forced by events to release Schindlmayr from his obligations. In fact, Himmler seems to have grown quite tired of this troublesome captain and strongly suggested that he be packed off to the front, a solution Himmler frequently relied on when his protégés failed to fulfill a given task. While Schindlmayr made some progress in Germanizing the Gerelick boys, Himmler also gave up any idea of expanding that project. It was Berger who managed to save Schindlmayr from total disgrace by retaining his services as an SS recruiter. A couple of years later he was promoted to chief of Berger's recruiting commission in Belgium. As late as March 1945 Schindlmayr received a medal for his achievements. To the end he remained a loyal Nazi functionary. His tarnished career symbolized the contradictory nature of LD objectives, compromised by war, the vagaries of bureaucratic infighting, and the irresistible forces of urbanization.[77]

### Blood and Soil to the Bitter End

To promote professionalization, the LD instructional farm was introduced in the fall of 1941, perhaps an antidote to the aborted Schindlmayr scheme but also an imitation of that SS idea. The HJ had its own model farm in Koppelsdorf (Saxony), where the results had been so encouraging that Axmann wanted the experiment reproduced in every region. Eighteen of them existed by the spring of 1942, including seven in the eastern territories. Another six were added the following year and several more in 1944. Financially underwritten by the party, they varied in size from 150 to 300 acres and were on the whole models of German agrarian order. Each year thirty male and thirty female leader-candidates were sent to these establishments, preceded by a year in the LD and a further year in a professional training situation. Thus, the third year would normally have been spent on an instructional farm, followed by service in the W-SS, attendance of an LD leadership school, and finally installation as a defense-peasant in the East.[78]

At the Munich conference of HJ leaders in December 1941, Schwarz promised "generous financial support" for the acquisition of instructional farms.[79] Axmann also singled them out as a promising development. Some youth leaders saw them as a marvelous opportunity to promote normal contact between the sexes, which LD camps did not provide, thus facilitating good marriages where both partners were fully committed to agrarian ideals. At the same time, they were afraid of deviant or premarital sexual activity, revealing typical Nazi ambivalence about sex. At the time Axmann had barely recovered from the loss of his right arm on the Eastern Front. His prestige enhanced and his fascination for the great events transpiring there led him to declare "Eastern Action and LD" as the motto for 1942. He delivered his New Year's message in the city of Posen, headquarters of the HJ in the Warthegau: "Youth must be closely tied in with this annexed territory. The East is Germany's fate." He praised Himmler's work and named him the "honorary leader" of the LD, thus camouflaging the abortive attempt to absorb it. Axmann clearly intended to push for a major expansion of an independent LD, but he also emphasized dependence on the SS by highlighting "new farmer certificates." BDM Leader Jutta Rüdiger followed suit by proclaiming "Eastern Action" as the most significant work of the girls in 1942, with the eventual goal of becoming defense-peasant consorts.[80]

There were cities and industrial areas in the East, and the HJ played a role in harnessing urban youth. But this was minor in view of the prevailing rural character. The LD was of greater importance to HJ leaders concerned with occupational preparation and eventual settlement on the land. Himmler's patronage made sure of that. In a challenge to youth he backed Axmann's priorities: "The wide acres of the East, which the German soldier is buying with his blood, must be occupied and exploited by German youth into the farthest future as good defense-peasants."[81]

Taking a cue from Gottlob Berger, who was recruiting thousands of foreign nationals for the W-SS, Axmann decided to do the same for the LD.

The RJF had already established "command posts" in the Hague, in Brussels, and continuous contact in other areas. The HJ strongly influenced the development of native fascist youth organizations in all occupied lands and these were used to recruit Germanic youths for the LD. At the model farm in Koppelsdorf and the female LD leadership school in Wünschendorf the first volunteers were trained, most of them coming from Holland, Belgium, Denmark, and Norway. All went to LD camps in the Warthegau, except the Dutch who were sent to Danzig-West Prussia. On 12 July 1942 they were formally initiated by Axmann at Posen with much fanfare about being the vanguard of a new agrarian European order. By the end of 1943, when Walloons were added to the Flemish volunteers, accompanied by others from Estonia and Latvia, their numbers increased to 1,725. The Norwegians gradually withdrew with the intent of forming their own LD.[82]

These Germanic youths, destined for W-SS service, were promised eventual settlement as defense-peasants in the eastern marches. They retained a sense of autonomy and their camps flew their own as well as HJ flags. Somewhat older than their German counterparts, they were genuine volunteers who performed their LD service with enthusiasm. Being part of a Teutonic struggle against the evils of Bolshevism appears to have been their basic motivation, rather than any mystical notions about the pristine qualities of the countryside and rural-racial values.[83]

Augmented by Germanics, LD organizers proceeded to recruit the 1943 contingent. Careful to inform parents about free occupational training available to LD volunteers, second-year repeaters were pressured to go to the East. First-year participants, generally fourteen years old, no longer received salaries, but their "pocket money" increased to 10.50 RM per month. Second-year volunteers continued to receive salaries equivalent to the prevailing local scale for agricultural workers. HJ unit leaders and party officials were drawn into the campaign, concentrating their efforts on elementary school graduates, directly competing with the Land Year. Using so-called selection camps, fairly severe criteria were applied to weed out potential shirkers and those who sought to escape into the countryside for a variety of personal reasons. The slogan "the best are good enough" produced results. Among 33,179 volunteers who underwent screening in the selection camps, 6,984 were weeded out, thus leaving a core of 26,195 (10,396 boys and 15,799 girls). These were more committed to the ideals of the LD than previous groups, according to the optimists in RJF.[84]

Recruitment still continued, particularly for leaders, who were harder and harder to get, despite Robert Ley's cancellation of Labor Service obligations. Even LD leader-candidates destined for instructional farms in

1944–45 were already sought and committed on paper. To get enough volunteers for service in the East, Axmann had determined earlier that second-year repeaters had to go east. Parents objected to their children going into that uncertain area, and the pressure of party officials had to be used to persuade them. Parents were invited to HJ functions and local HJ leaders visited them in their homes to promote service in the East.[85] Among existing LD-Scharen the RJF initiated "achievement competitions," which pitted them against each other on such matters as camp orderliness, influence in the villages, percent results in the effort to keep youngsters permanently on the land, and embarkation on formal occupational training. Achievements in sports and physical fitness, basic knowledge of politics, keeping of clan records inspired by SS practices, and amounts of money in savings accounts for eventual settlement purposes were all items for which points could be accumulated. As in all other HJ activities, the leadership had found a way to exploit the youthful zest for rivalry.[86]

These efforts made 1943–44 the best year for the LD, with nearly 40,000 youngsters joining the green army under the blood and soil banner. Simon Winter valiantly tried to maintain the old principles and pursue the original goals. The LD witnessed a conscious attempt to return to the ethos of the early "time of struggle." A fortress mentality became palpably evident. But the LD had reached its apogee and faced increasing pressure from two directions: parents and foreign workers. Parents appear to have been more courageous than before in resisting their children's commitment to permanent careers in agriculture, reasoning that they would have more promising opportunities in an urban environment. The other source of resentment among LD leaders was the increasingly large number of forced foreign laborers and prisoners of war, who were inundating German agriculture and overshadowing the LD to the point of making it irrelevant. Much time was spent in complaining about these two tendencies during the final two years of the LD's existence.[87]

In the absence of specific evidence it is hard to determine the exact number of volunteers for the 1944–45 LD year, when most HJ activities were drastically curtailed. But there is no doubt that the LD continued to operate during the final year of the war, with escape from bomb-ravaged cites undoubtedly playing a role. LD conferences continued to be held—one of them in HJ Region Baden-Alsace attracted 1,000 participants in February, and another in Franken had 800 participants in October 1944. The RJF tried to cancel the latter on grounds of "total war" necessities, but party leaders insisted it be held and it was, incurring a cost of 9,550 RM. Scattered evidence suggests that there were probably as many volunteers during the final year as there were in the preceding one and that the LD began to disintegrate gradually in the fall of 1944.[88]

## The Significance of the Land Service

Over the course of its ten-year history the LD involved 215,633 young people. Beginning with 500 volunteers in 1934 it expanded to 40,000 in 1944, overcoming a temporary decline at the outbreak of the war. Growth was slow and measured, because the objectives flew in the face of demographic trends and economic realities. When female youths were incorporated to counter the drain of military conscription, the LD became a more viable socioeconomic institution, since it promised an increase in the number of young peasant families committed to the revival of agriculture. The females gradually outnumbered the males, threatening a socially balanced evolution. The war perpetuated this, and it could only have been corrected after a military victory. Increasingly there was more geographic diffusion and a shift from landed estate to peasant village. During the first two years LD groups worked only in Mecklenburg, Pomerania, East Prussia, and Saxony-Anhalt, to which the Kurmark, Silesia, Hanover, Hessen-Nassau, Saxony, and Thuringia were added in 1936. In the following year LD groups were sent to all regions of the Reich, soon followed by Austria, the Sudetenland, and the Warthegau, although the General Government, Lorraine, Alsace, and Lower Styria did not receive their LD groups until 1942–43. For organizational reasons the LD followed its Artamanen predecessor and sent most of its groups to large landed estates during the initial years. A major shift to the more difficult rural villages was largely motivated by ideological and social considerations, involving 25 percent of the participants in 1936, 60 percent in 1937, 78 percent in 1938, 85 percent in 1940, and 90 percent during the remainder of the war.[89]

The LD as a promising experiment from the perspective of Nazi agrarian policy was reinforced by a decrease in the age of volunteers. The average age of eighteen to twenty in the early years receded sharply in 1937, when 63 percent of the boys and 71 percent of the girls were sixteen. In 1938 some 80 percent of participants were sixteen or younger, and during the war most volunteers were fourteen and fifteen years old.[90] This downward trend was stimulated by shortage of older youths and a desire to eliminate competition. The Land Year had more limited objectives, being simply an attempt to facilitate greater understanding and appreciation for agricultural work among urban youngsters, and it had less economic value in terms of the labor performed. The SS, however, encouraged the RJF, already moved by general hostility to the educational establishment, to compete with Rust's project in the hope of displacing it. This gambit failed, but the effort enhanced LD prestige, being officially sponsored by the SS, and changed its social structure. While estate managers and parents resisted the change to younger volunteers, HJ leaders turned it into a virtue. Younger participants were easier to recruit and more amenable to indoctrination and social molding. It was also easier to direct them toward permanent agricultural vocations once autarchy and reagrarianization superseded the battle against unemployment and land flight.[91]

Unlike Future Farmers of America, which contains farm children already committed to agriculture, the LD was imbued with the idea of transforming urban youth into peasants, thus reversing prevailing trends. The sheer irrationality of such an undertaking would appear to be no more than the expression of racial fantasy and economic naiveté. Yet a movement which could persuade an educated populace to accept a patently absurd romantic ideology and mobilize a whole nation for aggressive war could certainly persuade impressionable young people that blood and soil was more than propagandistic balderdash. Despite lack of apparent economic promise Nikita Khrushchev was able to persuade thousands of young Russians to participate in his "virgin lands" project; Mao Tse-tung drove millions of students into agricultural labor; and Fidel Castro transformed urban youths into sugar cane cutters. With less coercion the RJF managed to persuade a significant proportion of LD members to decide on future careers as German peasants.

In 1934 a mere 10 percent of the 500 volunteers declared a willingness to become hereditary peasants in the sense of the *Erbhofgesetz*, the entailed medium-sized farm. This figure varied in subsequent years, reaching a high of 30 percent in 1938–39 and averaging 20 percent for the prewar period. This average rose during the war to slightly more than 25 percent, meaning that some 50,000 out of 200,000 participants were prepared to become nazified German peasants, most of them anticipating free land as SS defense-peasants in the colonized East. These conclusions are based on declarations of intent, sidetracked by military conscription and the W-SS.[92]

In its relentless pursuit of the *Volksgemeinschaft*, the RJF tried to structure the LD so as to reflect that ideal. It was to be an instrument for demographic diffusion and help to break down traditional social barriers between urban and rural societies. The social composition of the LD suggests that the HJ was making considerable progress toward that evasive goal. In 1937, when unemployment was still a problem for teenagers not in school, more than half of a representative sample of 10,000 LD boys came into the organization from the ranks of the unemployed or from occasional jobs, but the rest came from quite diverse occupational groups. There was no clear class pattern, although on the whole they constituted a socially and economically disadvantaged group of teenagers, for whom the LD represented a certain degree of social mobility. This becomes evident when the occupational breakdown of the fathers is compared with that of the sons. Nearly half of the former were industrial workers or miners, whereas only 10.5 percent of the sons had been engaged in similar work before joining the LD. The large number of fatherless sons in this sample and the fact that 36.5 percent came from families of four or more children indicates that the LD was to some degree an instrument of social welfare (Table 5.1).[93]

When this prewar social profile is compared with the 1942–43 LD contingent of 11,415 boys and 18,189 girls, all of whom were fourteen to fifteen years old, it becomes clear that a diffuse social pattern had developed. The LD had become a microcosm of adult society. The only missing social group is the aristocracy, unless some may have been included under the categories of civil servants and professional soldiers. This diffuse social structure is also evident in the urban distribution of LD volunteers, with 45.9 percent coming from cities with over 50,000 inhabitants. Another ten years of a similar social development might have made the LD an effective solvent of class distinctions and given various urban social groups an important stake in the revitalization of agriculture (Table 5.2).

In an organization ruled by the leadership principle, a leader by his exemplary attitude could have decisive effect on a youngster's resolve to join the new peasantry. While the HJ generally tended to favor middle-class leaders with a secondary school education, a few years older than the age groups under their control, the LD leadership before the war contained a strong agrarian element, was on the whole vocationally oriented, and was older than the leadership corps of the HJ as a whole. In 1937, among 800 LD group leaders 29 percent were agrarian workers or sons of peasants and another 10 percent were rural civil servants. Only 14 percent had been unemployed and had not undergone any kind of occupational training. The remaining 47 percent had completed widely scattered types of vocational training. They tended to be older than HJ leaders normally were at this level: 30 percent were between eighteen and twenty; 38 percent between twenty and twenty-five; 25 percent between twenty-five and thirty; and 7 percent were over thirty years of age. Less than half had long LD experience; 14 percent were holdovers from the Artamanen; 15 percent had been in the LD since 1934; 13 percent since 1935; 27 percent since 1936;

and 31 percent had entered the LD in 1937 as group leaders. A promising compromise between stability and mobility appears to have been struck. It is interesting that only 36 percent were members of the party. The LD was not perceived mainly as an instrument of indoctrination. It was taken seriously.[94]

At a training seminar for seventy-four LD leaders in 1939 the following pattern emerged: twenty-one of them were between eighteen and twenty; thirty-two were between twenty-one and twenty-five; and twenty-one between twenty-six and thirty. Sixteen were sons of peasants and seven were sons of agrarian workers. All of them had completed vocational training, mostly of the handicraft variety. Fifty-three of them had spent at least two years in the LD and only seven were not interested in remaining in agriculture—two of these were sons of peasants. Thirty-eight leaders had made a firm decision to become peasants on their own plots of land, although they did not have the means to do so and depended on the state or the SS to fulfill their dreams.[95]

This social profile of the leadership changed significantly with the outbreak of war, when 90 percent were drafted, forcing reliance on younger individuals. The average age of the new crop of some 2,000 was nineteen, with 35 percent of them previously engaged in urban occupations, 33 percent in agrarian vocations, and 32 percent without any previous training. The latter third were mostly graduates of secondary schools (*Abiturienten*) and agrarian laborers who had not yet taken the agrarian workers' examination. They averaged only a year-and-a-half of LD experience before being named LD-Scharführer. Slightly more than half (63 percent) had received brief training for their tasks, and 75 percent declared a willingness to remain in the LD indefinitely. But that was wishful thinking, since the majority joined the W-SS at the end of each year. This extraordinary mobility threatened LD stability and forced the RJF to rely on the instructional farm and LD leadership schools to train new batches of leaders periodically. The cost of these operations indicates that the HJ still took the LD seriously and would have been able to maintain it as a viable institution.[96]

In this context alliance with the SS became the decisive factor. It was largely responsible for the institutionalization of the LD by lending it ideological justification and political prestige, by encouraging financial support by the party, and by promising free land for future settlement. Total absorption would have destroyed the LD, since it would have become a mere appendage supplying needed personnel for the far-flung SS enterprise. The attempt revealed that the SS was more opportunistic than the

HJ, committed to immediate organizational efficiency rather than long-range economic and social ends. As it was, the SS diverted the Land Service from its primary goals into military combat, which would make those future defense-peasant homesteads available, but which also brought about defeat and an end to the blood and soil adventure.

# 6 | Imperialists, Colonists, Exploiters

Ethnic politics were not invented by the Nazi party. At least as old as integral nationalism, they go back to the race-conscious nineteenth century. Under the aegis of national socialism, however, ethnicity or "blood" was elevated to a principle of primary value. The vague concept of race became an operative notion that lay behind the vast project designed to restructure the demography of Eastern Europe. Annexed parts of western Poland were selected by Hitler as a laboratory for forceful transfer of populations and massive Germanization, so that the area would become a new frontier with pristine Germanic racial characteristics. It is perversely logical that Hitler should have chosen Himmler to implement these policies. He in turn realized that the durability of any large-scale demographic transmutation would have to take children into account. Already bound to the SS through the LD and SRD, the HJ got entangled with the Reich Commission for the Strengthening of Germandom (RKFDV). The HJ enmeshed itself in colonial endeavors that turned idealistic young women and men into exploiters of "inferior" people and manipulators of Germanizable ethnics.[1]

## From Ethnic Politics to Imperial Expansion

Both Himmler and Axmann envisaged extensive HJ involvement in territories annexed or occupied in the course of imperial expansion. The build-up of the native HJ organization in the Warthegau, the annexed part of southwestern Poland, began as soon as the area was attached to the Reich. The same was true for Eupen-Malmédy and Alsace, but Lorraine provided obstacles attributed to insufficient numbers of Germans who had retained their ethnicity. Luxemburg had no HJ at first, but a sympathetic Boy Scout organization had established contact with the RJF before the war. Soon after occupation, Axmann's deputy, Kurt Petter, the head of the Adolf Hitler Schools, began to build a youth organization in Norway under the guidance of Paul Wegener, head of the party organization in that country. Inside the Mussert movement in Holland, a youth organization was developing with RJF assistance. In fact, some of the leaders of this movement visited HJ camps during the summer of 1940 and went home with good impressions.[2] The RJF developed a strong organization in Holland under Hermann Lindenberger, who sought to politicize the children of German nationals and indoctrinate selected Dutch youths with the advantages of becoming full-fledged Germans. The latter came under the auspices of the RKFDV and took on the same racist connotations as the more concerted effort of the same nature in the Warthegau.[3]

These ventures into ethnic and foreign policy, which Germans referred to as *Volkstumspolitik*, were not exactly new to the HJ. A Foreign Office existed before 1933, and during the 1930s Karl Nabersberg, its energetic chief, had been Schirach's agent in a vigorous pursuit of ethnic politics among youth in border countries.[4] Nabersberg and Schirach played important roles in wresting control of the Association for Germans Abroad (VDA). In fact, wherever German minorities were to be found, as in several Latin American countries, the HJ encouraged the organization of youth as a way of stimulating loyalty to the "Fatherland."[5]

The emerging cooperation of the RKFDV and its affiliated agencies with the RJF in the East was a logical development. The Nazis felt the Greater German Reich could only remain in existence if the upcoming generation were won over to their cause and provided the janissaries to keep it in being. The practice of carrying on its own foreign policy, the special relationship with the SS, and long involvement in reagrarianization gave the RJF an opportunity to participate in a major demographic experiment. The vicious character that Nazi population policy was to attain was not anticipated by youth leaders. After all, as Robert Koehl has said, pursuing "traditional irredentism with a bold program of ethnic consolidation via resettlement, which was brutal and inhumane, was not lacking in common sense."[6]

Rhetoric and flattery were used to recruit young people for the hard work of demographic reconstruction. Ulrich Greifelt, Himmler's chief of staff at RKFDV headquarters in Berlin, wrote: "Never before did our . . . youth receive a greater and pleasanter task. . . . Never before . . . was the task in the German East of such a fateful magnitude and clarity."[7] A spokesman for Arthur Greiser, governor of the Warthegau, said: "It is the task of youth to open the eyes of the young generation to the racial necessity of our eastern policy and to put in their hands by education the necessary weapons for a clear and uncompromising attitude in the ethnic struggle. Only the young generation, which carries within itself the characteristics for an effective eastern policy and has the toughness to endure, can pursue this struggle in the German East to successful conclusion. The youth of Germany has the means to make a decisive contribution, through communal education, to the recovery of German blood, which is in danger of being suppressed by hostile races."[8]

What Hitler meant by "living space" became amply clear after the defeat of Poland. Four new Gaue were created out of territory annexed to the Reich. Danzig-West Prussia, the former "Polish Corridor," was handed over to Albert Forster as governor, who sought to make it fully German by indiscriminate Germanization in disregard of SS racial sensitivities. An expanded East Prussia went to Erich Koch, who was mainly interested in the agricultural economics of his bailiwick. Fritz Bracht took over the heavily industrial new Gau of Upper Silesia and sought to exploit it for the Greater Reich. The remnant of central Poland, what was left of it after the Russian annexations to the east, was dubbed the General Government and handed to Hans Frank, chief of the Nazi Association of Lawyers. In the west and southwest a sizable piece of territory, stretching along the Warthe river with the capital at Posen, became the Warthegau, and was ruled by Arthur Greiser, a Danzig senator, who firmly believed in the necessity of a rigorous sorting out of ethnic types. He helped to turn the Warthegau into a boiling pot of administrative confusion, jurisdictional infighting, exploitative competition, and unspeakable human suffering.[9]

These modern-day robber barons contended with endless numbers of officials from the Berlin ministries and a host of greedy businessmen. The most intense struggle occurred with Himmler's HSSPF appointed for each new Gau and his plenipotentiaries and their retinues attached to the RKFDV. The most important of the RKFDV affiliates was the Ethnic German Liaison Office (VoMi), which originated in the early 1930s and attained a richly financed predominance in ethnic politics when it literally deposed the traditionalist Association for Germans Abroad (VDA) in 1937, a political victory for the SS that the RJF helped to achieve. Ethnic politics under traditionalist tutelage meant maintaining ethnic identity among German minorities abroad, but ethnic politics under SS control meant demographic manipulation on a massive scale.[10]

The decree Hitler released on 7 October 1939 gave Himmler three related tasks: (1) the repatriation of persons of German "race" and nationality resident abroad who were considered suitable for permanent return to the Reich; (2) the elimination of those sections of the population of foreign origin constituting a danger to the German community; (3) the formation of new settlement areas by transfers of populations and by giving land entitlement to persons of German "race" returning from abroad. Thus armed with sole authority, Himmler called himself Reich Commissar, set up the RKFDV, and began to use state agencies and organizations under his control to achieve Hitler's goals. The most important of these ancillaries were the VoMi under Werner Lorenz, the RSHA under Heydrich and Kaltenbrunner, and the RuSHA under Hofmann and Hildebrandt.[11] The functions of these three organizations matched aspects of the RKFDV decree, and they were the SS agencies with which the RJF had to deal in achieving the "strengthening of Germandom" on the junior level. The HJ defined its role more modestly: to "prevent the dissolution of German blood among foreign nationalities"; to "win back German blood which has been dissipated among foreign nationalities"; to "support the reception measures in the new regions of the East."[12]

Some 200,000 ethnic Germans from the Baltic countries and parts of eastern Poland annexed by the Soviet Union had been repatriated and congregated in transit camps by the end of 1939. They were being "processed" during the winter and spring of 1940 by the SS. This occurred while more than 300,000 Poles who had tracked east to escape the combat zone, and thousands of Jews, were being forcibly evacuated by RSHA to make room for the ethnic Germans.[13] Russian pressure on the Baltic states and on Rumania, leading to the eventual incorporation into the Soviet Union of Estonia, Latvia, Bessarabia, and Northern Bukovina, created a second wave of settlers. Agreements with Rumania brought in settlers from parts of that country, and additional ethnic Germans were transferred from the General Government over Hans Frank's objections. By the spring of 1941 another 270,744 potential settlers had been added to the bulging transit camps, creating an unbelievably confusing movement of people with all of its hardships, brutalities, and individual agonies.[14] While an "ethos of reconstruction" pervaded the 60,000 ethnic Germans left in the annexed parts of western Poland, the several hundred thousand Reich German officials and businessmen, who swarmed into the region seeking influence, power, and wealth, were eager to shape events to Germany's advantage.[15]

**Indoctrination and Training of Immigrant Youth**

At the end of 1940, when many BDM girls had already gone east to help new immigrants, Ulrich Greifelt and Werner Lorenz asked Artur Axmann to get the HJ involved in resettlement. The new youth leader needed little prodding. He immediately set up a Resettlement Bureau and picked Hans Menzel, a resourceful young staffer from the RJF Foreign Office, to run it.

For a while Menzel operated out of the large office dealing with evacuation of children (KLV). The latter had been formed in 1933 to provide vacations for school children. In 1940 the KLV became a major project when hundreds of thousands of children from large cities were evacuated to relatively bomb-proof camps in the country. Here they were under the care of BDM girls and Nazi teachers. It was logical to connect resettlement with the KLV, since both entailed painful separation from the security of the family home. Although the latter could at least be justified on grounds of wartime danger, the former had no such justification and required force based on racial motives.[16]

Menzel soon acquired a staff of over 500 and issued guidelines in consultation with Himmler's demographic agencies. Transit camps for ethnic German youth, meanwhile, were organized by the VoMi. The belated entry of the RJF, the shortage of youth leaders, the failure to get military deferments, and trying negotiations for adequate financing made Menzel's task difficult. Since he was expected to indoctrinate, train, and Germanize nearly 100,000 youths, his organizational achievement was remarkable. When he began in January 1941, nearly a half million ethnic Germans had been moved into transit camps in the East and the Reich. A sizable number from the "first wave" of 1939–40 had already been settled. Most of the older ones had been drafted, while younger ones were organized into standard HJ units. Menzel, therefore, concentrated on youth in the "second wave" from Bessarabia, Bukovina, Lithuania, the Dobrudja, Vohlhynia, and the Southern Tyrol. Among the quarter million immigrants in this category, there were about 50,000 youngsters. The VoMi herded them into 500 transit camps, where Menzel's staff began the process of Germanization, lasting six months.[17]

The VoMi camps, scattered among two dozen Gaue of the old Reich, were off limits to all except Resettlement Bureau employees and local HJ leaders who had to provide equipment and facilities. Full-time HJ leaders, designated by Menzel's office as "resettlement experts," reported to regional VoMi settlement officials. Twenty-two of them had been appointed by March 1941. The work in the camps themselves was done by native ethnic youth leaders, many of whom had to be quickly trained in the standard forms of HJ work. This kind of instant training was a perpetual problem, since the older boys kept disappearing—thanks to W-SS recruitment—which forced dependence on boys of seventeen and younger. The most qualified ethnic youth leaders were sent to the RJF and various regional directorates to gain practical experience. Afterward they were shipped to the settlement areas to provide a native corps of youth leaders.

The essence of the work in the camps consisted of indoctrination, physical exercises, cultural schooling, health instruction, and some occupational guidance, with emphasis on agrarian economics. A weekly "service plan" kept them busy from 7:00 in the morning until 9:00 at night.[18]

The heaviest emphasis fell on political indoctrination. For this purpose Menzel's office issued a series of *Heimabendmappen*, which contained interesting points of departure to be used by regional HJ settlement officials and camp directors. Charlemagne, Henry the Fowler, and Ulrich von Hutten, for instance, were singled out as the primary builders of the German Reich, fulfilling a dream and yearning presumably shared by all who spoke the German language. The peasant wars during the Reformation and the wars against Napoleon were erroneously pictured as motivated by the same popular desire to include all Germans in a single giant empire, containing and preserving "inner freedom, German mores, and Germanic ethnicity." The Hohenstauffen kings and the Teutonic Knights became heroic figures beyond recognizable proportion, as did Charles V, Prince Eugene of Savoy, Frederick the Great, and Bismarck. But Bismarck's Germany had only had the external form of a great power; the "internal growth into unity," necessary for a new European order, had had to wait for Hitler. Considerable attention was paid to the idea that "discord among brothers leads to impotence," illustrated by Henry VI's humbling trip to Canossa, forced on him by discord among German princes. National socialism, after all, recognized only Germans and non-Germans, ignoring class distinctions. The long struggle between Prussia and Austria was treated in the same vein, and ethnic Germans were pictured as suffering even more than Reich Germans from political weakness and social disunity.[19]

At this point the propaganda booklets launched into emotional portrayals of Hitler, the very "embodiment of German yearnings for the Reich." Then followed a standard summary of events since the Beer Hall Putsch, emphasizing the "highest manly virtues" of honor, loyalty, obedience, discipline, camaraderie, and sacrifice. Special sections contained conventional anti-Semitic diatribes, holding an international Jewish conspiracy (including Albert Einstein and Leon Blum) responsible for almost every existing problem and the war itself. The pamphlets concluded with projections of an egalitarian new social order in the East, which would be the "most German of all," and to the building of which the German Labor Front, the Food Estate, and most of all the HJ Land Service would contribute. Ethnic youth now returning to the "homeland" had a special role to play in this monumental historic task. At the end there was praise for the prowess of the German soldier forged by the HJ experience.[20]

How effective this kind of transparent propaganda was is difficult to determine, but it was probably more telling than it would be with less impressionable teenagers living in less structured environments and in less disturbing times. This intensive political drilling was stretched over a six-month period, reinforced daily by discussions, flag roll calls, song-fests, plays, and Sunday "morning festivals," substituted for church services. For the purpose of this "cultural guidance," Himmler contributed an initial sum of 150,000 RM. Altogether Menzel spent 696,340 RM during the first three months of the program, mostly for sports equipment and library materials. Some of the assistance was provided free of charge. A group of singers from the High School of Folk and Youth Music performed in sixteen camps in Saxony and the Sudetengau, and another group from the German Radio Network played in fourteen camps in Oberdonau.[21]

In the summer of 1941 the RJF moved from indoctrination of leaders to regular schooling and occupational training for all ethnic youngsters. Even those who came from urban settings and whose parents had been industrial workers were switched to agricultural careers. Special courses trained assistant medical officers, medical orderlies, welfare nurses, kindergarten workers, teachers' aides, and other typical career options promoted by the HJ during the war. The overriding aim of "organically incorporating" settler youth, conveniently contained within the structure of tightly controlled camps, within the HJ organization, emerged as the predominant motivation. Menzel forbade "independent negotiations" with VoMi and RKFDV officials even in the eastern settlement areas. In HJ regions that had several ethnic German youth camps, planning sections under full-time HJ leaders were created to deal exclusively with problems of resettlement and camp activities.[22]

It soon became apparent that resettled ethnic Germans had "enormous respect for all things in the Reich." This was substantiated by all who had contact with them. The SS realized that this attitude could be exploited to achieve the aims of Germanization.[23] VoMi officials ordered in April 1941 that all girls in the camps, even those who had found temporary jobs, were to be gathered during designated days when BDM leaders could visit, lecture, and engage in informal discussion. These contacts were followed up by selecting suitable young women and preparing them to pursue agricultural, handicraft, and artisan training. The selected girls were first taken into initiation courses by the BDM, then transferred to agricultural and artisan schools for a preparatory course, and finally installed in standard apprenticeships. Most of them never returned to the camps. For those who successfully completed the preparatory course, Duty Year obligations were canceled. The VoMi absorbed initial costs of this cumbersome scheme, designed to utilize the available female labor and meet racial-agrarian aims at the same time.[24] Circumvention of the Duty Year and drastic abbreviation of the established route to agricultural apprenticeships contradicted the assumptions of the Food Estate's training program, but no one was in a position to challenge the dynamic SS, adept at implementing workable shortcuts.

The VoMi went a step further in July when it asked the RJF's Borderland and Foreign Office to furnish HJ leaders for its work within the remaining German minority groups in Slovakia, Hungary, Rumania, Yugoslavia, and Northern Schleswig. A grant from RKFDV allowed the RJF to provide settler youth who participated in HJ training courses with spending money, although HJ funds were still used to cover travel costs. These friendly gestures on the part of sometimes reluctant VoMi and RKFDV functionaries were not attained easily and came only after Himmler personally put pressure on them to support Menzel's operation, emphasizing the "special significance" of HJ Lagerbetreuung (camp care and control). As a result the VoMi made a number of additional camps for settler youth and additional money available to the HJ for the period from November 1941 to March 1942.[25]

It was at first assumed that Menzel's work would consist mainly of indoctrination and that it could be completed within the span of a year. Settlement, however, turned out to be slower than anticipated, keeping many youngsters in the transit camps longer then the projected six months. For this reason it was decided to begin occupational training in the camps. At the height of the operation, in the fall of 1941, VoMi maintained 1,250 camps scattered over twenty-two Gaue. By this time over 50,000 youths had undergone indoctrination, and thousands had been guided into occupational training. It was done in a climate not conducive to such endeavors. By comparison with normal HJ camps, these transit facilities were primitive. The transient environment, with constant influx and outflow, created many problems, exacerbated by almost immediate military induction of young men when they reached their eighteenth birthday. This forced reliance on younger boys and girls for routine tasks. An attempt was made to enable those who had begun some professional training to pursue these careers. Some 700 teacher trainees were channeled into pedagogical schools, and over 7,000 girls were directed into apprenticeships in agriculture and welfare work, including the profession of midwife. The great majority of youths came from farm families, which led to strenuous recruitment within the camps for leaders of the Eastern LD. Some 165 leader candidates were sent to the Reich LD Leadership School in Gross-Gurek in Upper Silesia, and most of them soon found their way into LD camps in the East, providing badly needed reinforcement. Because new HJ organizations in the East needed leaders, the best immigrant young-sters were shipped off to the newly established Reich Leadership School for Resettlers in Steinau an der Oder and a complementary facility for the BDM in Tieffensee near Berlin.[26]

On 1 June 1942 only 14,383 youth remained in some 432 transit camps. Menzel still had 142 full-time and 375 part-time leaders employed in the endeavor. By that time 9,245 youths had completed special training in vari-ous national and regional short-term courses. At the Reichsschule in Steinau, 709 boys had been certified as professional HJ leaders and another 92 had been trained as LD leaders in Gross-Gurek. At the Reichsschule Tieffensee and at Freiburg 691 girls had been trained as medical assistants, while some 50 had successfully completed courses leading to social welfare occupations, artisan professions, educational careers, and agricultural employment. So-called Settler Schools and Settler Student Homes, as well as a secondary school at Litzmannstadt, had been set up for resettled young people.[27]

Demographic policy now began to focus more directly on Germaniza-tion and naturalization. All efforts were bent on speeding up these pro-cedures and creating a stable population of full-fledged German character. To consolidate the work of the BDM Eastern Action with the administrative measures of resettlement, Axmann abolished Menzel's bureau in the spring of 1942 and created a new one, known as Festigung deutschen Volkstums (FdV). It was a junior version of Himmler's RKFDV and prac-tically became an extension of the latter. HJ officials soon were attached to all RKFDV agencies.[28]

## BDM Eastern Action and Settler Care

The "Eastern Action" actually antedated Menzel's project. It began unobtrusively in the spring of 1940, when elementary school teachers, not fully certified, were recruited by the RJF to serve in the occupied part of Poland. During the summer Arthur Greiser invited the BDM into the War-thegau to assist nascent HJ organizations in aiding new settlers. Enthusi-astic early reports led to expansion of this new HJ-SS collaboration. It was closely related to the work of the Land Service because most settlers were poor farmers and because this was the area where Himmler's defense-peasant scheme was to be realized. After brief initiation by the SS Settlement Staff in Litzmannstadt (Lódz), BDM leaders between the ages of fifteen and twenty-one went from village to village and farm to farm helping new settlers get established. These early settlers came mostly from the ethnic German enclaves of Galicia, Vohlhynia, Bessarabia, and the Baltic states. The girls performed physical labor for them, did household chores, cared for babies, told stories about Germany, sang folk songs, and taught them the German language. They also staged convivial evening gatherings, put on plays, festivals, and other assorted communal and quasi-cultural events designed to indoctrinate and Germanize these forced returnees to the Greater German Reich. A total of 1,400 girls were engaged in this work by the end of the year.[29]

It was to be the culmination of the blood and soil ideology institutionalized in the LD. In fact, LD camps for girls had already been set up in the Wartheland in 1940, and by March 1941 a total of 106 camps with 3,000 participants functioned in the Wartheland, Danzig-West Prussia, Upper Silesia, and the Protectorate of Bohemia-Moravia. These LD girls came from the old Reich and performed their regular land service under extremely difficult conditions. When Menzel organized the Resettlement Bureau, he was ordered to recruit male LD leaders among settler youth because of shortages created by the draft at home. He tried to do that by appealing to boys who came from families with two or more sons and thus had little hope of getting their own farms, and by citing Himmler's promise of eventually acquiring a homestead as SS defense-peasants. There was little response.[30]

The Eastern Action of the BDM was more successful and quickly expanded to include Danzig-West Prussia and Upper Silesia. "Sponsorships" were introduced by which old Reich BDM Regions adopted a certain number of villages in the Warthegau and kept sending over girls on a rotation basis. To create continuity, these services were extended from six weeks to a full year. Many BDM leaders served as settlement specialists in home HJ Districts and worked closely with RKFDV officials in the East.[31] From a fund provided by BDM Gau Silesia, district organizers were installed in the Warthegau with a salary of 200 to 250 RM. Most old Reich Gaue provided at least one or two leaders for this purpose, and thirty of them went to the East in the spring of 1941. Since there was an estimated shortage of some 1,000 teachers in the Warthegau, BDM leaders were recruited as teachers' aides with the promise of eventual full certification.

These aides also had to assist settler families and build up BDM units in the villages. Considering the duties imposed on them, the pay of 146 RM per month was meager.[32]

For some time the BDM had obligated its members to undergo home economics training, which could be fulfilled during the Duty Year. But the latter did not yet exist in the new territories, and so an attempt was made to extend a year of basic training in home economics to all upper level BDM members in the eastern units. The obligation could be met by attending a BDM Home Economics School for a year, half of which could be credited to the Duty Year. One half of the latter could also be met by participation in the "home economics working association" of the BDM-Work Faith and Beauty, sponsored in part by the Youth Department of the German Labor Front. It could be fulfilled by attending state-run home economics schools, or the Land Year, sponsored by the Ministry of Education. Only those girls who spent a full year in the Labor Service or the LD could have their Duty Year obligation canceled entirely. In this complicated fashion the BDM tried to help ethnic girls become authentic German housewives.[33]

At home the Duty Year could be met by a full year of service in the Eastern Action, which undoubtedly had something to do with the success of that venture. During 1941, 2,695 BDM leaders served in the Warthegau for a period of six weeks, another 468 went to Danzig-West Prussia, and 201 to the General Government. They came from most regions of the old Reich, although the Warthegau provided a number of its own BDM leaders for the program, and many of those were ethnic girls being resettled.[34]

The emphasis during the year fell on assistance in home and field, in school and kindergarten. New BDM units were established in sixty-four settler villages. The BDM conducted 213 *Morgenfeier* (the Nazi substitute for religious services), ran 329 *Kindernachmittage* (a kind of Montessori approach to education for preschoolers), and staged 1,045 village festivals of various types, from communal singing to de-Christianized yuletide celebrations. Incongruously enough, BDM girls also performed weddings and baptismals, replacing outlawed priests. The BDM became the dominant force in the community. Over 400 of them worked with 171 existing kindergartens and helped to establish ninety-one new ones, assisted by the NSV. At the time there were only eighty-five elementary schools in the Warthegau, and the BDM assisted in all of them by conducting sport exercises, musical instruction, and supervising homework. Some fifty-five new schools were staffed by 178 teachers' aides. Work with children was difficult enough for uncertified and inexperienced young women, but they also helped settlers by cooking, cleaning, darning, caring for babies and the sick, tending barnyard animals, and harvesting hay, cereal crops, and potatoes. Nearly 5,000 settlers scattered over 968 different villages were aided in this way, sometimes requiring that BDM girls travel on foot for distances of ten kilometers. In Eastern Action camps ethnic women and girls were taught how to sew and cook properly. Evening classes in basic German were conducted even during the harvest season. Thousands of NSV boxes containing toys, books, and clothes were distributed. The operation was supervised by thirty-two BDM district agents led by Bann-mädelführerin Freimann, whose skill and dedication put many HJ leaders to shame. It was the Nazi version of female liberation, conditioned by wartime necessity, which produced its own kind of equality.[35]

Many resettlers were held in transit camps in the East before final settlement. Because of political and military contingencies as well as the sorting and naturalization procedures, their stay in these various camps was frequently prolonged. The BDM was called in to help. Ten camps were set aside for ethnic girls in the Wartheland, containing an average of 1,650 young women for varied periods of time. Most of the camp staff were ethnic women trained by the RJF, of whom there were 695 by September 1941. Through typical BDM activities the ethnic girls were initiated into the communal mores and practices of Nazi youth. The time was too short for systematic educational efforts, but thousands were directed toward agrarian careers, welfare occupations, and teacher training. Later, more strenuous attempts were made to conduct instruction in the German language, mostly by some thirty graduates of secondary schools sent over from Germany. This work was both complementary and a follow-up to that engaged in by Menzel in the Reich camps.[36]

When Hitler invaded Russia, all eyes were focused on the East. In his traditional New Year's message, Axmann declared 1941 to be the year of a major "build-up in the new territories," and that is where the RJF put its primary emphasis. The build-up proceeded with the introduction of the "youth service obligation" in Eupen-Malmédy, the incorporation of 90 percent of the youth in that annexed region, and the integration of the ethnic youth of Luxemburg with the HJ. In Lorraine 75 percent of the youth entered the HJ, in southern Styria it was 95 percent, and in western Upper Silesia, the part that had been annexed, incorporation proceeded according to the outcome of Germanization procedures controlled by the SS. The ethnic German youth of Alsace had already been incorporated in September 1940. Then, in 1942, the Eastern Action of the BDM and the Eastern LD received priority rating among HJ activities. When rank-and-file girls are added to the leaders, it is clear that nearly 10,000 BDM girls served in the Eastern Action program during the course of 1941. While many of these girls remained in the East, another 16,022 went there during the course of 1942.[37]

Beside the standard four-week terms, running consecutively from March through November, simultaneous six-month, even full-year terms, were introduced in March 1942. The former was designed for older BDM leaders who were supposed to use their vacations to acquaint themselves with the problems and challenges of the East, whereas the longer terms were intended to give younger girls an opportunity to become fully committed to the East. In each HJ District in the East "specialists for settler care" were installed to coordinate relations with party, SS, and VDA officials, as well as to supervise BDM camp leaders, teachers' aides, and kindergarten helpers. Many decided to settle in the East permanently.[38] The "sponsorship circles" became a firm feature of the project by ministerial decree. HJ Region Hamburg, for example, received two districts in Danzig-West Prussia, Bromberg and Wirzig, and one in Upper Silesia, Bendsburg, as its permanent client areas. All BDM girls involved in the Eastern Action from Hamburg went only to these districts. It made for efficient recruitment and orderly administration. Strong personal ties between the home and frontier regions were created. This was particularly true for BDM girls who served as teachers' aides in the schools and in Germanizing activities in the villages composed primarily of new settlers.[39] The East was fast becoming a training ground for many professions favored by the HJ leadership. Volunteers were enticed by offers of rapid advancement, "eastern salary supplements," and "living cost equalizations."[40]

Indoctrination and education were not infrequently confused. The teachers' aides of the BDM thus played a key role on the forefront of Germanization. Arthur Greiser saw a new identity forming between settler school children and BDM teachers' aides, based on unencumbered youthful idealism. He was proud of the fact that the whole idea of the Eastern Action had been his. He believed that effective teachers could only be trained by practical work in primitive villages. But Albert Forster thought teachers' aides ought to have at least some training. He introduced three-month preparation for them in the Educational Institute at Elbing. The RJF saw these aides as a positive outgrowth of a teacher shortage in the Reich, since service in the East qualified many aides for early admission to pedagogical schools. The BDM made it possible for some women to assume careers denied them for financial or other reasons. Three months at Elbing, supplemented by three weeks of practice teaching in the villages and two weeks of initiation under HJ auspices, was hardly adequate substitution for formal training, but it was better than no career at all.[41]

Who were these teachers' aides? Among the 700 active in 1944, all probably in their early twenties, 58 percent came from commercial occupations, 16 percent from household work, 11 percent were still students, 2 percent came from industry, and 7 percent had no occupational backgrounds. All of them had been part-time BDM unit leaders at home for a long time. Their educational qualifications were relatively meager: 72 percent had completed the *Volksschule* and some technical training in *Aufbauschulen*; 26 percent had gone halfway through secondary schools; and a mere 2 percent had received the *Abitur*. The demands placed on them were stiff: 68 percent were simultaneously active in party work; 15 percent worked with the Red Cross; 24 percent ran local libraries; and 25 percent conducted adult education classes.[42]

Teachers' aides were expected to be front-line agents for the "strengthening of Germandom" by enlivening the communal culture of the villages. They were expected to maintain "a struggle against cultural rubbish and trash." They were to introduce a superior culture by way of music, reading matter, and theatrical performances. They also had to teach settler women to grow vegetable gardens and prepare nutritional meals, make their own clothes, repair household items, and make toys for their children. In doing all this, they were expected to spread a feeling for the superior qualities of German customs. That some parents did not always respond with appreciation was dismissed with the argument that the children responded well enough.[43]

As part of the eastern priority of 1942, Axmann decided to send a thousand male HJ leaders to assist the BDM in the task of settler care and control, the full meaning of the German word *Betreuung*. In 1943, when Germanization and naturalization were fully underway, this male Eastern Action was rapidly expanded by the addition of another 5,326 HJ leaders, most of whom volunteered because their Labor Service obligations had been canceled. Since most of them were eighteen, it is surprising that that many volunteers could be found in a year when the demand for military manpower was more intense than it had ever been. Their main responsibility was the supervision, education, indoctrination, and occupational counseling of settler youth in the process of being Germanized. They also helped in final settlement, in building up HJ units, in teaching language courses, and engaging in sports. Many of the HJ leaders appear to have had a commercial, artisan, or agrarian inclination, and they were expected to foster these types of careers among their immigrant charges.[44]

The threatening military situation at the end of 1943 caused the Eastern Action of the HJ to gradually fade away, although the Eastern Land Service survived until the spring of 1944. Altogether nearly 46,700 young women and men of the HJ participated in the Eastern Action project, while some 16,000 served in the LD. They all played important roles in the process of introducing the newcomers to the German and Nazi way of life, although the retreating German armies of 1944 must have made it seem as if their laborious efforts had all been in vain.[45]

**Germanization and Naturalization of Ethnics**

Turning to the final phase of Germanization, we find that this intricate process was unbelievably complex and confused. All SS agencies involved in it were headquartered at Litzmannstadt in the Warthegau. That dingy industrial city became the center of Himmler's demographic policy. Here too the RJF set up its own administration to deal with settler youth, the so-called HJ Action Staff, headed by Herwarth Düppe. Actually, the rubric came into use only after Axmann changed Menzel's Resettlement Bureau into the FdV, although Düppe had been chief of the Litzmannstadt extension of Menzel's office in 1941. Düppe was the key man in the HJ population policy when it reached its final phase in 1943 to 1944.[46]

Himself born in the East at Castorp-Rauxel in 1909, Herwarth Düppe was typical among young men involved in population policy. He joined the HJ at twenty and the party at twenty-four. Instead of completing secondary school, he opted for a career as youth leader. His goal of becoming an architect never went beyond temporary employment as a mason. He was married in 1937 to Elisabeth Büchel of Düsseldorf. He was Evangelical and she was Catholic, but both left the church, he in 1935 and she in 1940, and became *gottgläubig*, the euphemism employed by most SS members who wanted to meet Himmler's agnostic requirements but still retain some semblance of religious belief. Düppe served in the army on and off from 1936 to 1940 and then in the W-SS reserve from 1943, finally took an officer training course, was promoted to SS-Untersturmführer, and finished his Nazi career in the notorious Third SS Panzer Division "Totenkopf." His wife was employed by the NSV during most of the war, when their two children did not demand her time. Düppe's W-SS training supervisor characterized him as an "experienced," "quiet," and "responsible person," "eager to serve." He was articulate and self-assured in matters of ideology, although his capacity for combat command was questioned. He was well suited to head the HJ Action Staff.[47]

During a span of over two years, beginning in 1941, Menzel, Düppe, and a host of HJ coworkers supervised the reception of 186,100 youth of German origin into the new and old parts of the Reich. Among these were 6,760 young people from the "politically unstable German element" in the new territories of the West and South, as well as some areas of the East. Even northern France yielded 1,557 youth of Germanic extraction, and the Low Countries provided additional contingents. By the end of 1943 some 7,780 Germanized youngsters from foreign lands had been permanently settled in the Reich. The latter process was still going on in 1944, and the number therefore was probably higher by the end of the war, especially since the receding fronts brought hordes of refugees into central Germany. The RJF even found 18,530 Germanizable young people in the General Government, which the SS regarded as a dumping ground for racial "misfits."[48]

Since racial hubris was the driving force behind population policy, an invidious sorting and grading of human types became the basis of eligibility for naturalization. The racial experts of the SS developed a four-fold classification system which they called the German Nationality List (Deutsche Volksliste: DVL). In category one fell individuals who were clearly recognized as members of the German minority in Poland; category two included Polish citizens for whom German was the prevailing language, excluding, of course, Jews and "renegades"; category three was a miscellaneous classification which incorporated German spouses and children of mixed German-Polish marriages; category four was composed of German-speaking pro-Polish or anti-Nazi persons, known as "renegades."[49] Out of 729,200 youth subject to the HJ in the East, this scheme produced 139,550 Reich German youth; 64,300 ethnic German youth who had already been resettled; and 501,950 who were in the process of being sorted on the DVL, not counting two special groups in the General Government where no DVL existed.[50]

In order to "stabilize society," the HJ sought to encompass all young people. This was more difficult than appears on the surface. It involved for different groups various types of decisions about naturalization, placement on the DVL, and exclusion of those deemed to belong to "foreign ethnicity." While these procedures took their excruciatingly slow course, the HJ sought to influence the hordes of young people in the enclosed environment of camp life. They were examined to determine racial qualities, occupational preference, and previous economic circumstances. For this purpose there was an HJ Action Commando attached to Himmler's Immigration Center (EWZ) at Litzmannstadt. The EWZ, founded by

Reinhard Heydrich in 1939, was composed of SIPO and SD personnel from the RSHA, as well as other SS agencies. Branch offices also existed in Danzig, Stettin, Krakow, and Paris. So-called "flying commissions" traveled from camp to camp conducting naturalization procedures. The HJ Action Staff received information from its own examining commissions and then passed it to relevant HJ offices so that a decision about acceptance into membership could be made. They were guided in this effort by their EWZ superiors.[51]

More intensely concerned with racial selection was the HJ Action Commando attached to the RuSHA branch in Litzmannstadt, which processed youngsters from annexed territories to the west, southwest, and some eastern territories. These youths were considered to be akin to full-fledged Germans, which made subtle racial differentiation more difficult. Once those were made, naturalization followed rapidly. This Commando worked with the HSSPF in preparing lists of candidates and passing them on to HJ regional headquarters for eventual incorporation. For those most difficult to Germanize, the process was far more cumbersome, since they were included in the complex sorting schemes of the DVL. Those in categories one and two became HJ members automatically, as did most youngsters in categories three and four when they had completed a certain period of probation. Some in categories three and four had their "service cards" or naturalization papers stamped "subject to revocation," since the HJ wanted to reserve the right to expel those who subsequently revealed signs of having been inadequately Germanized. The insidiousness of all this expressed itself in attempts by many parents and their children to get into classes one and two by almost any ruse. It was a tricky game to which the SS and HJ subjected thousands of young people in the foolish effort to sort and filter human beings as if they were natural phenomena amenable to scientific classification.[52]

The "service card" introduced by Axmann in October 1943 sprang from the effort to keep a rein on young people during the hectic conditions of war. Those who had undergone Germanization received an official card that identified them as HJ candidates with one of the following qualifications: "eligible for naturalization," "immediate naturalization," or "naturalization subject to revocation." A second group received cards identifying them as "potential HJ members" with three qualifications: (1) "proscription"—for members of families not naturalized, not yet Germanized, politically unreliable, of foreign origin, or from homes whose head had been recruited by the partisans; (2) "exception"—for youth from fatherless families, or those whose family relationship was unclear, those whose citizenship could not be determined, and "open cases," i.e., individuals from the General Government; (3) "foster child"—for those under eighteen who had been resettled without parents and had no guardian. Decisions to place young people in one of these categories were made by the HSSPF and RuSHA with the assistance of the HJ Action Commando.[53]

At the beginning of 1944, following Forster's earlier example in Danzig-West Prussia, special youth camps were arranged for youngsters whose families had been classified as DVL three and four cases. Aimed at preventing the "revocation" of citizenship for these products of mixed marriages and "renegades," the HJ tried to correct linguistic and occupational deficiencies, as well as shortcomings in "character," physical fitness, and ideological and political orientation. Forster already had five camps with 400 inmates, while Greiser planned forty camps for this purpose. In southeast Prussia 1,400 DVL group three and four youngsters had gone through similar camps since 1943, and in Upper Silesia the HJ took strong measures to re-Germanize these youngsters, depending on the youth service law as a means of coercion. Behind it all lay the aim of creating "a dynamic and defensive farming community" in the East. Kinship with the LD was clearly maintained.[54]

Another way to expedite Germanization was dreamed up by Düppe's Action Staff for individuals deemed "capable of re-Germanization." These young people showed no external signs of being German, but their forebears were thought to have been at least partially German. An experimental camp erected for them at Litzmannstadt proved to be so successful that similar camps were arranged for by the HSSPF in each of their fifteen jurisdictions within the old Reich. Early in 1944 they contained 4,446 of these belated converts to German ethnicity. Increasing the thinning ranks of the German labor force appears to have been as important a motive as any other.[55]

The DVL and HSSPF camps were opportunistic devices designed to deal with specific naturalization problems created by a minority of ethnic youth. The majority experienced Germanization while housed in one of two basic types of camps. Until the summer of 1943 the prevailing type was known as the "communal camp," where youngsters were simply separated from parents and housed in separate rooms or separate buildings. They attended local schools and engaged in standard HJ activities. Occasionally they were allowed to visit their parents. For the most part those parents and children who had been sorted by EWZ commissions were sent to the communal camps for final naturalization. But Axmann, always uncomfortable with the proximity of parents, persuaded Himmler in April

1943 to set up independent *Jugendlager* where settler youth could be submitted to complete HJ control. These "youth camps," organized along standard HJ lines, were regarded as the ideal type of Germanizing environment where immigrant youngsters could be raised to the level of Reich youth.[56]

Since the camp population was extremely fluid—in March 1944 there were 15,234 youngsters in 293 communal camps and 2,939 in thirty-seven "youth camps"—effective leadership was a serious problem. Native leaders, who had come with the various ethnic groups and those who emerged during the sojourn in the early reception camps quickly disappeared into the W-SS, the regular army, and the various demographic agencies. Heavy reliance was placed, therefore, on HJ and BDM leaders who came to the East under the Eastern Action program. Then, through the various short training courses sufficient numbers of potential leaders were selected from the resettler groups themselves—some 35,000, in fact, were thus selected by 1944. The HJ Action Commando attached to the EWZ also initiated leader selection courses and sent gifted youngsters to the KLV-School at Steinau/Oder and the Resettler School for Girls at Tieffensee. The Leadership School for Resettlers at Litzmannstadt began to train high-ranking HJ leaders at the end of 1942. Among some 700 who completed the course of study by early 1944, almost half came from Bosnia, and a sizable group were ethnic Germans from Russia, but there were also students from the Baltic states, Galicia, Bessarabia, Rumania, and Lower Styria. This institution was the special project of Herwarth Düppe, who founded it with the cooperation of RKFDV officials and local civil authorities. It was located in a pleasant wooded area in the outskirts of Litzmannstadt.[57]

Düppe also had a hand in establishing a secondary school for resettlers at Litzmannstadt. This school began in May 1942. The courses were conducted by assistant school master, Dr. Herbert Schmidt, who also served as education expert on the HJ Action Staff. The students were grouped according to ability and mastery of the conventional curricula for such schools. One such group in the summer of 1942 had twenty-one young people varying in age from eighteen to twenty-six, who had immigrated from Rumania, Estonia, Yugoslavia, Lithuania, and the old Poland. They wanted to become certified farmers, military officers, teachers, engineers and technicians, physicians, and jurists. Only three failed to pass the examination, which was carefully adjusted to the differing educational and linguistic backgrounds of the students. Many selected a quite improbable question for the main examination essay: "How was Kant's categorical imperative implemented during this course?" Düppe recruited the teachers from the Adolf Hitler Schools in Germany. By 1943 this Settler School of Litzmannstadt had a full complement of classes, maintained a relatively high standard of instruction, and had approximately 300 students working for the traditional *Abitur*.[58]

The practical work in settler camps took the conventional HJ form. Premilitary training, for which special camps were organized in 1942, acquired special emphasis in the East. Physical exercises and even sport competitions were conducted, involving over 3,000 participants by 1943. Indoctrination was aided by thousands of books and propaganda material supplied by various old Reich agencies. So-called "cultural work" took the form mostly of HJ-Spielscharen sent over from Germany proper to perform conventional HJ plays, songs, and more or less amateur theatrical affairs, particularly at Christmastime. In conjunction with the RKFDV and the Ministry of Labor, systematic career counseling and preliminary occupational instruction were given to some 28,000 settler youths by early 1944. Since constant movement and relatively primitive living conditions created their own health problems, efforts were made to solve these, and a sizable number of youngsters were transferred to the old Reich for recovery purposes. Clothing problems were partially solved by putting hundreds of thousands into HJ uniforms.[59]

Involved in the re-Germanizing process from the initial emigration actions of the VoMi to the final naturalization under the HSSPF and RSHA, HJ leaders helped to determine classification of individual youths and even asked from time to time to have decisions revoked. The HJ was more fully involved in Himmler's population policies than any other party affiliate and more important to its success than most of the state ministries. The task of Germanization was not an easy one, since the goals were based on irrational assumptions. How, for instance, was one to prevent that "not a single drop of German blood be lost and become useful to foreign ethnicity?" It meant receiving the status of German ethnicity despite oneself. A term frequently used in the documents was *Umvolkung*, suggesting a kind of magical transformation that amounted to changing a person's attitude toward Germany, German culture, and Nazi politics, since the racial criteria used to determine ethnicity were not subject to logical analysis. In order to bring about such a change, the HJ deemed it necessary to separate young people from the unreliable influence of their parents, and then hope that the parents' attitudes would be changed by their transformed offspring. A complete break of relations with parents was considered to be "bolshevistic." Hence the *Jugendlager* became the appropriate means to achieve the aims of Germanization.

Occupation Policy and Cultural Infiltration

HJ involvement in ethnic politics included German youth of the Baltic states and occupied Russia not being resettled in the annexed territories of Poland. Officially this aspect fell under the jurisdiction of Alfred Rosenberg's ministry for occupied eastern territories. Axmann and Rosenberg arranged for HJ leaders to be included at all levels of the ministry's administrative network. While this work was outside the purview of the HJ-SS alliance, some of the personnel belonged to the SS, and Rosenberg himself did not remain free of SS influence in occupation policy. In 1943 none other than that peripatetic SS bureaucrat Gottlob Berger persuaded Rosenberg to put all political matters in his hands, making Rosenberg a mere figurehead.[60]

Rosenberg had established Youth Departments at his headquarters in Berlin and at the offices of his regional *Generalkommissaren* in the occupied areas. This occurred in May 1942, followed by Axmann's order in August which created the Administrative Center East of the RJF with branches in Riga, Rowno, Reval, Kauen, Minsk, Lusk, Shitomir, Kiev, Nikolaev, and Dneperpetrovsk.[61] Hauptbannführer Siegfried Nickel, at twenty-nine a veteran HJ leader, headed the Administrative Center East. Interestingly enough he did not join the party until 1936, but he did join the SS in 1940 and served in the Body Guard, becoming a reserve Untersturmführer in November 1941. He had been active in the late 1930s as HJ representative in Yugoslavia and Italy, probably as a kind of ambassador to native fascist youth groups. On the surface he was well qualified, since he spoke one foreign language and held a secondary school certificate.[62]

Nickel did not begin his work without precedent. The RJF had promoted sympathetic youth organizations in the Baltic states and in Memel since these areas came under German control. The former chief of the SRD, Heinrich Lüer, who ran the Riga office after 1942, managed to stimulate thriving youth activities in that region. In White Russia, which together with the Baltic states was administered under the so-called *Kommissariat Ostland* by Rosenberg's ministry, and in the Ukraine, under a similar rubric, youth work did not get underway until 1942. Nickel and Lüer concentrated on the "German element" in these areas, which meant, according to SS standards, some 300,000 ethnics, 5,000 of them in the Minsk region, 120,000 west of the Dnieper, 45,000 east of the river, and 130,000 in Transnistria. HJ and BDM leaders from the old Reich proceeded to organize youth groups in most of these regions. The primary goal, according to Nickel, was liberation from the Bolshevik ideological system and the introduction of new life styles. If Nickel is to be believed, the ethnic German youth of the Baltic and Russia accorded his workers a curious and cordial reception. German fairy tales, sagas, heroic historical deeds, and German music were imbibed with uncommon eagerness by young people who had grown tired of communist lore.[63]

So-called "Action Squads," consisting of teachers and students from the Adolf Hitler Schools, traveled through these regions. One group of eighty-five left Berlin in July 1942 and went to Estonia, Latvia, and Lithuania, where they propagated German values, frequently before wounded soldiers and families of officials. A second group of twenty did the same for ethnic German families in the districts of Shitomir, Kiev, and Transnistria. A third group of 110 teacher trainees from an educational school in East Prussia spent six weeks in the Nikolaev region. This "Action Squad" scattered to various camps to help organize local youth groups during the last week of their tour. Together these groups were thought to have reached almost 200,000 people.[64]

Since the "Action Squads" were supposed to be part of a long-range exchange program, several groups of selected native youth were brought to Germany. Some thirty carefully selected boys of fourteen to seventeen from White Russia were put into a short training program at the Volkswagen Works in Braunschweig. Girls from Estonia were introduced to KLV camps in southern Swabia, and native youth leaders from Estonia and Latvia were brought in as guests and observers in various HJ headquarters. Although plans were afoot to extend this program in 1943, it is unlikely that any significant expansion occurred. Plans were at least partially implemented in 1943 and 1944, however, to place Ruthenian and Ukrainian children in special "juvenile villages" and then in army camps and factories in Germany as air force auxiliaries and munitions workers. At Nuremberg a half-hearted attempt was made to tie Baldur von Schirach to this so-called "Hay Action." Yet there was nothing criminal about seeking to take care of thousands of war-created vagrants who wandered about the countryside without parents, homes, or living quarters. Among the older of these war-waifs, the SS and air force eventually employed some 56,000 as menial helpers. Only 3,000 had come to Germany by June 1944 and were employed as planned.[65]

Hitler's more fantastic schemes, such as bringing half a million ruddy-cheeked Ukrainian girls to Germany as domestic servants, finding them German husbands, and finally incorporating them in the master race, never fully materialized. Only about 15,000 volunteer Ukrainian peasant girls actually did come to Germany, and a substantial part of the 300,000

ethnic Germans eventually tracked west after the German defeat at Stalingrad—more the result of military defeat than a demographic master
plan.[66]

**The Impact and Effect of Racial Indoctrination**

The effectiveness of HJ population policy was more crucial than that of
the SS. While Hitler and Himmler determined general policy and SS officials shuffled paper, maintained quotas, and organized camps and trans-
port, it was the young men and women of the FdV and the Eastern Action
who served on the cutting edge of the policy, face to face with hostile Poles,
confused native ethnics, and bewildered settlers. As most leaders were
keenly aware, the success of Nazi population policy depended on the
degree of success the HJ colonizers achieved in their efforts to enculturate
the upcoming generation of ethnic German natives and new immigrants.
How successful they might have been in the long run can be assessed from
the results of their work during the four years that the policy was in effect.
Concentrating on the demographic microcosm of the Wartheland, the
essential elements of the policy can be examined: the physical and material
environment, the racist assumptions of superiority and misguided "civi-
lizing" mission, the "obstacle" of residual religious belief, the fatuous characterization and degrading of the Poles, the artificial glorification of ethnic
settlers and natives, and the ambiguous and insidious nature of Germanization.

By Western material standards the Wartheland and West Prussia was a
genuine economic frontier that impressed itself on the young colonizers as
a stimulating challenge and depressing obstacle. Posen, Litzmannstadt,
and Bromberg, the three largest cities excepting Danzig, were anything
but German in architecture, facilities, services, and inhabitants. One BDM
leader described the old textile center of Litzmannstadt as "the ugliest city"
she had ever seen, leaving an impression of unmitigated "squalor." The
towns, villages and "colonial settlements" must indeed have appeared to
be primitive compared to the meticulous agrarian scene regarded as typical of Teutonic order. Young girls from large German cities were appalled
by the two-room wattle-and-daub houses with dirt floors and straw roofs
and the irregular and ill-kept gardens, which greeted them as the prevailing features of the Eastern landscape. Villages seemed to be no more than
small dusty wastelands punctuating the sprawling, undulating plains. No
wonder the Eastern Action girls packed everything from kerchiefs to wash-
basins when they moved East. Households there had few utensils and little

furniture, forcing the colonizers to sleep on mattresses filled with straw and eat at tables made of rough wood. Health and sanitary conditions were so abominable, fed by ancient superstition and irrational practices, that many HJ volunteers were reminded of the medieval towns described in history books.[67]

Cultural missionaries are never popular. What made the HJ and BDM pioneers more effective than most self-conscious bearers of a "superior" culture was the hard physical labor they came to perform. This gradually opened the minds of suspicious settlers and native ethnics and frequently even evoked some friendliness from the generally hostile Polish "enemy." Early each morning the girls of the Eastern Action scattered from their communal camps to the various farmsteads. They peeled potatoes; fed the cattle, goats, and geese; milked the cows; and hoed rows upon rows of beets together with Polish and "Germanized" field hands. Everybody wanted to know everything the girls knew about Germany, the Führer, the HJ, and the BDM. There was endless work and talk. A girl from metropolitan Hamburg, barely fifteen, managed to milk three cows and deliver two calves during her third day on the farm of an ethnic German village elder. Stimulated by collective effort, the harvest season was the happiest time despite the backbreaking work it entailed. From 7:00 in the morning until 8:00 at night they bound and stacked sheaves of rye and oats. Some of the girls became sick, others grew very tired. Some had to ask their parents to send them gloves for their lacerated hands. But they still found time, as teenagers inevitably will, to practice dances and songs, take evening walks, and wonder at the wide open spaces of the new German East. It was a romantic adventure despite hard physical exertions. The end of the harvest was celebrated with good food and occasionally some rare schnapps.[68]

Melita Maschmann, who did all of these things voluntarily even though she could have spent her time writing articles for the HJ press, theorized that "fanatical hard work had become a passion" that was used "to create a self-assertiveness which we lacked." BDM leaders in their early twenties, like conventional pioneers, were forced to assume unaccustomed roles by force of circumstance. As representatives of the party and the conquering Reich, they became "parish clerks," "justices of the peace," "doctors," "teachers," "village constables," even incongruous village "priests." Maschmann recalls how she bicycled from village to village with her sparse "medicine bag" to administer basic care to her admiring "patients." She was able on one occasion to stem an epidemic of diarrhea that threatened to wipe out all the babies in a village, but only after eliminating competition from a faith healer.[69]

There was room on this Nazi frontier for personal initiative because the restraints of bureaucracy had not yet materialized. Rules were frequently circumvented when it came to meeting idealized objectives. When newly arrived settlers were found to be without furniture and household utensils, ingenious BDM and HJ leaders used "doctored" papers to "confiscate" the needed items from whoever appeared to be able to spare them, whether they were Poles or fellow ethnic Germans. After all, they were engaged in colonizing the advance posts of empire. Germany required of them not merely that they perform an important task, but that they surrender themselves to it without restraint and hesitation. "This feeling," Maschmann recalled, "rose on many occasions to a sensation of intoxication." They romanticized their austere existence and developed the familiar colonizer's disdain for those who stayed behind. It was "the arrogant enthusiasm of the cultural missionary." Thus they became accomplices in a policy of hatred and exploitation—fed by their SS superiors and tutors—but without really becoming as individuals viciously hateful and cruel.[70]

Religion created ambiguous attitudes, resulting from the party's anti-church indoctrination and the atheistic stance of the SS. Since most clergy had been driven out or drafted, BDM leaders were frequently compelled to preside over weddings and funerals, giving improvised speeches on pseudoreligious topics that unavoidably sounded like anemic sermons. One peasant woman commented after Miss Maschmann had conducted a funeral: "The Frau Führerin talked as lovely as the Reverend Father used to." The emotional strain of these situations took their toll on inner peace. Most villages had at least two churches, one Evangelical, attended by ethnic Germans, Reich Germans, and settlers, another Catholic, for Poles and "Germanized" families. Religion thus created another fissure in a divided and conflict-ridden society. But there was no attempt to close the churches down. Many officials appear to have concluded that churches were essential as instruments of political control, especially since they were relatively harmless without sufficient clergymen. There were more subtle ways to defuse religious influence. The villagers were invited to attend the Sunday morning rituals of the HJ and BDM, followed in the afternoons by popular festivals. There was a conscious campaign to convert the capacity for faith among these humble peasants from religious fidelity to the politicized myths of Nazi ideology.[71]

The demographic experts of the SS treated ethnic Germans as quotas that had to be extracted, transported, organized in camps, sorted and filed, and then dumped in the chosen areas of settlement. Each government district in the Warthegau had its own SS Settlement Staff, which supervised the relocation of some half a dozen ethnic groups, beginning with Volhynians in 1940 and ending with ethnic Germans from the Black Sea region in 1944. They were squeezed in between native ethnics and remaining Poles, in total disregard for communal life, availability of school facilities, and sanitary considerations. The SS usually dumped the settlers near the most convenient roads and communication centers. They also initiated each new Eastern Action contingent when it arrived. But all work beyond that point was in the hands of the HJ and BDM. At first the BDM girls were met with suspicion and some hostility from Poles and some native ethnic Germans. Some village elders regarded them as intruders, arrogant urban loafers, who would merely exhaust the village food supply. Suspicions usually evaporated when the girls patiently explained why they had come and then demonstrated their sincerity by physical labor. Rivalries, jealousies, and endless squabbles prevailed among the varied ethnic groups so artificially thrown together in most villages. This was one of the most difficult problems the BDM faced.[72]

The reasons for this internecine conflict are readily discernible. Younger settlers received larger plots of land than they had owned in their homeland, whereas older ones got smaller parcels but hoped to change that situation after the war. The earlier settlers received better houses and more fertile land than later ones, who had to take what was left over. Methods of cultivation and agrarian habits differed from one national group to another, and from prevailing German practices. The fact that all of them had a common German heritage, which had brought them together in the first place, although hardly by choice, was not always enough to prevent disputes from erupting. The relatively backward native ethnic Germans were frequently degraded as "*Volkspolen*" or "Wood-Poles," while they in turn referred to Volhynian immigrants as "Vanilla-Germans." It was no easy task for young girls to arbitrate between "these hostile brethren," playing down "instincts of greed and . . . desire for political . . . advantage" and arousing feelings of pride for a common tradition. Being surrounded by a hostile Polish majority created an atmosphere of ominous uncertainty. While outwardly submissive, the Poles were clearly waiting for an opportunity to reclaim expropriated land. Toward the end of the war Polish guerrillas raided German settlements and burned down the new farmsteads of immigrant settlers.[73]

The prevailing attitude among the cultural missionaries toward their clients was a mixture of disdain and sympathy. Many put them on racial pedestals and saw them consciously as manipulable material. Melita Maschmann said this about a Volhynian settler: "It was remarkable in what old fashioned, almost biblical sounding German he would express his praises. He was firmly convinced that the Führer would think of him quite personally and see to his children's welfare as soon as the war was over." Hildegard Friese, Eastern Action leader in the district of Welun, was constantly struck by the strength of the mother tongue. Everywhere ethnic parents wanted their children to learn German. They sent them to improvised BDM "language schools" in shacks and railroad stations. Friese was impressed with the "racial purity" of the Volhynians and their linguistic identity, enhanced by the habit of siring large families, which she found to be exemplary among ethnic minorities. In fact, she found "less Polish, Ukrainian, or Rumanian blood" among settlers from Eastern Europe than "French blood among West Germans or Italian blood among South Germans." This ethnic "cleanliness" stood in stark contrast to "Polanized" native Germans. It was, in her view, based on "biological and confessional" considerations and revealed itself by "instinctive . . . economy of words and . . . direct forms of expression."[74]

Welun District Leader Oldwig von Natzmer expressed a common belief when he said that "one had to educate these settlers and ethnic Germans to accept the German work ethic." That was a task which a few thousand BDM girls could not achieve in a few years. "The essential thing was," as Friese saw it, "that the young people . . . grew and matured in the right direction," pointing towards an "authentic peasant attitude" and the conversion of inherited religious fidelity into a nationalistic faith. In the process the well-known shortcomings of settlers, "superstition, insecurity, and insensitivity," not to mention a certain "primitive" ethos, would be overcome. Here the BDM Eastern Action, the HJ as a whole, and their SS patrons could play a decisive role.[75]

There were a number of solidly German settlements in the Welun district. These Germans had maintained their ethnic identity and enjoyed material advantages over their Polish neighbors, partially the result of governmental favor under Josef Beck and Smigly-Rydz. Toward the end of her stay Friese concentrated her work on these neglected "colonies." One of the enclaves, the Swabian village of Konstantinov, located on the only paved road in the district between Welun and Radomsko, gave Friese cause for optimism. The colony had been settled in 1772 and typical Swabian surnames could still be recognized, while some older women were capable of conversing with Friese in homespun dialect. This village was the only one in the district where all landowners were German. Kindergarten, set up by the BDM and later taken over by the NSV, schools, and HJ and BDM units thrived here and made ethnic politics largely superfluous.

Other colonies provided serious problems for Germanization agents and made Konstantinov a notable exception.[76]

The Poles, on whose soil HJ imperialists were building a new society, were officially designated as racial aliens, even though they constituted 60 to 80 percent of the population. This created extraordinary emotional and conceptual dilemmas. Many Poles were openly hostile and threatened to even scores with the invaders. "It took courage," wrote BDM Eastern Action Leader A. Lumpp, "to regard the Poles as inferior and defeated people." But the glowing pride in representing Germany on this challenging frontier "did not permit" the cultural missionaries "to betray any human weakness vis-à-vis the Poles." Rumors spread by the SS that proscribed Polish priests were clandestinely encouraging Polish women to produce numerous children, even illegitimately, produced fear and hatred of the biologically dangerous enemy. Without realizing that the Polish intelligentsia was being liquidated by SS-Einsatzgruppen, many HJ and BDM youngsters assumed the Polish nation consisted of workers, peasants, and tradespeople, which enhanced their sense of superiority.[77]

Although the expulsion of Polish families from their homes and farms was the task of the SS, members of the HJ and BDM occasionally were drawn into that painful process. As soon as the houses were empty, the BDM had to make them ready for German occupants. Confronting understandable disorder, their notions about "Polish mismanagement" and "Polish dirt" were confirmed. So they considered it quite natural that "orderly German farmers took over the country and the farms." Some Hitler youths found it difficult to maintain an air of detachment from the Polish people they came in contact with. Feelings of sympathy could not always be suppressed. But party propaganda stiffened their backbones. Most of them showed little moral compunction about the suffering caused in the effort to secure "living space" for a nation whose "biological survival" was in the balance. As Maschmann put it, "a group which believes itself to be called and chosen by God, as we did, has no inhibitions when it comes to taking territory from 'inferior elements.' " It is no wonder that "the Poles had misery written on their faces. In their eyes one encountered all gradations of antipathy from cool reserve to hatred. Even the few who behaved subserviently had an oppressive air of dejection."[78]

The task of Germanizing was made particularly difficult, according to Friese, because the prevailing ethos of the Poles exuded an aura of laziness, filth, and stupidity. She philosophized:

One has to be reminded that every primitive culture has more tenacity than a higher one. The Pole in this fruitful sense is primitive, tireless, frugal, yes not infrequently even diligent and clean, especially if he was touched by these virtues in the Reich. Peasants, above all Polish peasant women, are more instinctive, cunning, cautious, even if out of coward-ice, unrestrained, adaptable and in their torpor still more tied to nature, its artifices and forces, than we are. The Pole will never be free; if we do not dominate him with an iron hand, then his own leaders—be they intellectuals, priests, or partisan chiefs—will turn him into an illegal instrument. It is not inappropriate to make this observation, gathered on lonely journeys through heath, forest and bog. . . . It is provoked by the insidious or obsequious but never straight-forward glances of nameless Polish children at every cottage door.[79]

Was it the conqueror's lingering fascination with the victim's stamina? The oppressor's strange reverence for the subjects of his oppression? Impa-tience with the unwelcome need to dominate? It was certainly more than German rejoicing in other people's misfortune that inspired Hildegard Friese's acute observation.

How effective then was the process of Germanization? Considering that any success in such endeavors usually takes generations, the bearers of German culture made more progress in four years than one might have expected. Their youthful enthusiasm, total commitment, and the relatively innocuous instruments they chose to use had much to do with their partial success. A few examples will demonstrate why such a guarded judgment is reasonable.

A group of BDM girls from Hamburg, led by twenty-year-old Edhi Abban, spent an Eastern Action term in the village of Lubiewo in the Gau of Danzig-West Prussia during the summer of 1942. Besides all the other required tasks, they visited the local kindergarten with dramatic effect. They managed to teach the diverse group of children folksongs, even though most of them understood little German, a feat their teacher with her broad Saxon accent, had been unable to achieve. The mishmash of languages and accents gave this kindergarten a droll character, but the good-natured enthusiasm of the Hamburg girls won the hearts of the chil-dren. The same thing occurred with the village population when the girls put on a Sunday evening songfest in the schoolyard. The Bessarabians, in particular, joined in the singing when the girls switched to the Hamburg dialect. Halfway through their stay the girls staged a dramatic production, a kind of political and cultural amateur hour, including songs, dances, a fairy tale, and a charade of local personalities in homemade costumes.

Local Polish citizens were barred from the event, leading to loud protests, although ethnic Germans and Germanized Poles from neighboring villages were brought in. The event stimulated much enthusiasm and comment, partially because much beer had been consumed during the afternoon and partially because village children had been trained to do their own skit and were prominently featured in the program.[80]

In 1942 Lubiewo held twenty Bessarabian families who had been settled there in May, seven ethnic German families of Polish origin, and one old German family headed by the district farm chief. The rest of the 500 villagers were Polish by any definition, although a number of them were in the process of being Germanized. The latter spoke German only when they felt themselves to be under observation and gave the impression that they had allowed themselves to be Germanized only to get additional ration cards. Edhi Abban found "real Poles" to be more "sympathetic and characterful" than the Germanized individuals whose sincerity she questioned, since they behaved in a subservient manner. "But in Danzig-West Prussia," she complained, "everything that walks and once might have had a drop of German blood is being Germanized, unlike in other Eastern Gaue." In the light of such observations, Abban and her girls spent many hours discussing the problems of Germanization, without reaching any firm conclusions.[81]

While the results of indiscriminate Germanization in Danzig-West Prussia were fraught with ambiguity, in the Warthegau the effects were only slightly less questionable. Dr. Friese was constantly amazed how many tall, blond, and blue-eyed people had been "Polified"—the German word "verpolt" implying a form of ethnic and racial disease more serious than measles. In Welun clearly distinguishable lines between Germans and Poles could not always be made. To take illiterate men into the SA and then throw them out again when they revealed unexpected Polish traits only created enemies. A typical case, indicating the vagaries of Germanization, was an "outwardly Nordic" farmer who spoke perfect German but was considered Polish, even though he had two brothers in the Wehrmacht. He was sent back to Welun to manage the hereditary farm, but could not marry a German and had no desire to marry a Pole. While Friese avoided a direct attack on the DVL procedures and the youth camps of category three and four, she clearly implied that they were artificial and inhuman, resulting in bad public morale. She cited the case of a former estate manager by the name of Kutz, who was tall and slender, with a small head and light blue eyes, a paragon of Aryan physique, but whose mother and wife were Polish. Kutz was glad to be able to speak German with someone again and asked that his two small sons be admitted to the BDM-run school. That was in 1941. During the following year his Polish wife and their daughter of sixteen, "a picture of Aryan beauty," arrived from the General Government. The daughter spent some time in a BDM camp, reading Polish novels, clattering on the piano, and avoiding work. After a few days she "escaped," and in 1943 the entire family disappeared, led by the "energetic Polish wife," despite the fact that the two boys had made "good progress" under BDM tutelage. Friese commented: "How did the factors of race, external fate, and free, personal will, interact with each other? Who knows the border between pure blood and mixed blood? Can 75 percent Polish blood, as in the case of the Kutz children, justify the demand to become German or merely permit it?"[82]

The District of Welun in the southeastern corner of the Warthegau bordered on the General Government in the east, Upper Silesia in the south, the old Prussian District of Kempen in the west, and several old Polish districts to the north. It was purely agrarian, with only three medium-sized towns and several small market centers scattered among 1,000 villages and "colonial settlements." There were few large estates in this "forgotten hinterland" of the industrial regions of Upper Silesia and Litzmannstadt. In 1940 Welun contained approximately 25,000 ethnic Germans scattered among 250,000 Poles and a sizable Jewish minority in the towns and market centers. The original Landrat and Nazi District Leader Oldwig von Natzmer believed the district had "the best Poles and worst ethnic Germans." Friese thought it was the "most Polish district of the Warthegau" and therefore posed the greatest challenge to the agents of Germanization, requiring "different means" than elsewhere. By 1944, when 27,000 ethnic settlers and 3,000 Germans from the old Reich had been added to native ethnics, the German-Polish population ratio of 1:10 changed to 1:5; many Poles and all Jews had been expelled in 1942. The settlers from Germany proper, while still merely a trickle, were looked upon as the salt of the earth. They gradually assumed positions of leadership, forming a new elite to be expanded by defense-peasants from the W-SS.[83]

Friese believed that an observable social structure was emerging in the District of Welun and the Warthegau:

> The Poles, who are foreign people and numerically in the majority, can never be ignored, but neither should they be feared. Biologically and politically they constitute a hostile substratum. (The same holds true for Jews and Russians, who are no more than dead witnesses to a necessary sacrifice.) Above this is the first German layer of ethnic Germans, in

every way matted together with the substratum. It is THE TASK of our generation to effect a clear separation between these layers without any regard for painful individual cases. The honor and future of the ethnic Germans demands this and their leaders provide the possibility by their very existence. Then above this comes the next highest layer of resettlers from the farther East, who are the largest German group, although by no means tightly integrated. By retaining a nearly pure bloodline and authentic mother tongue, despite existence in a foreign environment, they have proven themselves as much by sacrificing their old homeland as by building up their new one. The thin upper layer is composed of Germans from the old Reich, who have to prove their right to leadership like wise fathers by gradually surrendering responsibility to their maturing children.[84]

No doubt Friese expressed the prevailing view when she portrayed the social situation in a corporate-biological way by labeling Germans from the old Reich as "adults," the settlers as "youth," and the native ethnic Germans as "children." Common blood, faith, and soil, were to be the social cement that held this artificial society together. Not surprisingly, she thought the BDM, HJ, and SS were the social masons.[85]

HJ representatives involved in all aspects of Nazi population policy saw themselves as "an authentic elite of German youth." The Eastern Action School of the RJF was a kind of school for carriers of a "superior" culture. This young army of colonial agents did their work where it counted most, in households and fields, in kindergarten and schools, and in communal welfare work. Most BDM teachers' aides decided to stay in the Warthegau after their initial terms of service ran out. The established "sponsorship circles" provided a steady and regular flow of colonial agents from patron districts in the old Reich. These agents made their contribution to the "strengthening of Germandom" by working in the various camps and with the settled immigrant families themselves. Thus thousands of Hitler's children under the guidance of the SS became a new version of the Teutonic Knights, crusading for German culture with racial ideology substituted for religious fanaticism.

# 7 | Contestants, Boxers, Combatants

Anything but robust, and given to hypochondria all his life, Hitler projected for Germany's young people an ideal physical model that was the direct opposite. As early as 1920, when he helped Gottfried Feder compose the party program, physical fitness had been an inseparable part of Nazi ideology. "The state," the program announced, "must see to raising the standards of health in the nation by protecting mothers and infants, prohibiting child labor, increasing bodily efficiency by obligatory gymnastics and sports." To 54,000 Hitler youths assembled at the party rally in 1935 Hitler proclaimed that he wanted them to be "slim and slender as greyhounds, tough as leather, and hard as Krupp steel." The young were to dedicate every moment of free time to "the useful training of their bodies," instead of "loitering in streets and movie houses."[1]

Professional youth leaders in the Third Reich clearly placed physical fitness above training the intellect as a priority in their educational curriculum. Unable to come to terms with his own physical inadequacies, Hitler lost himself in a world of emotional hyperbole when he described his educational goals shortly after assuming the chancellorship: "I want to see once more in the eyes of youth the gleam of pride and independence of the beast of prey. Strong and handsome must my young men be. I will have them fully trained in all physical exercises. I intend to have an athletic youth—that is the first and the chief thing. In this way I shall eradicate the thousands of years of human domestication. Then I shall have in front of me the pure and noble natural material. With that I can create the new order."[2] It has not been generally recognized how close the leaders of the HJ and their fanatical SS patrons came to making Hitler's inhuman dream come true.

## A Racial Ideology of Sports and Fitness

When the Hitlerian rhetoric is boiled down, several practical motivations for a national policy emerge: physical training is a primary duty of a rising

**173**

nation-state; state education must cultivate "the biological substance" of the citizen as a member of the superior race; public health, self-conscious strength, and a combative soldierly attitude are the specific goals of physical training. The locker room was to be turned into a racial hothouse for breeding ideal physical specimens and creating a nation of combatants. The attitude of the pugilist was consciously promoted as the ethos of a bellicose new generation.[3] The Nazis tapped a rich source of contagious enthusiasm in positing competitive sports and physical fitness as a desirable social activity. While a sense of fair play, spurred by sports, can transfer to life and contribute to ideas of social justice, games and exercises can also serve as an escape from the complex situations of the real world into the ordered life of the sports clubhouse. A different form of escape offered by sports is that of fleeing from the drudgery of everyday life into a world of action and heroics. Sports provide opportunity to assert oneself, to expend boundless energies, and to reap immediate rewards and glory.[4]

The philosophers of sport have found putative justification for physical competition, since "young men are attracted by athletics because it offers them the most promising means for becoming excellent." In achieving excellence, the successful athlete provides the rest of us with an opportunity "to identify ourselves with the athlete, as one who is what a man ought to be." Sport "catches the interest and elicits the devotion of both the young and the old, the wise and foolish, the educated and the uneducated." The physically fit individual is raised above the average run of individuals, a heroic epitome of man qua man. By disciplined action and the suppression of distracting impulses, the athlete "uses his native freedom with maximum effort, to place himself for a moment alongside artists, religious men, and inquirers of every stripe."[5]

Instinctively Hitler was aware of these surrogate qualities in sports both for himself and the German people. Somehow the HJ was to be what he as a youth had never been and never would be as an adult. Prominent Nazi philosopher, Alfred Bäumler, systematized the party's ideological preoccupation with physical training by comparing the Greek concepts of spirit (*Logos*) and nature (*Physis*) and elevating the latter over the former. "Retaining the purity of nature," thus became "the basis of National Socialist communal life." This was the first and most important political inference he drew from his new "philosophy of the spirit." Bäumler believed a "new age had arrived," characterized by "the gymnasiums of the HJ and SA as the focal points of the state." The HJ leadership was flattered by such attention from gray-haired sages and made physical culture the basis for effective indoctrination of the young.[6]

As Eugen Weber discovered in his study of the sports revival in fin de siècle France, "sports were integrated and integrating activities, part of the contemporary scene, reflecting social and ideological preoccupations, and very likely affecting them in turn." The revival of sports was part of a nationalist revival and contributed to the spread of chauvinism. The Nazis found an older tradition to build on, that of "Turnvater" Jahn, whose slogan "from the gymnasium to a new national life" became the theme for a "Jahn Renaissance." The Jahn heritage had given exercise enthusiasts a taste for adventure, self-discipline, and effort, which Jahn had promoted as moral tools for building character. For Thomas Hughes, Jahn's English imitator, games fostered patriotism and self-reliance and had a tempering effect on body and character. While both looked upon sports as a way of "harnessing young energies and instincts to social ends," the German tradition tended to stress nationalist commitment and the English, elitist individualism. Physical exercises went beyond muscle-building and impulsive competition to satisfy private needs. To the HJ, physical exercise "expressed a patriotic spirit, a spirit of manliness, as did camping, hiking, games in the open country, and youthful pranks." As activities in the national interest they were not ordered by achievement for its own sake, but "determined by leadership and following, subordination and service, order and obedience, fidelity and virility."[7]

Far from being politically neutral, sports and physical training were the most licit and docile of social activities. "The opportunities opened for social control," as Weber observed, "appear more powerful than those making for self-liberation or self-expression." Physical exercise was seen by some HJ ideologists as a revolutionary instrument, having been rescued from its purely technical utility and politicized to help "preserve the new values of Germany's racial-historical life." Hans Surén, in a poetic flight of fancy, even found a symbolic new color for a physically shipshape nation: "Yes—as if bronzed the skin must glow, not sickly, yellowish or white as paper, but brown—weather-brown and tough must be the future bodies of German men and women! This must be the future national color of honor!"[8]

As the Nazi regime unfolded and every affiliate developed its own fitness program, it became clear that the Nazi sports policy was to go far beyond the nationalist flavor of its French and English predecessors. Distinctively Germanic concepts of *Volk*, race, defense, and leadership served as guidelines for the structuring of physical education in the schools, the HJ, the Labor Front, and the SS. These programs invariably included the following goals: education in community, serving the goal of racial eugenics, and forging individual will and character. These objectives made German sports different from English endeavors, where sports were regarded as teaching individual traits like fairness. A "German ethos" that put individual striving for excellence in the service of a greater good, the community, was regarded as superior to the English notions of fair play in competition. English sports were rejected along with capitalism, pragmatism, puritanism, positivism, and the ideal of "the gentlemen." A new vision of German society and culture exhibited far different traits than English utilitarianism and functionalism.[9]

Nazi society was based on the fundamental premise, according to one theoretician, that the minimally educated person who was physically healthy and possessed solid character filled with unencumbered decisiveness and willpower was more valuable to the community than a highly educated weakling. The types of physical exercises and the nature of sports and fitness activities as a whole were thus patterned to conform to Germanic social principles and life styles. The apparently spontaneous play of young boys was organized to develop leader-follower relationships. Those who took the lead in games became leaders of HJ units as a matter of course. Command and obedience in one situation transferred automatically to others. The rough practices of children at play were nevertheless governed by certain unstated, commonly accepted assumptions, such as loyalty, honor, and courage, regarded as "laws of youthful association," which laid the foundation for subsequent roles of leadership in the state. Muscular performance brought about hardening and produced the mature sloughing of "hyper-sensitive timidity," while encouraging "daring action." The HJ deliberately promoted fatiguing exertions, which, commonly endured with friends and cohorts, created binding ties of camaraderie.[10]

An essential element of the Nazi philosophy of physical education was the idea that political power, physical prowess, and racial purity were inextricably connected. R. Walther Darré thought that agrarian youth had to engage in physical exercise not only to maintain good health but to enhance "selective breeding." Rudolf Bode believed physical training should be anchored in "the physical and spiritual sources of the German mother-womb and the circulating bloodstream." He anticipated contemporary notions of "biorhythms," since he thought "German physical training, like all education, must meet two demands: it must renew physical strength through intellectual discipline and the power of the soul through a culture of rhythmic patterns." It was believed, mostly by Nazis themselves, that people tended "to think in biological terms and act in heroic fashions," because prime values in education focused on race, community, militancy, and leadership. Somehow, these familiar *völkisch* prerequisites were "to be realized through a program of physical exercises" saturated by the appropriate ideological environment. Physical education recast in this sense, the Nazis thought, would finally repair the damage done by Jews who were accused of "undermining and misdirecting the political importance of physical instruction."[11]

The affinity between physical training and militarism was not a German phenomenon. Johan Huizinga found it to be a general phenomenon: "An ideal of noble strife, fulfilled in myth and legend, is one of the strongest incentives to civilization. It has more than once given rise to a system of martial athletics and ceremonial social play which together adorned real life with poetry, as in medieval chivalry and Japanese bushido." In France Weber noted how sports created a mood of patriotic optimism among middle-class youth and helped "to develop and maintain a warlike atmosphere among young people." It was socially desirable because "competitive games offered a means of channeling and regulating violence, especially the savage violence of adolescence. To individuals too ready to follow some subversive drummer, games offered opportunities for self-assertion and sometimes also for indulging in competitive violence in any number of ways that society condemns off the battle-field."[12]

To the HJ a generation later, all activities were structured to imitate competitive sports, while the drive for achievement and excellence and the preoccupation with physical exertions and training were regarded as preparation for inevitable military service. Youth was thought to have a natural predisposition for the austerities of the soldierly life. But there was to be no *Soldatenspielerei*, because youth from childhood were to accept war as necessary and serious business. Every young boy, when he entered the HJ at ten, completed a six-month probation by undergoing the so-called *Pimpfenprobe*, which involved a difficult series of physical tests. He had to run 60 meters in twelve seconds, make a long-jump of 2.5 meters, throw a ball 25 meters, pack a knapsack with essentials for survival, and take part in a day-and-a-half-long hike. The test also included knowledge of key HJ slogans, the Horst-Wessel Song, and other musical staples of Nazi culture, militaristic in tone and content.[13]

The Nazis assumed from the start that soldiers could not be made in a couple of years of training but that one had to begin the process in the formative years of childhood. Once obligatory HJ service was introduced, a decade of physical preparation for military performance could be systematized. Helmut Stellrecht wrote in 1936: "The rifle should fit the hand as naturally as the pen." Capitalizing on "autonomous leadership," which encouraged self-confident physical performance, competitive activism was easily converted into aggressive bellicosity required for combat.[14]

The Prussian military tradition became a Nazi caricature. Hans Wichmann announced that "the new Germany saw its highest life-form in the soldier who became the ideal model of education, . . . so that German military training could never have purely technical utility but expressed youthful nurturing in the spirit of the race." The HJ believed its task was the "development of manliness and political instincts," which could only be realized by segregating youngsters into age groups and sex groups. Biological differences called for different methods of training. As motherhood was the natural function of girls, so warfare was a native predisposition to be fully developed among boys. This had nothing to do with playing soldiers' games, since "militarism was corrupted soldiering, soldiering with a bad conscience, bereft of soul and inner conviction." A German man was thought to be a soldier throughout his daily existence. Education that elicited the spirit of the soldier thereby strengthened what were believed to be the "most advantageous aspects of the German national character." It was, perhaps, no exaggeration when one observer proclaimed proudly that "the love of weaponry and military service is for us Germans in the blood."[15]

### From Physical Exercise to Military Preparedness

Himself awkward, flabby, slightly effeminate, and resembling more the man of leisure than the Führer's sleek "greyhound," Baldur von Schirach made fitness and sports an HJ trademark. Thoroughly organized from the start, sports became one of the early appeals of the HJ and contributed to its expansion. Sports were part of the "demand for totality," which meant that the RJF tried to get all competitive sports and fitness programs under its control.

In 1934 Schirach wrested control over basic physical exercises for young teenagers from the National Association for Physical Exercise (DRL). Even "voluntary fitness sports," conducted by constituent clubs that made up the membership of the DRL, were taken over when the HJ Law of 1936 made the RJF responsible for the "entire physical . . . education" of youth. What followed was predictable. Hans von Tschammer und Osten, whom Hitler had appointed Reich sport leader, became Schirach's deputy and proceeded to integrate all sports activity within the HJ. To spice up the competition and to attract increasing numbers of participants, Schirach created "achievement medals" for the HJ, JV, BDM, and JM. Detailed instruction books for systematic physical training in HJ units, graded by age and sex, were soon issued in regular and abundant profusion, while all HJ regions set up leadership schools to train sport, terrain, and marksmanship supervisors. Sports were touted and propagandized in every available medium. The National Sport Competition attracted enormous numbers of teenage contestants. From 1.5 million participants in 1933, the army of competitors grew to 7 million in 1939. In the year the war began, nearly 80 percent of all teenagers competed in these national contests of physical prowess and personal achievement. It was not an idle boast when Schirach claimed to have physically mobilized German youth.[16]

The physical fitness program that led to national competition was rigorously structured. Jumping, running, discus throwing, swimming, ball playing, and gymnastics were required of all youngsters regardless of ability, as were so-called terrain maneuvers, target shooting, and long hikes. At least four hours during the week and three weekends per month were dedicated to these endeavors. Target shooting with small caliber rifles for boys fourteen to eighteen and air rifles for JV boys was an essential element of a program steeped in militaristic ideology, although in the early 1930s it was done more for fun than conscious preparation for soldiering. While there is no evidence that any of the boys objected to systematic familiarization with lethal weaponry, some parents became concerned when accidents occurred on the rifle ranges. This led to increased employment of marksmanship teachers and supervisors and the imposition of accident insurance.[17]

The most unusual part of the program, terrain exercises, went further than outdoor survival techniques learned by Boy Scouts. Capitalizing on the proverbial wanderlust, boys were taught to read maps, to recognize typical landmarks, to judge distances, to describe terrain characteristics, to utilize varied types of camouflage, and to learn orientation in all types of natural environments. Groups of boys even learned how to reconnoiter by engaging in fairly realistic terrain maneuvers, which were more like cowboy and Indian tussles than military exercises.[18]

Enthusiasm was maintained by focusing all physical feats on official competitions. These were scheduled uniformly in June for local units, in July and August for district meets, and in September for regional sport festivals. The excitement of competition, from which few stood aside, had its own intrinsic rewards, while the regime's larger purposes were achieved with little conscious indoctrination. Much of the élan was spurred by the convenient fact that the Olympic Games took place in Germany. It has been said that the 1936 Olympics demonstrated as never before that "the better an athlete was as an athlete, the less he was allowed individualism and the more he was cast as an allegorical, ideological battler." This was more true in Nazi Germany than any other country. Activity in preparation for the Berlin games and the reverberating effects of the outstanding performance of German athletes made sports a national cause.[19]

The militaristic trend in sports, stimulated by the reintroduction of conscription and the Olympic Games, was reflected in an organizational change. An older office in the RJF was divided: the Office for Physical Exercises now dealt with competitive sports in the broad sense, while the Office for Physical Fitness was publicly designated as headquarters for "military sports." Headed by Dr. Helmut Stellrecht, this bureau became an unabashed center of ideologically charged militarism. Born in 1898, Stellrecht held a doctorate in engineering and had a background in the Free Corps and Labor Service. He served in the Ministry of Labor and the RJF simultaneously throughout the 1930s. In 1940 he joined the W-SS for a year with the rank of Brigadeführer, and between 1941 and 1945 he was chief of staff in Rosenberg's Office for Ideological Education. Typical of older professionals in the RJF before the war, he was well suited to get the training program launched.[20]

Stellrecht's slogans, "defense readiness" and "defense capacity," expressed the general aims of a program that concentrated on target shooting and terrain maneuvers. The emphasis fell, at first, on the development of marksmanship among HJ boys. But Stellrecht ran into a legal difficulty, since use of firearms by youngsters under eighteen was prohibited unless supervised by competent adults. This provision was circumvented when Himmler, as national police chief, reinterpreted "competent adult" to include HJ marksmanship supervisors, most of whom were seventeen and eighteen. In 1936 Himmler also began to furnish the HJ with SS trainers and weapons instructors. It marked the unobtrusive entrance of the SS into the HJ premilitary training program.[21]

Most of the marksmanship supervisors, however, were trained by the army at the HJ Rifle School in Thuringia. The success of this endeavor was partially the result of enthusiastic promotion by the famed Erwin Rommel, who for a time served as war ministry liaison. During 1937 Rommel toured HJ meetings and encampments lecturing on "German soldiering," while privately pressuring Schirach to make an agreement that would have turned the HJ into a "junior army," according to Schirach. The latter's fear of Rommel's influence led to his withdrawal from the liaison post, but an agreement was made with the army command in October 1937. More limited in scope than Rommel had wanted, it provided the HJ with several hundred marksmanship supervisors and experienced instructors for the Rifle School. By 1939 the HJ had 20,000 marksmanship supervisors.[22]

Symbolic of the growing militarization of HJ sports, new rifle ranges sprung up across the country like mushrooms, especially in smaller towns and rural areas, which had seen few of them previously. They were built on an extensive scale because Schirach had persuaded the German Municipal Association to furnish land and building materials and the NSKK, SA, and SS to supply free labor. While all party formations who helped to build them were supposed to be able to use these ranges rent-free, the HJ monopolized them. In 1938 alone some 1,250,000 HJ boys did some target-shooting, and 950,000 participated in the second annual marksmanship competition. By 1939, 51,500 boys had earned the HJ Marksmanship Medal, which required 90 percent accuracy in hitting a target from a distance of 50 meters with half of the shots being executed freehand from a prone position.[23]

Terrain maneuvers, the other side of the training coin, were less successful. Since the infantry is the queen of any army, terrain maneuvers received more attention as the war approached. But the HJ managed to train only 10,000 terrain maneuver supervisors before the war. Some of them were not fully competent, which led to fatal accidents, largely because illegal flare pistols were used by some groups during terrain games. It soon became apparent that if the premilitary training program was to be fully realized, something would have to be done about training all HJ leaders in the physical skills related to military performance in the field.[24]

Once the military command had been restructured to suit Hitler's ambitions and the new OKW was under the direction of General Keitel, the HJ no longer had to fear an army takeover. Some seven months before the outbreak of war, Schirach and Keitel came to an understanding that envisaged premilitary training for all HJ leaders. Two-week courses were set up to meet army specifications. They were conducted mainly in HJ facilities with the cost borne by OKW, which also furnished equipment and personnel, assisted by HJ marksmanship and terrain sport supervisors. The emphasis in this case fell more heavily on terrain familiarization.[25] Had this project been adopted earlier, it might have led to systematic training of the entire HJ. But the massive drafts of 1939 and 1940 put a nearly fatal squeeze on training personnel, facilities, and equipment. Determined to give every boy between sixteen and eighteen some premilitary training, the RJF resorted to use of so-called war-training leaders to replace experienced supervisors. While these new leaders were supposed to receive over one hundred hours of instruction, many were too young and inexperienced to do their jobs.[26]

New training schedules released in the fall of 1940 made it clear that the RJF remained adamantly committed to the program of preparedness and was not ready to surrender these tasks to anyone else. JV and JM were to perform physical exercises two hours a week and participate in "voluntary achievement sports" four hours a week. The latter were scheduled on Sunday morning. Those who were fourteen and fifteen had a similar schedule, whether they were students or employees, while school officials and employers were forced to provide opportunities to meet these requirements. For older boys, sixteen to eighteen, marksmanship practice and terrain maneuvers replaced conventional exercises four hours weekly. They also spent four to six hours a month in "voluntary achievement sports," which in the nature of things were more compulsory than voluntary, since peer-group pressure made volunteering a social necessity. Once every two months this older group of HJ boys was required to spend three hours participating in "terrain games," usually on Sunday afternoons.[27]

Terrain games were in some ways a unique invention, designed to exploit a typical tendency in most young boys. What red-blooded seventeen-year-old could resist the chance to express his natural inclination in the company of cohorts to romp through forest and glen, searching for opponents, defending his territory, waylaying enemies, scuffling and wrestling in wild abandon? Loosely structured, terrain games tested what boys had learned about the use of terrain and encouraged fierce group conflict by having one group assault another with the object of capturing certain symbols of victory such as hat decorations, arm bands, or swagger sticks. What Karl May, in his popular novels about cowboy and Indian warfare in the romanticized American West, had taught millions of German boys—including the young Hitler—the HJ converted into vicarious experiences. With "Indian-like maneuverability, cleverly camouflaged, with exploitation of even the smallest natural advantage, frequently through the application of a cunning sally" adept terrain gamesters outfoxed their opponents and in the process learned skills and techniques that any infantryman can appreciate. It is no wonder that terrain sports were regarded as "the queen of physical training in the HJ." Army leaders had high regard for these terrain games, remembering that the English Boy Scouts had emerged from the Boer War.[28]

Giving every boy premilitary training was difficult under existing circumstances. There were simply too many demands to satisfy. Many of the lower-ranking leaders in the HJ were employed and had to get released by employers through cumbersome procedures. Weeks spent in premilitary training were usually deducted from vacation time, which had a deleterious effect on health. The Ministry of the Interior was eager to avoid undue strain on the war economy and held the RJF to monthly quotas for premilitary training courses. The result of all this was that the HJ put only some half million boys through premilitary training in 1940 and 1941. The 23,000 "war-training leaders" and 34,000 marksmanship monitors the HJ had in 1941 were not enough to make the program comprehensive. In the HJ Region Swabia, for instance, only 5 percent of 53,728 boys between fourteen and eighteen received training in 1941, even though courses were conducted in regional leadership schools, army and air force barracks, and SS establishments on a fairly regular basis. Swabia was not an isolated case.[29]

In part these problems resulted from weak leadership in Berlin. Helmut Stellrecht left the RJF in 1940 to join the W-SS, and his replacement, Dr. Ernst Schlünder, was slow to take hold. Stellrecht had been theoretical in his approach, interested in the importance of physical education for military preparedness. Schlünder's practical and technical bent of mind reflected his background as a sports instructor. With a doctorate in physical education and as a decorated army veteran, he concentrated on premilitary training per se. Gradually Schlünder changed the Office for Physical Fitness into the Office for Premilitary Training and expanded its control to include technical training in the HJ special formations. Another change was designed to deal with the shortage of trainers, inadequate facilities, and scheduling problems by organizing a series of national training camps (RAL).[30] The HJ intended to use the RAL, largely staffed by army reservists, to prepare the various types of supervisors. Six camps were planned and three were ready by the summer of 1941, taking some 480 boys at a time in courses running for twenty-one days. For a while this arrangement functioned well enough, but the RJF soon discovered that many army trainers were trying to influence the boys politically. Schlünder was so incensed that he urged Axmann to replace army trainers with W-SS veterans.[31]

Suffering from chronic personnel shortages, the SS could not immediately second the sixty trainers it had promised to send to the RAL. Yet the SS slipped into the premilitary training program by way of the back door. In numerous localities scattered throughout the country, individual SS units assisted the HJ by providing sports instructors, gymnastics coaches, and exercise supervisors. This had been done through most of the late 1930s. Himmler, at one point, personally ordered the ORPO and SD to supply the HJ with marksmanship instructors. The SS, as has been mentioned, was a major contributor to the building of new rifle ranges. Gottlob Berger's Main SS Office transferred at least 160 trainers to the HJ before 1942. In HJ Region Swabia the SS ran one series of training courses at rural police headquarters in Kempten. There may have been others in Swabia, and there certainly were similar courses in other HJ Regions. These SS trainers provided the basis for more systematic SS involvement in subsequent years.[32]

### Organization of the WEL and the Intrusion of the SS

Early in 1942 it had become apparent that something fairly drastic would have to be done if premilitary training for older teenagers was ever to be universal. Since the RAL seemed to function well for the training of supervisors and leaders, Schlünder concluded that similar facilities should be organized to train the vast number of HJ boys between sixteen and eighteen. Putting every boy in the group through twenty-one days of concentrated training was an enormous task requiring the equivalent of legislative action. In Nazi Germany a decree by Hitler, issued on 13 March 1942, was sufficient to set the wheels in motion.[33] The Wehrertüchtigungslager der Hitler-Jugend (WEL) thus created proved to be a successful innovation in terms of meeting what the Nazis felt to be necessary psychological conditioning for military combat. In a way, they were ideologically charged basic training camps, less pragmatic, technical, and brutal than such camps for older draftees usually are, but more effective in fostering the attitudes that make military service more than a tolerable endurance test.

Building on a decade of physical fitness training, Schlünder structured the WEL to deemphasize their military purpose by highlighting values appropriate to the age of the trainees. Foremost among these were promotion of physical health and dexterity, nurturing manly character and self-confidence, and the old goals of "combat readiness" and "combat capacity" first declared by Stellrecht. By "development of character," Schlünder had certain natural "emotional and spiritual tendencies" in mind that could be conditioned to create a "happy willingness to make decisions." "Nurturing combat readiness" was regarded by him as "a basic law of life," which he claimed had made the HJ "more imbued with martial virtues and enthusiasm for military service at the beginning of the war than any other youth in the world."[34]

The organization of the camps proceeded rapidly. As Hitler had indicated, administration, discipline, and indoctrination were left in the hands of the RJF. Camp directors were mostly wounded army officers and W-SS veterans with substantial experience as leaders in the HJ. Trainers were army and SS NCOs with reserve status or on temporary domestic assignment while recovering from battle wounds. The RJF conducted an orientation conference for WEL personnel early in April, and Axmann announced that attendance of the camps was to be regarded as an order from the Führer. To avoid "straining the war economy," Axmann demanded apprentices use their vacation time to complete the training. His claim that schedules would allow for sufficient rest, implying that time spent in a WEL could be regarded in part as a vacation, hardly fit subsequent developments. He felt compelled to say it, to sweeten what was a bitter pill to swallow for many overburdened teenagers.[35]

Government ministries and party agencies cooperated to get the camps established as soon as possible. Regional HJ leaders were made responsible for induction in two stages, an alert order followed several weeks later by the actual call-up. This allowed employed youth to apply for leave and employees to ask for postponement if factory conditions required it. Changes were granted by local labor offices on the recommendations of armaments bureaus, food offices, or industrial and commercial boards. Secondary school students were drafted for courses corporately during summer vacations, while students at technical schools and teacher training institutions took their training during semester breaks. If some tried to avoid the courses, the "youth service law" could be used to force compliance. Without consulting parents, the police could deliver recalcitrant boys to the camps or penalize them. Transportation costs were borne by the state, and accident insurance was provided by the HJ. The Labor Ministry extended vacation periods if they were used for training, and the Interior and Economics Ministries ordered that no vacations be granted unless youngsters presented alert orders, so as to avoid the use of leaves for other purposes. All of these measures combined made it difficult to evade WEL training.[36]

The training cycle began on 10 May 1942. By the end of the following year the HJ operated a total of 226 WELs and seventeen RALs. Another twenty-seven national camps conducted specialized training for youths from occupied countries. By the end of 1943 nearly every boy of seventeen was undergoing premilitary training, while 361,477 youngsters had earned the "war-training certificate" and 141,322 had received the more prestigious HJ Achievement Medal. Nearly 60,000 boys had performed well enough to be

classified as "war-training leaders." The youngsters in the special formations earned a variety of certificates appropriate to their particular expertise—6,610, for instance, had earned driver's licenses. Roughly 10 percent
of the boys went through the training experience without mastering the
basic skills required to graduate "with results." But on the whole the WELs
had turned out to be a successful way to implement universal premilitary
training for Germany's adolescent population.[37] It was a testimony to
Schlünder's organizational ability and to the dedicated WEL inspectors he
appointed to keep the camps functioning properly. The post of chief inspector for a time was held by Willi Blomquist, who assumed an HJ administrative appointment in the Netherlands and was replaced by Gerhard
Hein in December 1942. Later regional inspectors were appointed to help
maintain the quality of training and to correct deviations from RJF guidelines.[38]

Hein came close to exemplifying the heroic ideal propagandized relent-
lessly by HJ leaders during the war. He came from modest social circumstances, was an old HJ leader, and a highly decorated veteran of both army
and W-SS. He was born in Upper Silesia into a family of miners, which he
himself had intended to become until he joined the local HJ in 1931, then the
Labor Service in 1933, and finally the new army in 1936. He did not join the
party until 1936, but his commitment to the ideals of the HJ came to the fore
in 1938 when he decided to attend a Land Service Leadership School, after
which he became an LD camp director in rural Schleswig-Holstein. His
agrarian career was cut short by the draft in September 1939. In the western
campaign he earned all the preliminary medals and the Oak Leaves for
the Knight's Cross in short order. Then in the eastern campaign he was
wounded three times, making him more suitable for the home front.
Meanwhile, he had attained the rank of captain and was now ideally prepared to assume the post of chief inspector. In that capacity he played an
important role in recruiting and training the Hitler Youth Division of the
W-SS. He was so enthused about this unit that he left the inspectorate and
took command of a battalion in the Twenty-sixth Regiment during its
heavy engagement on the Normandy front. Hein's career was one the HJ
tried to have emulated through the instrumentality of the WEL.[39]

Schlünder and Hein tried to make the WEL experience a meaningful
contribution to a boy's readiness for combat and the hard life of a soldier.
Hein spent many hours on the rifle ranges and field installations of the
camps, easily associating with boys for whom such personal contact with
certified war heroes was probably more effective than endless lectures and
drills. But for Gottlob Berger, Himmler's Pied Piper, the WELs were little

Gerhard Hein, inspector of WEL, and Germanic trainees from northern Europe (Bundesarchiv Koblenz)

more than recruiting corrals. Shortly after Hitler issued his decree, Berger persuaded Schlünder to set aside at least one camp in every HJ Region for the exclusive use of the SS, which provided all of the trainers and thus had ample opportunity to recruit for the W-SS.[40]

The SS staffed forty camps by August 1942 with roughly 500 trainers, most of whom were qualified veterans supplied by Hans Jüttner's W-SS Operations Office, but at least 135 of them were old NCOs rejected by field divisions whom Berger commandeered and tried to turn into trainers. These hard-bitten and embittered characters were wholly unsuited for dealing with young boys, alienated many of them, and created widespread animosity toward the SS. At the insistence of the RJF, Berger tried to counter this unanticipated development by preparing future SS trainers in a special orientation program run by SS Colonel Herbert Edler von Daniels and SS Captain Paul Ehlert. Once this got underway the performance of SS trainers improved, although the damaged SS image was hard to repair.[41]

Two things complicated HJ-SS relations. One was a conflict between Berger and Jüttner. The other was a deliberate policy of the RJF, which filled the SS camps with troublemakers in the hope that stern methods and fanatic indoctrination would improve HJ discipline. The Jüttner-Berger conflict forced the latter to scour the SS for men no one wanted and use them as trainers. Thus the worst SS men and problem HJ boys confronted each other in many camps, creating extraordinary problems and more than one scandal. Jüttner and Berger represented two types of personalities in the SS, the technical realist versus the ideological enthusiast. While both were interested in the recruitment possibilities of the camps— in itself a potential source of conflict with the RJF, which put effective premilitary training first—Jüttner was not persuaded the camps would increase the number of SS volunteers. Supplying trainers for 42 SS camps compared with the army's 120 was unrealistic, in Jüttner's view, when the W-SS constituted only 3 percent of army strength. Furthermore, most of the 90,000 youths who filtered through these forty camps were compelled to join the army because of OKW's quota system. Since the W-SS needed 10,000 NCOs in 1942, the 500 trainers seconded to the WELs represented an unnecessarily "heavy sacrifice." Jüttner wanted to reduce SS camps to fifteen, but Berger adamantly pushed to get more of them.[42]

Berger blamed unsatisfactory recruitment on the deliberate policy of the RJF, which, "in complete misunderstanding of the situation, sent precisely to SS camps the most unreliable types, especially those with religious inclinations and those who wanted to become parsons." Berger had no quarrel with the antireligious policies of the HJ, but he was not about to support these policies at the expense of SS recruitment. He was able to demonstrate that his aim of opening new recruitment opportunities through the WEL program was beginning to bear fruit. In one camp near Linz, where his trainers had come under heavy criticism because of their degrading methods, nearly 50 percent of the boys joined the W-SS. In response to a searing SD report on the insensitive behavior of SS trainers in the Linz camp, Berger did weed out the worst offenders and placed more emphasis on careful preparation of other SS trainers. He also cultivated HJ goodwill by supplying them with vehicles and gasoline from his shrinking rations. The RJF, in turn, agreed to stop its policy of sending problem boys to SS camps, although Schlünder refused to follow Berger's sarcastic suggestion of "sticking all varieties of priests in the camps of the army" and sending him more "farm boys and sons of workers from the cities."[43]

Appalled by the Linz SD report and incensed with the debilitating feud between Jüttner and Berger, Himmler demanded that Berger correct his trainers, since "especially with the HJ we must always put our best foot forward." Himmler refused to follow Jüttner's suggestion and insisted the latter change his negative attitude toward the WELs, at least one of which had to be kept under SS control in each HJ Region. A reduction in SS camps nevertheless occurred after the fall of 1943, when the RJF agreed to send to them only members of the HJ Patrol Service and boys who had already been found to be suitable for the SS.[44]

The reduction of SS camps from forty-two to thirty was made up by Berger in other ways. The W-SS was rapidly becoming a multinational elite guard with thousands of recruits and conscripts flooding the ranks from Northern, Western, and Eastern Europe. A study commissioned by Berger revealed a tempting pool of draft-age youth: 78,430 in Norway, 65,401 in Denmark, 246,636 in the Netherlands, and 204,344 in Belgium. In a joint effort with Helmut Möckel, Berger convinced Himmler and Hitler to set up special WELs for Germanic youths willing to join the W-SS. By the fall of 1943 three camps for youths from Norway, Denmark, the Netherlands, and Belgium had been established on German soil. Another four camps were arranged for ethnic German boys from the Ukraine, Estonia, Czechoslovakia, Hungary, and Croatia. Aided by local fascist youth leaders, this program met with remarkable success and helped to swell the ranks of the W-SS.[45]

The SS share of the HJ premilitary training program far exceeded the relative size of the W-SS. With thirty-one WELs staffed by the SS in 1944, it had 13 percent of them under its control. With roughly 700 trainers in the field, as compared to OKW's 3,000 in 200 camps, the SS provided 23 percent of the total training personnel. These statistics do not include the seven WELs for Germanics and ethnics, two national training camps for NCOs, two for specialists from the Signal HJ, one for motor and driver training at Buchenwald, one for mountain training at Rautz on the Arlberg, and one national camp for the training of SRD leaders. Since the W-SS took in only 3 percent of the armed forces, it is clear that Berger's policy enabled the SS to gain a disproportionately large opportunity to influence the HJ and recruit in their midst.[46]

**Character of Camp Directors and Trainers**

The character of camp directors and trainers had a significant impact on the effectiveness of premilitary training, its immediate impression on the youthful trainee, and his subsequent performance in battle. As a group they were young men under thirty, with backgrounds as HJ leaders and front-line service with the army or W-SS. Directors were professional youth leaders with relatively brief military experience; their main loyalty was to the HJ organization. Trainers were army or SS NCOs in their early twenties, most of whom had HJ experience as lower-ranking leaders. They were basically professional soldiers, assigned to WEL training because of wounds sustained in combat. After a while many were recalled to active duty, thus creating considerable turnover.

In general, army trainers were better prepared, more experienced, and temperamentally better suited to work with teenagers than their SS counterparts, many of whom lacked significant combat experience and revealed minimal sympathy for the HJ ethos. The contrast came into sharp focus in the Linz SD report. Made in the fall of 1942, that analysis was based on several WELs near Linz. Contrary to general practice, one large Linz camp had a mixture of army and SS trainers, thus inviting unavoidable comparisons, from which the SS emerged as definite loser. Most army and air force trainers were fine soldiers, who dropped the conventional "barracks mentality" when they became trainers and adjusted themselves to the camp community with its specific HJ character. As a result they worked congenially with HJ leaders and still maintained soldierly qualities. Most SS trainers, however, remained coarse and insensitive, frequently displaying a defiant, egotistical, and swaggering image that many boys found unpalatable. And yet "one would have expected something very extraordinary from the Waffen-SS," one HJ leader mused sardonically.[47]

HJ and SS trainers in a premilitary training camp (Bundesarchiv Koblenz)

Army recruiters, even generals and Iron Cross medalists, carefully ingratiated themselves with HJ leaders by adopting appropriate formalities, while SS recruiters, mostly lower ranks, inspected and propagandized with "an unhappy and decidedly vulgar air" about them. One SS officer addressed HJ boys in the manner of a "market huckster," condemning those who refused to volunteer as "cowardly dogs and misfits." As a group, SS trainers in one camp refused to adjust to camp life, demeaned the HJ, and failed to submit to the discipline of HJ superiors. The SD informers claimed that the inappropriate behavior of SS trainers had affected recruitment, but Berger later insisted that precisely in the WEL where this type of behavior had prevailed half of the boys decided for the W-SS. Obviously many boys were either intimidated or impressed with the macho image of the SS.[48]

The character of SS trainers can be extrapolated by analyzing the correspondence of one camp director, Kurt Ziegler, who was in the unusual situation of being an army reservist but working throughout most of his term of three years with SS trainers. We can see the SS trainer here through the eyes and values of an army colleague, who by all appearances was one of the best administrators the HJ had. Ziegler headed the Unter-

joch WEL in the mountainous region of southern Swabia in 1942 and thereafter WEL Harburg in northern Swabia. In his profuse correspondence,
Ziegler, who had been severely wounded in battle, revealed egoism, enthusiasm, and much of the surrealistic wartime ethos in the consuming
quest for combat manpower.[49]

When Ziegler took over Unterjoch in August 1942, the camp was staffed
with ten SS trainers who were eager to serve, but only seven of whom had
seen active military duty. In terms of personality and experience, all were
less qualified than army trainers in Swabian camps. The senior SS trainer
at Unterjoch came from Berlin and had a difficult time adjusting to the
mountainous terrain and the isolation of the camp. He was slow in developing empathy with local boys. Being an experienced youth leader, Ziegler managed to improve the performance of his SS trainers and stimulate
cooperation between trainers and trainees. SS trainers met their severest
challenge in training farm boys who had never engaged in organized
physical exercises. Yet the SS preferred recruits from the country, officially
because of its blood and soil ideology, but realistically because young rus-
tics were more susceptible to indoctrination. In this instance Ziegler
shared the official SS attitude, while his trainers appeared unaware of SS
ideology.[50]

Ziegler's encouragement of congeniality between SS and army was not
practiced at the top. Annual workshops for senior WEL trainers were held
separately under the auspices of the Main SS Office, OKW, and the Air
Force Command. In Bavaria army reserve authorities even objected to
indiscriminate mixing of trainers in the same WEL. In most regions SS
trainers were segregated, but not in Swabia. Ziegler took his SS contingent with him to Harburg in the spring of 1943. Since most trainers at
Harburg were SS men, Ziegler should have been replaced, but the available W-SS veterans were not qualified. One was no more than a clerk and
the other had been fired because of unexplained absences. At Harburg
Ziegler had to contend with a nearly continuous turnover of SS training
personnel. As soon as Ziegler had them oriented, the SS Recruiting Office
transferred his trainers to active field units or other camps. The army and
air force could afford to select better men and keep them in the camps
longer. They also rewarded trainers for good work and promoted them
with greater rapidity. This disadvantaged SS trainers and hurt their image
with the HJ. In one instance an SS private had to be replaced because he
abused the relative freedom of camp life by "odorous exploits with the
opposite sex." An SS corporal had to be transferred because his utterly

lethargic conduct made him somewhat less than an inspiration to the boys under his care.[51]

More serious than these peccadillos was Ziegler's inability to get along with the senior SS trainer assigned to him, Josef Gartner. As a single son Gartner had been deferred from active duty and made a career for himself in the A-SS and the Death's Head Units. Ten years as a concentration camp guard was indeed strange preparation for training teenage boys, as Ziegler pointed out. Gartner was devious, manipulative, and primarily interested in advancing his career, although not entirely without talent. He had been a ski instructor and staff sergeant of an A-SS battalion. In his evaluations Ziegler deplored Gartner's crude way of dealing with trainers and trainees. In his frequent trips to Berlin, Gartner used a friend in the Main SS Office to have himself appointed director of a new WEL in the Tirol. Ziegler was incensed, because Gartner used the occasion to denigrate Ziegler's austere personality and inflated HJ loyalties. Gartner had never been in the HJ. He and Ziegler symbolized the conflict between two extremes in the character of camp directors and premilitary trainers: the amoral, semitalented career-hunter versus the deeply committed, naively sincere patriot.[52]

When, because of personnel shortages, the SS decided to pare down its WELs to one for every two HJ Regions, the SS training contingent at Harburg was phased out. It was in Ziegler's nature to make one final comradely request. He wanted week-long leaves for his departing trainers and to celebrate their association with an early Christmas party and an excursion into the mountains. All past rivalries apparently forgotten, Josef Gartner offered the facilities at his camp on the Arlberg. Ziegler's party included the entire regional staff and army and SS liaison officers. The mayor of Augsburg joined the festivities and brought along seventy-five bottles of fine wine.[53]

Early in 1944 Berger and Axmann agreed to staff the SS camps only with NCOs who had been HJ leaders. Purportedly this was done to clarify "disciplinary subordination," but in reality it was an unavoidable move to improve the quality of SS trainers and to make them more competitive with those of the regular army and air force. Berger promised that no more transfers would be ordered unless absolutely necessary and that such necessities would be determined by HJ authorities. Emphasis on pure sports was renewed by providing every camp with a sport trainer prepared in RJF sport schools. From the spring of 1944 inductions for SS camps were based on lists of SRD members and W-SS volunteers. In this way the SS guaranteed that HJ trainees in its camps were already committed to service with the Black Corps when they began their premilitary training.[54]

## Curriculum, Discipline, and Morale in the WEL

True to its purpose, the curriculum of the WELs incorporated an exaggerated Darwinian ideology infused with the youthful élan of the HJ, physical exercises highlighting its combative ethos, and the basic techniques of war making. Individual prowess and inner resolve was fostered within the general context of group solidarity and communal responsibility. As in sports, teamwork was the essence of the soldierly game. Orderly procedures, promptness, and cleanliness were thought of as essential virtues of the good warrior. Every trainee had to realize that the common good took precedence over individual interests and learn to practice genuine camaraderie in his daily affairs. This emphasis on orderliness helped to instill a sense of discipline, unquestioning obedience, and clear subordination. "Troop-like drills" were avoided, not only because they were inappropriate for young boys, but also because they were less practical than exercises designed to instill martial attitudes. While "natural tendencies to excess" were restrained, endurance and toughness were the primary goals.[55]

Ideology assumed special significance for teenagers about to fight a war consciously styled as a struggle of ideas. Much of the curriculum was devoted to strengthening basic Nazi precepts. Lectures on martial political themes, lively group discussions, and elaborate patriotic ceremonials were all structured to have maximum psychological impact. A uniform weekly lecture, prepared in Berlin, was delivered by camp directors and served as theme and motto around which other weekly activities were patterned. The first week's theme, "We Fight," conveyed a feeling for war as nature's ineluctable law and the central role wars have played in the lives of dominant peoples. "We Sacrifice," the second week's motto, sought to engender a sense of total personal commitment to the point of giving up one's life. "If you never put your life on the line, you will never learn to live" was a dictum repeated ad nauseam. The final week's motto, "We Triumph," glorified "the Greater German struggle for freedom," the historic eastern migration of the German people, and the specific aims of the current war as implementations of Germany's historic mission to civilize the barbaric East.[56]

After every evening meal there was a "political hour" consisting of questions put to trainees to test their knowledge of current political events and the progress of the various fronts. Later in the evening the more articulate boys led bull sessions. As relatively open exchanges of opinion, these discussions were intended to imbed in the consciousness of trainees essential points stressed in lectures and during the day's training. It is doubtful that many boys remained immune to this ideological blitz and gradually came to accept ideas they might have rejected in normal circumstances. While indoctrination per se took only 14 hours out of a total training schedule of 166 hours, the basic notions permeated the entire curriculum whether it was implemented in the barracks, on the shooting range, exercise area, or field. Nothing was left to chance. Even some nine hours of "free time" were supervised.[57]

Since this was not basic training but rather intensive orientation designed to awaken a boy's "instinctive identity with nature," nearly half of the allotted time was taken up with terrain exercises. These included night training, patrolling, and terrain games. Instinctive reactions to signs of danger and opportunity were to be sharpened so that human actions were hardly distinguishable from those of animals in their natural habitat. Gerhard Hein believed if there were no physical contact or group conflict in the fields and woods, the terrain games would lose their intrinsic appeal for hyperactive teenagers. WEL training thus "released natural youthful propensities, polished innate adroitness, strengthened the will to endure hardships, and taught youngsters to be self-reliant and confident."[58] These qualities were most useful when combined with skillful handling of the soldier's best friend, the rifle. Use and care of small caliber weapons and target shooting took up another fourth of the training time. From age ten these boys had practiced shooting with air guns, and after fifteen, with small caliber guns. WEL training perfected this experience and shortened the time devoted to it during basic training. The Nazis were driven to this concentration on shooting skills by the relatively poor performance of young German soldiers in World War I. To round off premilitary training, fourteen hours were devoted to physical exercises, six hours to first aid instruction, and four hours to housekeeping.[59]

For boys of sixteen and seventeen these were difficult goals to reach, requiring strong motivation and persistent effort. Schlünder and Hein were clever enough to structure training in a way that capitalized on the native play element. Although channeled to serious ends, an air of "roughhousing" was not absent from effective training. An array of rewards helped to make it attractive to most and endurable to all. Not only was the food rich and generous, but medals were handed out liberally. Nearly everyone earned the war-training certificate, and the best shots received the Marksmanship Medal. The most prized award was the HJ Achievement Medal, normally earned after lengthy and faithful service in HJ units, but now awarded to the best trainees after three weeks of intensified physical and mental exertions. Those boys whose native talent for leadership had been brought out during training were given the War-Training Leader Certificate. Competition for these and other medals, in itself conducive to good morale, was so strong that it occasioned considerable jealousy and led to complaints from leaders of regular HJ groups who feared their own programs would be affected.[60]

While discipline varied from camp to camp, in general it proved to be more of a problem in camps staffed by the SS, who proclaimed themselves relentless disciplinarians. SS trainers in a WEL near Mönchen-Gladbach submitted teenage boys to the kind of discipline one might have expected to find in a penal institution. From morning until night they were drilled and harangued in a merciless fashion, frequently receiving "kicks in the pants." Noon rest periods were shortened, and other HJ regulations were completely ignored in the effort to turn awkward teenagers into men of precision. The result was that morale was shaken beyond repair. Trainers in the camp featured in the Linz SD report reaped the fruits of harsh discipline by having to contend with collective animosity toward the SS. Klaus Granzow found the tight discipline of the SS camp he attended literally unbearable. One of his colleagues on guard duty one night slipped a girl into the guardhouse and received a severe prison sentence. For his bad performance on the shooting range, Granzow was humiliated in front of his fellow trainees by the SS training superior. As an army officer candidate, Granzow suffered maltreatment by SS trainers, who seemed to regard him and his fellow secondary school students as natural enemies. Not only SS trainers occasionally resorted to extreme measures. "Tests of courage" were set up by forcing nonswimmers to jump into deep water and compelling clumsy boys to attempt difficult feats of gymnastics.[61]

The WEL were conscious attempts to simulate the conditions of actual combat. The 200-odd boys in each camp were separated into HJ groups in imitation of tactical squads and platoons, with appropriate leaders selected by trainers, who drove them constantly to be the very best. To encourage reliance on each other and to cut any remaining apron strings, the camps were wrapped in ominous secrecy and nearly total isolation. Trainers were forbidden to house their spouses on the grounds or in nearby towns. Some camp directors prepared innocuously optimistic form letters that trainees were ordered to copy and send home. While Schlünder prohibited this form of thought control, he clamped censorship on all correspondence in

1943. It was done to prevent disaffected trainees from exaggerating unpleasant incidents, but probably also to prevent increasing war-weariness of parents from infecting the boys and weakening morale. Leaves or visits to local movie theaters were rare and usually led to conspicuous behavior.[62]

Demonstrating that boys will be boys, no matter what regulations may exist, many of them rebelled against constricting rules. It was not unusual for camp directors to put from 5 to 10 percent of a course contingent temporarily in guarded custody. At Harburg, Kurt Ziegler—by comparison with SS camp directors a mild disciplinarian—found that some boys incurred disciplinary measures in order to enjoy the relative comforts of the indoors during inclement weather. He asked that the disciplinary regulations be loosened so that he could have a freer hand to deal with infractions in a discretionary manner. Existing rules gave him little guidance in dealing with boys who revealed negative attitudes, slept through ideological lectures, or could not be stimulated to participate enthusiastically. He recommended official approval of stronger disciplinary measures in order to avoid resort to "illegal use" of extreme coercion, a bit of typical Zieglerian sophistry that escaped the bureaucrats in Berlin.[63]

The RJF refused to allow stronger penalties than house arrest. In fact, Dr. Richard Liebenow, chief physician of the HJ, was concerned that insensitive trainers might put excessive physical demands on growing teenage boys. He warned camp directors that army duty regulations were designed for adults and no more than 25 percent of the physical demands of these regulations could reasonably be applied in the camps. He reminded trainers that they were dealing with Hitler youths, not recruits. It was more important to stress combat performance than the highest possible physical achievement.[64] The health of trainees was a major concern of most camp administrators if not most trainers. All camps had resident doctors or Red Cross nurses who examined the boys regularly. Dental deficiencies, which were prevalent in some groups during the end of the war, were corrected before the boys left camp. As one might have expected, the SS, claiming a shortage of medical officers, was less concerned with health problems. But in general WEL trainees probably received better medical attention than most of the civilian population. Their food rations certainly were better than most civilians enjoyed, since they received the same rations as military personnel not in combat. Camp directors reported that most of the trainees gained weight despite constant physical exertions.[65]

Good food and medical care, fair treatment by trainers for most trainees, the excitement and encouragement of engaging in war games with age-group cohorts—all worked together to maintain discipline and good morale. Most of the thousands of boys who filtered through the WEL during the three years of its existence had been so thoroughly indoctrinated that they honestly believed in the necessity of premilitary training and willingly accepted the challenges it presented. Many probably merely endured it because there was no escape from it without drastic consequences. A few found it utterly unbearable.

Some disaffected boys were prepared to express their opposition, particularly against SS trainers. Karl Jochem and Peter Ledermann, never especially enamored with the party or the HJ, freely expressed their anti-Nazi feelings and then joined the SS division made up exclusively of Hitler Youths to save themselves from punishment. Jacob Geri had volunteered for the HJD but reneged when SS trainers suggested he leave the Catholic church. Ziegler thought his request to be released should be granted since he could not imagine a religious person like Geri functioning as a W-SS officer. Robert Kaap, on the other hand, devised a clever scheme to escape from a WEL at Hauenstein in Baden. Kaap persuaded a friend, Andreas Edighoffer, to send a telegram to the camp director, saying that Kaap's mother was very ill and required his assistance at home. Unfortunately, the director checked the story and found out that Mrs. Kaap had died some time ago. Kaap was immediately demoted and put in jail, while co-conspirator Edighoffer was merely thrown out of the HJ orchestra, after showing abject remorse. Kaap and Edighoffer regretted that the HJ had become militaristic and found WEL training utterly repulsive. Edighoffer later told Kaap that he felt they "had to support each other" if they were to survive in an unsympathetic world, run by "the artists of death." "This noon I wrote for a few hours in the forest," he went on, "and thought deeply. I submit myself to life indifferently. I read Rousseau and other 'prophets' . . . but . . . I cannot imagine any life more boring."[66]

The sharpest expression of the kind of animosity SS trainers were capable of stimulating came from a boy who underwent premilitary training at WEL Mausbach near Stolberg in HJ Region Cologne-Aachen. He sent this unsigned letter to training superior SS Sergeant Georg Lanninger:

> Finally we have reached precious freedom again. These three weeks were for all of us a living hell. If I should ever meet one of you trainers at night, I would beat the shit out of you, so that you would never again dare to mishandle freedom-loving people. A time will come when we will even scores with you SS swine. Then no SS big-shot will escape with his life. It would have been better for you to have stayed on the Eastern Front. But it always happens that the biggest pigs and dogs bum

around behind the front and enslave free people. Few of us volunteered for the SS because we despise this pigsty and because I carried on effective hate propaganda against you. You will not find out who I am, because you are too stupid. Hopefully you have the courage to read this letter to the other SS big-shots. Now I have a request: please stop SS Corporal Bohr's dumb ideological lectures! That is the greatest nonsense I have ever heard. So, this is about the impression we have of you and your camp.

> Greetings in the name of God,
> [Signed] A free German.[67]

This remarkable example of insight and courage, unfortunately, is not typical. Letters written by other trainees to SS men in the same camp express satisfaction with the training, even enjoyment. Heinz Steeg wrote to SS Sergeant Alberts thanking the trainer for turning him into "a real fellow," something "the stupid rhetoric of the schools" had never been able to do. Steeg was prepared to return for another stint. Much the same attitude was expressed by Hubert Hudgen who wrote SS-Sturmmann Kopp in an adulatory and respectful vein, saying that they had "all been very satisfied with camp life, especially with the trainers." Having heard only "gruesome" tales about the SS before coming to Mausbach, Hudgen "had learned to know SS men in the camp to be quite different individuals." "A better camaraderie of both boys and soldiers," Hudgen said, he "had never experienced before." Even Klaus Granzow, who was no friend of the SS, admitted that SS trainers, for whose intelligence he had little respect, had helped to make him "harder, more self-assured, and courageous." He was glad to be rid of his "formerly soft and dreamy tendencies."[68]

As far as Lanninger's correspondent is concerned, he undoubtedly had been influenced by the surprisingly persistent anti-SS sentiment in many areas during the war, and an equally unexpected pacifism among students. At thirty Lanninger was older, better educated, less opportunistic, and more committed to the elitist ideology of the SS and its cultural pretensions than most SS trainers, essentially technicians of war and ideological conflict. Lanninger was a good leader and effective teacher, according to his superior, the chief of the SS Recruiting Station in Düsseldorf, who gave him three months leave to finish his studies and take the examination for toll inspectors. Lanninger, who was subsequently promoted and encouraged to become even more assiduous in his indoctrination efforts, told his superior that the anonymous letter "shocked him deeply" and blamed it on the prevalent religious antipathy toward the SS in that western region of the Ruhr. As a result, Lanninger never missed a chance to talk to his boys about the "mission of the SS"—even during pauses in terrain games.[69]

The curriculum of the WEL highlighted those aspects of the HJ physical fitness program that lent themselves to maximum preparation for military combat and compressed those elements into an intensified and demanding three-week schedule. To achieve the mental, emotional, and physical results desired, it was necessary to impose strict discipline and control without crushing initiative and enthusiasm. Instances of minor indiscipline and prankish rebellion merely demonstrate that discipline was generally maintained. With the notable exception of a few sensational reactions to inept SS trainers, morale in the WELs was probably higher than it was in the civilian population.

**Waffen-SS Recruitment in the WEL**

Relying on the WELs for recruits, the SS constantly carped about inadequate results. The disproportionately large number of SS camps, nevertheless, made a significant contribution to W-SS expansion after 1942. Camp Harburg in Swabia may serve as an example. Between April and December 1943, 1,735 boys passed through Harburg; 1,424 of these were seventeen, 291 were only sixteen, and the remaining twenty were eighteen and nineteen. Out of the total, 690 were classified as "war volunteers," while the rest decided to wait for the draft. Among those who decided to volunteer in the camp, 173 opted for the army and 133 for the W-SS, but another 200 had already committed themselves to the SS before they arrived at Harburg, and 184 had done so for the army. Thus nearly 50 percent of the boys decided to volunteer and capitalize on the prestige and choice of unit that entailed. Since the SS managed to get 48 percent of the volunteers in a camp run by an army veteran and in part staffed by army trainers, there was little reason for the SS to complain. In camps staffed entirely by the SS and directed by HJ leaders who were SS veterans, almost all joined the W-SS.[70]

Recruitment in SS camps was assiduous. Camp directors and trainers pitched for volunteers during so-called free hours, at lunch time, and during afternoon breaks. At night trainers visited the sleeping quarters with pen and paper in hand. Movies and lectures by agents of SS recruiting stations were arranged by HJ regional leaders on a regular basis. Winners of the coveted Knight's Cross were frequent visitors. Their colorful accounts of individual exploits and valorous deeds hardly ever failed to induce raptured attention and produced scores of new recruits.[71]

Since the SS could not draft soldiers, it depended completely on volunteers. This frequently led to appeals and methods that bordered on coercion. Officially both HJ and SS forbade threat and force. They even prohibited musterings on camp grounds in the effort to make enlistment genuinely voluntary. The RJF was concerned that those who chose to enlist in the army or air force would not be discriminated against by the SS, yet that was precisely what happened in many camps with SS training personnel. Klaus Granzow confided these bitter feelings to his diary on 25 July 1943:

> Few in our group volunteered for the SS. The SS sergeant appears every day in our rooms. . . . Klaus Odefey and I then immediately leave the room, since we have both signed up to become officer candidates in the army. They cannot force us into the SS. The others in our group have until tomorrow to think it over. Then they will probably be forced to sign up. In other groups most of the boys signed up with the W-SS for twelve years. They can choose their own type of service. Most of them choose tank units. They will now push a light load and have an easy time. Only we officer candidates will be further pushed around. That is absolutely wrong. Why are those of us who are going into the army treated worse than the boys who are pulled into the SS? Are we not all fighting for Germany, the same Fatherland?[72]

The prejudicial behavior of SS trainers forced Schlünder to exclude them from active recruitment late in 1943. Their relationship to the trainees was thus no longer soured by the need to produce volunteers. But camp directors frequently resorted to devious schemes.[73]

Fritz Reinbacher, a camp director in Swabia, began the first day with a speech that stressed volunteering as a denial of the enemy's claim that German youth was war-weary and as a declaration of manful honor. Besides, voluntary enlistment would open opportunities for postwar careers. In the evening all boys wrote papers on Reinbacher's theme, the best receiving prizes, and outstanding compositions were read and discussed. Those who wrote "nonsense" had to keep their papers a while longer. Made conspicuous, they became the object of general merriment and disapproval. By casually referring to unacceptable papers, Reinbacher created fear of consequences. This produced continuous talk about volunteering. Those who did not volunteer were forced by peer-group pressure to explain themselves. Later Reinbacher once more used collective pressure when the papers of those who still had not volunteered were collected, read aloud, and discussed in an acrimonious fashion. Holdouts were informed that their themes would go into HJ files so that no one could claim ignorance. At this, many of the most adamant begged permission to revise their themes. Reinbacher did not press them further, except to ask that the volunteers assist the nonvolunteers in revising compositions. Another well-timed speech by Reinbacher painted scenes of Germans turned into slaves by victorious barbarians. "Is it not better then," he cried, "to spend a few years in combat than to submit to this Jew-ridden rabble?" Conquering Russians would murder more people than Germany was losing in the war. Real fellows would rather be partisans than submit to a foreign yoke. Such dire events could be avoided if all had the resolution to fight and to win. A somber atmosphere having been created, all joined in singing, "When rotting bones do quiver and quake," and went off to bed. The next morning more application papers arrived, and Reinbacher claimed they were "truly voluntary."[74]

Reinbacher's scheme was recommended, since it usually harvested around 80 percent of the course contingent. Most recruiters sent to the camps by the SS were less successful. One such case was recorded by Swabian camp director Karl Waiblinger. In anticipation of a visit by an SS recruiter, Waiblinger carefully prepared his trainees by stressing the crucial role of the W-SS, focusing on the "honor" and "challenge" that would require "regular guys" who would enjoy a "glorious fellowship in the true Nazi spirit." But the recruiting corporal blabbered about specific advantages in the W-SS not to be had in the army. Few boys volunteered, leading a humiliated Waiblinger to suggest he "could do without such characters."[75]

The best ambassador the SS had was probably Corporal Fritz Christen. As the first SS enlisted man to receive the Knight's Cross, he had been decorated by the Führer himself. A gunner in the Death's Head Division, Christen was the sole survivor of his battery when he held off repeated Russian tank assaults. Under constant fire, without food and water, carrying shells from knocked out batteries at night, he blazed away at Soviet tanks and infantry during the day. After seventy-two hours of a living inferno, he had destroyed thirteen tanks and killed almost one hundred men. This feat made him an instant celebrity, although it was not atypical of the abandon with which SS soldiers fought, particularly in the notorious division of concentration camp guards.[76] Christen repeatedly toured WELs with great success. In August 1944 he visited Harburg and the regional leadership schools in Swabia, telling colorful stories of war in Russia and harvesting large numbers of volunteers for the W-SS even at that late date. Unaware that many of his fellow soldiers were criminals, HJ boys responded to his appeals with greater enthusiasm than high ranking officers were able to evoke. His low rank conveyed the impression that even common soldiers could earn fame and glory.[77]

## The Impact and Value of Premilitary Training

Army leaders were the first to acknowledge the achievements of the HJ in preparing recruits for the battlefield. The Army Personnel Office collected evidence which revealed that young men who had held leadership positions in the HJ were "the most qualified candidates for the officer corps." Soldiers in the technical support units invariably had gotten a head start in the WEL. Commanders of replacement units as well as front-line officers "confirmed" the militarily significant impact of early training in the WELs, whose "graduates" as a rule were "superior front-line soldiers." The Knight's Cross winners, whom the RJF never failed to parade before its charges, had high praise for the quality of training conducted there. Prominent staff officers and generals, after initial doubts, came to realize that premilitary training was an essential part of a soldier's education.[78]

Combat readiness, according to Schlünder, simply meant to be able to shoot straight and know one's way about any type of terrain. In the WEL the majority of boys learned these skills well. The chief of staff of the Munich Military District reported to OKH in 1943 that "those recruits who went through the Premilitary Training Camps were superior to those who did not." They were "particularly superior in their knowledge of firearms and sharpshooting." After the war B. H. Liddell Hart, the famous English military expert, asked General Otto Elfeldt, former commander of the Eighty-fourth German Army Corps, to explain why the generation that had grown up under national socialism demonstrated more individual initiative on the battlefield than their fathers had shown in World War I. It was the result, Elfeldt answered, of "the kind of scout training these young soldiers had received in the HJ organization." What both commentators left unsaid was observed by the keen eye of Major von Hirschfeld, decorated with the Knight's Cross and frequent WEL visitor: "In every WEL that I saw, one could physically sense the energy and enthusiasm of the boys, who revealed a rare openness in their first contact with the soldier's life."[79]

Barely below the surface is a sense that military officers were pleasantly surprised the HJ had been able to organize and implement effective training normally reserved to themselves. Departing from traditional methods, the HJ tailored premilitary training to the particular needs and potentials of sixteen- and seventeen-year-old boys, which one officer thought to be "something new and revolutionary." With the exception of a few coarse SS veterans, there were no hard-bitten drill sergeants in the WELs. Most trainers were sensitive young soldiers with substantial HJ experience. Most group leaders, "room supervisors," and training assistants were themselves seventeen- and eighteen-year-old HJ leaders. The camp directors, while experienced soldiers, were professional youth leaders. Without HJ assistants the goals of the program could not have been reached, giving substance to the claim that German youth was, in effect, training itself. As Ernst Schlünder proclaimed, "The readiness to do battle with weapons was the most striking essential characteristic of Hitler's boys."[80]

Like combat itself, the experience in the WEL brought an indirect social bonus. The camps served as solvents of social distinctions. They forcefully threw together and compelled cooperation and mutuality among those who joined the HJ voluntarily and those who came by force of law; they brought together in close collaboration boys from the cities and the country, middle-class students and working-class apprentices. The fairly equal class distribution among volunteers for the W-SS further confirmed this leveling process. Once again an institutional means was found to make the sense of community more than mere propaganda.[81]

There is little doubt that German soldiers of World War II were much better prepared for the rigors of military combat than their fathers had been for the Great War. They fought with greater professional skill, resourcefulness, and independent initiative than their opponents in the enemy lines. While there clearly was a certain degree of weariness and apathy in German ranks toward the end of the war, few Allied units could match the fanatical commitment and suicidal aggressiveness of the elite SS divisions, whose cadres were constantly refurbished with new recruits from the HJ. Between the springs of 1942 and 1945 literally every German volunteer and draftee filtered through the WELs before he put on the field gray uniform. In this way he may have gained an advantage his opponents did not have, but he also experienced a form of coercion and indoctrination that made him more prone to the type of "barbarization" actual combat would entail. The early difficulties the RJF had in getting premilitary training off the ground, and the clear distaste for the soldier's life many trainees from the upper middle class revealed, suggests that the reluctance of some to engage in obligatory military service, characteristic of democratic societies, was not entirely absent in Hitler's Germany.

# 8 | Pied Pipers for an Elite

Hitler's attack on Poland stimulated vigorous activity in the SS and the HJ. Streamlining for a war all seemed to have anticipated was the order of the day. While a sense of confident truculence pervaded the SS, in the RJF there was confusion, infighting, and a sense of doom. A strange kind of ambivalence infected many youth leaders. For a decade they had propagated a militant spirit within the HJ that could only be realized in combat. At the same time they sensed the end of the cherished cultural and political activities that had given them unheard of prestige. Now they would be soldiers like everyone else and have to surrender the comfortable life to which they had become accustomed. The rank and file for the most part simply submitted to the inevitable demands of war. Fanatical propaganda once more replaced more considered socialization. Every activity took on a somber tone as the HJ experienced the tension of the old "time of struggle," converted into deadly earnest.[1]

The HJ-SS alliance held firm, providing the rapidly expanding Waffen-SS with its main source of recruits. Without this reservoir, the SS would have had to depend on foreign personnel, making it a questionable fighting force and contradicting its elitist ideology. Even so, half of all SS soldiers came from outside Germany's borders in the end. But available HJ manpower enabled the SS to replenish the cadre of its core divisions with the best young men any army could have desired. HJ indoctrination was good preparation for the aggressive performance expected of the W-SS. Berger's pied pipers, meanwhile, faced a real test. He urged them to look in every nook and cranny of German society to find perceptive individuals who knew how to entice boys for military careers. Berger thought these persuaders would most likely be deferred A-SS veterans, but certainly one could find them also among mayors, teachers, and policemen. The important thing was to convey the notion that the W-SS was a guard formation and that it was an honor to fight in its ranks. Methods and techniques should be flexible and appropriate to local conditions and moods.[2]

## Initial Tests of the HJ-SS Alliance

SS recruiting stations were beehives of activity during the spring and summer of 1940. They processed recruiting results, organized acceptance examinations, initiated call-ups, negotiated releases from WBKs, and examined applicants for the A-SS and the HJ-SRD. Radio advertisements, placards, and posters were prepared in Berger's recruiting office. To expedite matters only a certificate of acceptance, a picture, and a basic questionnaire were required for an applicant to have an SS number assigned. For practical and ideological reasons, Sundays were considered to be the best days for recruitment. From 200 to 300 men could be mustered in a single day. Recruiting teams included a station representative, HJ and SS physicians, a "suitability examiner," clerks, drivers, and medical orderlies. A preliminary examination eliminated the "obviously unsuitable," although care was supposed to be taken not to embarrass those judged to be racially inferior, the most frequent reason for rejection.[3]

Recruiting sessions in the HJ stressed distinctions between army and W-SS, "special tasks" of the SS (mostly police work), the concept of "political soldier," utilization of the W-SS in the war, and stories of HJ veterans who had earned the Knight's Cross in the W-SS. HJ response to SS appeals in 1940 were good. In Frankfurt, for instance, HJ leaders were simply "waiting for the call of SS recruiting officers" in their eagerness to get their boys into SS uniforms. The fact that all SS units were fully motorized was particularly attractive. The voluntary fire-fighting auxiliary, attached to the SRD, responded well because they saw a way of improving their standing vis-à-vis the HJ "police." Some of the best "material" was found among HJ leaders in the *Oberschulen*, where school administrators provided unused classrooms to Berger's pied pipers. Doubts expressed by parents were usually answered by reminding them that no one would be called up until his age group was inducted—not entirely true even in 1940. The RJF, in fact, informed HJ leaders that long-term volunteers could enlist in the W-SS at seventeen.[4]

Throughout 1940 Berger battled with OKW, which resisted the development of the W-SS into a "parallel army."[5] The exigencies of this struggle produced some unusual expedients, forcing Berger to complain about "stupid and tactless recruiting." One HJ leader ordered a group of students to an SS mustering session, even though they had already been accepted by the army. They were informed that the SS was "building a new army of 100,000 men in the East and that all Hitler youths, especially graduates of *Hochschulen* who refused to enlist would be prosecuted for . . . treason."

Gottlob Berger, SS recruiting chief (Bundesarchiv Koblenz)

Berger denounced such tactics, fearing, no doubt, that his relationship with the RJF would be jeopardized and the uncertain image of the SS among students would lead to open hostility.[6] To make the W-SS more attractive to HJ leaders, Himmler improved their advancement in the officer corps. After nine months of active service, candidates could embark on training as unit leaders and then attend SS cadet schools. Upon graduation the officer candidate would be returned to the W-SS or choose a career with the SD, ORPO, RuSHA, SS Administration, or Medical Corps—at least he was promised such a choice. He had to sign up for at least four and a half years, be 5'6" tall, and be between seventeen and twenty-three years old. The other requirements were the same as before the war, except that defective eyesight was no longer a hindrance. Instead of producing the ancestral chart, he merely promised that he would do so at some point. Impressed with these enticements, many HJ leaders were soon scattered among reserve units. In August operations chief Hans Jüttner ordered their expedition to the front.[7]

Berger proved his mettle by securing 59,526 new soldiers between 15 January and 29 June 1940. The Death's Head Division actually had 10,000 men above the number authorized by Hitler. Recruiting continued at a slightly reduced pace because OKW made frantic efforts to contain the SS.[8] One way to circumvent OKW was the transfer of Hitler Youths to the A-SS. The elaborate transfer ceremonials had already become infrequent. Papers were simply exchanged by local offices. After an examination, conducted by the SS recruiting stations, they received status as SS candidates, but remained in the HJ until called up by the W-SS. This was done to prevent other party formations and the army from snatching them up. These candidates were expected to spend a few months in the A-SS, however, and undergo indoctrination. SRD members, already led and trained by SS men, were given SS status on their eighteenth birthday.[9]

SS recruiting stations, meanwhile, conducted musterings of Hitler Youths throughout 1940. The Munich station examined 3,000 boys of seventeen, although only 1,300 of these proved to be "suitable." Even if 400 fell by the wayside later, the results were still thought to be satisfactory, considering the deplorable "racial situation" in Bavaria, where frequent "Dinaric," "Mongoloid," and even "Negroid" features had been detected by the hysterical "suitability examiner." Altogether, the W-SS called up 48,894 men in 1940 from within Germany, most of them freshly recruited. The majority came from the classes of 1920 and later. This meant that most of them had undergone the HJ experience, and over 16,000 were still in the HJ when they enlisted—in fact, 168 were barely sixteen. An almost equal number of police reinforcements were also called up. By the end of the year the W-SS had become an army of 150,000 men. It was an expansion of unprecedented proportions, unthinkable without the HJ-SS alliance.[10]

### New Arrangements and Agreements

In 1941 considerable activity took place at SS headquarters, where new divisional cadres were being organized. In January Himmler demanded the cooperation of Main Sector leaders in securing "young recruits" and activating SS reservists to "reinforce new formations." Young volunteers should be mustered and called up immediately. Suggestions that these call-ups should be staggered in order not to alarm the army were to be ignored. "For the build-up of the W-SS," Himmler declared, "I am responsible to the Führer and to no one else." He wanted every free hour devoted to recruitment.[11] Hitler, the RJF, and OKW did not share Himmler's urgency. On 26 February Hess, Schirach, Axmann, and Friessner, representing OKW, held a discussion with Hitler. They agreed to defer all full-time HJ leaders for the time being, although campaigns for part-time leaders were conducted in May and June. The army, meanwhile, countered SS tactics by assigning officers to conduct training courses for HJ leaders. While Berger tried to circumvent restrictions decreed by OKW, the latter instructed its district commanders to watch SS recruiters. OKW was particularly irked because the SS defamed the army and used police officers as recruiters. Since Himmler controlled the police, OKW was unable to prevent their use, but there were other ways to retard SS expansion. One of these took the form of delaying the processing of papers in the WBKs.[12]

Army and SS recruiters competed vigorously for a shrinking number of young men. When it became clear that Hitler was going to invade the Soviet Union, OKW allowed Berger to recruit an unlimited number provided they enlisted for twelve years. He got 22,361 men by ignoring what OKW thought would be a safe deterrent and telling recruits they would serve only for the duration of the war, probably two years. Most of them came from the class of 1923, not yet subject to conscription. In September Berger told OKW that the SS needed 6,000 new men within the month. OKW doubted that many could be found, but made available those born in 1923 to 1925. As usual, OKW underestimated Berger. He managed to get most of what he wanted. Even with this coup, the recruiting numbers for 1941 within Germany were two-thirds below those of 1940. Aided by friendly fascist youth movements, foreign recruitment helped to raise the size of the W-SS to 171,215.[13]

Since 1941 was not a good year for Berger's manhunters, he was eager to enhance the HJ connection. This he attempted to do at the Munich conference of HJ regional leaders in December. Major General Friessner got a cool reception at Munich, since he implied that youth was ill-prepared for military service. He called for "fewer speeches and more technical precision." Berger's representative at the conference recalled that the HJ itself had initiated premilitary training long ago and "without any noticeable assistance from the Wehrmacht, at times even in defiance of army opposition." As head of the Education and Training Department Friessner had clout, but he was soon replaced by Lieutenant General Ludwig Wolff, who took a less critical attitude toward the HJ and their SS allies.[14] Berger capitalized on the favorable mood within the HJ. Sometime in 1941 OKW had made a preliminary agreement with the RJF to exchange draftable HJ leaders for wounded veterans. In January 1942 OKW reneged without offering a reasonable excuse. Axmann then turned to Berger, suggesting that he request the transfer of some 300 army reservists with HJ background to the W-SS. Berger was rebuffed by OKW and asked Himmler to contact Keitel personally. Apparently Himmler had no more success. But in February the RJF reached an independent agreement with the SS by which W-SS veterans could be assigned to full-time HJ work, if they were former HJ leaders and if they were classified for "garrison duty on the home front."[15]

Suddenly the army became eager to provide the HJ with trainers. In April OKH offered to furnish any number desired provided the RJF canceled its agreement with the SS regarding the SRD as a "feeder" organization. OKH officers implied the Führer intended for the army to be responsible for premilitary training of youth below draft age, playing a game many other operators played in light of the ambiguities Hitler preferred. The politicians in the RJF knew how to play that game of "interpretation" too, and Helmut Möckel wasted no time in putting Berger on the trail. The latter simply told Möckel that similar intimations by "these gentlemen" of OKH be referred to him personally. But cultivation of HJ goodwill did not always filter down to the ranks. At one point the RJF complained about SS soldiers who refused to salute HJ leaders, most of whom were very sensitive about such amenities. Hans Jüttner, ever aware how "large a part of W-SS reinforcement came from the HJ," ordered all HJ leaders to be properly saluted and required instruction about HJ rank and insignia. The SS managed to secure its recruiting base in the HJ through a variety of such small measures, cementing the generational relationship.[16]

The war with OKW, meanwhile, continued. Reports about "illegal" SS recruiting methods continued to surface, leading to a new approach in the fall of 1942. Rudolf Schmundt, chief of the Army Personnel Office and Hitler's adjutant, wrote Maximilian von Herff, chief of the SS Personnel Main Office, complaining about recruiting irregularities. Herff immediately consulted Berger, who assured him that the WBKs and the SS recruiting stations were working together "without friction"—a blatant dissimulation. As to the specific indictment that the SS was recruiting volunteers who had already been mustered by the armed forces, Herff pointed to existing regulations, which allowed this procedure as long as the men in question had not been called up. In response to Schmundt's further charge that the SS was accepting volunteers "without parental permission," Herff pointed to an order of Hitler's which specifically allowed the SS to do so. It is hard to believe that OKW was unaware of this decree, since Artur Axmann informed the leadership of this "secret" directive in 1942. The decree in question had been issued on 17 February 1942 at the suggestion of Himmler, and it specifically allowed the W-SS to "recruit and call up underage youth without the permission of legal guardians or parents." Once again the SS outmaneuvered the professionals in OKW.[17]

Irregular recruiting techniques that OKW seems not to have noticed were used by the HJ leaders themselves, many of whom were W-SS veterans by this time and not particularly well attuned to legal niceties. In April 1942 SS Sergeant Ernst Bingger, newly appointed leader of HJ District 312 in Memmingen, simply called a meeting of all boys aged sixteen to eighteen, making attendance compulsory under the Youth Service Law of 1939. The purpose of the meeting was kept secret until the boys actually assembled, when they were confronted with appeals to sign up with the W-SS.[18]

At the end of 1942 the SS made arrangements that promised more substantial results in securing reinforcements from HJ special formations for the technical field units of the W-SS. One year previously, the army managed to skim off the best leaders from the Motor-HJ and the Signal-HJ for officer candidates. The latter were excused from labor service, and those who enlisted before finishing the *Oberschule* received their diploma prematurely. The SS Recruiting Office (SSEA) then made a similar arrangement with the Signal-HJ, but could not get many volunteers because labor duty was not canceled. A month later the RJF and the Central SS Office (SSHA) agreed to supply mechanically inclined boys of seventeen and sixteen for the motorized units of the W-SS. The HJ regions, as usual, were expected to supply a set number of contingents. A novel feature called for the transfer of Motor-HJ members to the SRD units after their preliminary examination for suitability. This was done to prevent the army from poaching before the W-SS could call them up. Most of these recruits came to the W-SS with mechanic's licenses already in hand, since they had to undergo special training in the newly established WEL. Signal-HJ and Motor-HJ were originally intended as steps to the army, but conditions being what they were, the SS was able to use its relationship with the HJ to get access to these suborganizations as well.[19]

### Success of Coercive Methods and Ploys

In February 1943, when the battle of Stalingrad had changed the war into a prolonged retreat, Himmler was authorized to form two new divisions. To do this he recruited in the labor service camps where most of the eligibles were fulfilling three-month duty. These young men were drafted unceremoniously by the SS, OKW having granted special permission to circumvent normal procedures. Inductees quickly complained about this peremptory action. Hitler appears to have given permission to "draft" in the camps, but the enthusiasm of SS recruiters strained the bounds even of Nazi propriety and stimulated vigorous protest from party quarters. Martin Bormann informed Himmler that he was receiving widespread complaints about "methods employed by the W-SS." Men were forced to enlist "against their will," he said, while "pencils were pressed into their hands accompanied by accusations of treason if they refused to sign up." Young men were not permitted to consult parents, according to Bormann, revealing surprising ignorance of Hitler's special permission to cancel these prerogatives. He went on to accuse the SS of eliciting signatures under false pretexts, e.g., they were told that the signature merely confirmed that they had read and understood the literature, or that they confirmed the accuracy of personal data. Unless Himmler stopped these infractions, Bormann feared "substantial consequences." Unaffected by Bormann's threat, Himmler insisted Hitler had given permission to induct every man from the 1925 class fulfilling labor duty. Most had enlisted voluntarily, although "here and there pressure had been used." The complaints had not come from recruits, but from their common bête noire, "fanatical Catholic parents." Since the Führer had to have two divisions in France by 15 February, this was the only way to meet the emergency. Furthermore, Himmler suggested a little more assistance from party chiefs, instead of "constant carping criticism."[20]

Coercive methods continued and so did criticism. A young SS NCO by the name of Härtewig conducted a recruiting session at the Agricultural School in Halle. After a lecture he ordered the pupils to get writing materials, but some 30 percent failed to return. The angry sergeant then screamed: "When these people finally come to the SS they will be shot forthwith, for this is nothing else but sabotage and desertion of the flag. I will get their names from the director of the school and will see to it that they are inducted into the SS immediately and assigned as mine stumpers." When Härtewig calmed down he had the remaining students fill out application forms. One of them was Werner Kallmeyer, son of labor leader Siegfried Kallmeyer, associated with the RAD reporting office. Werner refused to sign the papers before consulting his father, provoking Härtewig to explode again: "We will take no more nonsense from these old camels. All of you will sign or no one leaves this room." Then another student, named Beyer, struck up an exchange with Härtewig. Beyer: "My father told me not to sign anything without his consent." Härtewig: "Your father, apparently, was never a soldier." Beyer: "He was a soldier for seven years and experienced the whole world war." Härtewig: "Your father was never a real soldier—please sign!" Beyer still refused, whereupon the NCO once more opened fire: "You pigs think that your comrades out there permit themselves to be shot to hell so that you can evade the war!" Beyer left the room but was immediately forced to return. Beyer: "This is pure force; yet we want to volunteer freely." Härtewig: "I take that to be an insult directed at a German officer. Get out of here! I don't want to see you again!" When other students still resisted, Härtewig cried: "You cowards! You just want to avoid the war! I will see to it that those who refuse to sign will become human mine detectors and soon kick the bucket." Most of the boys then signed. Härtewig collected the forms, mumbling, "Those who don't come voluntarily we can force in any case. Their value as human beings is immaterial to us." Kallmeyer eventually signed too, with the proviso that his father would have to approve.[21]

Reich Labor Leader Konstantin Hierl then sent Himmler a letter relating the Kallmeyer incident and similar events. He was sure that the Reichsführer disapproved and would do everything in his power to prevent recurrences, since men recruited under such circumstances certainly would do the SS little good and might even be "dangerous." Hierl then went on to suggest an orderly plan to assist the W-SS in its recruiting efforts. Himmler thanked Hierl for his "frank discussion as among old party comrades" and hoped Hierl understood the "pressures under which the SS had sought to fulfill the Führer's wishes." In his complaint of 24 February, Bormann specifically named four boys of fifteen who had been enlisted under false pretenses. This had occurred in a WEL staffed by the SS, according to Bormann's informant. Berger soon got to the bottom of that charge. He informed Himmler that the boys in question had been recruited by the HJ in a regional leadership school, not a WEL. Since these schools were under HJ control, the SSEA was innocent.[22]

Berger was irritated with party functionaries for interfering with his operation, but general party resentment could not be disposed of so easily. The clamor soon reached the highest seats of power. Hans Lammers, chief of the Reich Chancellery, requested a copy from Himmler of the Führer's alleged order that "empowered him to draft the class of 1925." Numerous complaints from labor camps had been addressed to the Führer himself, and Lammers wanted to squelch them. Himmler had no such document, but "surmised Hitler's order had been given orally" and then passed on to him through OKW and the RAD. That Hitler actually gave permission to "draft the entire class of 1925" is unlikely, although permission to recruit in the camps must have been given. Himmler overstepped his authorization and then created confusion to avoid consequences. Berger, meanwhile, investigated the Kallmeyer incident himself and found the SS recruiter in question to be a "veteran HJ leader with the necessary experience to handle boys," although it is not clear whether he acquired this particular insight in the HJ or the SS. Berger's resourcefulness in defending his own men while discrediting his detractors once more saved the situation for Himmler.[23]

Not all parents of SS inductees found recruiting methods unacceptable. A farmer in Neuendorf wrote: "My son, who was doing his labor service, was mustered by an SS commission . . . and a few days later drafted by the W-SS and shipped to Shitomir. . . . At first this . . . disturbed me greatly. . . . I resolved . . . to protest. . . . But a recent letter . . . changed my mind. . . . My son is excited about life in the W-SS . . . the good companionship . . . the care with which the trainers . . . inculcate the precepts of soldiering . . . the good food rations. . . . I congratulate the W-SS for being able to inspire young recruits so quickly with the proper esprit de corps."[24] This change of heart must have struck a welcome chord. A national report compiled by the operations office of the W-SS adopted a decidedly different tone. It found the physical and racial characteristics of recruits far below those of the prewar generation, apparently ignoring what was found to be true in Frankfurt and other cities. Some 40 percent of the youths examined in the RAD camps were automatically rejected. The reason was not malnutrition but hard labor. What really disturbed the SS, however, was the prevailing attitude: few volunteered; most came because they had to, meanwhile fearing disapproval of parents and priests and combat itself. Some signed papers tearfully; others expressed happiness at being rejected. Various causes were deduced: heavy casualty rates in the W-SS, its engagement at critical points, sharp drill during training, little chance of promotion, and the duty to leave the church. Unwilling to face reality, the SS could do no more than blame "rumors" spread by "boasting" W-SS veterans. Many had been used as recruiters among the HJ, and now that policy was backfiring, since the HJ too received pointed criticism. Nearly all reporters, including ex-HJ leaders, complained about the "complete failure" of the HJ to foster "idealism and . . . the joys of combat."[25]

SS recruiters found some differences in their experience depending on the geographic region. In the northeast many recruits were found to be short of stature. In Berlin HJ boys were bright and critical, but responsive to a film on the locally based SS Body Guard. In Dresden they appeared with written parental prohibitions against joining the SS and stated that "they would become soldiers soon enough." In an apprentice shop of 300 boys free from parental influence, however, the response was uniformly positive. At Munich the SS speaker tried a little humor by referring to the "Mounted Mountain Marine," whereupon four boys promptly volunteered. Church and HJ in Bavaria were criticized for creating a "negative attitude." HJ leaders, members of the SRD, and "graduates" of the WEL were conspicuously absent from recruiting sessions. At Nuremberg recruiters found the unwillingness to join "catastrophic." In Vienna priests had threatened volunteers with hell, saying "the SS is godless." The recruiting station at Salzburg suggested fewer combat films and more emphasis on "genial aspects" of the soldier's life. Despite varying receptions, the school, the HJ, and the church were condemned uniformly for failing to indoctrinate youth in the appropriate political fashion.[26]

When Himmler got a hold of this report, he was disturbed and hastened to inform Martin Bormann, his fellow anticlerical fanatic. Failing to mention the imprudent behavior of his SS recruiters and also exempting the RJF from criticism, Himmler laid all blame for the "systematic poisoning of youth" at the door of the church. He did not recommend a direct attack on the church, but a carefully camouflaged counterreligious propaganda program. Unlike Stalin, who softened his antireligious stance in order to build patriotic morale during the war, Himmler and Bormann plunged ahead in their neo-pagan campaign, divisive and counterproductive as it was.[27]

War-weariness was not only infecting the home front. SS First Lieutenant Herbert König, who headed the SRD for a while, sent a depressing account to his colleagues in the recruiting office from the battlefield of Kharkov. He saw all the signs of "approaching tragedy," a replay of 1918. The hordes of retreating soldiers filled him with horror and "reinforced the arguments for the rightness of our ideology." His regiment had lost 1,800 men in a battle trumpeted as a great SS victory, despite the eventual outcome. But König was more concerned with inculcating ideology and related how eagerly his men read SS literature and responded to his lectures during lulls in the fighting. He felt that the Central SS Office was the agency that could prevent Germany's funeral. If the soldiers of the army had experienced the kind of training given to SS recruits, there would not have been any retreat on the Eastern Front, in König's view.[28] When in many minds the eventual defeat was no longer in question, SS stalwarts found no other solution than renewed efforts to inject an ideology of racial superiority and the triumph of willpower over reality.

Desperation bred ideological rigor and more forceful recruiting. The garrison commander of Königsberg received reports "that recruiting for the W-SS was again taking forms that exclude any voluntary action," especially in technical schools and government bureaus. Since the SS recruiting station had promised not to accept any recruit who had been forced to sign up, the commander ordered an investigation. When the litany of complaints continued, Berger was forced to admit that the notion of volunteering was losing any semblance of truth, especially when OKW sent General Schmundt to see Himmler. The latter ordered his Legal Office to investigate charges against Berger's recruiters. His response was typical. He did not fear untoward discoveries, but deplored the inevitable "disturbance and uncertainty." The "enemies within" would be encouraged to resume their attacks. SS Main Sector leaders, Berger charged, would use the inquiry to renew their assaults on the recruiting stations.[29] In reality Berger had little reason for concern. Hearings were held for a few recruiters accused by Schmundt and regional SS leaders, but penalties were mild. Himmler made sure of this by instructing his legal experts to produce uniform findings amounting to reprimands and transfers to other duties. Himmler's lawyers believed the public was no longer aroused by "the chosen recruiting methods."[30]

Undeterred, the W-SS engaged in furious recruitment during the winter and spring of 1943. The first recruiting efforts for the HJ division got started in February. In March and April "extended recruiting action" within the HJ as a whole got underway. Artur Axmann issued the basic orders late in January, while the RJF assigned the contingents for the regions early in February. The importance of this campaign was underscored by the fact that the entire party apparatus was mobilized to assist in the effort to build up the W-SS. This may have been done in part to counteract the former reluctance of certain party officials to support or even to resist SS recruiting efforts.[31]

HJ Region Swabia, for instance, received a quota of 600 suitable boys. HJ Regional Chief of Staff Walter Ludwig and SS-Hauptsturmführer Willy Schraub, from the recruiting station in Munich, agreed on details of the operation. Under the guise of "area roll calls" two recruiting sessions, lasting approximately half a day each, were held within each HJ District, with decorated SS veterans giving speeches and using film clips depicting heroic W-SS exploits. All boys of sixteen and seventeen were "invited" to the meetings and given "health examinations" to determine their suitability for the SRD. This stratagem allowed the SS to carry acceptable candidates in SRD files, even though the SRD had nothing to do with this campaign. Pro forma statements that "the principle of voluntarism would . . . be respected" was mere eyewash.[32]

The thirteen districts in Swabia were given contingents depending on the distribution of the age group in question, ranging from thirty to fifty each. In the city of Augsburg this operation apparently got confused with earlier actions carried out by SS Captain Bertl Schindlmayr, not one of the three sergeants—Schulte, Sohr, and Tinnacher—assigned to the current campaign. Schindlmayr, that independent SS entrepreneur with special ties to Himmler, had recruited 140 boys for the W-SS on his own. Police Captain Spangenberg had managed to "invite" boys individually to the police station and thus captured another 180 recruits. After examinations, however, only thirty out of Schindlmayr's group turned out to be acceptable and similar results emerged from Spangenberg's effort. The SS recruiting station then renewed the effort. In Donauwörth, District Leader Jürgens reported seven boys for the HJ division and six for the W-SS, falling far short of the quota. Gustav Tinnacher was certainly a "first-class fellow," wrote Jürgens, and the campaign had been well organized, but the "pronounced anti-SS attitude of a strongly religious population" was hard to overcome. Kempten was more successful, producing sixty-four prospects, while Nördlingen delivered twenty-one and Memmingen seventeen. Altogether Swabia came up with 1,000 prospects, of which 180 met SS standards when the examinations were almost concluded. While final results may have raised the total, Swabia did not fulfill its 600-man quota. Yet a device had been discovered whereby all seventeen-year-olds could be subjected to the appeals of SS propagandists. The "area roll call" idea originated in the RJF and was used throughout the country. This may explain why Berger was able to collect over 60,000 recruits from the class of 1926 during 1943.[33]

Waffen-SS recruiting poster, 1943 (Bundesarchiv Koblenz)

Beginning to realize that the SS was picking off the best, OKH initiated a recruiting expedition for the Grossdeutschland division. The replacement brigade of this elite outfit began to furnish trainers for the WEL and the regional leadership schools as a way of creating HJ goodwill. The HJ in turn was asked to establish "sponsoring relationships" between front units and their home HJ segments by maintaining a traffic in letters, packages, and visits by soldiers on leave. These measures were designed to counteract successful recruiting by the SS. Bluntly condoning counterraiding, OKW suggested that since formal call-ups of W-SS volunteers filtered through military reserve offices, one could contain the flood. If it "were known" that volunteers for the SS had signed under "duress" or "misrepresentation," they could be "taken over" by the Wehrmacht. The WBKs "were not responsible for assuring the filling of SS quotas." Above all, "the HJ should be taught to have the courage not to sign anything that contradicted their wishes."[34]

The army consistently underestimated Gottlob Berger. In August he made another agreement with the RJF "to obtain a certain percentage of volunteers for the W-SS in order to counteract the highly pressurized recruiting of OKH." The national health law, which required periodic examinations, was used to examine sixteen-year-old boys by the SS X-ray Battalion, thus capitalizing on an ad hoc scheme used in Swabia and probably other HJ regions. No actual recruiting was done by examiners, who did not identify themselves as SS men. A "suitability-examiner" simply coded cards in such a way as to indicate potentially suitable boys. These prospects were then shuffled to WELs staffed by the SS. The scheme was more or less secret. Berger told Himmler: "Officially the RJF knows only that we will examine the whole 1927 class through the SS X-ray Battalion." Eventually Berger planned the same procedure for the 1928 and 1929 classes, thus assuring "early registration" and "concentrated recruiting."[35]

### Crisis in Manpower Recruitment and SS Conscription

The campaign of 1943 was successful enough to warrant repetition in 1944. Ernst Schlünder informed HJ regions that Axmann and Berger had agreed to schedule the effort from February to April. This time, however, it was combined with recruitment for the HJ division, for Grossdeutschland, and for the SA regiment Feldherrnhalle, largely to give the appearance of impartiality. Originally it was directed primarily toward members of the SRD class of 1927, another stab at fatuous camouflage.[36]

Swabia was again given a contingent of 600 by Schlünder, who warned

that the SS was now dependent almost exclusively on the HJ for replacements. Regional Leader Ludwig Stinglwagner was expected "personally
to support" the campaign "with all his might." The campaign was conducted exactly as in 1943, except that the SRD inspectors replaced regional
chiefs of staff in carrying primary responsibility. SS recruiters were involved in all aspects of HJ activity: youth film hours, "home evenings,"
service roll calls, and instruction sessions. Most members of the 1927 class
had undergone preliminary examinations under Berger's "health test roll
call," which made the task easier. Each district received a contingent of
approximately forty recruits, except Wertach and Augsburg-Land, which
received sixty, and Augsburg-Stadt, which got a quota of one hundred.
The boys were to be impressed with the notion that it was "a great honor to
double the volunteers," this time because the Führer had personally ordered "an enlargement of the W-SS" and because the latter was the "only
arms bearer of the party." A district leader's responsibility did not end
when the requested number was reached. He was expected to get as many
of the 2,000 suitable boys in Swabia as possible. This time recruits had to
sign "volunteer certificates," to ward off charges of coercion. There is little
evidence that other than SS recruiters went to HJ districts. The boys, furthermore, were told that voluntary enlistment in the W-SS would give
them a choice in the type of field unit they desired, which would not be the
case should they wait a few months to be drafted by the army.[37]

In some areas the Grossdeutschland did send its own recruiters. For
instance, in Südhannover-Braunschweig, Baldur von Schirach's adjutant
invited an assault squad to enlist HJ boys in "his" division. Provincial chief
Hartmann Lauterbacher, who had not yet forgotten his slight by the former
youth leader, reported to Himmler that this division had been traditionally
antipathetic to the SS. Since many HJ leaders in the region collaborated
with the anti-SS propaganda of the Grossdeutschland, Lauterbacher
stopped its recruiting efforts. "Pride in one's own unit had always existed,"
he wrote, "but this incident has its origin in . . . politically motivated rejection of the W-SS." Himmler found this report of Lauterbacher's "very interesting," and expressed his gratitude. Two years later, however, Lauterbacher's antipathy toward Schirach was forgotten when he became a prime
defense witness for his former superior at the Nuremberg trials.[38]

The response of HJ boys was slow. Axmann had demanded a preliminary accounting by 15 March, but Stinglwagner's report of 1,061 volunteers
from Swabia must have been unsatisfactory. A few days later he sent a
personal letter to each district leader, suggesting that they should know by
this time "what methods were most effective." One simply had to call

every unit together, without publicizing the purpose of the muster, and apply the necessary pressure. District leaders were expected to attend recruiting sessions themselves and inspire requisite responses. On 19 April Axmann informed Stinglwagner that only 300 of the reported volunteers had been found suitable. Some of these would probably be eliminated later. Since many other regions had produced two or three times as many as their original quota, he could not understand why Swabia fell behind. Axmann ordered: "You must immediately use every method you deem appropriate to get better results. If there are not enough boys of seventeen, take those who are sixteen." Cumulative results in Swabia developed as follows: The HJ division started with 312 recruits on 15 April and acquired a total of 429 by 26 July; the W-SS as a whole began with 202 on 15 April and ended up with 533 on 26 July; the Feldherrnhalle only got three volunteers and Grossdeutschland twenty-seven, while various other volunteers amounted to 517; this brought the total at the end of July to 962.

Among those deemed suitable, 60 were eighteen, 154 were seventeen, and 89 were sixteen. Thus 31 percent of those recruited in Swabia were eventually accepted, indicating that elitism was maintained. It could also mean that despite coercion the boys were not all that unwilling to join the W-SS. Special efforts were made to keep qualified "volunteers" who did not possess permission from parents, suggesting that coercive methods had been used. While Hitler had secretly allowed underage boys to be recruited without permission of parents back in 1942, it was still thought advisable to get this permission, even in 1944.[39]

In the summer of 1944 the campaign fused at points with a new one to enlist the class of 1928. Normally this age group would not have been the focus of SS recruiting efforts until the spring of 1945, but the impending military collapse drove the SS further toward younger groups. HJ leaders in Swabia seem to have been quite successful in this effort. At least five of them received commendations for committing between 80 and 92 percent of all sixteen-year-old boys in their districts. The enlistment of sixteen-year-old boys by the W-SS had occurred as early as 1940. Four years later it seems to have become a general practice. Hitler's decree of 25 September 1944 creating the Popular Militia then made it a matter of law. But even Nazi "law" meant little to the SS in general and Berger in particular. There is some evidence to suggest that boys of fifteen and even fourteen were recruited by the SS in certain areas as early as the spring of 1944.[40]

The army, meanwhile, assigned wounded veterans to regional and district staffs of the HJ. Liaison officers of local replacement units arranged recruiting meetings, where decorated veterans made appeals. Some of these kept a careful watch on SS recruiting techniques. Lieutenant Bremme, the "specialist for volunteer replacements" in Coesfeld, discovered that the W-SS had mustered all boys of seventeen and sixteen in Westphalia under the guise of an obligatory tooth examination. The local police had conducted "air raid courses" for the HJ and used them to recruit "volunteers." Although some regional HJ leaders sought to avoid the "use of force," most district leaders supported coercion. Other army recruiters revealed sympathy for the "difficult position" of HJ district leaders, assaulted by masses of recruiting literature from every conceivable military unit demanding its "best boys." Reports from a variety of army-HJ liaison officers indicate that sponsorships aided the army's efforts in constricting the flow of W-SS recruits from the HJ. The SS attempted to mimic the sponsorship idea but failed. Most W-SS units were not composed of men from the same geographic area. The SS had to depend on such other expedients as recruiting young war correspondents. Once Himmler became the commander of the replacement army, following the July 1944 plot against Hitler, these sponsorships lost some of their importance.[41]

Continuous competition between W-SS and army was only one aspect of a multifaceted rivalry for a diminishing supply of manpower. Considering the wastefulness of these battles, it is surprising that the war lasted as long as it did. There would seem to have been only one rational answer: the concentration of manpower allocation within the hands of a single agency. This idea occurred to Gottlob Berger. In August 1944 he addressed a lengthy memorandum to SS Major General Werner Naumann, chief of the ministerial office in the Ministry of Propaganda and Enlightenment. With Himmler's consent Berger proposed a "reorganization of the entire reserves of the German *Volkskraft*." This would have included armed forces, W-SS, police, labor service, Organization Todt, and the civilian labor sector. On the local level, a single new military report office was to incorporate the existing WBKs, SS recruiting stations, RAD report offices, and lower recruiting units of the Organization Todt, NSKK, air force, and navy. The proposed bureaus were to receive "substantial independence and responsibility," and be subordinated to a "manpower central" in Berlin. The latter was to be directed by Himmler or his deputy. Here Berger had himself in mind. Had his proposal been adopted, the RJF would have received requests for manpower from a single source, instead of the bewildering multitude of agencies and military formations. In January 1945 Berger was still urging Himmler to present this plan to Hitler.[42]

As things stood, Berger had to content himself with limited last-minute measures.[43] One of those sought to deal with the serious shortage of officers. In December 1944 Hitler had ordered that a number of potential army and SS officers be selected from the HJ for special training. The projected training at NAPOLAs, AHSs, and the *Reichsschule Feldafing* was to be directed by Himmler. The first courses began in February 1945, and recruitment commenced the month before, concentrating on boys who were fifteen. Although volunteers were preferred, local party leaders could "nominate boys of their acquaintance who . . . refused to volunteer freely." In such cases it would be necessary "to enlighten the parents." On 5 February Berger reported to Himmler that 2,000 officer candidates had been called up for the first course sessions. Of these, 1,500 were bound for the army and 500 for the W-SS. The response of the boys at this late date symbolized the success of HJ indoctrination, effectively exploited by SS recruiters.[44]

### The SS Female Assistance Corps and the BDM

The SS Female Assistance Corps (SSHK) was another example of those numerous last-minute expedients by which the SS sought to mobilize all remaining strength for the war effort. Himmler made full use of the HJ-SS alliance to implement an idea that was belated and contradictory. That a male-dominated elite should resort to creating a female counterpart at this stage no longer made any sense. Whatever the real motive, the effect was ominous, since it tied the BDM to the W-SS, along with their male colleagues. The necessities generated by total war thus had the unintended effect of tending to erase sexist distinctions so assiduously promoted up to that point, although the equality that might have come had BDM girls been drafted for actual combat never materialized.

The SSHK had its origins in the SS Signals Auxiliary, patterned on a similar organization in the German Air Force. An old veteran, Ernst Sachs, chief of the SS Communications Office, was picked by Himmler to head the SSHK when it was created in 1943. At the time Sachs was sixty-three years old and hardly known even within top SS ranks. He appears to have made a late career of sorts in SS Communications, although his rank, including that of W-SS general, would suggest some achievements earlier.[45] In March Jüttner's Operations Office, where Sachs was then located, attempted to systematize the use of signals women in SS offices and military headquarters. They were to be requested only if their employment freed men for front-line duty. They were not to serve merely as helpers. Himmler insisted decent housing and female companionship had to be provided before any of them could be employed. Earlier Himmler had invited Gertrud Scholtz-Klink, the leader of the Nazi Women's Organization, to comment on his guidelines, designed to protect the SS from malicious gossip as much as to protect young women from chauvinist abuse. That Himmler's guidelines were ignored by sex-starved SS men is confirmed in numerous complaints from signals women, leading to stern intervention by the SS Superior Court.[46]

Signals women could serve as telephone operators, telegraph clerks, and radio operators, but their activity was supervised by a low-ranking SS man who did not merely repair machinery but insured the confidentiality of communications.[47] In the effort to turn the signals women into a more substantial assistance corps, Himmler established a school to train leaders at Oberehnheim, near Strassburg, later known as *Reichsschule-SS Oberehnheim*. In August Sachs worked out procedures with Scholtz-Klink and the "female specialist" in his own office, Ilse Staiger. It soon became evident that Scholtz-Klink, whose rapid rise in the Nazi hierarchy revealed considerable political acumen, wanted to "keep male influence" at the school "to a minimum," since women could do everything that men could do. She suggested that the school be headed by a *Schulleiterin* instead of a *Heimleiterin*. Sachs told Himmler this was out of the question, since the school already had a male commander.[48]

For nearly a year an extensive volume of letters and memoranda was exchanged among HSSPF, SS Main Sector leaders, chiefs of various SS offices, and the Nazi Women's Organization, dealing with the issue of who should be the "national representative" for all women in the SS and the "protection of young women" as specified by Himmler's guidelines. That the Women's Organization should have been consulted at all is indicative of an interesting vulnerability on the part of certain SS leaders and Himmler himself with regard to the awkward position forced on them by the need for female assistance and the effort to maintain the SS as an exclusive male club. Himmler's position was further complicated by Scholtz-Klink's aggressive promotion of female competence and the fact that she was married to August Heissmeyer, an HSSPF, former head of the Central SS Office, and NAPOLA inspector.[49]

Himmler's concern became acute when BDM girls began to be recruited for the planned Assistance Corps and the *Reichsschule-SS*. From his "field command post" in October 1943 he instructed his minions to apply the guidelines with particular care to young women under twenty-one who were employed outside Reich borders, although in matters of housing and welfare, responsibility rested with the RJF. The SS was asked to support the efforts of the RJF in this respect "to the best of their abilities." Nothing was done except to send Himmler's guidelines to Reichsreferentin Jutta Rüdiger of the BDM.[50]

Gradually raising Himmler's ire, Ernst Sachs was slow to issue regulations, but when he did so they delineated matters in precious detail. Service in the SSHK was considered "honorary" and assumed successful completion of the *Reichsschule-SS*. Each request for an "assistant" had to specify exact need, available transportation, equipment, housing, and living conditions. Requests would be honored only if proof existed that men would be freed for the frontline. All assistants remained under the control of Sachs unless he released them to the HSSPF or male supervisors. The assistants were expected to work a fifty-six-hour week, within three rotating shifts, thus keeping each office in operation around the clock. A single assistant could remain in a building at night if it were deemed secure, otherwise two had to be present. Assistants had to be housed in "homes," usually confiscated houses or rented premises. A universal curfew of 10:00 P.M. was ordered unless pressing local reasons demanded some other arrangement, which required previous written permission. After intensive training at the *Reichsschule-SS*, continuous technical instruction was ordered for all full-time employees. This dealt with official secrecy, spies, saboteurs, enemy propaganda, chain of command, service regulations, grievance procedures, military law, air raid precautions, and first aid. Leaders in the SSHK were expected to take advice from "home supervisors" on "behavior and mental attitude." Special emphasis was placed on professional relationships with male members of the SS, who were expected to deal with female assistants in a "clean, decent, and knightly-comradely fashion," as one would deal with "a sister." Assistants who wanted to get married had to get permission from Himmler and the RuSHA.[51]

Himmler was dissatisfied. He was ready to grant Ilse Staiger as Reichsbeauftragte im SS-Helferinnenkorps complete control over purely female matters, and he increased the decision-making power of office supervisors in matters of exceptions to the curfew, but he demanded that everything written about the SSHK be submitted to him in advance. He was determined to prevent "avoidable difficulties for the SS." In dealing with relationships between the sexes, Himmler feared "ominous implications for our recruiting efforts" if "explicit tenderness of feeling" were openly revealed. SS assistants who expected a child had to inform the home supervisor or the national representative by word of mouth or personal letter. The latter had specific directions on how to deal with unwanted pregnancies, probably by sending the women to a home for unwed mothers.[52]

The SS Indoctrination Office and representatives of Oberehnheim determined the curriculum of the school, placing heavy emphasis on ideology. For reasons of security and SS corps spirit, now endangered by the "intrusion" of females, indoctrination was considered to be crucial. At the moment it did not seem purposeful to request the assignment of indoctrination girls from the HJ, since it had recently asked that all of the SS indoctrination materials be sent to the RJF, a clear indication that the latter was now depending completely on the SS to carry out indoctrination. The SS Indoctrination Office meanwhile agreed to find a suitable female indoctrination officer for Oberehnheim from the Female Colonial School in Redsburg, "famous for its outstanding corps spirit and impeccable collaboration."[53]

The commander of Oberehnheim, SS-Obersturmbannführer Karl Mutschler, changed the curriculum to suit the new function of the school as a training center for the SSHK. The new curriculum had "to reflect the SSHK as the sister organization of the Elite Echelon, so that there is no longer any other significant, representative career for a woman, beside wife and mother, than that of SS assistant." The training supervisor had to have a broad view of the curriculum, so that trainees would be effective in their jobs. He was expected to create a mix of ideology and practical skills. Instruction in physics replaced signals technology. They were also to acquire basic knowledge of administrative procedures in the SS. Home economics was a third important element. It was particularly important that women who sacrificed their personal life by working in the SSHK would have the opportunity to find appropriate employment after the war. Sports played the usual role. General initiation outside classroom instruction, even under extraordinary wartime conditions, was considered to be important. Care had to be taken that special speakers, festivities, social gatherings, and cultural activities rounded off the program. Trainees and SSHK candidates were to receive a full introduction to "the whole life of the nation in dynamic relationships."[54]

At Oberehnheim indoctrination took precedence over practical training. Basic classes took up twelve hours per week, while telegraph operation and radio operation consumed only four hours each. Assistants transferred from the army received a refresher course of thirteen hours. About half of the teaching was conducted by the head of the indoctrination staff, SS-Hauptsturmführer Hess. Newly installed Training Assistant Lössel assumed a quarter of the duties, and the rest reverted to three home supervisors, Princess Stephan zu Schaumburg-Lippe, Frau Brinkmann, and Frau Laun. Because of her diplomatic experience in Latin America, the princess, quite a catch for Himmler, got a prominent role in indoctrination, especially when it came to anti-American propaganda. Her husband, a prime aristocratic showpiece for the Nazi Party, was Goebbels's adjutant. Brinkmann and Laun had to take a back seat because they were outclassed and because of frequent alarms and the general uncertainties produced by proximity to the front. Hess was forced to cut corners. Running classes of one hundred girls at a time was not the best way to proceed, but one had to make do under emergency conditions.[55]

Recruitment, surprisingly, was easier than one would have expected at this late hour. At the end of August 1943 every SS Main Sector reported success, with Südwest producing the highest number (235) and Warthe the lowest (5). The campaign as a whole harvested 859 recruits for the SSHK. The poor results in SS Main Sector Warthe is no surprise, since the resettlement program was making extraordinary demands on the BDM there, but the large number of volunteers from the Southwest is unusual and probably had to do with the fact that Gauleiter Wagner was a keen supporter of Frau Scholtz-Klink, who may have had a hand in this campaign.[56] Southwest, of course, also included Alsace, and the *Reichsschule-SS* was located there until it had to be moved because of the receding front. Sachs insisted that ideology, good grasp of grammar, and general perceptiveness be criteria of selection. He was also concerned with physical qualifications, since a number of deficiencies had been detected in earlier volunteers. Those rejected complained bitterly because many of them had given up good positions in order to enter the SSHK.[57]

The new influx hardly matched increasing demand for female assistants. SS offices as of 1 October 1943 requested 329 telephone operators, 109 telegraph clerks, 379 radio operators, and 132 female assistants for special purposes. If these 949 assistants are added to the 301 already installed in new positions and the 223 then training at Oberehnheim, it appears that the SSHK consisted of roughly 1,500 members at the time. The demand for female assistants was so great that one can hardly avoid suspecting it went beyond professional need and had something to do with the jocular rumors about the BDM becoming an "association of German soldiers' mattresses" toward the end of the war. Sachs, who may have regarded himself as some sort of official procurer in his semisenile old age, had to stagger his call-ups in four-week intervals and promise that some 1,200 female assistants would be supplied during 1944.[58]

The HSSPF were called upon to assist in recruitment. SS-Oberführer Zittel in Würzburg requested the cooperation of the local BDM leader, Gebietsmädelführerin Schäffer, in recruiting more assistants. In this case the search was for holders of secondary school certificates, aged eighteen to thirty-five, who revealed the required physical, racial, and ethical qualities, and also displayed a certain "physical and spiritual freshness," with quickness to learn, legible handwriting, good hearing, and error-free speech as understood prerequisites.[59] Himmler was not satisfied with results and made a special plea for renewed efforts, especially for daughters of SS and police families. He thought if young girls were dealt with in a decent and knightly fashion in the SSHK, more would be willing to become a part of the SS family. This letter was widely distributed and affected subsequent recruiting.[60] Since most female assistants in the first campaign had been recruited without regard for racial prerequisites, all members of the SSHK had to undergo a post hoc examination in the spring of 1944. These took place in the offices where the assistants were employed. Great stress was laid on keeping negative results secret, without stipulating whether such controversial results were to lead to dismissal, an event quite unlikely under the circumstances.[61]

Once Himmler rapped a few knuckles, recruiting got serious. In the Southeast, HSSPF E. H. Schmauser stimulated "intensive recruiting" all across the board, including the involvement of police agencies, local military reserve units, RKFDV and VoMi offices, RuSHA offices, A-SS offices, HJ liaison officers, and even administrators of the two concentration camps in the region, Auschwitz and Gross-Rosen.[62] Himmler's paterfamilias approach worked. The Gauleiter of Upper Silesia, acting as representative for the RKFDV, mobilized his forces to recruit for the SSHK. Schmauser thought, following the Reichsführer, that "first of all, efforts had to be made to recruit the daughters of our SS families after they had completed their labor service." He emphasized that recruits would be employed as "war helpers" upon graduating from the *Reichsschule-SS*. They would be installed in SS offices and facilities in the old Reich and in the occupied areas of West and East.[63]

The main source of female assistants had to be the BDM. Most BDM leaders, it appears, were quite willing to cut corners in order to satisfy Himmler. Gebietsmädelführerin Schäffer, for instance, instructed Bann leaders to take girls of seventeen if necessary, although most candidates undoubtedly came from the "Faith and Beauty" auxiliary. Even girls who were employed in work not absolutely necessary for the larger war effort were pursued. Experience gained in setting up the new BDM signals units had shown that a number of capable girls had considerable interest in tasks reserved for the SSHK. Schäffer demanded that the three districts in her region that had signals units were each to provide at least four recruits and one girl from each of the other districts.[64]

It soon became obvious why recruitment took on a familiar efficiency. In May 1944 Himmler transferred the whole SSHK project to Berger's SSHA. He delegated recruitment to Heinrich Jürs, the head of the SSEA. Once more Jüttner's Operations Office and A-SS chieftains, even if they were HSSPF, were displaced. Methods tested on the HJ were applied to the BDM. Since open advertisement was forbidden, the following procedure was adopted: (1) recruitment through the BDM, (2) recruitment and assignment of girls for the SSHK through the BDM Signals units, (3) physical examination of recruits for the SSHK through BDM doctors, and (4) installation of BDM representatives for the signals business in the regions as liaison to the recruiting stations of the SS. RuSHA criteria were applied rigorously. If candidates were married, they had to get the agreement of husbands, and if they had underage children, these were housed in homes attached to the renamed *SS-Helferinnenschule*. To provide "a general impression," each candidate had to appear before a group of observers consisting of the HSSPF, the leader of the recruiting station, and the BDM-liaison. She had to state in writing that she was neither pregnant nor aware of any illness and provide evidence of being "genetically sound." When all conditions were satisfied, the candidate was inducted on the basis of the "emergency service law." The SD subjected candidates to a kind of security clearance.[65]

Never lax in responding to Berger's overtures, the RJF promised to deliver 3,300 SSHK candidates from the BDM signals units in early 1945. The BDM experts in the RJF suggested that the training time could be shortened because these girls already knew the rudiments of the job. The same optimism revealed itself in the statement that should need arise, this contingent could be enlarged, especially since labor duty had now been canceled for volunteers.[66]

Oblivious to the deteriorating military situation, Berger moved swiftly to create new career possibilities for the BDM. Training programs were designed to prepare women for specific careers, varying in length and location. The career chosen attached the individual to a specific training group, while all had to undergo the eight-week "basic curriculum." Swearing in as a member of the SSHK followed successful completion of the basic curriculum. Subsequent technical training fit the actual situation of future employment. There was a training group designated for telegraph and one for radio. Further groups for staff and bureau service and for home economics were in the planning stage. A separate school for SSHK leaders was established at Niederehnheim, soon moved further east because of bombing raids. Special training was planned for vehicle drivers, dental assistants, medical orderlies, and infant nurses, among others.[67]

A revealing telephone conversation took place on 22 November 1944 between two SS-Standartenführer, Dr. Karl Dambach, Berger's ideological expert, and Robert Brill, Jürs deputy in the SSEA, dealing with problems generated by Karl Mutschler. Brill complained that Oberehnheim seemed to focus on criticism of Berger's successful recruitment. Since the old system produced no more than fifty to seventy girls per month and the SSEA had in a single stroke provided the necessary numbers, one could only attribute the criticism to jealousy. He justified Berger's methods of using war-emergency powers on the grounds of utility. After all, large numbers of candidates gave Mutschler a chance to be more selective. Berger had to recruit girls of seventeen because teenagers were assuming adult tasks out of necessity all over the country. Teenagers, after all, could be more easily trained than the older women preferred by the elderly Sachs. On the issue of height Brill was ready to go to 5'2", since girls of seventeen were still growing. Speaking for Jürs and Berger, Brill summarized: "We are now in the sixth year of war, and it is more important to win the war soon than that the home supervisor of an SS school should have to complain about having more or less work to do in order to initiate her girls."[68]

Despite Brill's bravura, recruiting problems were not that easily solved. SS-Hauptsturmführer Sonnen in Berlin-Lichterfelde contacted Brill with a whole list of problems. In the signals units of the BDM, one found at the moment mostly girls age seventeen to nineteen and those of twenty-five who had fulfilled their labor duty but were subject to induction as RAD "air defense assistants." Some 200 girls had recently been released by Oberehnheim without explanation. Since these had not done their labor duty but were sent home after RAD induction time, Sonnen was in a bind. In her training group of eighty, one girl complained, only fourteen had been kept. Since the SSHK school had been evacuated suddenly, the released girls had lost all of their personal belongings. The girls now wanted to know if they would be installed in the SSHK when they completed their labor service. Under these conditions, not a single girl would report for induction. There was, however, no shortage of candidates. Those completing labor duty on 1 January 1945 were eager to join up, but they were not members of BDM signals units. Unless discrepancies were rectified, such as whether the war-emergency conditions were lifted, allowing these girls to find jobs, all sorts of illegal activity was to be expected. Among the girls who had been released, Sonnen noticed that some were obtaining food stamps by ruse and bumming around the city with nothing to do. Ilse Staiger soon got wind of this difficulty and demanded the released girls be drafted back into the school forthwith, and that labor duty be ignored.[69]

While it must have been obvious that the situation was hopeless, there was no sign of giving up on the idea of creating a Female SS Corps. In January 1945 the chief of the Order Police arranged for all female police helpers to be transferred to the SSHK. This applied to girls who had been through the Police School at Erfurt and had given some indication that they wanted to join the SSHK. The SSHA now had jurisdiction over recruitment and reserves; selection of home supervisors; supplies; housing; and leadership and care, indoctrination, and technical training in the SSHK. Actual assignments still remained under the control of police officials, but the Erfurt School soon became an SSHA facility under Berger.[70]

The SSHK became the focal point at the final conference of SS recruiting station officers in Eipel on 19 January 1945. Meanwhile, a uniform news release with numerous illustrations was given to the press through the party propaganda office in Stuttgart. Berger was finally ready to go public when there could have been little reason for doing so, conditions being what they were after the failure of the Ardennes offensive. Thus the belated and contradictory effort to create a female counterpart to the male SS corps continued to the very last minute.[71]

### The Effect of Recruitment on the HJ-SS Alliance

Toward the end of the war the HJ was little more than a convenient conduit for W-SS personnel, both male and female. In 1944 Hitler even revoked the compulsory labor service, and Berger no longer had to worry about OKW quotas. The 1944 "Just You" recruiting campaign continued throughout the spring and summer, concentrating on boys of eighteen and seventeen, although it included a good proportion of sixteen-year-olds. The latter two classes were certainly underage, and the SS share from these had not been determined, but that did not bother Berger. Himmler became commander-in-chief of the replacement army in September and soon persuaded Keitel to eliminate the WBKs from the cumbersome process of recruitment. In December the last vestige of OKW control vanished when Berger received authority to draft outright 20 percent of all boys of seventeen and eighteen. Most of them were called up immediately, which meant that the SS was able to induct probably more than 150,000 teenagers during the last six months of the war. It was a belated victory for Himmler's chief pied piper, who was more than pleased with himself. "The battle which I began in 1940," he wrote to Himmler, "and which SS General Jürs continued with toughness and endurance, has reached a conclusion."[72]

More than 900,000 men and women served in the W-SS during World War II. Over half of them were ethnic Germans, Germanics, or foreigners from occupied or friendly countries, where Berger's recruiters worked with particular zeal and reckless efficiency. At home methods were somewhat milder but just as effective, despite opposition within the SS, from the party, and from OKW. The divisions of the W-SS could not have been what they were, brutal and efficient fighting machines, without the dependence of the SS on the HJ, which provided the core for most of these divisions to the very end.

The Hitler Youth, its ethos, activities, and generational consciousness changed during the war. The war made demands on the organization that it could not fully meet even though it was designed in part for those demands. The SS by virtue of its alliance with the HJ did more than make demands. It nearly destroyed the independent existence of the HJ, having earlier saved the RJF, under assault from other quarters. Driven by the obsession to expand its armed force and extend its influence, the SS was forced willy-nilly to infiltrate the HJ in order to find the "human material" to feed that obsession. In the process Germany's younger generation became a kind of junior SS; although many HJ members managed to stay out of the W-SS, few were able to avoid contact with the SS altogether. The SS helped to destroy the original intent of the HJ as an organized generation by diverting its energies toward martial and sinister purposes. This was more true for the male HJ, but belatedly it also began to impact the BDM, as the Eastern Action and the SSHK demonstrate. At the same time, it is apparent that there were limits to SS influence. The reluctance to volunteer and the indifference of many youths to the appeals of W-SS recruiters partially confirms conclusions reached by students of youth opposition. The evidence suggests, nonetheless, that the SS essentially succeeded in extracting the personnel it needed to fuel its imperial expansion.

# 9 | The Final Sacrifice

In his study of human behavior on the Eastern Front, Omer Bartov has delineated the "barbarization of warfare,"[1] a characterization that fits aspects of other fronts and the exploitation of children in the final months of war. After the Stalingrad disaster, bewildered HJ leaders and determined SS officers conspired to generate a children's crusade to shore up crumbling defenses and offer thousands of teenagers as a final sacrifice to the god of war. That the HJ-SS alliance should have concluded this way is no surprise. For years the SS had inducted underage youth, and millions of HJ members already found themselves in ill-fitting SS uniforms doing men's jobs at home and in combat. Millions of emaciated boys were digging tank traps and manning antiaircraft batteries. Young girls were replacing nurses in hospitals. Armies of children were collecting scrap metal and old clothes, fighting fires caused by bombing raids, policing streets and railroad stations, and serving as couriers and messengers. Normal activity for the young had become an afterthought.[2]

Goebbels's "total war" mobilized the younger generation as it did everyone else. The creation of the Hitler Youth Division (HJD) within the W-SS expressed a sense of desperation and foreboding doom.[3] The HJ was also an essential element in the so-called People's Militia (*Volkssturm*), which was supposed to incorporate all able-bodied males. In the end, more sinister and brutal schemes were hatched that envisioned the formation of a clandestine guerrilla army, made up largely of HJ boys and BDM girls. These children were expected to conduct sabotage and assassination behind enemy lines, wreaking havoc on occupation troops and Allied collaborators. That such schemes should have been thought of is a natural concomitant of the ideology which informed the HJ-SS alliance. That these schemes should actually have begun to emerge in the twilight of Hitler's empire is proof of the effectiveness of that collaboration. The HJ-SS symbiosis climaxed in blood and destruction during the chaotic death throes of the Third Reich and extended beyond total surrender to radical political activity in the postwar years.

HJ units march off to dig tank traps on the frontier (Bundesarchiv Koblenz)

## The Hitler Youth in the Volkssturm

The People's Militia was patterned on spontaneous resistance during the Napoleonic Wars, although there was little that was spontaneous about it in 1944. It appears to have emerged from Himmler's fertile brain and was under his control as commander of the Home Army, with the ubiquitous Gottlob Berger as chief of staff. The "third wave" of the People's Militia was reserved for boys of sixteen to nineteen not already in uniform. Since most of these youths were under the authority of the HJ or the Labor Service, these affiliates were made responsible for their induction. Party, SS, and HJ were supposed to work in harmony to implement this final sacrifice of the younger generation.[4]

The idea of creating an "iron reserve" of 100,000 sixteen-year-old boys was first broached by RJF Chief of Staff Helmut Möckel in a telegram of 2 August 1944 to Dr. Wilhelm Stuckart, the state secretary in Himmler's Ministry of the Interior. Pressured by defense commissars, Möckel requested a decision from Himmler, barely containing his enthusiasm for "self-defense squads" to fight acts of terror by enemy guerrillas. Stuckart agreed that a nationwide network of adolescent squads should be organized on a volunteer basis, but with the understanding that compulsion could be used to enforce uniform training. It was assumed that SS officers would train and command these units. In order to outmaneuver Albert Speer and Fritz Sauckel, both of whom were bruiting about similar projects, Stuckart and Möckel wanted to mobilize a contingent of 40,000 immediately. Ever alert to competition, Martin Bormann soon joined the contest against the minister of armaments (Speer) and the plenipotentiary general for the utilization of labor (Sauckel).[5]

In the fall of 1944 Bormann had issued standing orders that all party officials, including HJ leaders, were to drop their paperwork, grasp available weapons, and join the nearest military units to defend every inch of German-held territory. That order was designed, no doubt, to scoop up anyone not mobilized by some other special order or general project, like the People's Militia. Artur Axmann, among others, was impatient to implement the HJ part of the Volkssturm decree. In January 1945 he sent an urgent telegram to Himmler demanding to know if the "third wave," composed of seventeen-year-olds, was to be mobilized for action on the receding Eastern Front. At the time Himmler could not give him a definite answer.[6]

It is amazing how many officials were prepared to launch a children's crusade. Even General Director Budin, the maker of the *Panzerfaust*, the primitive weapon modeled on the American "bazooka," got into the act. His friend Gottlob Berger passed Budin's suggestion to Himmler. Budin thought that manpower was no problem. Two Hungarian and two Russian divisions and a large Ukrainian one could be organized immediately, provided they had weapons. It was therefore crucial to keep all available personnel occupied in the manufacture of arms. Tens of thousands of returning German soldiers could always be mobilized again and returned to the front. In January 1945 the Labor Service still held 62,000 young men of nineteen and eighteen in reserve, as well as 160,000 boys of seventeen who had completed premilitary training. In Berlin alone some 25,000 air force and navy personnel could be sent to the front. Berger once more complained that a general mobilization center under his guidance could make full use of all these unemployed soldiers. Himmler, however, could do little except promise Berger that Admiral Dönitz would cooperate.[7]

In their eagerness to contribute to the war effort, the pencil-pushing bureaucrats of the RJF began to train a host of boys who had done well in small caliber shooting competitions by sending them to special training courses designed to create a pool of sharpshooters and snipers. These crack shots were then offered to the army and the W-SS. The army showed interest and OKH instructed reserve units to use them, making sure that they were actually installed as snipers. The W-SS made no special effort; it did not have the patience for snipers in the heedless aggression of its combat style.[8]

Among last minute child-crusaders Martin Bormann and Heinrich Himmler made quite a pair. On the evening of 27 February Himmler, who had just emerged from a conference with Hitler, proudly informed Bormann that the Führer had just approved the induction of 6,000 boys of fifteen and sixteen to "beef-up the rear defense line." But that was not all. Hitler also gave Himmler permission to set up special women's battalions, with training to begin immediately, after consulting the NS Women's Organization to aid in recruitment. Aware of Russian female units, Hitler was eager to use female soldiers to put pressure on males, the ultimate form of sexual politics. Himmler and Bormann were concerned that some 500,000 to 600,000 men were then stationed in the Reich as military support troops. If some way could be found to send them all to the front, there would not be a shortage of combat soldiers. Putting boys and women into uniform was designed to embarrass these paper soldiers. Ignoring that most armies have relatively small numbers of soldiers actually engaged in combat, they both thought all would go well if these "shirkers" were forced to fight.[9]

Early in March the RJF offered 500 selected youths as assistant reserve trainers under a special project appropriately entitled "Spring Action." These boys of seventeen and eighteen were supposed to become NCO candidates for the army and the W-SS. They were exempted from labor service and assigned to an infantry training battalion in Oldenburg. This particular project got underway at about the same time that American troops were crossing the Remagen Bridge and penetrating into the interior of Germany. The famous battle at the bridge was conducted by an odd assortment of forces, revealing how desperate things had become. There were 1,176 men in the immediate vicinity of the bridge, among them 500 members of the People's Militia, 200 antiaircraft personnel, 120 "Eastern volunteers," 120 members of an engineering company, 36 security troops, 20 members of the air force manning a rocket battery, and 180 Hitler Youths from local units. This motley company could not hold the bridge, but their attempt reveals how much the war effort had come to depend on teenagers.[10]

What gave these last-ditch efforts plausibility was the ominous fact that the basic machinery of party and government remained intact. Especially those institutional arrangements that supported the HJ-SS alliance seem to have functioned to the very end. Two months before the German surrender, the HSSPF was still issuing orders to recruit SRD boys for a special training course at Bad Ems by activating the HJ-SS liaison officers of local districts and the regional inspectors of the SRD, neither one of whom showed any signs of deserting their posts. Detailed plans were even made to assure prompt delivery of mail. Courier service was organized so that orders and reports could be quickly carried from Bann to Bann and back and forth to regional and national HJ headquarters.[11]

Acting as presumptive commander of the children's crusade, Artur Axmann left no stone unturned. On 3 April he presented a plan for tank destroyer troops (TDTs) to Bormann. The order to create these units had already been issued to the HJ, and model units had been trained and sent into action. A battalion of 700 Berlin boys had been hauled off to Gotha. They were part of a larger brigade of 4,200 boys who had undergone three weeks of haphazard training. Subsequently 2,000 of them were attached to the Ninth German Army fighting on the Beeskow-Storkau-Strausberg line. The remaining 1,500 TDTs were put at the disposal of the Berlin commandant and committed to defense on the perimeter. A Bormann subordinate, Dr. Metzner, along with Ernst Schlünder, the premilitary training chief in the RJF, and the regional HJ leader inspected these bazooka boys during the day of 3 April with apparent satisfaction. While the Berlin HJ was getting ready for the final battle, in the Pomeranian town of Pyritz im

Weizacker a TDT went into action against forward units of the Ninth Russian Armored Guard Corps. When all resistance seemed to crumble, the HJ dug into the ground and defiantly held out for several weeks. Few were left to surrender. Similar action occurred north of Stettin. These incidents are examples of HJ resistance all along the Eastern Front.[12]

The organizational concept was convenient enough. By equating the HJ *Stamm* with the military battalion, the *Gefolgschaft* with the company, the *Schar* with the *Zug*, and the *Kameradschaft* with the *Trupp*, the HJ local structure was simply metamorphosed into a combat organization. The actual combat unit, or Troop, consisted of nine boys, two groups of three manning *Panzerfausts* and the remaining three carrying machine guns for protection. Since a Kameradschaft normally contained ten to fifteen boys, this scheme exploited the familiar organizational structure of the HJ and took in a substantial part of its membership, leaving a skeleton administrative crew to maintain the remaining part of the organization for other war-related activities. On the company level, three-quarters of the boys were to erect tank traps and one-quarter were to be engaged in destroying tanks with bazookas. Within the HJ regional commands, WELs were ordered to train tank destroyer units during the month of April. Much of the remaining HJ organization was gradually turned into a combat-ready defensive system.[13]

The Bavarian HJ managed to put at least one-fifth of the entire membership into the various People's Militia units: 811 boys and girls in tank destroyer troops, 2,246 in alarm units, 727 in communication groups, 918 in courier squads, 4,726 in general support units, 1,119 in supply units, 1,036 in BDM sanitation units, and 361 in BDM signal groups. Rather ad hoc in the way it developed, the plan nevertheless clearly envisioned substantial involvement of the HJ in the People's Militia.[14]

On the district level plans were well underway. In Bann Wasserberg there was a tank destroyer unit of 20 boys, an alarm squad of 50, a signals squad of 25, a courier unit with 30, and assorted supply and service units totaling 303 boys and girls. There were no bazookas available yet, but the unit had two standard issue 98-caliber guns with 500 rounds of ammunition and eight small caliber guns with 600 rounds. The signals boys had four field radios, 1,500 meters of cable, and a telegraph. Early in April the TDT was in training at the district camp, and the signals squad had been well prepared by army trainers. Members of the courier unit were all fifteen or fourteen. In case of mobilization Gefolgschaftsführer Hans Hofmeister was prepared to send his couriers to secretly designated places, bringing about an assembly of all available units of the People's Militia's "third wave." Appropriate clothing was laid aside and every boy knew he had to bring a supply bag with food for at least a day. Bann 336 in Berchtesgaden was in even better shape. Proximity to one of Hitler's official residences meant that an SS unit was housed there and was prepared to arm the HJ to the teeth. The courier unit had 84 boys, while a total of 512 boys in all were ready to receive arms whenever the SS decided to issue them. Cooperation between the district training camp, the Youth Home in Einring, the LD Camp, and the KLV camps had been planned in detail.[15]

The Bavarian HJ was never called to action. By the time George Patton's American tanks got there it was all over. In Berlin, however, it was a different story. Klaus Küster was not yet sixteen. He specialized in knocking out Russian tanks at a range of less than sixty yards. There were more than a thousand boys like Klaus doing the same thing in those final days of April, while the man who inspired such senseless sacrifice slowly played out the final pathetic strains of his life, deep beneath the ruins. Himself only twenty-six, SS Captain Dieter Kersten commanded a battalion of 300 HJ boys during April. After vicious house-to-house combat, a mere fifty of them were left, but these found a Werewolf nest near Halensee and fought on beyond 2 May, when Berlin had already capitulated.[16]

The man responsible for this turn of events was none other than the thirty-two-year-old youth leader, Artur Axmann. Apparently on his own initiative he had decided to commit his TDT in the Battle of Berlin. One bleak April day he stormed into Hitler's bunker to announce to the commander of the Fifty-sixth Panzer Corps, General Karl Weidling, that the HJ was ready to fight and was even then manning the roads in the rear of the Fifty-sixth Corps. The general's reaction was not what Axmann expected. Weidling was so enraged that he became temporarily inarticulate, but finally denounced Axmann's plans for the stupidity that they represented: "You cannot sacrifice these children for a cause that is already lost. . . . I will not use them and I demand that the order . . . be rescinded." But Axmann's flustered promise to countermand the order never reached the boys, if it was in fact ever issued. The units remained in their positions on 18 April. In the following two days they were ground to bits by Russian tanks.[17]

> In the darkness Private Willy Feldheim grasped his bulky *Panzerfaust* more firmly. . . . Crouched in the damp foxhole, Willy thought about the days when he was bugler. He remembered in particular one brilliant, sunshiny day in 1943 when Hitler spoke in Olympia Stadium and Willy had been among the massed buglers who had sounded the fanfare at the Führer's entrance. He would never forget the Leader's words . . . : "You

are the guarantee of the future . . ." and the crowds had yelled "Führer Befiehl! Führer Befiehl!" It had been the most memorable day of Willy's life. On that afternoon he had known beyond doubt that the Reich had the best army, the best weapons, the best generals and, above all, the greatest leader in the world. The dream was gone in the sudden flash that illuminated the night sky. Willy peered out toward the front and now he heard again the low rumbling of the guns he had momentarily forgotten, and he felt the cold. His stomach began to ache and he wanted to cry. Fifteen year-old Willy Feldheim was badly scared, and all the noble aims and the stirring words could not help him now.

Willy Feldheim and his company of 130 HJ boys were swamped by Russian tanks, forcing them to fall back pell-mell. They made a final stand in a ditch and eventually crawled into a bunker. After forty-eight hours of continuous combat they were drained of energy and fell asleep as best they could. When they emerged hours later they were met by a fantastic sight, like some "incredible scene" from "an old painting of the Napoleonic wars." There was nothing but ruined buildings and dead bodies all around them, smoldering in the brilliant sunshine. The bodies of their HJ colleagues brought a shocking realization that they were "all alone," deserted and sacrificed.[18]

Willy and his cohorts were among 5,000 other children who took part in that "twilight of the gods" amidst the ruins of Berlin, which the trembling Siegfried, ensconced in his Bunker-Morgue, was determined to thrust on the German people, not the least of whom were the young members of his own generation. On the afternoon of 20 April, during Hitler's last birthday celebration, a tragic ceremony took place in the Chancellery garden. Axmann brought some HJ boys to the bunker. In the presence of Himmler, Göring, and Goebbels, the Führer thanked his young warriors and pinned decorations on their ill-fitting uniforms. No real soldiers were there to note how much Germany had come to depend on mere children. Because of them an unrealistic Führer kept telling his visitors all day that he was sure the Russians would meet their final defeat in Berlin. Two days later Goebbels cynically proclaimed that Keitel and Jodl themselves would lead the defense of Berlin with every available man and woman, including "every last Hitler Youth." A hasty cordon was thrown around the capital, sparsely manned by all available SS men, commanded by SS General Wilhelm Mohnke. The latter had been a battalion commander in the HJD and now served as Hitler's adjutant. Once more he found himself commanding the HJ, even younger than before, some merely twelve, with steel helmets dropping over their frightened faces.[19]

It was a moment of truth for young warriors if not for their Führer. While

SS commanders shot looters and deserters on sight, HJ boys like Klaus Küster discovered weapons could be used for all sorts of actions. He took his starving aunt to a store and confronted the owner with a loaded pistol. Then he helped his flabbergasted aunt to carry boxes of foodstuffs out into broad daylight. His aunt denounced him for using "American gangster methods," but Klaus merely told her to "shut up!" Aribert Schulz, sixteen, reported to his headquarters in a deserted movie house and saw an SS trooper marching a man out the door to be shot. The victim was an army sergeant who had been caught in civilian clothes. Schulz soon realized that the SS trooper at his HJ headquarters was not an advisor, but the official executioner. In other sections of Berlin the HJ fought alongside French and Walloon members of the W-SS and Russians from Vlassov's army, led by the SS. The HJ fought as fanatically as their international partners, although for quite different reasons.[20]

Melita Maschmann spent that last month in Berlin. She and her BDM girls, no older than the boys in the trenches, were given various impossible jobs by Axmann, setting up temporary hostels for wounded soldiers right behind the front lines, keeping order in chaotic railroad stations, which all other officials seem to have deserted, helping bewildered refugees, and caring for civilian wounded. Her comment has the authenticity of an eyewitness: "I shall never forget my encounters with the youngest of them, still half children, who did what they believed to be their duty until they were literally ready to drop. They had been fed on legends of heroism for as long as they could remember. For them the call to the 'ultimate sacrifice' was no empty phrase. It went straight to their hearts and they felt that now their hour had come, the moment when they really counted and were no longer dismissed because they were still too young. . . . If there is anything that forces us to examine the principles on which we operated as leaders in the Hitler Youth and in the Labor Service, it is this senseless sacrifice of young people."[21]

With Axmann in command, a battalion of 1,000 Hitler Youths, aged fifteen to sixteen, were sent out on 23 April to defend the Wansee bridges against the arrival of a relieving army commanded by General Wenck. Jodl passed this order on directly from Hitler, but other army leaders would have nothing to do with it. General Steiner declared that they were untrained and would be murdered in battle, so he sent the boys back to their bases. Axmann had no such reservations. He set up his headquarters at 86 Kaiserdamm and later in the cellar of the party chancellery at 64 Wilhelmstrasse. He and his boys held on until 30 April, when Hitler and Eva Braun committed suicide. On the night of 29 April, Willi Johannmeier, Heinz

Lorenz, and Wilhelm Zander, who carried Hitler's last will and testament out of a burning Berlin, were sheltered in an HJ bunker near the Pichelsdorf bridge. Wenck's army was defeated before it could get to Berlin. Axmann deserted his boys and escaped by himself on 1 May to join the remnants of another HJ troop in the Bavarian Alps. Here they held out for six months. Back in Berlin a group of HJ tank destroyers withdrew from fierce battles near the main railroad station on 2 May, leaving behind 140 knocked-out Russian tanks. A total of 5,000 Hitler Youths were involved in the Battle of Berlin. A mere 500 survived.[22]

In Vienna Baldur von Schirach was in a quandary. He was always less decisive than Axmann. Now he appeared to waver in committing the HJ to actual combat, trying no doubt to salve his conscience and find a convenient postwar alibi. The Defense Commissar, Rudolf von Bünau, deprived Schirach of his authority over the People's Militia and was prepared, at the end of March, to commit the HJ portion of the militia. But Schirach used his authority as Reichsleiter to prohibit the induction of the HJ. Instead he ordered the HJ leader of Vienna, Hans Lauterbacher, to organize an HJ battalion out of volunteers who were about to be drafted. They were thoroughly trained, according to Schirach, and committed to a section far behind the front line, near Pressburg. When the Soviet army came near Pressburg at the end of March, Schirach withdrew the battalion to Vienna proper, although Lauterbacher and his commanders objected strenuously. They wanted to fight. In his memoirs Schirach claims that he, despite protests and without authority, kept withdrawing the HJ battalion until they were outside the combat area at Gmunden. Other evidence suggests, however, that Schirach's memory is unreliable. On 30 March, when the Russians had broken through the line of defense southeast of Vienna and were only eight miles from the suburbs, Schirach called up the People's Militia and declared Vienna a fortress. HJ boys built tank traps and street barriers. They got *Panzerfäuste* and dug foxholes. HJ newspapers screamed: "Hate is our prayer, revenge our password!"[23]

On 10 April, while the TDTs were sitting in their foxholes ready for action and the battered HJD under Sepp Dietrich was gradually withdrawing from before the Russian juggernaut, Baldur von Schirach sat in an elegant room brooding by candlelight. Otto Skorzeny, Hitler's Mr. Fixit, walked in and demanded to know why the streets were empty and why no one was manning roadblocks. Always the dreamer, Schirach did not believe that the city was undefended. When Skorzeny advised him to escape, he declared: "No, I will never leave my post and I will die in this spot." But he did exactly what Skorzeny advised. He disguised himself as an innocuous writer and slunk away into the mountains, an example of cowardice rather than the maudlin heroic action he had spent two decades purveying to the youth he forsook without a thought to their fate. He claimed later that the combat of the HJ on the Oder, in Breslau, and in Berlin was not the result of an order from him, although he was willing to admit that it might have been the "ominous consequence" of his educational activity. The youthful combatants, he thought, were trying to set an example for adults![24]

In Breslau the final battle began at the end of January. Among the thirty-eight People's Militia battalions which participated in this adamant struggle, four distinguished themselves particularly well, the Forty-fourth, whose leader received the Knight's Cross; the Seventy-fourth, made up of railroad employees; and HJ battalions Fifty-five and Fifty-six, who fought on well beyond Hitler's death—until 6 May. A native Silesian HJ leader, Günter Fraschka, has given a vivid eyewitness account:

> I was there when Silesia disappeared in bloody rape. I saw . . . how Silesia's youth was driven to the front and sacrificed in the fire storm. . . . The boys who fell beside me were fourteen and fifteen years old. . . . I led a combat group that was made up almost exclusively of children. I am one of the few who survived. The others perished, died in atrocious agony. . . . They believed in their Fatherland, remained faithful to him whom they called Führer; they carried his name in their hearts. . . . Their home is lost, but they do not know that and have faith in victory. A net of lies has enveloped them; their courage is not the result of lies, but springs from love of their Silesian home. Their sacrifice becomes meaningless as the red storm consumes them. . . . And he who gave them his name and promised that the future was theirs, he has long since betrayed them. He warms himself by the arsonists fire, for Silesia's boys are to him no more than kindling for the furnace. . . . For those kids . . . the dream of life vanishes like a soap bubble as the order to attack is given.

In Silesia as in Berlin twelve- to sixteen-year-old boys were driven to make suicidal attacks and die "heroic" deaths for a cause they had been taught to espouse. This criminal sacrifice was instigated by HJ leaders who had utter contempt for Baldur von Schirach. He had ceased to be any kind of example to them, and he delivered the survivors to further brutalities at the hands of Allied secret agents in Czechoslovakia who feared Werewolf activity after the collapse.[25]

## The Hitler Youth and the Werewolf

At 9:00 o'clock in the evening of 20 March 1945, a captured Boeing-17 lifted off the runway of a deserted airfield in Hildesheim, flying west. The "Flying Fortress" was one of several foreign airplanes utilized by Himmler's RSHA for clandestine tasks, usually allotted to Otto Skorzeny's "Hunter Packs." On this occasion it carried a Werewolf Commando of six individuals on a secret mission to assassinate the first American-appointed mayor of a German city, Dr. Franz Oppenhoff of occupied Aachen. Operation "Carnival" was ordered by Himmler, planned by SS-Obergruppenführer Hans-Adolf Prützmann, and carried out by a Werewolf Commando made up of four SS men and two members of the HJ. SS-Untersturmführer Herbert Wenzel, leader of the assassination squad, was a veteran of the army's Brandenburg Division, which Admiral Canaris of the Abwehr favored as a recruiting ground, and had been drafted by Skorzeny's Hunter Packs, currently serving as a trainer at Prützmann's Werewolf training center in Hülchrath Castle near Grevenbroich. He secured the necessary weapons and equipment and determined clandestine methods. SS-Unterscharführer Josef Leitgeb, a thirty-two-year-old trainer at Hülchrath, served as second-in-command, with the unencumbered determination of a professional killer. A twenty-three-year-old Hauptgruppenführerin in the BDM, Ilse Hirsch, was supposed to provide supplies, but turned out to be an important link in the successful execution of the mission. She was picked for Operation Carnival by a trainer at Hülchrath. Wenzel picked one of the young trainees at Hülchrath, a sixteen-year-old veteran SRD leader from Aachen, Erich Morgenschweiss, as courier and communications expert. Two older members of the Border Patrol and experienced "frontier-crossers" for the Gestapo served as guides through alien territory.[26]

The Commando parachuted into a Belgian forest and moved toward Aachen. At the frontier they killed a young Belgian border guard, hid their foreign currency, and moved on to set up camp near the target. Ilse Hirsch got separated, made it to Aachen on her own, and contacted a friend in the BDM. By devious ways she determined the whereabouts of Oppenhoff, important information she conveyed to the others when they arrived in the city on 25 March. While the HJ members and one of the border policemen waited in the camp, Wenzel, Leitgeb, and the other policemen confronted Oppenhoff in his own house, after he was fetched by a frightened maid from a party at the neighbors' house. They masqueraded as German fliers who were looking for the German lines. Oppenhoff tried to persuade them to surrender to the Americans. When Wenzel hesitated, Leitgeb screamed "Heil Hitler" and shot the mayor point blank in the head. Just before an American patrol arrived to check the telephone line which Wenzel had cut, the three assassins scattered in different directions. Only Leitgeb showed up at the secret camp. Later he stepped on a mine and died. Hirsch and Morgenschweiss also stepped on mines and ended up in a local hospital severely wounded.[27]

This first successful Werewolf operation soon became a sensation. A so-called Werewolf Radio, apparently initiated by Bormann and promoted by Goebbels, broadcast the astounding news. The Allied press eagerly picked up the exaggerated propaganda claims about widespread guerrilla operations by fanatical Hitler Youths, trained and led by the SS. This Werewolf propaganda, combined with reports of resistance by civilians, was intended to convey the idea that spontaneous daily deeds of heroism were mere isolated instances of a widespread rising against occupation troops that was about to explode. In reality most Germans were eager to cooperate with British and American troops and not the least interested in Goebbels's nihilistic call to sacrifice. These Werewolves were not intended for guerrilla warfare in the conventional sense, since that implied defeat. They were supposed to operate behind enemy lines in uniform, as soldiers sabotaging and distracting the enemy, while the regular armies fought on. Neither the Allies nor the German public realized that the Werewolf organization envisioned by Goebbels and Bormann in their radio broadcasts had nothing to do with Himmler and Prützmann's actual use of the group. This confusion misled the Western press and Allied intelligence officers.[28]

*Colliers* Magazine was taken in by Goebbels's propaganda. At the end of February it carried a detailed account that spoke of a huge guerrilla warfare program hatched by Ernst Kaltenbrunner. The article envisioned a large army of fanatical SS and HJ warriors, using the latest technical wonders in weaponry then being stored in the hidden recesses of the Alps. They were alleged to be involved in an intensive training program, which was thought to capitalize on the German experience with partisans. There was fear that secret headquarters for these intrepid guerrillas were to be set up even higher in the mountains and perhaps even in neutral countries so that the occupation troops would never quite know where to expect harassment and sabotage. The piece concluded by predicting that the movement would fail because the German people were unlikely to support it—the only part of the article that turned out to be accurate.[29]

There were reports from other quarters to feed these illusions. On 28

March the *Manchester Guardian* reported that a German girl of twenty who had given first aid to wounded American soldiers had been shot by Werewolves in revenge. A German newspaper carried an account of a teacher who had accepted appointment as mayor of Muetzenich and was then killed by Werewolves, who pinned a message on his body: "Anyone who lifts his little finger to help the enemy betrays the flag and will be extirpated from the people's community!" The German armed forces radio broadcast this incident and the Werewolf Radio later carried an account of an attack on American soldiers in Koblenz by ten-year-old boys. In Frankfurt am Main three high-ranking American officers had been killed by alleged Werewolves.[30]

Prützmann had been appointed plenipotentiary for the Werewolf Organization by Himmler early in November 1944 at a meeting in his Hohenlychen headquarters. Otto Skorzeny, Walter Schellenberg (SD), and Ernst Kaltenbrunner (RSHA) were present for the occasion. Earlier plans for guerrilla activity by party officials were unacceptable to Himmler. Now Skorzeny and the SS would take matters in hand and utilize the HJ. Prützmann soon set up a Werewolf Staff, headquartered at Hülchrath Castle, used by the HSSPF West, Karl Gutenberger. Some 200 Hitler Youth and other recruits began to train as Werewolf commandos under the guise of W-SS volunteers. Trainers were seconded from Skorzeny's guerrilla units, the regular army, and from the RSHA and Gestapo. The RSHA organized a "Center for Secret Demolition Equipment," intended as a supply depot for Werewolf operations. At the turn of the year a conference of Werewolf leaders was held in Potsdam, including numerous HJ leaders. There was even talk about creating a female branch of the Werewolf to be staffed by BDM girls. At the time some 5,000 young men and women were thought to be eager to join.[31]

Gutenberger was ready to train volunteers sent to him by the Gauleiters of Cologne, Düsseldorf, and Essen. Almost all came from full-time positions in the HJ and BDM, where they had learned to use revolvers, machine pistols, and bazookas. Now they were taught about explosives and deceptive behavior needed to operate behind enemy lines. Gutenberger handed the actual training to two SS colonels, both trusted subordinates. Colonel Raddatz was a former schoolmaster who had volunteered for the LSSAH at a young age and quickly rose to captain. He fought in the Battle of Caen with the HJD, was wounded, and was then assigned to Gutenberger's staff. Lieutenant Colonel Neinhaus was an old party friend, a veteran officer from World War I. After serving as a W-SS recruiter in Cologne, where he had ample contact with the HJ, he got into a major conflict with other SS recruiters and became persona non grata, making him available for this task. These two decided that Hülchrath Castle was an ideal location, being near the small Rhenish town of Erkelenz, away from prying public eyes.[32]

When the first group of volunteers arrived, they were outfitted in W-SS uniforms. Neinhaus made contact with intelligence officers of Field Marshal Model's Army Group B. Well-camouflaged bunkers dug into the hills of the rugged Eifel were located and reserved for Werewolf squads. These were to hide food, weapons, and equipment until the Allied forces rolled over them. Then at night they were to sally forth, harassing and sabotaging enemy communication lines and supply depots. During the day they were to wander through the towns in civilian clothes armed with false passes supplied by the Gestapo.[33]

Prützmann's staff set up other training centers for volunteers from the HJ. Some were located in the suburbs of Berlin, others in the so-called Alpine Redoubt. They were taught to sabotage vehicles and communication facilities and to poison wells and food supplies. Some were issued large quantities of arsenic. If Bavaria is an adequate guide, it is clear that most HJ leaders took the Werewolf project quite seriously. In a report of 6 April 1945, the mobilization chief of the region emphasized the Werewolf among other formations, such as tank destroyer squads and courier units. A substantial number of boys were involved in training for Werewolf activities at the time. Martin Bormann was not put off by Himmler's Werewolf activities. At a conference of party officials at the end of April, previously elaborated plans for guerrilla resistance were discussed, although it had become obvious that party stalwarts feared fatigue, hunger, and war-weariness. While specific individuals in the party apparatus had been given assignments, no one could point to any results. The SS and their HJ allies, however, actually engaged in Werewolf actions.[34]

While there is no indication of an impending spontaneous uprising, there is the evidence of individual actions to suggest the HJ had been primed for resistance. In Cologne-Deutz a boy of seventeen obeyed an order to shoot a Ukrainian laborer whom he found sitting on a toilet. A Bannführer in a Hanoverian town shot the mayor point blank when the latter ridiculed his attempt to form an HJ resistance group as the Allies approached the gates. In Quedlinburg, Himmler's mystical retreat, the HJ district leader organized a Werewolf unit that hid in a forest glen and made daily reports to party officials. The district leader shot a physician who had attempted to flee on 17 April. The doctor's bloody coat was hung on the wall of the Werewolf den to remind everyone "what happens to betrayers" and

Four fighting HJ boys (eight to fourteen years old) captured by U.S. troops (Bundesarchiv Koblenz)

deserters. Near Rothenburg an der Tauber three civilians were executed for daring to disarm a group of twenty-five HJ boys who had armed themselves and decided to join a beleaguered SS unit in the vicinity. The former HJ-Gebietsführer of Mansfeld, now an SS-Hauptsturmführer barely recovered from wounds received in the battle of Kharkov, organized 600 HJ boys into Battle Group Harz. They collected W-SS veterans from a military hospital, students from a NAPOLA, remaining members of the Air-HJ, and boys from a nearby WEL. When the Werewolf Radio proclaimed defiance on 1 April, they went into action against American troops. Within twenty days seventy combatants were left, reduced to fifty shortly thereafter. A desperate attempt to ambush an American supplies convoy was unsuccessful. Most of these starving boys were wiped out by air raids, when American patrols could not find them. Heinz Petry, sixteen, and Josef Schörner, seventeen, survived until 5 June, when they were tried as spies by American troops and executed.[35]

North of Hamburg, toward the end of April, an entrenched group of Werewolves and their SS commanders refused to surrender to two battalions of the British Eleventh Armored Division. When Admiral Karl Dönitz ordered them to lay down their arms on 1 May, they still persisted.

A unit of the German Eighth Parachute Division was finally brought in to subdue them. They found mainly dead bodies, scattered around the forest den. On the eastern side of the Elbe, isolated groups of youngsters from the Werewolf center at Gatow offered feeble resistance to a swarm of Russian tanks. A few survivors remained hidden in bunkers and were later turned in by angry and hungry civilians, whom the Russian troops rewarded by allowing them to plunder Werewolf food dumps.[36]

In Berlin, when panic suffused the city and thousands of soldiers started to desert, SS squads caught whom they could, executed them on the spot, or hung them from the nearest tree in their underclothes, with placards hung around their necks saying: "We betrayed the Führer!" The Werewolves posted signs on houses: "Dirty cowards and defeatists! We've got them all on our lists!" In Hitler's bunker Bormann was eager to buy time for a planned escape. He ordered the SS to suspend Werewolf activity on pain of death. It is unlikely that Prützmann received such an order, and even if he had, it would have been ignored, just as Dönitz's order given at the same time was largely ignored. Most of the Werewolves gave up not because they were ordered to do so, but because there simply was no longer any reason to go on fighting.[37]

In the mountains of the Tyrol a grim determination among HJ and SS remnants still prevailed. Melita Maschmann recalls:

> My last meeting with the Tyrolean Hitler Youth took place under the aegis of the so-called Werewolf training in which SS officers schooled us in sabotage techniques. We all looked towards a dark future with the helplessness of children. Only one thing seemed certain to us: that no power on earth would succeed in destroying our community, the fellowship of the corps of HJ leaders. Many of my Tyrolean friends had had experience of illegal youth work from the period before the union of their country with Germany. With them I sought salvation in the idea that now a new period of illegal activity would begin, although no one knew what its political purpose would be. So we adjusted ourselves to the idea of "fighting on."[38]

Dönitz finally made a proclamation on 5 May over Radio Copenhagen, Flensburg, and Prague: "The fact that at present an armistice reigns means that I must ask every German man and woman to stop any illegal activity in the Werewolf or other such organizations in those territories occupied by the Western Allies because this can only injure our people." Nothing was said about territories occupied by Russian troops. Himmler's adjutant, Rudolf Brandt, also said nothing about the East, when he passed this order to Prützmann. As late as 31 July, when Germany lay supine and in ruins, the Reuters correspondent in Czechoslovakia, Guy A. Bettany, reported defiant Werewolf activity among the sullen Sudeten German population. Factories in Usti nad Labem had been blown up; a shortwave transmitter was broadcasting defiance from the frontier town of Decin; Czech officers had been shot; and attempts had been made to free prisoners from an Allied internment camp. All of this was attributed by nervous Czech authorities to the still feared Werewolf organization.[39]

## The Aftermath

A decade of close association was difficult to break over night. The cord that held the HJ and SS continued to tug even while the International Military Tribunal at Nuremberg condemned the entire SS organization as criminal, thus implicating the HJ in crime and aggression. Several Hitler Youth leaders found themselves in the Alps right after the German surrender, playing their SS association to the end.

Melita Maschmann and three associates, including the head of the BDM, Dr. Juta Rüdiger, hid themselves until 13 July, when they were arrested by American troops. On 30 April, while Maschmann was planting trees, doing something typically useful to avoid facing the ominous inevitabilities of her situation, she was confronted by a tough-looking SS visitor. It was Otto Skorzeny. He and a band of his "hunters" were hiding out in a remote valley and needed someone to cook and wash clothes. The BDM leaders agreed to perform these menial tasks. On 1 May, the day before the Americans occupied Innsbruck, they drove through a blinding snowstorm in an army amphibious craft to the Skorzeny redoubt and found a few months of peace and quiet. There were other clumps of SS men, hiding in other Alpine valleys, but there were few signs of planned resistance. It was many years before Melita Maschmann gained enough perspective to write her memoirs, one of the more valuable and responsible inside accounts to come from any youth leader.[40]

Baldur von Schirach and Artur Axmann, not burdened with the same degree of criminal culpability as their chief alliance partner, Heinrich Himmler, took divergent paths after the war. Himmler followed his surrogate "father" into melodramatic suicide by biting down on a cyanide capsule while in British captivity, although he was slow to recognize that secret surrender negotiations with Allied agents could not soften the universal outrage at his handiwork. Schirach made a pathetic attempt to escape responsibility by masquerading as a writer. He finally realized the hopelessness of that route and surrendered himself to American authorities. He took the onus upon himself, somewhat disingenuously, for miseducating

and misleading German youth, but remained forgetful about his involvement in the holocaust, particularly the transportation of Austrian Jews to
the concentration camps. His testimony at Nuremberg, his twenty years in
Spandau prison, and his commercially successful memoir reveal no particular moral sensitivity or insight and remain totally silent when it comes to
explaining the HJ-SS collaboration. He died in 1974, finishing his remarkable career as an employee of a small business firm.[41]

Axmann avoided arrest until December. During the winter of 1945–46 he
and Willi Heidemann organized transportation, under the guise of legiti-
mate trucking companies, to speed prominent former Nazis into remote
hiding places. In March 1946 a combined Allied intelligence project, known
as "Operation Nursery," arrested nearly 1,000 suspects and put the trucking
firms out of business, although other means were soon found to continue the
project. In May 1949 a Nuremberg "denazification" court finally got around
to trying him as a "major offender," imposing a sentence of thirty-nine
months in prison. His previous internment was counted as sufficient
punishment. He got off with forfeiture of property above 3,000 DM and a
prohibition against political activity. The latter was ineffective. Axmann was
found soon to be in the inner circle of a right-wing organization known as
the "Brotherhood." Purporting to be a veterans organization, the Brotherhood operated secretly during the first two years of occupation. Among its
membership were former top W-SS officers; General Staff officers; former
commanders of elite army divisions; former employees of the RSHA; former
HJ Leader Gottfried Griesmayr; ex-RJF Chief of Staff Hartmann Lauterbacher, who directed the external affairs of the Brotherhood from Italy; and
even the former Gauleiter of Hamburg, Karl Kaufmann.[42]

Typical of a substantial number of former HJ leaders and relatively invis-
ible functionaries are Alfred Zitzmann and Gottfried Griesmayr. Zitzmann, a former member of the W-SS, was squad leader of the Werewolf
unit that bombed a Nuremberg denazification tribunal. After spending a
year in prison, he became active in right-wing politics and rose to become a
local chairman in the neo-Nazi Socialist Reich Party. As a functionary in
the RJF, Griesmayr wrote much of the "educational material" used in the
systematic indoctrination of the HJ. He also served on Martin Bormann's
staff and wrote speeches for Hitler. The memoirs he coauthored with Otto
Würschinger purport to be an objective account but fall short of that mark.
The work reveals how uneducated most of the "educators" of the HJ really
were. Toward the end, Griesmayr was in the unoccupied part of the Sudetenland and participated in sending HJ youngsters into combat as tank
destroyer troops and werewolves.[43]

The *Volksgemeinschaft* ideal continued to exist. A former editor of *Wille und Macht* and Far Eastern correspondent of the *Völkischer Beobachter,* Wolf Schenke, organized the "Third Front" in 1950, which once more promoted ideas for a party which transcended occupational, regional, and social lines of division. Erstwhile Oberbannführer Wilhelm Jurzeck and Siegfried Zantke and one-time Gebietsführer Johann M. G. Schmitz joined him in the campaign. The leaders of the group had connections to officials of the "Eastern Zone" and responded with alacrity to Walter Ulbricht's call for negotiations by launching a letter-writing campaign in the "name of thousands of former comrades." Jurzeck eventually accepted an invitation from East Berlin and was absorbed by the Free German Youth. He was not alone. As in the early 1930s, right and left merged under the banner of political radicalism.[44]

It is remarkable how much of the impetus behind the new right activity in the 1950s and 1960s was provided by veteran SS and HJ leaders. Former SS leader Kurt Döhring organized a youth group for one of the radical right parties that took on a strange resemblance to the HJ. Gerhard Hein, the former inspector of the WEL and battalion commander in the HJD, was one of several prominent leaders engaged in organizing a conference that sought to coalesce right-wing groups in the "national front" of 1951. The prominent former HJ ideologue Gottfried Neesse published a book in 1957 calling for an authoritarian state. Nostalgia for the "good old days" was also detectable in the right-wing journal *Die Deutsche Zukunft,* edited by former HJ leader and W-SS Lieutenant, Siegfried Zoglmann. The old notions of "a leadership elite" and a "virile German policy" resurfaced in the Bund Deutscher Jugend, attached to a right-wing splinter party. This group was conspicuous because of the large number of former HJ and W-SS members in the ranks and the leadership, forcing the parent party to distance itself from its juvenile appendage.[45]

For most of the millions of former members of the HJ and BDM, the immediate postwar years were a time of physical and psychological hardship. Only a few looked back upon their experience with positive feelings, and then only to bits of experience that somehow had helped to mature them. For the majority, the realization that they had worked and slaved for a criminal cause came with devastating slowness. But for all it left indelible marks, carried for a lifetime. They reacted in a variety of ways. Some regarded the loss of freedom, especially toward the end of the war, as the greatest deprivation. The HJ had robbed them of a normal childhood. A boy of seventeen felt he could never escape the murderous experience of the final Battle of Berlin, a cruel recurring nightmare. Another sought solace in the fact that he had attempted to help others whose suffering had been greater than his during the course of the ever-present bombing raids. One boy recalled how he had lost himself in the hard work of digging tank traps near a concentration camp, telling himself the abuse the inmates endured must somehow have been earned, and only later was willing to admit that he had been wrong. Until the end some continued to believe that national socialism was "something special," even if the HJ itself had been intolerable. This reaction was reversed by others. For one W-SS soldier, severely wounded in the Battle of Caen, the harrowing experience of being shunted from one field hospital to another while in constant pain was the most enduring memory. The enveloping panic, while fleeing from the Russian front, was most memorable for another boy, who also remembered that the W-SS units, egging everyone on to resist, inspired equal fear.[46]

For BDM girls the most memorable impression was the presence or absence of a feeling of community in the RAD camps or the hospital work during the war. Few developed relatively mature political sensibilities and thus reaffirm the strongly sexist experience of the Hitler years. Communal life in camps, play and sport, even agricultural work and collective digging of tank traps, were uppermost in their immediate recollections. Somehow the HJ and BDM made them count for something, even if the demands adults made had deprived them of normal girlhood experiences. Other girls had made efforts to avoid the BDM, seeking solitude whenever they could, a goal girls probably found easier to accomplish than did the boys.[47]

Those who served as Luftwaffenhelfer, manning antiaircraft batteries, uniformly found that experience less onerous than other duties. This may be because such tasks were less dangerous than combat, although in the end they also fought on the ground, particularly those serving in Berlin. Because they were shielded from direct influence by the SS and because their war was conducted at arm's length, this duty retained an adventurous element. Few saw death and mutilation first hand, except in isolated cases where fliers had not been able to bail out in time. Most of the 200,000 air force and marine aids were taken out of normal school routine. The attempt to provide substitute education on the spot was a failure. Some, no doubt, welcomed this escape from the classroom, while others found time to pursue independent reading. Officially still subject to normal HJ duty, the nearly continuous air raids toward the end made formal HJ service largely impractical for the secondary school pupils who made up the bulk of these auxiliaries. According to personal accounts, these sons of the upper middle class regarded themselves as "soldiers," welcomed the coincidental release from HJ regimentation, and said they had looked upon much HJ activity as mere child's play.[48]

There were some HJ veterans who came to regret that the anticlerical propaganda had erased their religious upbringing and turned them into nihilistic pessimists. A few seem to have found the strength of character to resort to "inner migration" during the Third Reich, steeling themselves against infection by the conforming majority or maintaining a clandestine religious faith as antidote to the prevailing amorality and irreligion. Kurt Gerstein was a good example of the latter tendency. Strangely enough, among the material distractions of the economic miracle, there was no notable revival of religious faith in postwar Germany among members of the HJ generation.[49]

Most former members of the HJ avoided all politics for nearly a quarter century. This stands in stark contrast to the radical activism of unreconstructed former HJ leaders. The radical left-wing activism and terrorism of the 1960s and 1970s in the Federal Republic appears as a delayed reaction of those born after 1945 against the misguided activism of the HJ generation. The student revolts of 1968 have created a morally inspiring tradition, which now expresses itself in references to the "sixty-eighters," patterned on the "forty-eighters" of more than a century ago. The "Greens" have legitimized much of the left-wing political protest by entering the Bundestag, while their political perspective appears in the halls of academe by informing at least some of the new wave of *Alltagsgeschichte*. Much of the right-wing political activity of former HJ and SS leaders has faded, but the frequently rowdy annual conventions of the W-SS veterans' organization go on, and many of the greying old HJ and SS veterans seem to be engaged in writing tendentious memoirs devoid of wisdom, understanding, or regret. The controversy over Ronald Reagan's visit in 1985 to the military cemetery at Bitberg containing graves of W-SS soldiers once more rekindled old enmities, racial hatreds, and frightful emotional shadows from the HJ-SS alliance. Kurt Waldheim's publicized past and the trial of Klaus Barbie in France had the same effect. Maintaining an ominous life in the collective Jewish and German memory, this transgenerational alliance continues to encumber the widespread efforts at reconciliation.[50]

# 10 | Conclusion

The acceptance of guilt and the necessity of redemption for the German people has been in the back of my mind as this study developed. Contemporary political issues and the perpetual revisionist discourse among scholars is never absent from any historian's endeavor. Now the time has come to make explicit what has been implicit in the narrative text. I have never found moralistic obiter dicta to be particularly congenial. The old-fashioned search for objective historical reality has always been more acceptable to me. One does not have to subscribe to outworn historicist principles to believe that the determination of particular historical facts ought to take priority over eagerness to join popular new schools of interpretation. If a choice has to be made between intellectual enlightenment and political mobilization in determining the moral and didactic function of history, the former is preferable to the latter.[1]

Recent research on social aspects of the Third Reich has highlighted heterogeneity, diversity, resistance, apathy, and inefficiency.[2] Different approaches have been used to modify previous assumptions about national socialism, including the lower-middle-class origins of Hitler's movement and the social composition of his party. The history of "every-day life" has side-stepped most of the interpretational discourse and set the prosaic facts of mundane existence in stark relief. By dwelling on indifference to official ideology, the presence of widespread dissatisfaction and dissent, and frequently, the persistence of class conflict, the degree of actual consensus and control has been obscured. Noting the constant stream of books about opposition, Horst Krüger has openly wondered how Hitler ever came to power and stayed there when Germany appears to have been a nation of resisters and opponents.[3] It is more satisfying to write about the few who saw the inherent evil in national socialism and had the rare courage to oppose and object. It is harder to write about Hitler's successes and the great majority who either ignored the evils they saw or were ignorant and naive in their enthusiasm for a cause that appeared good and right to them at the time. If Ian Kershaw and Sebastian Haffner are correct in their

**255**

estimate that 80 or 90 percent of the population remained committed to Hitler until his victories in Russia came to an end,[4] and if my estimate is accurate that 95 percent of the younger generation remained faithful to the cause even beyond Stalingrad,[5] then caution ought to be exercised in departing too far from the realities of domination and consent.

This study has exposed aspects of life in the Third Reich hitherto left unexplored. The evidence suggests that the appeal to the ideal of a *Volksgemeinschaft*, reinforced by a surprising degree of social heterogeneity within the SS and particularly the HJ, was effective in the short run. While limited, the amount of success attained in creating a sense of national communal solidarity among the young helps to explain why the crimes committed in its name were and are possible in modern society.

The national socialist movement appealed to a wide range of special interest groups and all social classes. Its very diversity was a source of strength in a period of political disillusionment and economic uncertainty. Personal and national crisis engenders not only individual pessimism and collective fear, but also the capacity for dramatic loyalty and unified assertion of superiority. A few simple ideas, no matter how absurd, if they promise salvation through the power and freedom to correct wrongs, demonstrate rights, and dominate enemies can trigger mass movement and a joint willingness to make individual sacrifices. A kind of supraclass revolution can take root, particularly if its motive force is the younger generation, not yet hardened by time and habit or familiarity with qualified success or failure. The Nazi party was a party of the young. They gave it its first political success and provided the energy and drive to seize power, establish predominance in society and state, and mount and maintain a war against overwhelming odds. That youthful vitality and short-sighted, dynamic impatience with older and more sophisticated ideas was the motor behind Hitler's brazen challenge to human values and the European balance of power.

Resistance was neutralized by the propagandistic application of Hitler's manufactured charisma and by his party's multiple thrust embodied in the affiliates and annexed organizations. These penetrated practically all professions, social groups, and institutions. It was the politics of assimilation. Besides the Labor Front, two of the most important instruments of this policy of social integration after the SA had been broken were to be the SS and the HJ. After 1933, when many old fighters were slowly growing weary and fat, eager to enjoy the comforts and pleasures of power, the SS and HJ provided a wellspring of youthful élan. Without them Hitler could not have withstood the skeptical old officers of the army. The army needed the

HJ as well. It tolerated the SS because national unity was not only something the officers valued for its own sake, but which was also necessary to build a strong army and conduct successful war. The SS maintained unity, and army leaders were willing to tolerate the means it employed to do so. At least they were prepared to ignore SS terrorism until it was too late to do anything about it or until they realized that the war would be lost. The Nazi movement could not have expanded and kept its youthful character without SS terrorism and without the HJ becoming an important element in the movement before the assumption of power. As a mass organization, incorporating nearly the entire younger generation in the twelve years that followed, the HJ sustained the movement's vitality.

The SS fed its insatiable thirst for power and its penetration into the collective mind and social fabric by replenishing its personnel from the politically conditioned HJ. The SS pandered to the natural curiosity of the *Jungvolk* by indulging their fascination with tall physical types wrapped in splendid black uniforms. Himmler made assiduous efforts to entice HJ leaders with sparkling careers in the exclusive Black Corps. Institutional links to the HJ were established at all levels in order to influence the younger generation and stimulate their interest in eventual transfer to the Elite Echelon. Attraction was made more potent by setting high standards of acceptance and thus assuring the desired physical, mental, and "racial" type of reinforcement. Regional and local HJ leaders were not always adept in making organizational arrangements or eager to promote SS interests because they were imbued with the notion that youth should be led by youth—should be autonomous. The boys themselves were not overwhelmed by SS appeals to join the armed formations, although before the war a significant number of those who could qualify joined the Special Duty Troops and the Death's Head Formations, as well as the General-SS and the Security Service.

Rearmament and the army's inevitable interest in future soldiers led the SS to restructure its recruiting apparatus under the clever guidance of Gottlob Berger. This SS operator par excellence resisted few temptations to manipulate the tangled strings of party and state in order to achieve Himmler's aims. First an alliance was formed between SS and HJ by making the HJ Patrol Service and the HJ Land Service automatic feeder-organizations for the SS, thus assuring normal transfers to SS branches of the best young men and women the HJ had to offer. Then Berger and Himmler drove off belated and feeble SA attempts and renewed efforts by the army to gain control over the entire HJ organization on the eve of war. When this succeeded, Himmler and his pet manipulator also injected themselves in the successor crisis of the National Youth Directorate. While their candidate, Hartmann Lauterbacher, did not win, the winner, Artur Axmann, soon became even more responsive to SS demands than Schirach, largely because he lacked the independent political status his predecessor enjoyed. This HJ-SS alliance, partially a result of wartime manpower pressures, and partially a development motivated by ideology, affected tens of thousands of German teenagers and involved many of them in the sinister and fatal projects of the SS.

During the war Berger went all out to exploit the HJ alliance. Veteran SS men and wounded reservists assigned to HJ administrative posts competed with army and air force counterparts to influence the HJ ideologically and to gather cannon fodder for new W-SS divisions. Aided by devices to make the SS attractive to ambitious HJ leaders and starry-eyed idealists in the ranks, the efforts of SS recruiters were more successful after Hitler unleashed SS expansionists. When the war took a turn for the worse, SS recruiting became coercive. This was also partly the result of indifference to the special pleading of the SS. Many recruiters were inept, brutal, and careless about youthful sensitivities. Others believed in the special mission of the SS as a European defender from bolshevism and were more successful in persuading HJ boys that they should join to become leaders in elite SS divisions that would save Germany from defeat. A manpower crisis in the end, when OKW no longer resisted W-SS expansion, again drove SS pied pipers into the thinning ranks of the HJ. The army still got most of them, but the SS got more than what would have been a reasonable share of recruits. Many of those who were recruited at the end were barely seventeen or even sixteen. SS campaigns in 1943 to 1945 were cradle-robbing expeditions, which brutally exploited fatalistic resignation within the HJ that expressed itself in eagerness for a final moment of adventure, danger, and heroic death.

There is no way the SS could have become the most significant single element in the Nazi system without the HJ alliance, because that alliance provided the Black Corps with a steady stream of committed loyalists and ideologically pure functionaries and soldiers. The SS could not have become a state within a state if the alliance with the HJ had not been struck in 1936 and Himmler and Berger had not preserved the independence of the National Youth Directorate at the beginning of the war.

The HJ-SS alliance, however, was based on more than recruiting arrangements for the W-SS. Himmler's power was dependent primarily on his internal and external police functions. The HJ had its juvenile police force, which emerged quite independent of SS influence. It was an outgrowth of the campaign to incorporate all young Germans in the HJ and to enforce internal discipline without reliance on adult supervision. The Patrol Service did its share of spying and informing, but it did not have an elaborate system of spies and informers; it pursued delinquents, rebels, and deviants, but it did not arrest and torture them to extract confessions; it helped to establish and staff detention camps, but it did not run concentration camps and exterminate young Jews, although it certainly aided the SS and state in collaring ideological deviants, social delinquents, political opponents, and nonconformists. The Patrol Service was supposed to enforce RJF guidelines; maintain order at HJ meetings, marches, and encampments; discourage disinterest; and promote youthful respectability. These relatively laudable goals were hard to reach, and from the beginning Patrol Service leaders were bound to depend on adult police cooperation. The Criminal Police and the Security Service soon discovered the utility of this juvenile police force for purposes not initially envisioned. Once Himmler had become national police chief, he tied the Patrol Service to his multifaceted police empire by specific agreement, which made the Patrol Service a reservoir for SS police reinforcements as well as for other SS branches. Even before Reinhard Heydrich had created the Central Security Agency, he eagerly recruited security police personnel through the Patrol Service and involved them in domestic surveillance.

There was certainly more social deviance, ordinary crime, and rebellion within the ranks of the younger generation than has hitherto been realized, but Himmler's police apparatus, feeble as it appeared to be in dealing with juvenile delinquency and political resistance during the later war years, nevertheless kept the degree of resistance and rebellion within limits. The new evidence brought to light in the current research suggests that social control could not have been maintained to the degree that it was without the SS sponsorship of the HJ Patrol Service, which protected the reservoir of future SS men more effectively than has hitherto been supposed. The church and the bureaucracy would hardly have tolerated the Nazis as much as they did without the atheistic policies and racist pseudo-religious ideology of the SS being assiduously conveyed to and imprinted in the collective mind of the younger generation through the institutionalized channels forged between HJ and SS.

The experiment with a juvenile police failed to live up to its promise, not because there was a lack of ideological commitment or organizational skill, but because wartime priorities turned the Patrol Service into a supplier of elite combat soldiers. At the same time fire-fighting groups and speed commandos assisted the Order Police and Fire-Fighting Police in a host of war-related activities. In this way thousands of Patrol Service members became involved in SS-controlled activities and were exposed to doctrines of racial prejudice, clandestine surveillance, and repressive measures. Those who joined SS branches responsible for systematic extermination, such as the Death's Head Formations, the Security Service, and the Gestapo, could hardly have dreamed that the romantic spying roles that enticed them initially into the Patrol Service would lead to such ends.

The economic and social aims of the HJ Land Service were not sinister. Based initially on unrealistic notions, the LD envisaged the farmer as an authentic agrarian innocent, formed by tooth and claw of raw nature, capable of acting without the debilitating artificial restraints of urban civilization. But the Land Service became a practical economic and social device that sought to build a stable and loyal peasantry. This was intended to help assure a reliable food supply and to confirm the promise of economic autarchy. During its early years the LD made a contribution to efforts at alleviating the effects of unemployment, particularly for new entrants into the labor market. The "battle against flight from the land," a much more ambitious effort with long-range implications for the economy and the structure of society, was another matter. The Land Service may have been the first significant official effort to reverse the typical twentieth-century migration from the land to the city by persuading urban youth to embark on agrarian careers and perpetuate hereditary lines of committed farm families. These efforts were more ambitious than those of Future Farmers of America. As with all other HJ projects, it was the intrusion of the SS which forced both an artificial burgeoning of the effort and at the same time a displacement of sounder earlier goals inspired by R. Walther Darré.[6] Aside from welcome financial support, the SS introduced the attractive bucolic mirage of free farmsteads for those willing to become members of Himmler's anachronistic future army of defense-peasants, farming the soil and defending the homeland all at once. This introduced an element of colonial exploitation into a purely domestic endeavor and sidetracked the Land Service into the W-SS. Nevertheless, the suggestive idealism represented by the Land Service, in alliance with SS "blood and soil" enthusiasts, made a significant contribution to Nazi agrarian and economic policies. By adding its efforts to confiscation of food supplies in occupied regions and foreign slave labor on the land, the LD helped to avert famine and starvation during the war.

Noble on the surface, but just as corruptive in its effect, were the demographic operations of Himmler's Reich Commission for the Strengthening of Germandom. This awkward euphemism stood for the empire building and Germanizing activities, in which the HJ participated with unreserved energy. The work of the BDM Eastern Action in its practical expression was socially progressive, but it was anchored in racist preconceptions. These led to policies which sought to displace people deemed inferior and establish Germanic dominance in conquered eastern territories. The arrogant notion of a *Herrenvolk* crusade against alien barbarism surreptitiously and by systematic, explicit indoctrination was conveyed to thousands of young people who participated in this destructive project. The idealism and unselfishness that politically innocent young people have always demonstrated was not absent from the efforts of the BDM and HJ to assist the Germanic immigrants imported into the occupied regions of Eastern Europe. Concerted efforts to educate their children and improve their living conditions, even to inculcate Germanic standards of domesticity and agrarian orderliness, were in themselves sincere. But these practical aims sprang from a policy designed to sort out valuable racial "human material" capable of Germanization and destroy the remaining human chaff. The nobility of spirit that inspired many young people was destroyed, since the policy had essentially exploitative aims. The HJ in this case was no more than a convenient adjunct to Himmler's disastrous goals. It has not been generally recognized how much Himmler's demographic engineering depended on the BDM and HJ.

The SS never attained complete control over the HJ, and its influence over the ten million youngsters within it had limitations. This is clearly illustrated by the development of the premilitary training camps. Organized physical exercise and competitive sports have always been important aspects of any youth organization with state functions, but the HJ made it more rigorous, comprehensive, and politically significant than others. With the reintroduction of conscription, these activities became largely protomilitary and soon attracted the attention of the army and gradually the SS. HJ leaders tried at first to train all of its members within existing programs. But that proved to be impossible, despite the aid of OKW chief Wilhelm Keitel, whose agreement with Schirach provided trainers and facilities ultimately deemed inadequate or ideologically unreliable. Hitler was then persuaded by Axmann to establish the premilitary training camps that all boys were forced to attend.

Once the camps were established, the SS lost no time in mounting another piratical raid by persuading the HJ to reserve for them some forty camps. It was obvious from the beginning that the SS training program did not extend beyond the shortsighted notion that the WELs were convenient recruiting corrals. OKW, which staffed four times as many camps, had a more genuine interest in preparing youths for combat. This dilatory and deceptive SS policy became apparent in Kurt Ziegler's camp at Harburg. In all the camps, particularly those staffed by the SS, German adolescents received a form of training that was heavily larded with psychological priming and indoctrination. By teaching them that the war was one of competing ideologies culminating in victory or annihilation, it encouraged fatalistic sacrifice. The puzzling continuation of the German military effort, long after most outsiders and many insiders thought the Nazi cause a lost one, becomes less puzzling when it is realized how effective the psychological conditioning was. The WEL and the disproportionately large involvement of the SS in the enterprise made this possible.

In the end, victimization of children and the betrayal of their infinite capacity for fidelity and loyalty, so assiduously and successfully promoted, led to the criminal sacrifice of adolescent "soldiers" in the Volkssturm and juvenile guerrillas in the abortive Werewolf project. The nihilistic children's crusaders who commanded the SS and the HJ instigated this "final sacrifice." The bloody tie that bound the SS and HJ through the final moments of defeat and destruction continued as a warning even beyond 1945.

The HJ was a generation of misguided idealists. Hitler's children demonstrated a youthful capacity for fidelity. That loyalty was abused. In the name of perverted ideals, the SS exploited and misled millions of them. They were betrayed, deserted, and sacrificed by a party and a regime that had used them to attain power. The bewildered and disoriented survivors found themselves shunned by a society which, once more, exploited them as alibis for past errors and mass amnesia. The HJ generation experienced a peculiar form of socialization. It was characterized by intense regimentation and forceful indoctrination, designed to inculcate an artificially defined social heritage. Bureaucratic regulation affected every aspect of adolescent adjustment to life. It constricted youthful spontaneity and deflected the thirst for action into mechanized competition and limitless warfare. Under the misguidance of the SS, a large segment of the HJ generation was not socialized in the normal sense, but compelled to assume predetermined roles without the freedom to consider alternatives.

The HJ and BDM were more than streamlined German versions of the Boy Scouts and Girl Scouts, decked out in knee-pants and brown shirts, marching in massed formation through cobblestoned streets and picturesque landscapes. It was more than an incongruous and amusing *Kinderkorps* infatuated with a newfangled Siegfried, who, in the end, turned out to be a tragicomic reincarnation of the Pied Piper of Hamelin. That popular notion about the HJ fades rapidly when its history is examined.

The experience of this generation, instead of evoking a picture of sardonic relief from the somber realities of Himmler's black-coated engineers of terror and death, reveals a new dimension of the Third Reich. Far from representing merely the two extremes of innocence and guilt in the morally compromised world of Hitler's Germany, the separate growth of the HJ and SS as organizations depended on the active collaboration of the elites who controlled them. The Third Reich, in turn, could hardly have existed without them as individual institutions or as a collective foundation for the social and political edifice. Yet the house Hitler built with the optimism and energy of the young, and the discipline and coercion of those who prefer force over persuasion, was rotten to the core. It collapsed not only because military defeat brought it down, but because its foundation was unsound and the premises that inspired the architects were false and inhumane. Horst Krüger's house[7] was broken before Allied bombs and Russian guns turned it into rubble.

# Appendix

Table 1.1. Membership of Nazi Party and Primary Affiliates, 1923–1934

| Year | Party | SA | SS | HJ | Total |
|------|-------|-----|-----|-----|-------|
| 1923 | 55,000 | 2,000 | 100 | 1,200 | 58,300 |
| 1924 | 20,000[a] | 3,000[a] | 125[a] | 2,400 | 25,525 |
| 1925 | 27,117 | 6,000 | 800[a] | 5,000[a] | 38,917 |
| 1926 | 50,000 | 8,000[a] | 900[a] | 6,000[a] | 64,900 |
| 1927 | 70,000 | 10,000[a] | 951 | 8,000[a] | 88,951 |
| 1928 | 100,000 | 15,000[a] | 1,000[a] | 10,000 | 126,000 |
| 1929 | 150,000 | 25,000[a] | 2,000 | 13,000 | 190,000 |
| 1930 | 300,000 | 77,000 | 2,727 | 26,000[b] | 405,727 |
| 1931 | 375,000 | 260,000 | 14,964 | 63,700[b] | 713,664 |
| 1932 | 450,000[a] | 470,000 | 52,048 | 99,586[b] | 1,071,634 |
| 1933 | 849,000 | 700,000 | 209,000 | 2,292,041 | 4,050,041 |
| 1934 | 1,500,000[a] | 3,550,000 | 210,000 | 3,577,565 | 8,837,565 |

Sources: *VHB-HJ*, 1068–70. Orlow, *Nazi Party*, 1:45, 76, 109, 239; 2:18, n. 1. Merkl, *Stormtrooper,* 179–90. Diehl, *Paramilitary Politics*, 295. Horn, *Führerideologie*, 280, 298, 379, 395, 414. Stachura, *Nazi Youth*, 269. Wegner, *Hitlers Politische Soldaten*, 80–81, n. 8, 96, n. 86. Kaufmann, *Kommende*, 33–42. Brandenburg, *Die Geschichte der HJ*, 51–52, 58. Giles, *Students and National Socialism,* 69, 94–95.

[a]Estimates. SA and SS memberships might overlap with party membership. Merkl estimates that one-fourth of the SA and one-half of the SS members in 1934 were also members of the party.

[b]Figures include NSS and NSDStB with the inevitable overlapping memberships.

Table 1.2. Membership of Nazi Youth Groups (Date of Founding), 1930–1933

| Year | HJ (1922) | BDM (1927) | JV (1931) | JM (1931) | NSS (1929) | NSDStB (1925) | Total |
|---|---|---|---|---|---|---|---|
| 1930 | 21,000 | 5,000a | | | 5,075 | 3,000a | 34,075 |
| 1931 | 28,000 | 10,000a | 700 | 5,000a | 16,000 | 4,000 | 63,700 |
| 1932 | 48,000 | 15,000a | 10,000a | 4,000a | 13,786 | 8,800 | 99,586 |
| 1933b | 55,365 | 19,244 | 28,691 | 4,656 | 14,000a | 10,000c | 131,956 |

Sources: Stachura, *Nazi Youth,* 269. Brandenburg, *Die Geschichte der HJ,* 51–52, 58. Kaufmann, *Kommende,* 33. Kater, *Studentenschaft,* 117, 173–74. Horn, "The National Socialist Schülerbund," 363, 375. Giles, *Students and National Socialism,* 69, 94–95.
aEstimates. The NSS was abolished in April 1933.
bJanuary 1933, before the Nazi seizure of power.
cMore than 50 percent of university students voted Nazi and sympathized with the movement without actually joining the NSDStB. During 1932 it underwent considerable fluctuation: 11,000 members in October, 7,600 in November, and 8,800 in December.

Table 1.3. Hitler Youth Membership, 1933–1939

| Year | HJ | BDM | JV | JM | Total | Census Age 10–18 | Percent of Age Group |
|------|-----|-----|-----|-----|-------|---------|---------|
| 1933 | 568,288 | 243,570 | 1,130,521 | 349,482 | 2,291,861 | 7,529,000 | 30.44 |
| 1934 | 786,000 | 471,944 | 1,457,304 | 862,317 | 3,577,565 | 7,682,000 | 46.57 |
| 1935 | 828,361 | 569,599 | 1,498,209 | 1,046,134 | 3,942,303 | 8,172,000 | 48.24 |
| 1936 | 1,168,734 | 873,127 | 1,785,424 | 1,610,317 | 5,437,602 | 8,656,000 | 62.82 |
| 1937 | 1,237,078 | 1,035,804 | 1,884,883 | 1,722,190 | 5,879,955 | 9,060,000 | 64.90 |
| 1938 | 1,663,305 | 1,448,264 | 2,064,538 | 1,855,119 | 7,031,226 | 9,109,000 | 77.19 |
| 1939[a] | 1,723,886 | 1,502,571 | 2,137,594 | 1,923,419 | 7,287,470 | 8,870,000 | 82.16 |
| 1939[b] | 1,723,886 | 1,943,360[c] | 2,137,594 | 1,923,419 | 7,728,259 | 14,192,000[d] | 54.46 |

Sources: Kaufmann, *Kommende*, 42–43. Müller, "Hitler-Jugend," 13. Klönne, *Hitlerjugend*, 17. Klose, *Generation*, 138, 272. Brandenburg, *Die Geschichte der HJ*, 58, n. 7, 132, 181. Koch, *Hitler Youth*, 101, 113–14, 233. Stachura, *Nazi Youth*, 269. Stachura, *German Youth Movement*, 128, 131–37. Kater, "Bürgerliche Jugendbewegung und Hitlerjugend," 170–71. Siemering, *Deutschlands Jugend*, 10–12. *Statistisches Jahrbuch* (1935), 12, and ibid. (1941/42), 24. Mitchell, *European Historical Statistics*, 37.

[a]Without BDM-Werk Glaube und Schönheit, introduced in 1938 for young women nineteen to twenty-one, which Kaufmann includes in his total for early 1939. He thus arrives at the figure of 7,728,259 instead of the proper figure of 7,287,470.

[b]One could calculate the percent of the total age group the Hitler Youth as a whole included by incorporating the BDM-Werk Glaube und Schönheit, but such a procedure is unrealistic since the BDM-Werk was not intended to incorporate the entire age group but only those young women who preferred to remain associated with the HJ rather than some other party affiliate.

[c]Includes the 440,789 young women incorporated in the BDM-Werk Glaube und Schönheit.

[d]Estimate arrived at by dividing the ten-to-eighteen figure by five and multiplying by three to arrive at a probable figure for the total category of ten- to twenty-one-year-olds, a figure not available in the existing statistics.

Table 1.4. Social Profile of HJ Leaders, 1939

| Category[a] | Frequency | Percent |
|---|---|---|
| Occupation as youth leaders[b] | 19,125 | 2.5 |
| Secondary school teachers | 41,310 | 5.4 |
| University students | 45,135 | 5.9 |
| Secondary school students | 125,460 | 16.4 |
| Total upper middle class | 231,030 | 30.2 |
| Agrarian occupations[c] | 20,574 | 2.7 |
| Technical occupations[d] | 24,359 | 3.2 |
| Other occupations[e] | 86,445 | 11.3 |
| White-collar employees | 195,075 | 25.5 |
| Total lower middle class | 326,453 | 42.7 |
| Agrarian occupations[f] | 5,436 | 0.7 |
| Skilled workers[g] | 42,196 | 5.5 |
| Young blue-collar workers | 159,885 | 20.9 |
| Total lower class | 207,517 | 27.1 |
| Total | 765,000 | 100.0 |

Sources: Kater, *The Nazi Party*, 1–16. Kaufmann, *Kommende*, 45. Schultz, *Akademie*, 240. Klönne, *Hitlerjugend*, 42–43. Maschmann, *Fazit*, 149. Schoenbaum, *Hitler's Social Revolution*, 70–72.

[a]The ill-defined categories used by Kaufmann, the only available source, make exact determination of the social composition impossible but yield interesting results.

[b]Klönne estimates that the professional leadership from district leader upward divided itself into workers, farmers, and those without a career choice other than youth leader (25 percent); academics and university students (25 percent); and those belonging to the "gut bürgerliche Mittelstand" (50 percent).

[c]79.1 percent of *Landwirtschaftliche Berufe* (per Kater).

[d]36.6 percent of *Technische Berufe* (per Kater).

[e]What *sonstige Berufe* may entail is conjectural, but I have assumed that most of them are a kind of *Lumpenproletariat*, or semieducated unemployables who found a career opportunity in the HJ out of necessity. They could also be placed in the lower class.

[f]I have taken the 20.9 percent figure for Kaufmann's workers and applied it to agrarian occupations to determine a hypothetical proportion of agricultural laborers or their offspring.

[g]63.4 percent of *Technische Berufe*. I have used Kater's method in separating presumed skilled workers from technicians in the vague category of *Technische Berufe* used by Kaufmann.

Table 1.5. Social Profile of Total Hitler Youth, Early 1939

| Category | Frequency | Percent HJ | Reich[a] |
|---|---|---|---|
| University students, pupils, and teachers | 1,622,934 | 21.00 | 1.44 |
| Total upper middle class | 1,622,934 | 21.00 | 2.79 |
| | | | |
| Agrarian occupations[b] | 1,030,950 | 13.34 | 7.70 |
| Technical occupations[c] | 84,856 | 1.10 | 1.79 |
| Other occupations[d] | 463,696 | 6.00 | — |
| White-collar employees | 386,413 | 5.00 | 12.42 |
| Total lower middle class | 1,965,915 | 25.44 | 25.44 |
| | | | |
| Agrarian occupations[e] | 746,550 | 9.66 | — |
| Skilled workers[f] | 146,991 | 1.90 | 16.56 |
| Young blue-collar workers[g] | 3,245,869 | 42.00 | 37.25 |
| Total lower class | 4,139,410 | 53.56 | 54.56 |
| | | | |
| Total | 7,728,259[h] | 100.00 | — |

Sources: Kater, *The Nazi Party,* 1–16, 241. Schultz, *Akademie,* 240. RJF, *Die Organisation der Hitler-Jugend,* 56. Petrick, *Zur sozialen Lage der Arbeiterjugend,* 78.

[a]Reich percentages are based on the 1933 Census and are incomplete because categories for youth do not agree with those for adults.

[b]58 percent (per Kater).

[c]36.6 percent (per Kater).

[d]What *sonstige Berufe* may entail is conjectural, but I have assumed that most of them are a kind of *Lumpenproletariat,* or semieducated unemployables who found a career opportunity in the HJ as leaders.

[e]42 percent (per Kater).

[f]I have used Kater's method in separating presumed skilled workers (63.4 percent) from technicians (36.6 percent) in the vague category of *Technische Berufe.*

[g]The 42 percent figure for *Jungarbeiter,* cited in the RJF source and in Petrick, was used to separate the offspring of hypothetical agricultural laborers from those of landowning peasants.

[h]I have used the total HJ membership figure of 7,728,259 for this table because the only available listing by social category uses that figure.

Table 1.6. Social Profile of the SS, 1937

| Occupational Subgroup | Frequency[a] | Percent SS | Reich[b] |
|---|---|---|---|
| Managers | — | — | 0.53 |
| Higher civil servants | 5,149 | 3.30 | 0.48 |
| Academic professionals | 16,373 | 10.50 | 0.96 |
| Students | 7,156 | 4.59 | 0.48 |
| Entrepreneurs | 328 | .21 | 0.34 |
| Total elite | 29,006 | 18.60 | 2.79 |
| Master craftsmen (independent) | 16,836 | 10.80 | 9.56 |
| Nonacademic professionals | 3,534 | 2.27 | 1.79 |
| Lower and intermediate employees | 39,253 | 25.17 | 12.42 |
| Lower and intermediate civil servants | 10,658 | 6.83 | 5.18 |
| Merchants (self-employed) | 705 | .45 | 6.00 |
| Farmers | 11,682 | 7.49 | 7.70 |
| Total lower middle class | 82,668 | 53.01 | 42.65 |
| Unskilled workers | 15,357 | 9.85 | 37.25 |
| Skilled (craft) workers | 26,245 | 16.83 | 16.56 |
| Other skilled workers | 2,681 | 1.72 | 0.75 |
| Total lower class | 44,283 | 28.39 | 54.56 |
| Total | 155,957 | 100.00 | 100.00 |

Sources: CdSSEA, *Statistisches Jahrbuch, 1937*; T-175/205/4042275. Kater, *The Nazi Party 1–16*, 241. Shalka, "The General-SS," 424–26.

[a]This breakdown covers all categories of SS personnel: General-SS, *Verfügungstruppe*, *Totenkopfverbände*, and staff positions. Using Kater's guidelines and method of categorization, I have adjusted the horizontal listing of SS occupations in a vertical manner by using the principles of selection and determining percentages from aggregate figures recommended by him.

[b]Reich percentages are based on the German Census of 1933.

Table 4.1. Social Profile of Criminality in the Hitler Youth, January–June 1940

| Offense | Membership | | | | | Age | | | | Rank | | | Sex | | Home[a] | |
|---|---|---|---|---|---|---|---|---|---|---|---|---|---|---|---|---|
| | Total | HJ | DJ | BDM JM | Non-HJ | Under 14 | 14–18 | 19–25 | Over 25 | Regular members | Middle leaders | Professional leaders | Male | Female | Town | City |
| Homicide | 27 | 15 | 5 | — | 7 | — | 23 | 3 | 1 | 17 | 3 | — | 22 | 5 | 10 | 17 |
| Manslaughter | 29 | 17 | 3 | — | 9 | 5 | 14 | 8 | 2 | 17 | 3 | — | 28 | 1 | 14 | 15 |
| Suicide | 7 | 5 | — | — | 2 | — | 5 | 2 | — | 3 | 2 | — | 7 | — | 4 | 3 |
| Willful injury | 257 | 153 | 28 | — | 76 | 32 | 191 | 33 | 1 | 174 | 7 | — | 255 | 2 | 122 | 135 |
| Negligent injury | 266 | 128 | 69 | 1 | 68 | 63 | 177 | 22 | 4 | 187 | 10 | 1 | 260 | 6 | 97 | 169 |
| Robbery/extortion | 86 | 32 | 31 | — | 23 | 28 | 49 | 8 | 1 | 60 | 3 | — | 82 | 4 | 22 | 64 |
| Theft | 9,628 | 3,336 | 2,228 | 258 | 3,706 | 3,137 | 6,081 | 394 | 6 | 5,831 | 89 | 2 | 8,802 | 826 | 2,415 | 7,213 |
| Embezzlement | 864 | 403 | 130 | 35 | 296 | 182 | 585 | 90 | 7 | 531 | 37 | — | 800 | 64 | 172 | 692 |
| Embezzlement/HJ | 194 | 153 | 28 | 9 | 4 | 4 | 114 | 67 | 9 | 120 | 67 | 3 | 185 | 9 | 67 | 127 |
| Willful arson | 49 | 16 | 16 | 2 | 15 | 22 | 25 | 2 | — | 33 | 1 | — | 47 | 2 | 19 | 30 |
| Negligent arson | 137 | 34 | 40 | 2 | 61 | 64 | 70 | 3 | 1 | 73 | 2 | 1 | 131 | 6 | 73 | 64 |
| Miscellaneous charges | 2,766 | 1,220 | 576 | 54 | 916 | 828 | 1,683 | 233 | 22 | 1,782 | 66 | 2 | 2,653 | 113 | 843 | 1,923 |
| Missing persons | 137 | 72 | 20 | 9 | 36 | 32 | 98 | 7 | — | 98 | 3 | — | 126 | 11 | 29 | 108 |
| Moral offenses | 1,259 | 480 | 204 | 145 | 430 | 389 | 765 | 85 | 20 | 780 | 48 | 1 | 995 | 264 | 600 | 659 |
| Homosexuality | 1,467 | 631 | 269 | — | 567 | 276 | 878 | 198 | 115 | 855 | 41 | 5 | 1,464 | 3 | 273 | 1,194 |
| Total | 17,173 | 6,695 | 3,647 | 515 | 6,216 | 5,062 | 10,758 | 1,155 | 188 | 10,561 | 382 | 15 | 15,857 | 1,316 | 4,760 | 12,413 |

Source: Knopp, *Kriminalität*, 41.

Note: See Knopp, *Kriminalität*, 40, for comparisons with 1939 figures, and 42–43, for regional variations.

[a] Defined as town when the population is under 10,000 and city when it is over 10,000.

Table 4.2. Expulsions and Separations from the HJ, 1 July 1939–1 August 1941

| Cause | Expulsions Male | Female | Separations Male | Female | Total | Percent |
|---|---|---|---|---|---|---|
| Property violations | 283 | 31 | 747 | 266 | 1,327 | 49.13 |
| Moral offenses | 109 | 27 | 251 | 241 | 628 | 23.25 |
| Homosexuality | 116 | | 178 | | 294 | 10.88 |
| Bad attitude | 64 | 40 | 190 | 78 | 372 | 13.77 |
| Violent acts | 35 | 10 | 14 | | 59 | 2.18 |
| Abortion | 1 | 3 | 1 | 16 | 21 | 0.78 |
| Total | 608 | 111 | 1,381 | 601 | 2,701 | 100.00 |

Source: RJF, Amt HJ-Gerichtsbarkeit, *RB, Sonderdruck,* 35/41K (25.9.1941), T–81/114/133973–134024.

Table 4.3. HJ Crime Rates Compared with Adult Rates in the United States and West Germany per 100,000 Base Population

| Offense | North Central United States 1964 | West Germany 1964 | HJ[a] 1939 |
|---|---|---|---|
| Murder | 3.5 | 0.8 | 1.3 |
| Rape | 10.5 | 10.6 | 27.3[b] |
| Homosexuality | — | — | 60.1 |
| Robbery | 76.2 | 12.4 | 1.8 |
| Larceny | 1,337.3 | 1,628.2 | 177.9 |
| Auto theft | 234.7 | 78.2 | — |

Sources: Bleuel, *Sex and Society,* 31. Wilde, *Das Schicksal der Verfemten,* 8, n. 9, 22, nn. 42–43, 123, n. 9. Cressey and Ward, *Delinquency,* 32. Knopp, *Kriminalität,* 40.

[a]In the case of the HJ the base population is 8,868,559 teenagers between the ages of ten and eighteen inclusive.

[b]The figure for rape in the HJ indicates "moral offenses," which may include less serious crimes than rape, although they are all offenses in the sexual category excluding homosexuality.

Table 5.1. Occupations of LD Boys and Fathers, 1937

| Occupation | Boys | | Fathers | |
|---|---|---|---|---|
| | Percent | Number | Percent | Number |
| Unemployed | 28.5 | 2,850 | — | — |
| Occasional workers | 25.0 | 2,500 | 13.0 | 1,300 |
| Handicrafts and trades | 13.0 | 1,300 | — | — |
| Students | 11.5 | 1,150 | — | — |
| Industrial workers | 8.0 | 800 | 26.0 | 2,600 |
| Commercial employees | 6.5 | 650 | 11.0 | 1,100 |
| Agricultural employees | 5.0 | 500 | 5.0 | 500 |
| Mining employees/miners | 2.5 | 250 | 20.0 | 2,000 |
| Civil servants/free professions | — | — | 8.0 | 800 |
| Fatherless families | — | — | 17.0 | 1,700 |
| Total | 100.0 | 10,000 | 100.0 | 10,000 |

Source: Steindl, "Kritik," 24–25.
Note: In the case of the boys, it is previous occupations.

Table 5.2. Occupations of LD Fathers, 1942–1943

| Occupation | Boys | | Girls | |
|---|---|---|---|---|
| | Percent | Number | Percent | Number |
| Skilled workers and miners | 21.8 | 2,489 | 24.2 | 4,402 |
| Commercial employees (*Angestellte*) | 13.8 | 1,575 | 16.8 | 3,056 |
| Free professions | 13.5 | 1,541 | 11.0 | 2,001 |
| Occasional and unskilled workers | 12.2 | 1,393 | 12.2 | 2,219 |
| Rural handicraft and other vocations | 10.5 | 1,199 | 9.6 | 1,746 |
| Peasants and landowning farmers | 8.3 | 947 | 5.2 | 946 |
| Civil servants | 8.2 | 936 | 8.2 | 1,491 |
| Urban handicraft vocations | 5.6 | 639 | 7.0 | 1,273 |
| Professional soldiers | 1.9 | 217 | 1.5 | 273 |
| Unclassified | 4.2 | 479 | 4.3 | 782 |
| Total | 100.0 | 11,415 | 100.0 | 18,189 |

Sources: Winter, "Entscheidung für das Land," 166. RJF, "Kriegsjugend," 162,175.
Note: See Winter for urban distribution of LD volunteers in the same year.

# Notes

## Abbreviations

In addition to the abbreviations used in the text, the following abbreviations are used in the notes and the tables.

*ANBl* *Amtliches Nachrichtenblatt des Jugendführers des Deutschen Reiches,* Library of Congress

BDC  Berlin Document Center

CdFMW  Chef des Fernmeldewesen (Chief of Communications)

CdOrpo  Chef der Ordnungspolizei (Chief of the Order Police)

CdSSEA  Chef des SS-Egänzungsamtes (Chief of the SS Recruiting Office)

CdSSHA  Chef des SS-Hauptamtes (Chief of the Central SS Office)

DAI  Deutsches Auslands-Institut (German Foreign Institute)

*DAL* *Dienstalterliste der Schutzstaffel der NSDAP* (Personnel list with vital statistics of SS officers)

*DJD* *Das Junge Deutschland* (Periodical published by the RJF)

Est  Ergänzungsstelle (Recruiting Station of the SS)

Gbbf  Gebietsbefehl (Regional directive)

Gbi  Gebietsinspekteur (Regional inspector of SRD)

Geb  Gebiet (Region in HJ administrative scheme)

Gef  Gefolgschaft (Local unit of the HJ)

Gff  Gefolgschaftsführer (Leader of local HJ unit and rank designation)

GRS  Gebietsrundschreiben (Regional circular of the RJF)

HA  Hauptarchiv der NSDAP (Main Archive of the Nazi Party)

HJL  HJ-Leistungsabzeichen (HJ Achievement Medal)

IfZ  Institut für Zeitgeschichte (Institute of Contemporary History)

*IMT* *Trial of the Major War Criminals before the International Military Tribunal*

JfdDR  Jugendführer des Deutschen Reiches (Youth Leader of the German Nation)

K-F  Kriegsführer (wartime HJ leader)

Mitt  Mitteilungen (Newsletter)

NA  The National Archives (Washington, D.C.)

*NCA* *Nazi Conspiracy and Aggression*

NSDStB  Nationalsozialistischer Deutscher Studentenbund (Nazi Association of German University Students)

RAM  Reichsarbeitsminister (National Minister of Labor)

*RB* *Reichsbefehl der Reichsjugendführung der NSDAP: Befehle und Mitteilungen für die Führer und Führerinnen der Hitler-Jugend,* Library of Congress

Rderl  Runderlass (Circular directive)

Rdschr  Rundschreiben (Newsletter)

RFSS  Reichsführer-SS (National leader of the SS, i.e., Himmler)

**275**

RMdI Reichsministerium des Inneren (National Ministry of the Interior)
RMfWEV Reichsministerium für Weltanschauung, Erziehung und Volksaufklärung (National Ministry for Ideology, Education, and Public Opinion)
RNSt Reichsnährstand (National Food Estate)
RuS Rasse und Siedlung (Race and Settlement Office)
RWM Reichswirtschaftsminister (National Ministry of Economics)
Schw Schwaben (Swabia)
SSab SS-Abschnitt (Local SS administrative unit)
SSFHA SS-Führungshauptamt (Combat SS Operations Office)
SSOab SS-Oberabschnitt (Regional SS administrative unit)
SSSt SS-Standarte (SS Regiment/combat and administrative designation)
StGkm Stellvertretendes Generalkommando (Subordinate army corps headquarters)
Stubaf Sturmbannführer (SS rank designation, major)
*VHB-HJ* Reichsjugendführung. *Vorschriftenhandbuch der Hitler-Jugend* (RJF handbook)
*VOBl Verordnungsblatt der Reichsjugendführung der NSDAP,* (RJF circular), Library of Congress
*VOWSS Verordnungsblatt der Waffen-SS* (W-SS circular)
WELR Wehrertüchtigungslager Rundschreiben (WEL circular)
*WuM Wille und Macht* (Periodical published by the RJF)

## Chapter 1

1. Klönne, "Die Hitlerjugendgeneration." Stachura, *German Youth Movement.* Kater, "Generationskonflikt." Spitzer, "Generations." Esler, *The Youth Revolution.* Friedländer, *Reflections of Nazism,* 12.

2. Gordon, *Hitler and the Beer Hall Putsch,* 61. Stachura, *Nazi Youth,* 6–13. Klose, *Generation,* 262–63. Stachura, *German Youth Movement,* 1–9. Cf. Moller, "Youth as a Force in the Modern World"; Jarausch, "Restoring Youth to its Own History"; Gillis, *Youth and History.*

3. Rauschning, *The Voice of Destruction,* 251–52. Kater, "Generationskonflikt," 229.

4. In Brandenburg, *Die Geschichte der HJ,* 234. Cf. Borchert, *The Man Outside;* McClelland and Scher, *Postwar German Culture,* 198–201.

5. Maschmann, *Fazit,* translated as *Account Rendered,* the best of the group; Granzow, *Tagebuch eines Hitlerjungen;* B. von Schirach, *Ich glaubte an Hitler,* not always reliable; Finckh, *Mit uns zieht die neue Zeit;* and Heck, *A Child of Hitler.* While not strictly as a member of the HJ, the most insightful memoir is Krüger, *Das zerbrochene Haus,* translated as *A Crack in the Wall.* Less valuable is Shelton, *To Lose a War.* Moving individual reactions to the realities of late war and postwar times can be gleaned from Hass, *Jugend unterm Schicksal.*

6. Loewenberg, "The Psychohistorical Origins of the Nazi Youth Cohort." Cf. Spitzer, "Generations," 1366–67; Kater, "Generationskonflikt," 241–43.

7. For useful perspectives: Sauer, "National Socialism"; Buchheim, *Totalitarian Rule;* Schieder, *Faschismus als soziale Bewegung;* Bracher, *Zeitgeschichtliche Kontroversen;* Institut für Zeitgeschichte, *Totalitarismus und Faschismus;* Aycoberry, *The Nazi Question;* Hiden and Farquharson, *Explaining Hitler's Germany;* Hildebrand, *The Third Reich;* Kershaw, *The Nazi Dictatorship;* Haffner, *The Meaning of Hitler.*

8. Kater, *The Nazi Party,* 139–48, 200–203; idem, "Generationskonflikt," 240; Gordon, *Hitler and the Beer Hall Putsch,* 70–71; Merkl, *Political Violence under the Swastika,* 12–13,

286, 289, 13; Bracher, *The German Dictatorship,* 234; Broszat, "Zur Struktur der NS-Massenbewegung," 58–69.

9. Kater, "Die deutsche Elternschaft," 489–90; idem, "Hitlerjugend und Schule," 623.

10. Bracher, *The German Dictatorship,* 235; Broszat, "Zur Struktur der NS-Massenbewegung," 67–68.

11. Orlow, *Nazi Party,* 2:305–6, 152. Cf. Childers, *Nazi Voter,* 141; Kater, "Nazism and the Third Reich," 92.

12. Kater, *The Nazi Party,* 141–45.

13. Kershaw, *Popular Opinion and Political Dissent;* cf. Herzstein's criticism of Kershaw's work, *AHR* 89 (1984), 793–95, and Kater, "Nazism and the Third Reich," 95–98, who have pointed to such shortcomings as confusion of grumbling, dissent, and opposition; ill-defined social categories; and neglect of the later war years. See also Steinert, *Hitler's War and the Germans,* and D. Peukert, *Die KPD im Widerstand.*

14. Krausnick et al., *Anatomy of the SS State,* 140. On the function of the Führer myth, see Kershaw, *Der Hitler-Mythos,* the companion volume to his study of popular opinion, which explains at least in part why the effect of propaganda was neglected in his later book. Cf. idem, "Hitler and the Germans."

15. Koehl, *The Black Corps,* 224–47. Wegner, *Hitlers Politische Soldaten;* Stein, *The Waffen-SS;* Stachura, *German Youth Movement.* All have noted the special relationship between SS and HJ, although Koehl first instigated my pursuit of the theme.

16. Sauer, "National Socialism"; Koehl, "Feudal Aspects of National Socialism," 921–33; idem, "Toward an SS Typology"; Schoenbaum, *Hitler's Social Revolution,* 275–88; Peterson, *The Limits of Hitler's Power;* Nyomarkay, *Charisma and Factionalism;* Orlow, *Nazi Party,* 2:352–55; Aycoberry, *The Nazi Question,* 192–215; Mason, "Intention and Explanation," 23–40. Cf. Geyer, "The Nazi State Reconsidered."

17. Kershaw in *The Nazi Dictatorship* reveals how nearly every aspect of national socialism is still in scholarly dispute.

18. Hamilton, *Who Voted for Hitler?;* Kater, *The Nazi Party;* Childers, *Nazi Voter;* Allen, "Farewell to Class Analysis in the Rise of Nazism."

19. Kershaw, *Popular Opinion and Political Dissent,* 373–85; idem, *The Nazi Dictatorship,* 139–48; Mason, *Sozialpolitik im Dritten Reich,* 30, 113–15, 174; D. Peukert, *Volksgenossen und Gemeinschaftsfremde,* 13–17; Winkler, "Der entbehrliche Stand," 1–40; idem, "Vom Mythos der Volksgemeinschaft," 484–90. Even in some rather unusual contexts does Schoenbaum come under fire: Geyer, "Professionals and Junkers: German Rearmament and Politics," 79.

20. Schoenbaum, *Hitler's Social Revolution,* 280, 284. Cf. Stachura, *German Youth Movement,* 141, who finds some evidence that "the Volksgemeinschaft ideal had a populist base."

21. Broszat, "National Socialism, Its Social Basis and Psychological Impact," 137.

22. Broszat, "Zur Struktur der NS-Massenbewegung," 66. Cf. Kater, *The Nazi Party,* 236–39; Gordon, *Hitler and the Beer Hall Putsch,* 49–87; Bracher, *The German Dictatorship,* 152–60, 272–86; Stolleis, "Gemeinschaft und Volksgemeinschaft," 16–38. If the focus is placed on youth, then the importance of social class recedes; see Moller, "Rebellious Youth," 151; and Kater, "Generationskonflikt," 237.

23. Kershaw, *The Nazi Dictatorship,* 130; D. Peukert and Reulecke, *Die Reihen fast geschlossen;* Evans, *The German Working Class;* Huck, *Sozialgeschichte der Freizeit;* Niethammer, *Wohnen im Wandel;* Reulecke and Weber, *Fabrik Familie Feierabend;* Niethammer, "*Die Jahre weiss man nicht, wo man die heute hinsetzen sol.*" For perspective, see D. Peukert and Reulecke, *Die Reihen fast geschlossen,* 11–18; Kershaw, "Alltägliches und

Ausseralltägliches," 273–92; Bessel, "Living with the Nazis," 211–20. Cf. Jarausch, "German Social History."

24. Most of the authors in *Die Reihen* take this view. Cf. Bessel, "Living with the Nazis," 213.

25. Mason is the foremost proponent of this view, under fire from various quarters. Cf. Kater, *The Nazi Party,* 160, who found to his surprise that "as time went by, and especially during the war years, the workers found it increasingly easy to regard the Führer as one of them."

26. Jarausch, "German Social History," 359, n. 45, has put his finger on the central issue when he suggests that "it seems not only possible but desirable to develop an American variant of the history of people's daily lives which does not depart from theory and from quantifiable evidence and yet adds a dimension of personal experience, otherwise missing from analysis." For critiques of *Alltagsgeschichte,* see Tenfelde, "Schwierigkeiten mit dem Alltag," 376–94; Kocka, "Zurück zur Erzählung?"; G. Feldman, "German Economic History," 182; and a sort of internal criticism by Evans in *The German Working Class,* 31–32.

27. Messerschmidt, "The Wehrmacht and the Volksgemeinschaft"; Bracher, *The German Dictatorship,* 349–50; Mommsen, *Beamtentum im Dritten Reich,* 20–38; Broszat, *The Hitler State,* 241. Peterson, "The Bureaucracy and the Nazi Party." Orlow, *Nazi Party,* 2:3–17.

28. Volz, *Daten der Geschichte der NSDAP,* 67; Orlow, *Nazi Party,* 2: 6; Seidler, "Das Nationalsozialistische Kraftfahrkorps," 625–28. The *NS-Fliegerkorps* was a public body subordinate to the Reich minister for air, *Organisationsbuch,* 470; cf. Meier-Benneckenstein, *Das Dritte Reich,* 307–27. On the function of affiliates and auxiliaries as socially integrative forces, see Pridham, *Hitler's Rise to Power,* 320–21; Broszat, "Zur Struktur der NS-Massenbewegung," 68. Cf. Stephenson, *The Nazi Organisation of Women,* who emphasizes both the early appeal of the communal ideal and its failure during the war (156f, 201); and Giles, *Students and National Socialism,* who highlights the relative indifference of university students to indoctrination after the initial enthusiasm.

29. Schäfer, *NSDAP,* 52–56, 64–68; *Organisationsbuch,* 148–56, 286–94; Peterson, *The Limits of Hitler's Power,* 25, 27. Cf. Lingg, *Die Verwaltung,* and Lükemann, "Der Reichsschatzmeister."

30. *Organisationsbuch,* 70–77; Broszat, "Soziale Motivation und Führer-Bindung," 392–409; Hildebrand, "Monokratie oder Polykratie?" 73–96; Kettenacker, "Sozialpsychologische Aspekte der Führer-Herrschaft," 98–131; Kater, "Hitler in a Social Context."

31. Jacob, *German Administration,* 128–40; Diehl-Thiele, *Partei und Staat,* 8; Broszat, *The Hitler State,* 294–327. Cf. Caplan, "Civil Service Support for National Socialism," 167–91.

32. Schirach file, BDC. Orlow, *Nazi Party,* 2:317, 358, 425; Luža, *Austro-German Relations,* 297–358; Wortmann, *Baldur von Schirach,* 18–20; Fest, *The Face of the Third Reich,* 220–34; H. von Schirach, *The Price of Glory.* The old views of Schirach as a romantic lightweight and ineffectual administrator need to be tempered with the judgments of Luža and Wortmann, who portray him as a shrewd political infighter. In the end he had no friends left except Ley, but even the combined efforts of Goebbels and Bormann could not dislodge him from his Vienna post.

33. On Himmler, see Koehl, *The Black Corps,* 226, 242–45; Ackermann, *Heinrich Himmler.* On Goebbels, see Baird, *The Mythical World of Nazi War Propaganda*; Herzstein, *The War That Hitler Won.* On Bormann, see Lang, *The Secretary.* On Kaltenbrunner as Hitler's check on Himmler and direct relationship with Hitler, see Black, *Ernst Kaltenbrunner,* 130–31, 207–10, 212–14. M. Schmidt's *Albert Speer* has finally put the armaments minister in perspective.

34. Stachura, *Nazi Youth*, 9, 14, 269; idem, "Hitler Youth in Crisis," 332, 334, 347; H. W. Koch, *Hitler Youth*, 72, 74, 84–85, 89, 101; Brandenburg, *Die Geschichte der HJ*, 46–58, 122; Horn, "The National Socialist Schülerbund," 363, 375; G. Kaufmann, *Kommende*, 33; Kater, *Studentenschaft*, 117, 173–74, 209; Giles, *Students and National Socialism*, 69, 94–95. Cf. Table 1.3.

35. H. W. Koch, *Hitler Youth*, 41, 72. Brandenburg, *Die Geschichte der HJ*, 88, 90. Siemering, *Jugendverbände*. Eberts, *Arbeiterjugend 1904–1945*. Pietschmann, "Der KJVD 1927/28." On the attempt by communists to win "misguided" working-class youth over from the SA and HJ, see Fischer, "Class Enemies or Class Brothers?" 269–73.

36. G. Kaufmann, *Kommende*, 42–43; A. Müller, "Hitler-Jugend," 13; Klönne, *Hitler-jugend*, 17; Klose, *Generation*, 138, 272; Brandenburg, *Die Geschichte der HJ*, 58, n. 7; 132; 181; H. W. Koch, *Hitler Youth*, 101, 113–14, 233; Stachura, *Nazi Youth*, 269, and *German Youth Movement*, 128, 131–37; Kater, "Bürgerliche Jugendbewegung und Hitlerjugend," 170–71; Siemering, *Deutschlands Jugend*, 10–12; *Statistisches Jahrbuch* (1935), 12, and (1941/42), 24; Mitchell, *European Historical Statistics*, 37. There is general agreement in the basic HJ sources (G. Kaufmann and A. Müller) about membership, if one clearly distinguishes between the figures for the HJ proper (fourteen- to eighteen-year-old males), the BDM (fourteen- to eighteen-year-old females) and the JV and JM (ten- to fourteen-year-old males and females). Unfortunately, students of the HJ, excluding Klönne but including Kater, have ignored these factors in their calculations, stemming from an understandable reluctance to accept official figures by some, simply adopting the most convenient figure by others, or misreading figures. Koch, for example, takes Klose's figures of 8.8 million for ten- to eighteen-year-olds and turns it into a figure of HJ membership for the fall of 1939. Stachura restricts himself to figures for the HJ proper. Kater bases his calculations for percent of annual growth for the entire HJ on Stachura's limited figures, while ignoring the age differential between HJ (up to eighteen) and BDM (up to twenty-one after 1938 with the inclusion of the BDM-Werk). Kater's claim that no more than two-thirds of the relevant age group belonged to the HJ at the outbreak of the war in 1939 is based on his failure to detect the misprint in *VHB-HJ*, 1068. The figure of 3,445,815 youths belonging to non-HJ organizations applies to November 1933, not the fall of 1939! See *VHB-HJ*, 1070, and *VOBl* III/10 (14.3.1935). The problem of determining percentages lies in the habit of the Statistical Office to bunch age groups inconsistently. One is forced thus to estimate the strength of certain categories. This is important since girls up to age twenty-one belonged to the BDM-Werk after 1938 but were also included in the compulsory membership of the BDM proper after March 1939. For calculations based on these considerations, see Table 1.3.

37. See Table 1.1.

38. Stachura, *Nazi Youth*, 60; G. Kaufmann, *Kommende*, 46.

39. Jürgen Schultz's tacit admiration for the youth-oriented structure and "educational" system of the HJ—but not necessarily its ideology—especially Schirach's and Lauterbach's roles in creating it, is significant in that it probably represents a much wider, unexpressed view. See *Akademie*, passim, esp. 226. Maschmann and Heck have been more explicit in describing their former enthusiasm.

40. Conservative and pro-Nazi mothers may have played an important role in influencing their children to be favorably disposed toward the Nazis. While this interesting facet of domestic life needs to be established, hints of it do exist. See Bridenthal, "Beyond Kinder, Küche, Kirche"; Koonz, *Mothers in the Fatherland*; Krüger, *A Crack in the Wall*.

41. Shalka, "The General-SS," 227–28.

42. Ziegler, "The Demographic and Social Structure of the SS-Officer Corps," 192–98. Cf. White, "Outpropagandizing the Nazis."

43. Bernd Wegner, *Hitlers Politische Soldaten*, 214–16.

44. B. von Schirach, "An die Amtsleiter der NSDAP," 28.3.1933, HA/18/339; Stachura, *Nazi Youth*, 58–60; H. W. Koch, *Hitler Youth*, 85; Klose, *Generation*, 17; Stachura, "The Ideology of the Hitler Youth," 155–67.

45. To explain the divergence between rank-and-file proletarians and bourgeois leaders, an argument has been advanced by Horn ("The National Socialist Schülerbund") that the arrival of the NSS "established a solid bourgeois influence over the entire organization." This he thinks accounts for the expansion of the HJ from 28,700 to 55,400 members during the last 15 months of the Republic, suggesting a kind of petit bourgeois coup (358). If such had been the case, then the NSS would have had to merge with the HJ in October 1931, when Schirach replaced Gruber and Renteln took over the HJ in addition to the NSS, rather than being merely attached to it organizationally. The personnel changes initiated thereafter were not predicated so much on proletarian-bourgeois distinctions as they were symptoms of personal loyalty and power ploys on the part of Schirach, since most leaders before this date had been bourgeois. Horn himself states that "barely one percent of the NSS was incorporated into the HJ in this fashion while many of its former units were dissolved" (374). Such a conclusion is drawn in the effort to show that the middle-class NSS members were hostile to "the HJ's plebeian membership and manner" to the point of "deep-rooted class antagonism" and helped trigger widespread class conflict within the HJ. While there was some elitism in the NSS, as there was in the NSDStB, the majority must have accepted the communal ideals of the HJ. The decline in NSS membership from a peak of 16,000 at the end of 1931 to 13,786 a year later most likely was the result of Schirach's demand in July, after Renteln's resignation, that NSS members join the HJ, following an earlier policy that only leaders need do so. Between 12 April and 17 June it had been expedient to be an NSS member, rather than HJ, since the former had not been banned while the latter had, leading some HJ members to use the NSS as camouflage. This fluid situation came to an end in April 1933, when the NSS was abolished and all its members were enrolled in the HJ. By that time the HJ was so large that a few thousand elitist pupils hardly made a ripple.

46. Stachura, *Nazi Youth*, 59–60, 207–58. Klönne, *Hitlerjugend*, 42–43. G. Kaufmann, *Kommende*, 45. Maschmann, *Account*, 147–48. Schoenbaum, *Hitler's Social Revolution*, 70–72. Schultz, *Akademie*, 240. Kater, *The Nazi Party*, 241. Cf. Table 1.4.

47. G. Kaufmann, *Kommende*, 45. Schultz, *Akademie*, 240. RJF, *Die Organisation der Hitler-Jugend*, 56. Stachura, *Nazi Youth*, 61–62. Kater, *The Nazi Party*, 241. Stachura's misreading of statistics in Kaufmann is curious, since part of his argument is based on it. In *The German Youth Movement* he still insists that the "HJ lost its previous proletarian character following the large influx of bourgeois youth after 1933" (141), but in a note refers to an East German source which "estimates that in 1939 42 percent of the membership was working-class" (210, n. 21). That source, Fritz Petrick, *Zur sozialen Lage der Arbeiterjugend*, 78, no doubt got his information from the RJF document cited by Schultz. Note also that Stachura assumes Kaufmann's "ohne Berufe" category means they were "unemployed" and that Schultz collapses Kaufmann's "ohne Berufe" with "sonstige Berufe." Cf. Tables 1.4 and 1.5

48. Kater, "Zum gegenseitigen Verhältnis von SA und SS," 370–74; Wegner, *Hitlers Politische Soldaten*, 224, n. 44. Cf. Merkl, *Stormtrooper*, 153–59, who thinks it somewhat "simplistic to insist that the storm troopers were a predominantly bourgeois or lower-middle-class movement motivated by that economic class interest" (156); and Bessel, *Political Violence*, 33–53, esp. 44, where he argues that the SA "did not consist of any one of

the various class elements which formed the movement as a whole, but rather an age cohort" (i.e., youth), although he seems not to accept the notion that the SA was largely working-class in its social compositon. For Bessel's debate with Fischer about the proletarian nature of the SA, see Stachura, "Who Were the Nazis?" 312–14, 323–24. Stachura thinks Fischer has won the debate. On professionals in general, see Jarausch, "The Perils of Professionalism."

49. See sources listed in Table 1.6.

50. Ziegler, "The Demographic and Social Structure of the SS-Officer Corps," 195–98.

51. Boehnert, "The Third Reich and the Problem of 'Social Revolution,'" 213.

52. Wegner, *Hitlers Politische Soldaten*, 236–37, 256–59. Cf. Kater, *The Nazi Party*, 259; Koehl, *The Black Corps*, 237–41.

53. On the need for caution in the continuing debate about the utility of statistical analysis in the historical study of the Nazi movement, see Andrews, "The Social Composition of the NSDAP," and Stachura, "Who Were the Nazis?" Although both recommend further research, Andrews is less optimistic about its possibilities than Stachura.

## Chapter 2

1. *IMT*, 14:442; CdSSHA, "Parteikanzlei/Reichsjugendführung," 27.5.1944, T-175/155/2685702.

2. Grill, *The Nazi Movement in Baden*, 216–17, 226, 233, 308, 314–16, 322, 338–39, 342; Pridham, *Hitler's Rise to Power*, 197, 206–9; Noakes, *The Nazi Party in Lower Saxony*, 162, 190–95; W. S. Allen, *The Nazi Seizure of Power*, 73; Pauley, *Hitler and the Forgotten Nazis*, 42, 55, 59–60, 72, 76, 92, 205.

3. Wortmann, *Baldur von Schirach*, 118–19; Bessel, *Political Violence*, 121, 148; B. von Schirach, *Ich glaubte an Hitler*, 196–200; Fischer, *Stormtroopers*, 148.

4. "Verfügung," 6.11.1935, *VOBl* III/43 (28.11.1935), 1; "Überführung," *RB* 31/III (21.10. 1938), 813; Wortmann, *Baldur von Schirach*, 158–59; B. von Schirach, *Ich glaubte an Hitler*, 232–34.

5. RFSS to Bormann, 7.6.1938, T-175/80/2600435.

6. Hess, "Vormilitärische Ausbildung," 12.4.1939, *VHB-HJ*, 1352; Geb. Schw., "SA-Wehrmannschaften," 17.8.1939, T-81/103/120277; idem, "Vormilitärische Ausbildung," 1.12.1939, T-81/98/113818.

7. Hess, "Werbung," 20.11.1936, T-175/195/2734509-10; idem, "Verpflichtung," T-175/98/2618728-30; "Notiz für den Stabsführer," 1.11.1940, T-580/38/239; Orlow, *Nazi Party*, 2:148, 160, 204–5, 341–42, 353, 458. See also T-81/7/2725108f; T-81/23/20568.

8. Broszat, *The Hitler State*, 263, 268–70; A. Müller, "Hitler-Jugend," 29; RJF, "Kriegsjugend," 235.

9. A. Müller, "Hitler-Jugend," 15, 19, 22, 26, 32; Wortmann, *Baldur von Schirach*, 146, 211, 221.

10. A. Müller, "Hitler-Jugend," 8, 25–26; Wortmann, *Baldur von Schirach*, 141, 211, 221; RJF, "Kriegsjugend," 188–90. The best example of dual positions was Otto Schröder, who served as *K-Chef des Sozialen Amtes der RJF* and at the same time as *Leiter des Jugend-Amtes der DAF*.

11. Grundmann, *Agrarpolitik im Dritten Reich*, 22, 121–22; "Vorschriften über den Landdienstgruppeneinsatz," in *VHB-HJ*, 2926–49; "Vereinbarung zwischen RJF u. RNSt v. 8.1.1940," in *VHB-HJ*, 2921; "Anordn. d. Rmin. f. Ernährung," 27.1.1940, in *RB* 35/K (5.4.1940), 26; see also "Durchführung der Landarbeitslehre," in *VHB-HJ*, 2915–18.

12. A. Müller, "Hitler-Jugend," 15–16, 28; RJF, "Kriegsjugend," 88–100, 116–20, 154–64; Klaus, *Mädchen in der Hitlerjugend*, 12; Finckh, *Mit uns zieht die neue Zeit*, 74; Shelton, *To*

*Lose a War,* 31; Maschmann, *Account,* passim. For excellent studies of the NSV and Winterhilfswerk, see Grill, *The Nazi Movement in Baden,* 363–409; de Witt, "The Struggle against Hunger and Cold" and "The Economics and Politics of Welfare."

13. A. Müller, "Hitler-Jugend," 38; RJF, "Kriegsjugend," 117, 188; Klaus, *Mädchen in der Hitlerjugend,* 62–67, 72–74, 96–98; Stephenson, *The Nazi Organisation of Women,* 83–92.

14. RJF, "Kriegsjugend," 225; Smelser, *The Sudeten Problem,* 79–81, 140, 192–93, 245; cf. Bollmus, *Das Amt Rosenberg.*

15. A. Müller, "Hitler-Jugend," 12–13, 25, 28, 32, 35, 37; G. Kaufmann, *Kommende,* 118–25; *VHB-HJ,* 48–61, 881–990, 1354–1493; RJF, "Kriegsjugend," 121–53.

16. Wortmann, *Baldur von Schirach,* 127–29, 146–52; G. Kaufmann, *Kommende,* 156–73; Orlow, "Die Adolf-Hitler-Schulen," 272–84; RJF, "Kriegsjugend," 63–80, 195–224.

17. Krausnick et al., *Anatomy of the SS State,* 256; Wheeler-Bennett, *The Nemesis of Power,* 339–41; Reitlinger, *The SS,* 72–75, 81–82; Neusüss-Hunkel, *Die SS,* 34–38; Stein, *The Waffen-SS,* 15–27.

18. Klietmann, *Die Waffen-SS,* 15–27; Stein, *The Waffen-SS,* 8; Krausnick et al., *Anatomy of the SS State,* 158–59; Absolon, *Wehrgesetz und Wehrdienst,* 11. The SSVT had 6,383 men at the end of March 1935; the SS-Wachverbände, later SSTV, had 1,998 men on the same date; *Statistisches Jahrbuch der SS,* 1937, T-175/205/4042264–66.

19. Absolon, *Wehrgesetz und Wehrdienst,* 144–49; CdSSHA, "Einstellung in die SSVT," 9.12.1935, T-175/96/2616702–3; CdSSHA, "Einstellung in die SSVT und Entlassungen," 12.12.1935, T-175/96/2616701.

20. RFSS, Memo, n.d. (Jan. 1935?), T-175/96/2615952, and organization charts on 2615836, 2615888; Höhne, *Death's Head,* 134; CdSSHA, 14.5.1935, T-175/96/2615910; *DAL* for 1.10.1934 and 1.8.1935, T-175/204/2673864, 2673906; *Statistisches Jahrbuch der SS,* 1937, T-175/205/4042245, 4042304.

21. CdSSHA, 12.10.1935, T-175/152/2681130, and 23.4.1936, T-175/152/2681128.

22. CdSSHA, Nr. 07293/35, Oct. 1935, T-354/380/4082739; Lauterbacher in *VOBl* III/40 (7.11.1935), 3; SSab XI to SSOab Rhein, 2.5.1936; SSOab Rhein to SSab XI, 7.5.1936; T-354/380/4082729–30.

23. Ackermann, *Heinrich Himmler,* 243; B. von Schirach, *Revolution,* 33–36; Goethe, *Faust,* pt. 1.2113n.

24. "Rede des RFSS auf dem Brocken am 22.5.1936," T-175/89/2611557–76. The same speech was delivered to a group of army officers in 1937; RFSS, "Organization of the SS and the Police," *NCA,* 4:616–34. This version contains essentially the same ideas, but the emphases and forms of expression are different. There is more detail and greater frankness about internal SS organization, policy, and future plans in the Brocken speech. Himmler obviously made an attempt to be respectable to the quizzical and sophisticated army officers. He wanted the army to know that the SS was performing a significant function by relieving it of the duty of providing internal security for the regime.

25. RFSS, 4.2.1936, T-175/195/2734231; Lauterbacher in *RB* 43/I (4.12.1936), 941; RFSS, 26.3.1936, T-175/152/2681129; "Aktennotiz," SD Koblenz, 14.2.1938, T-81/101/117665; Hausser, 15.6.1936, T-175/96/2616442; Lauterbacher, "Teilnahme," *VHB-HJ,* 1167; Lauterbacher, "Ableistung," *RB* 15/I (24.4.1936), 307; CdSSHA, "Einstellung," 9.6.1936, T-175/195/2735054; *RB* 27/I (7.8.1936), 1; *RB* 28/I (14.8.1936), 626–27; Lauterbacher, "Anrechnung," *RB* 43/I (4.12.1936), 941.

26. In January 1935 the SSVT had 4,984 men, divided among LSSAH (2,531), SS regiment Deutschland (1,722), SS regiment Germania (526) and Cadet Schools (205). The addition of Engineer and Signals Battalions, plus increases in other units, brought total strength to 7,610 by the end of April. In August 1936 three new units appeared: SS Battalion "Nuremberg," Medical Detachment SSVT and Inspectorate SSVT. These

addenda plus normal increases brought the *Verfügungstruppe* to a total strength of 9,162 men; *Statistisches Jahrbuch der SS*, 1937, T-175/205/4042233. See also Klietmann, *Die Waffen-SS*, 23; SSEA, "Einstellung," 5.6.1936, T-175/96/2616695.

27. CdSSHA/VI, "Rekruiteneinstellung," 27.6.1936, T-175/195/2743997.

28. RuS, "Aufnahme von SS-Bewerber," 5.9.1936, T-175/148/2675353–54.

29. Merkblatt-Einstellungsbedingungen für die SSVT, 27.6.1936, T-175/195/2734993–99; RuS, "Aufnahme von SS-Bewerber," 5.9.1936, T-175/195/2735011–12. With the decline of RuSHA, after Himmler forced Darré to resign in 1938, less emphasis seems to have been placed on the *Ahnentafel*; Koehl, *The Black Corps*, 119–20.

30. SS regiment Deutschland, with headquarters in Munich, was confined to Military Districts V, VII, XII, and XIII; SS regiment Germania, centered in Hamburg, had to limit its recruiting to Military Districts IV–XI; A third recruiting center in Berlin, assigned to Districts I–VI and VIII, presumably, pursued personnel for the LSSAH and smaller units of the SSVT located in these areas; CdSSHA, "Einstellung," 4.9.1936, T-175/195/2735061; CdSSHA, "Rekruiteneinstellung," 16.9.1936, T-175/195/2735062; Krausnick et al., *Anatomy of the SS State*, 157–58.

31. RFSS, "Befehl über die Neuordnung der Befehlsverhältnisse der Gesamt-SS," 9.11.1936, T-175/152/2681093–95. A year later Himmler created the post of "Superior SS and Police Leader," one for each *Oberabschnitt*. Their purpose was to promote SS and police integration and direction on the local level. In some cases the new post was combined with that of the *Oberabschnittsführer*, thus further enhancing the power of the Main Sector leaders; see Buchheim, "Die Höheren SS- und Polizeiführer"; CdSSHA, "Bearbeitung des Sachgebietes VI," 11.11.1936, T-175/152/2681150–51. Cf. Birn, *Die Höheren SS- und Polizeiführer*.

32. All segments of the Nazi Party were purportedly voluntary organizations, although membership in the Hitler Youth was at least theoretically compulsory after December 1936. The SS, however, always emphasized its voluntary nature, even though a distinctly forceful manner was eventually to characterize the activities of the Recruiting Office. In Nov. 1936 Rudolf Hess admonished party leaders to keep their organizations truly voluntary. But he overlooked the fact that the special tasks allotted to the SS demanded careful selection. High entrance requirements intensified the search for appropriate "human material," thus leading, frequently, to coercive techniques, which would become more prevalent under the pressure of war. See "Werbung von Mitgliedern," 20.11.1936, T-175/195/2734509–10.

33. CdSSHA, "Neuordnung des Ergänzungswesen," 2.12.1936, T-175/195/2735023–25.

34. SSEA, "Merkblatt f. d. Einstellung b. d. SSVT u. SSTV," T-580/87/436; Absolon, *Wehrgesetz und Wehrdienst*, 16; CdSSHA, "Erfüllung der aktiven Dienstpflicht," 3.9.1936, T-175/96/261683f; Koehl, *The Black Corps*, 132–33.

35. Krausnick et al., *Anatomy of the SS State*, 271; Reitlinger, *The SS*, 82–84; Stein, *The Waffen-SS*, 23–24; Höhne, *Death's Head*, 422–23. In his speech to army officers in 1937 Himmler clearly stated his intention to exchange the men of the SSVT, SSTV, and police. Cf. Sydnor, "The History of the SS Totenkopfdivision and the Postwar Mythology of the Waffen-SS."

36. RJF, "Vereinbarung mit dem SS-Ergänzungsamt," *RB* 44/I (11.12.1936), 965; *RB* 45/I (19.12.1936), 991; *RB* 38/II (5.11.1937), 1025; SSEA, "Neuordnung des Ergänzungswesen," 12.1.1937, T-175/188/2725468.

37. CdSSHA, "HJ-Heime," 1.2.1937; CdSSHA, "Monate der Zusammenarbeit zwischen SS und HJ," 3.3.1937; RFSS, RuS, "Monate der Zusammenarbeit," 18.3.1937, T-354/431/4157501–3; Cerff, "Zusammenarbeit mit der SS," *RB* 21/II (11.6.1937), 531; Brennecke, "Führerheimabende der SS," *RB* 25/II (9.7.1937), 649; *RB* 38/II (5.11.1937), 1043; Karl

Cerff headed the RJF Culture Office between 1933 and 1939, when he joined the SS with the rank of *Oberführer* and served the Waffen-SS from 1940 to 1942, followed by service in the Propaganda Office until 1945. Fritz Brennecke, who wrote *The Nazi Primer*, was active in HJ indoctrination.

38. SSOab Fulda-Werra to SSHA, 10.6.1937; SSOab Fulda-Werra to SSOab XXII, 19.6.1937, T-354/431/4157475, 4157479; BDM Obergauführerin Hessen-Nassau to SSOab Fulda-Werra, 14.8.1937, T-354/431/4157467. Shalka, "The General-SS," 374–76.

39. "Tätigkeitsbericht des Schulungsleiters," T-354/420/4112260-61; "Tätigkeits-bericht," 9.7.1937, T-354/420/4142251. Cf. Mosse, *Nazi Culture*, 122–26.

40. CdSSHA, "Neuordnung des Ergänzungswesen," 30.4.1937, 11.6.1937, 17.6.1937, T-175/159/2690592, T-354/470/4212311, T-175/188/2725108.

41. Vita folders contained police leadership certificates, political leadership certifi-cates, transfers if the applicant was a member of another party affiliate, which included a *Führungsprädikat*, reports and marks on leadership, leadership certificates from the Labor Service or army, acceptance and obligation certificate, photographs, Race and Settlement Office questionnaires, hereditary health certificates, and *SS-Stammkarten*; CdSSHA, "Einreichung von AV-Papieren," 1.6.1937, T-175/152/2681167-68.

42. RFSS, "Neuordnung des Ergänzungswesen," 18.7.1937, 17.8.1937, T-175/159/2690588-89, T-580/87/436; CdSSHA, "Einstellung von Freiwilligen," 6.11.1937, T-175/195/2734661-62; CdSSHA, "Bestätigung zum Staffelmann," 17.12.1937, T-175/179/2715166.

43. SSOab Fulda-Werra, "Neuordnung des Ergänzungswesen," 7.5.1937, T-354/470/4212319; CdSSHA to SSOab Fulda-Werra, 8.11.1937, T-354/420/4142189; HJ Geb. 13 to SSOab Fulda-Werra, 12.11.1937, T-354/470/4212290-91; SSOab Fulda-Werra, "Übernahme von HJ-Angehörigen," 23.11.1937, T-354/420/4142191; SSOab Fulda-Werra to HJ Geb. 13, 23.11.1937, T-354/470/4212292; HJ Geb. Kurhessen to SSOab Fulda-Werra, 22.11.1937, T-354/470/4212289. For a demographic perspective on the Fulda-Werra *Oberabschnitt*, see Shalka, "The General-SS," 59–94.

44. RuS to SSOab Fulda-Werra, 3.3.1938, T-354/470/4212684; CdSSHA, "Übersicht," 11.5.1938, T-354/470/4212644-45; SSOab Fulda-Werra, "SS-Bewerber," T-354/470/4212646.

45. Hamilton, *Who Voted for Hitler?*, 199–204.

46. Stachura, *Nazi Youth*, 182.

47. Klönne, *Gegen den Strom*, 8, 24, 52–54, 57; "Aufstellung d. Streifendienstgefolg-schaften," T-354/454/4189616.

48. 2. SSSt, "Neuordnung des Ergänzungswesen," 4.3.1937, T-354/470/4212228-29.

49. "Bericht über HJ-Musterungen in Frankfurt a.M.," T-354/470/4221110-11.

50. SSOab Fulda-Werra to 2. SSSt, "Werbung für die SSVT," T-354/470/4212714; F. d. Bannes 166 to Moreth, 2.2.1938, T-354/470/4212692. See subsequent frames for examples of youth choosing business over the SS. Lindenburger to Moreth, "Überweisung zur SSVT," 18.2.1938, T-354/470/4212695. The 20 percent of the HJ in special formations is only slightly above the national average of 18 percent. Lindenburger, always eager to main-tain HJ autonomy, had been a functionary since 1933, serving in various HJ districts and the RJF. In 1940 he was transferred to the HJ organization in Holland where he fought with the bureaucrats of the party; Orlow, *Nazi Party*, 2:309-10.

51. 2. SSSt. to SSab XXX, "Besprechung mit der HJ in Wiesbaden," 19.2.1938, T-354/428/4152322-23; 2. SSSt to SSOab Fulda-Werra, "Werbung," 21.2.1938, T-354/470/4212680-81; SSab XXX to SSOab Fulda-Werra, "Besprechung," 5.3.1938, T-354/428/4152321. See 4152319 for the situation in the 83. SSSt in Giessen. 2. SSSt, "Verteilung," 23.5.1938, T-354/470/4212657; 2. SSSt, "Nachwuchsergänzung," 2.11.1938, T-354/470/4212380. Walter Moreth at thirty-four was an "old fighter" with a low SS number

(8767) who made colonel on 9.11.1938, shortly after this debacle; *DAL*, 9.11.1944, T-175/205/4042199.

52. Correspondence of the 57. (Meiningen), 67. (Erfurt), 35. (Kassel), and 47. (Jena) SSSt. with parallel HJ Banne and other SS units, 1937–1938; T-354/470/4212245–51, 4212393–94, 4212461–62, 4212627–31, 4212822–4. Cf. Shalka, "The General-SS," 372–78.

53. Hauser to Heissmeyer, "Ergänzung der VT und TV durch die A-SS," 25.11.1937, T-354/470/4212745–46; Est. Hamburg-Veddel, "Bericht über die Herbstmusterungen," 30.12.1937, T-354/470/4212739–43.

54. Koehl, *The Black Corps*, 141–53.

55. SSEA, "Einstellung von Freiwilligen," 25.1.1938, T-175/152/2681182 and similar documents dated 4.2 and 7.5.1938, T-175/98/2619465–67; *Statistisches Jahrbuch der SS*, 1937, T-175/205/4042288; SSEA, "Erstellung der Monatsmeldung," 14.4.1937, T-175/152/2681191–92; CdSSHA, "Bestimmungen über das Erfassungs- und Meldewesen," 15.1.1938, T-175/152/2681205–10; CdSSHA, "Neugestaltung," 16.1.1938; RFSS, "Neugestaltung," 27.3.1939, T-580/87/436; CdSSHA, Memo, 19.5.1938, T-175/37/2446542–43.

56. Berger file, BDC. I am indebted to Jost W. Schneider for data and letters written by Berger to Schneider in 1974.

57. Cf. Höhne, *Death's Head*, 511–13, and Koehl, "Toward an SS Typology," 113–14. It is Koehl's contention that SS careerists were "pitiable, inadequate specimens of humanity, who were nonetheless capable in their neurotic ways of using exactly those weaknesses of their fellowmen which were equally neurotic: suspicion, hatred, fear and sadism. It seems that the common human trait of pleasure in manipulating others is raised in such men to the nth degree, while the pathological aspects are masked by a cold rationalism." Koehl uses the fourteen SS defendants at Nuremberg as the basis for his study. While these men were involved in more sinister projects of the SS than Berger, he, nevertheless, seems to fit Koehl's general argument that SS careerists illustrate the manipulative ideal as a twentieth-century social trait.

58. RFSS, "Errichtung eines SS-Ergänzungsamtes," T-175/37/2546503–6.

59. CdSSHA, 29.7.1938, T-354/470/4212225–26; RFSS, "Ergänzung," 14.12.1938, T-175/39/2648926.

60. CdSSHA, "Führer für Ergänzung," 1.8.1938, T-175/131/2658210–11.

61. "Arbeitsrichtlinien . . . Dienstanweisung f. d. Streifendienst," *VHB-HJ*, 881–82; "Umgliederung des Streifendienstes als Nachwuchsorganisation f. d. Schutzstaffel v. 26.8.1938," *VHB-HJ*, 895–96; "Übernahme von HJ-Führern in die Schutzstaffel," 16.8.1938, T-175/42/2552747–48.

62. CdSSHA, "Lehrgang d. Führer f. Ergänzung," 1.9.1938 and 16.9.1938, T-354/470/4212197, 202–4; "Arbeitseinteilungsplan d. Führer f. Ergänzung," 15.11.1938, T-175/135/2663588. That the conferees should have been given a tour of Sachsenhausen is no surprise, since recruiters were to find enlistees for camp guards along with other units, but the convivial social visit to the theater on the same day strikes one as odd when confronted by it on a formal agenda. It only begins to make some sense when one realizes how important theater attendance was to Himmler's own socialization as a student in the upper bourgeois milieu of Munich and how much his own youthful experiences contribute to his subsequent conception of the SS as a clan. Ever the sycophant, Berger knew how to ingratiate himself with the boss. See Smith, *Heinrich Himmler*, 59, inter alia, and Ackermann, *Heinrich Himmler*, 242. Rubbing shoulders with young people, particularly in such harmless cultural pursuits as common theater attendance and film-viewing or amateur dramatics seems to have been very much a part of the social process in the emerging HJ-SS relationship. It is clear from Himmler's Dachau speech that this

was the way the SS sought to implement his conception of how the gap between generations could be bridged. See n. 69.

63. Warlimont, *Inside Hitler's Headquarters*, 6–11; Wheeler-Bennett, *The Nemesis of Power*, 374–82; Stein, *The Waffen-SS*, 18–24, 32; Klietmann, *Die Waffen-SS*, 26–31; Koehl, *The Black Corps*, 145–46.

64. RFSS, "Zweitschrift des Abkommen betr. SS u. LD," 17.12.1938, T-580/38/239; "Landdienst—Nachwuchsorganisation der SS," *DJD*, 33/2 (Feb. 1939), 93; see also T-175/ 45/2557209–10; for statistics, see A. Müller, "Die neue Epoche des Landdienstes," 73–74, and *Landdienst der Hitler-Jugend*, 11–13, 21.

65. "Dienstanweisung . . . Ergänzungsamt," 29.10.1939, T-175/104/ 2626774–806.

66. Berger, "Gegenüberstellung der Stärken," 1.12.1939; Berger, "Neuordnung d. Ergänzungswesen," 1.12.1939; T-175/104/2626770–72; Stein, *The Waffen-SS*, 38–42.

67. OKW, "Neuordnung des Ergänzungswesen der SS und Polizei," 30.11.1939, T-175/104/2626687. A revealing controversy with HSSPF and Oberabschnittsführer Southwest, Curt Kaul, who was shipped off to the front as company commander and his wife forced to perform common labor in an armaments factory, can be found in T-175/104/2626664–84, 110/2635116, 137/2664640.

68. CdSSEA, 1.2.1940, T-175/104/2626680–90.

69. B. von Schirach, *Revolution*, 33–36; CdSSHA, "Sonnenwendfeier d. SSHA am 21.6.39," T-175/36/2546107–9; RFSS to SSHA and RuSHA, 16.11.1937, in Heiber, *Reichsführer!*, 48; Ackermann, *Heinrich Himmler*, 64–71, 112, and 242–53 (excerpt from speech at Dachau, 8.11.1936).

70. Lauterbacher, "Nachwuchs für die SS," *RB* 4/IV (3.2.1939), T-175/45/2557240; B. von Schirach, *Ich glaubte an Hitler*, 232–34; "Vereinbarung zwischen d. OKW u. d. RJF," 20.1.1939, T-175/45/2557235–38.

71. Schirach to RFSS, 3.2.1939, T-175/20/2525137–38.

72. "Ernennung von HJ-Verbindungsführern zur SS," *RB* 22/IV (16.6.1939), and *RB* 4/K (Oct. 1939), T-81/113/132087, 132421.

73. Berger to RFSS, "Reichsjugendführung," 9.11.1939, T-175/20/2525133–35.

74. Lauterbacher, "Zustimmung der HJ-Führung bei freiwilligen Meldung für die SS," (10.11.1939), *VHB-HJ*, 1167; Berger to RFSS, "Besprechung mit Lauterbacher," 13.12.1939, T-175/20/2525129–31.

75. Berger to RFSS, "Besprechung mit Lauterbacher," 13.12.1939, T-175/20/2525129–31.

76. RFSS to Berger, 18.12.1939, T-175/20/2525124–25.

77. Berger to RFSS, "Reichsjugendführung," 3.5.1940; Berger to RFSS, "Amtsbesprechung in der RJF," 6.5.1940; T-175/20/2525119–22. Schirach, "Beauftragung des Obergebietsführers Axmann," *RB* 41/K (10.5.1940), T-81/113/132964–65. Lauterbacher to RFSS, 5.7.1940, T-175/20/2525117–18. G. Kaufmann, *Kommende*, 309. Lauterbacher's subsequent performance as *Gauleiter* seems to have made him everybody's favorite, including Hess, Bormann, Goebbels and Hitler. See Orlow, *Nazi Party*, 2:317, 358; Goebbels, *Diaries*, 564; Picker, *Hitlers Tischgespräche*, 239. Orlow's suggestion that he displaced Dietrich Klagges, the prime minister of Hanover, and a friend of the SS, cannot mean that he himself was not a friend of the SS. Cf. Speer, *Inside the Third Reich*, 176, where Speer recounts a joke Goebbels told Hitler cutting Lauterbacher's earlier pretensions down to size; and Wortmann, *Baldur von Schirach*, 137–38, 182, 184, 221, who suggests that Göring and Rosenberg also had designs on the RJF at the time, and confirms Lauterbacher's competence and popularity.

78. RFSS, "Aktennotiz," 14.8.1940, T-175/20/2525114–15.

79. Stachura, *Nazi Youth*, 207–58. Among 200 HJ *Altkämpfer*, 34 appear to have gone over to some branch of the SS or expressed sympathy with it by accepting "honorary" ranks.

## Chapter 3

1. Richardson, "Berlin Police in the Weimar Republic," 90–91; Douthit, "Police Professionalism and the War Against Crime," 317, 325–26; Kohler, "The Crisis in the Prussian Schutzpolizei," 131–50; Krausnick et al., *Anatomy of the SS State*, 195–96, 200; Liang, *The Berlin Police Force*, 20–25, 165–73; Heller, "The Remodeled Praetorians," 45–64; Browder, "The SD," 205–29, especially 216.

2. A. Müller, *Die Betreuung*, 54–55; Randel, *Die Jugenddienstpflicht*, 90. Cf. Pross, *Jugend-Eros-Politik*.

3. Horn, "Youth Resistance," 26–50, argues strongly for a significant opposition; Brandenburg, *Die Geschichte der HJ*, 194–227, and Stachura, "Machtergreifung," 269, discount its political importance and question its extent; Klönne, *Gegen den Strom*, made an early assessment, based on a collection of reports by opponents, reissued in 1978. For resistance or lack thereof anchored in religion, see works by Roth, von Lersner, Schellenberg, Kleinöder, Horn, Walker, Priepke, Riedel, and Schwersenz and Wolff. For opposition of socialist and communist youth, see works by Jahnke, D. Peukert, and Rosenhaft. On antisocial cliques, see works by Klönne, Muth, Gruchmann, Hehr and Hippe, D. Peukert, and von Hellfeld. A critical assessment of this growing body of literature is needed.

4. Stachura, "Machtergreifung," 256–74.

5. Seetzen, chief of Stapostelle Aachen, "Stapo Lagebericht von 23.12.1933"; Reeder report for February 1934; Stapo report for September 1934; in Vollmer, *Volksopposition*, 31–33, 102–3.

6. Vollmer, *Volksopposition*, 163, 202–3, 233–34. Cf. Walker, " 'Young Priests' as Opponents." On Rosenberg and his influence on HJ ideology see Wortmann, *Baldur von Schirach*, 53–55, 127, 168, 182, and Cecil, *The Myth of the Master Race*, 140–45, 151–53, 216.

7. Vollmer, *Volksopposition*, 220–21, 266–67, 360–61.

8. Klönne, *Gegen den Strom*, 26, 47, 51–52; idem, "Jugendprotest und Jugendopposition," 4:582. For the exceptional role of the Jungvolk and the strong influence of the Bünde style until 1936–37, see Klönne, *Hitlerjugend*, 71–73, and Stachura, *German Youth Movement*, 125.

9. Klönne, *Gegen den Strom*, 18; Scholl, *Six against Tyranny*, 5–6; Maschmann, *Account*, passim; Stachura, "Machtergreifung," 256.

10. Bleuel, *Sex and Society*, 159–60; Kohlrausch and Lange, *Strafgesetzbuch*, 411–15.

11. Vollmer, *Volksopposition*, 209, 226–27, 253.

12. Ibid., 203–4, 221. Report from Landjahrlager Friedrichsdorf, 2.7.1936, T-81/102/118722–24. Report of BDM leader Resel Frosch, 14.4.1934, T-580/540/375. Anonymous report addressed to Lydia Gottschewski, Bundesführerin of the BDM, T-580/540/375. Klaus, *Mädchen in der Hitlerjugend*, 104–14. Wolfson, "Constraint and Choice in the SS Leadership," 264.

13. Knopp, *Kriminalität*, 210–11. As the RJF liaison with the RSHA, Knopp compiled this revealing document by collating statistics from the Statistical Office, the Criminal Police Office, the Association of Juvenile Courts and Juvenile Court Assistants, the criminal statistics of the RJF, and the reports of the SRD regional inspectors. The variety of sources and the fact that the picture the report presents is not flattering to the RJF enhances the credibility of the findings. Ackermann, *Heinrich Himmler*, 140–41.

14. See BDC file for Lüer and biographic sketches for Lüer and John in Stachura, *Nazi Youth*, 226–27, 236.

15. Klose, *Generation*, 215. Lauterbacher, "SRD," *VOBl* III/9 (7.3.1935), 2. Schirach,

"Leitung der Abteilung Jugendverbände und Polizeiverbindungsstelle," *VOBl* III/26 (11.7.1935), 1. Lüer file, BDC. Stachura, *Nazi Youth,* 226–27.

16. Krausnick et al., *Anatomy of the SS State,* 145–56. Höhne, *Death's Head,* 205–8, 221–24. LKPA Berlin, "Umhertreiben von Jugendlichen," 14.11.1934, in *VHB-HJ,* 971–72. LKPA, "Bekämpfung homosexuellen Straftaten," 5.12. 1934, in *VHB-HJ,* 972. Lüer and John, "Zusammenarbeit m. d. Kriminalpolizei," *VOBl* III/15 (1935), 5–6.

17. Lüer and John, "Organisation des HJ-SRD," *VOBl* III/14 (11.4.1935), 3–4.

18. Lüer and John, "Streifendienstbefehl Nr. 1," *VOBl* III/18 (16.5.1935), 4–6. Idem, "Streifendienstbefehl Nr. 2," *VOBl* III/20 (31.5.1935), 3–4.

19. Lüer, "Streifendienstanordnung Nr. 1," *VOBl* III/21 (6.6.1935), 3–7.

20. For the *Heimtückegesetz* and its troublesome application, see Vollmer, *Volksopposition,* 163. Bleuel, *Sex and Society,* 182.

21. Aachen Stapo report by Heinz Seetzen for April 1935, and Reeder to Hans-Bernd Gisevius in the Ministry of the Interior, 21.6.1935, in Vollmer, *Volksopposition,* 210, 236. Reeder was a senior bureaucrat and a sponsoring member of the SS, but he strongly opposed Gestapo interference with the administration; see Höhne, *Death's Head,* 216–17.

22. John, "Streifendienstanordnung, Nr. 2," *VOBl* III/34 (26.9.1935), 6. LKPA, "Bettelwesen in der HJ," 4.11.1935, in *VHB-HJ,* 971. Lauterbacher, "Zusammenarbeit mit Polizei," *VOBl* III/39 (31.10.1935), 4. Lauterbacher, "Abkommandierung zum SRD," *RB* 23/1 (10.7.1936), 517. Lüer, Amt für Jugendverbände, "Einsatz des Streifendienstes" and "Halbjahr-Einsatzplan," *RB* 33/1 (25.9.1936), 721. Lüer, Amt für Jugendverbände, "SRD der HJ und Landjahr," *RB* 25/1 (24.7.1936), 583.

23. Lauterbacher, "Mitgliedersperre aufgehoben," *VOBl* III/9 (7.3.1935), 2.

24. Nabersberg, "Übersicht über den Stand der Jugendverbände," *VOBl* III/10 (14.3.1935), 6–7. (Nabersberg was chief of the Abteilung Verbände until Lüer took over, and he also headed the Abteilung Ausland, where he played an important role in the incorporation of the youth branch of the VDA.) Lüer, "Zusammenstellung abgeschlossener Verträge," *RB* 3/1 (24.1.1936), 41–42. For texts of all the police prohibitions, see "Polizeiverordnung gegen die konfessionellen Jugendverbände," *VHB-HJ,* 1097–1101; also "Doppelmitgliedschaft Hitler-Jugend und konfessionelle Verbände," ibid., 1095–97. Klönne, *Gegen den Strom,* 26, 44; idem, *Hitlerjugend,* 88–89. Cf. D. Peukert, *Die Edelweisspiraten,* 153, who found that "relatively few children of former SPD and KPD members appear to have belonged to the Edelweiss Pirates."

25. Muth, "Jugendopposition," 407; D. Peukert, *Die Edelweisspiraten,* 146–59; idem, "Edelweisspiraten, Meuten, Swing," 322–27; idem, *Die KPD im Wiederstand,* 388; Horn, "Youth Resistance," 32. Surely Peukert's suggestion that "deviating behavior" can be regarded as a series of steps beginning in the private realm of nonconformity, going on to rejection and protest, and finally ending in the public realm of resistance, has wider application than merely the "didactic" significance he intimates; see *Edelweisspiraten,* 236.

26. Neesse, "Die Einigung der deutschen Jugend," 12. For a description of the "d.j.1.11" and its mercurial leader, Eberhard Köbel, known as "tusk," see Brandenburg, *Die Geschichte der HJ,* 202–9. D. Peukert, *Die Edelweisspiraten,* 56. Muth, "Jugendopposition," 376. Gruchmann, "Jugendopposition," 107. For Schirach's letter of 3.8.1937 to the Gemeindetag, see Hellfeld, *Edelweisspiraten,* 20–21.

27. Klönne, *Gegen den Strom,* 24, 52–54, 57. Cf. idem, "Jugendprotest und Jugendopposition," 581–88; D. Peukert, *Edelweisspiraten,* 28–32.

28. Klönne, *Gegen den Strom,* 94–95, 59–65. Lüer, "Verbotene Schriften der Bündischen Jugend," and "Übersicht über das Bündische Schrifttum," 3.4.1936, in *VHB-HJ,* 1972–75. Klönne, *Gegen den Strom,* 122. On songs and literature used by the Edelweiss Pirates,

strangely devoid of traditional socialist style and content, see D. Peukert, *Edelweisspiraten*, chap. 6, and his *Volksgenossen und Gemeinschaftsfremde*, 188.

29. Kalinke, "Die Mitgliederentwicklung der Hitler-Jugend im Jahre 1935," *Statistik der Jugend*, 28.3.1936, HA/19/358. SD reports on "Führerfrage der HJ," 7.5., 13.7., and 5.8.1936, T-81/101/117669–92. RJF, "Führerordnung," n.d. (1935/1936), HA/18/336. "Das Gesetz über die Hitler-Jugend," *VHB-HJ*, 9–15.

30. Tetzlaff, *Das Disziplinarrecht*, 14–17. Schirach, "HJ-Disziplinarverordnung," *RB. Sonderdruck*, (14.12.1936), 1–7.

31. Hitler, *Mein Kampf*, 415. Bleuel, *Sex and Society*, 179–80. Muth, "Jugendopposition," 415.

32. Klönne, *Gegen den Strom*, 8, 44, 50, 58, 148.

33. "Berliner Streifendienst an der Arbeit," *Die HJ* (16.10.1937), 4–5. On the brutal nature of Gestapo interrogation of dissidents from the Bünde, see Ebeling and Hespers, *Jugend contra Nationalsozialismus*, 144–46.

34. Klönne, *Gegen den Strom*, 56–57, 63.

35. "Anordnung des Stabsführers," 20.8.1937, RB 31/II, in *VHB-HJ*, 916–17. Hellfeld, *Edelweisspiraten*, 21. "Überwachung der HJ durch den SRD," (19.3.1937), *VHB-HJ*, 923. "Ausgabe von Ausweisen, Geheimanweisungen usw. durch den SRD," (15.10.1937), *VHB-HJ*, 907. "Bestrafung von gemeldeten Jgg.," (15.10.1937), *VHB-HJ*, 960. John, "Verbindung zu den Kriminalpolizei-Leitstellen u. Stellen," *RB* 41/III (25.11.1937), 1123. RFSS, "Neuordnung der Weiblichen Kriminalpolizei," 24.11.1937, *VHB-HJ*, 975–76. Axmann, "Nachwuchs für die Weibliche Kriminalpolizei," *RB* 38/III (9.12.1938), 970–71. A. Müller, *Die Betreuung*, 57.

36. "Richtlinien für den HJ-SRD," AR. HJ v. 1.6.1938, with preceding and succeeding addenda, in *VHB-HJ*, 916–35.

37. Ibid. The RJF was certainly right about grooming and apparel, which the dissidents used to provoke both party and HJ officials and especially the SRD; see works by Klönne, Gruchmann, D. Peukert, and Muth.

38. Stokes, "Otto Ohlendorf," 231. Secret exchange between SD-Oab. Rhein and its subordinate office in Koblenz regarding "Zusammenarbeit zwischen HJ and SD," Nov. 1936, T-175/506/9370866–70.

39. "Arbeitsrichtlinien der HJ 16/41, Dienstanweisung für den SRD," *VHB-HJ*, 881–82. In order to secure this pact, Himmler apparently had to satisfy the political ambitions of HJ leaders by promising them more or less equivalent rank in the A-SS and SD; see "Anordnung des Reichsführers SS über die Übernahme von HJ-Führern in die Schutzstaffel," 16.8.1938, T-175/42/2552747–48. "Anordnung des Reichsjugendführers über die Umgliederung des Streifendienstes als Nachwuchsorganisation für die Schutzstaffel v. 26.8.1938," *ANBl* VI/19 (7.10.1938), in *VHB-HJ*, 895–96.

40. "Ernennung von HJ-Verbindungsführern zur SS," *RB* 22/IV (16.6.1939), and *RB* 4/K (1939), T-81/113/132087, 132421.

41. *RB* 4/K (1939), T-81/113/132421. John, "SRD als Sonderformation," *RB. Sonderdruck* I/39 (21.2.1939), T-175/45/2557165–72, 2557208. Lüer, "Das Erfassungswesen des Streifendienstes," T-354/454/4190032–40. RFSS, "Aktennotiz," 14.8.1940, T-175/20/2525114–15.

42. RuS Fulda-Werra to RuSHA, "SS-Eignungsuntersuchungen," T-354/454/4190098. See also reports by the Führer für Ergänzung, the Rasse und Siedlungs Führer, and the Führer themselves of the 2. (Frankfurt), 14. (Gotha), 35. (Kassel), 47. (Jena), 57. (Meiningen), 67. (Erfurt), and 83. (Giessen) *SS-Standarte* of the A-SS. They deal with the "Aufstellung der Streifendienstgefolgschaften . . . 15. Juni 1939," including correspondence with lower SS units and with HJ offices and SRD-Gebietsinspekteure. T-354/454/4189616, 4189505–8, 4189536, 4189542–48, 4190042–60.

43. See references in the previous note. For difficulties in larger cities see the exchange between SRD Gbi. Fischer in Halle with Prince Waldeck-Pyrmont's chief of staff, "Ausmusterung des HJ-SRD durch die SS," Apr. 1939, T-354/454/4189945–48.

44. See the sources mentioned in note 41.

45. See the sources mentioned in note 41. For 1938 recruiting figures, see "SS-Bewerber die zum Reichsparteitag 1938 von der HJ übernommen werden," T-354/470/4212646. For Frankfurt and Kassel, see "Stand der Streifendienstgefolgschaften am 15.6.1939," and "Aufstellung der SRD-Gefolgschaften," 25.6.1939, T-354/454/4190044–46. In Schwaben SRD strength before mustering stood at 1,400—100 per Bann—in 1941, with Augsburg having 70 members at the time, while HJ Region Westmark had 1,200 after mustering in June 1940.

46. Berger to Wolff, 1.11.1939; Berger to RFSS, "Reichsjugendführung," 1.11.1939; RFSS to Berger, 9.11.1939; T-175/20/2525133–36.

47. Berger to RFSS, "Besprechung . . . Lauterbacher," 13.12.1939, T-175/2525129–31.

48. Ibid. RFSS to Berger, "Besprechung," 18.12.1939, T-175/2525124–25.

49. A. Müller, "Hitler-Jugend," 40.

50. Lauterbacher, "Überweisung in den SRD," *RB* 19/K (21.12.1939), T-81/113/132376–77. The detailed directives contained in the above reflect almost exactly the scheme Berger had proposed, including the JV transfer and the secrecy of the numbers involved. In 1941 the issue of leadership shortage became moot, since Hitler agreed to give military deferments to most full-time HJ leaders.

51. For text of *Jugenddienstpflicht*, see A. Müller, *Die Betreuung*, 85–87. The Reich Citizenship Law is quoted in Randel, *Die Jugenddienstpflicht*, 96.

52. Randel, *Die Jugenddienstpflicht*, 13–15, 78–82.

53. H. Schulz, "Die Durchführung der Jugenddienstpflicht," 198–201.

54. Bormann, "Verpflichtung der Hitler Jugend am 31.3.1940," T-175/98/2618728–30.

55. "Dienststrafordnung der Hitler-Jugend für die Dauer des Krieges," in A. Müller, *Die Betreuung*, 87–89. An interesting clarification can be found in *Zucht und Ehre* (26.4.1940), T-81/115/135131–38. J. Wolff, "Hitlerjugend und Jugendgerichtsbarkeit," 655–60.

56. Ibid. Tetzlaff, *Das Disziplinarrecht*, 102–3. See report of Amt HJ-Gerichtsbarkeit for statistics on expulsions, *RB. Sonderdruck*, 35/41K (25.9.1941), T-81/114/133973–134024.

57. A. Müller, *Die Betreuung*, 64–65. Tetzlaff, *Das Disziplinarrecht*, 56. Klönne, *Gegen den Strom*, 58, 148. P. Werner, "Die Polizei," 243–45. Muth, "Jugendopposition," 373, 382–87. Gruchmann, "Jugendopposition," 105.

58. RFSS, "Polizeiverordnung zum Schutze der Jugend," 9.3.1940, T-81/98/1113782–85. On legal status of police orders, *Reichsgesetzblatt*, I (1938), 1582.

59. RJF, "Zusammenarbeit Zwischen HJ-SRD und Sozialstellen," *RB* 36/K (12.4.1940), T-81/113/132907. A. Müller, *Die Betreuung*, 58. Randel, *Die Jugenddienstpflicht*, 93. P. Werner, "Die Polizei," 245. See newspaper article "Jugendschutzgesetz, eine völkische Pflicht," by Hans Gelber, leader of HJ Bann Wertach in Kaufbeuren, rebutting an article entitled "Was die Jugend nicht darf," 5.5.1941, T-81/103/120577–80. Vornefeld, "Gebote und Verbote," 19–22. Knopp, *Kriminalität*, 157–59. "Die Überwachung der Gefährdung der Jugend," Arbeitsrichtlinien der HJ 8/40, 1.6.1940, in *VHB-HJ*, 936–79.

60. Lüer, "Der Jugenddienstarrest," 250–54. Axmann, "Das modernste nationalsozialistische Erziehungsmittel," 277–79.

61. RFSS, "Arrest als Dienststrafe der HJ," 25.6.1941, T-580/38/239. Tetzlaff, *Das Disziplinarrecht*, 20–21, 101. Lüer, "Der Jugenddienstarrest." A. Müller, *Die Betreuung*, 90–91.

62. Regierungspräsident (Bavaria), "Vollzug der Jugenddienstverordnung," 13.8.1941,

T-580/38/239. Bohler, "Polizeiliche Massnahmen zur Erzwingung der Jugenddienst-pflicht," 8.3.1943, T-81/100/116046.

## Chapter 4

1. RJF, "Einsatz des SRD auf dem RPT 1939," 12.8.1939, T-81/103/119422–23. More information on the rally can be found in HA/23/474.

2. SD Fulda-Werra to SD Kassel, Wiesbaden, Hessen, Koblenz, Trier, Frankfurt, "Rdschr. d. RSHA . . . der HJ zur Kenntnis gekommen," 9.3.1939; HJ Westmark to SD Koblenz, 31.3.1939, T-175/506/9370879–80. Ebert to Springs, "Arbeitstagung d. SRD-Gff.," 27.6.1939; Koblenz SD Aktennotiz, "Arbeitstagung d. SRD-Gff. in Bingerbrück," 12.7.1939; SD Koblenz, "Aktenvermerk . . . Zusammenarbeit mit dem HJ-SRD," 3.9.1940; T-175/506/9370882, 9370885–86, 9370995–96.

3. Heydrich, "Hilfeleistung . . . d. SRD . . . bei d. Behörden d. SIPO," 8.9.1939, T-175/506/9370887–89. RJF, "Einsatz d. HJ-SRD," RB 3/K (23.9.1939), T-81/113/132073–75. See also VHB-HJ, 584.

4. Heydrich, "Hilfeleistung," 14.9.1939; SD Insp. Rhein, "Dienstleistung v. Angehörigen d. SRD," 20.9.1939; SD Koblenz to Insp. SIPO u. SD, "Dienstleistung," 27.9.1939; Heydrich, "Hilfeleistung," 5.10.1939; Best, "Hilfeleistung," 12.10.1939; T-175/506/9370891, 9370893–901.

5. Krausnick et al., Anatomy of the SS State, 246–47. Tesmer, "Hilfeleistung," 24.10.1939, T-175/506/9370907–12. This document includes a list of 116 recruits for the second session at Pretzsch beginning 2.11.1939.

6. Krausnick et al., Anatomy of the SS State, 547. Best, "Hilfeleistung," 16.1.1940; Best, "4. Kurzlehrgang f. Angehörige d. HJ-SRD," 20.2.1940; T-175/506/9370953, 9370962–63. See also Stokes, "Otto Ohlendorf," 231.

7. Best, Memo Nr. 315 X/39, 10.11.1939; SD Koblenz, "Aktenvermerk," 4.12.1939; SD Koblenz, "Aktenvermerke," 5.–6.12.1939; T-175/506/9370924–26, 9370939, 9370944–45.

8. Ebert to SD Koblenz, "SRD-Mitglied Hermann Konzen," 6.11.1939; SD Koblenz, "Aktennotiz," 9.11.1939; Best, "Hilfeleistung," 17.11.1939; SD Köln to SD Koblenz, "Hilfeleistung," 12.12.1939; Best, "Befreiung," 21.12.1939; T-175/506/9370918, 9370921–23, 9370930–31, 9370938, 0370949–50.

9. Möckel, "Dienstanweisung für den SRD," RB 32/41K (5.8.1941), T-81/114/133886–87. RJF, "Einsatz d. HJ-SRD z. Überwachung der Gefährdung der Jugend," RB 46/41K (15.12.1941), T-81/113/132073–75.

10. Boberach, Meldungen aus dem Reich, 78–79. Bann Obermosel to Gebietsführung Koblenz, "Konfessionelle Überwachung der Jugend im Kriege," 4.10.1940, T-506/9370997. SD Koblenz-Luxemburg to SD Esch, et al., "Kirche und HJ," 7.8.1944, T-175/272/2768814. Steinert, Hitler's War and the Germans, 91, 153–54.

11. SD Koblenz, "Organisation d. Gottesdienstüberwachung," 29.11.1940, T-175/506/9371000–9371003. SD Stuttgart, "Organisationierung einer weltanschaulicher Gegner-beobachtung in der HJ," 21.8.1940, Steinert, Hitler's War and the Germans, 24, n. 92, and 16. Bleuel, Sex and Society, 175.

12. RJF, "SRD Dienstplan," RB 47/K (12.8.1940), T-81/103/119826. Heuser, "Anw. f. d. Durchführung d. Innendienstes," (1940), T-81/103/119498–510.

13. Heuser, "Anw. f. d. Durchführung d. HJ-Dienstes," (1940), T-81/103/119552–63.

14. On variety, locations, and call-ups for SRD training courses, see VHB-HJ, 897; T-175/36/2545360–63; T-81: 114/133875; 101/117709, 117085–86; 103/119373, 119677; 115/134650; 100/115758–59.

15. Stachura, *Nazi Youth*, 226–27. See also *RB* 15/I (24.4.1936), 311, and entry in Stockhorst, *Fünftausend Köpfe*. Lüer file, BDC. Berger to RFSS, "Reichsjugendführung," 3 May 1940, T-175/20/2525120. *RB* 62/K (28.10.1940), T-81/114/133280. *DJD* (1940), inside cover and 250–54. Cf. Stachura, *Nazi Youth*, 236, who is mistaken about Lüer's rank in 1935 and his position in 1942. Schultz, *Akademie*, 24.

16. RJF, "Arbeitsrichtl. d. HJ v. 15.12.1941, Dienstanw. f. d. SRD," *VHB-HJ*, 881–98; for new organizational chart see 883–84.

17. Ibid. Cf. "Arbeitsrichtl. d. HJ v. 1.6.1940, Die Überwachung der Gefährdung der Jugend," *VHB-HJ*, 936–79.

18. Rubouf, "Gebietsführertagung der HJ in München von 5. bis 7.12.1941," T-175/123/2648490–99. See also *RB* 46/41K (15.12.1941), T-81/ 114/134244.

19. SSEA, "Arbeitsanweisung Nr. 1," 23.3.1942, T-81/103/119628–43.

20. SRD reports by Bingger, Sept. 1941 to Jan. 1942, T-81/103/119841–54. Jürgens to Geb. Schw., 4.6.1942, T-580/348/#3. Reports for Apr., June, Dec., 1942 and Jan., Mar., July, Sept., Oct. 1943; Bingger file, BDC.

21. Bingger file, BDC: Certificates for various awards, application for marriage permit from RuSHA, R.u.S Fragebogen, handwritten *Lebenslauf* with several portraits, SS-*Stammrolle* and salary records; the files also contain monthly SRD reports for 1942 and 1943. Schw. SRD Rdschr. Nr. 2/42, 24.7.1942, T-81/103/119691. Bingger's SS Nr. was 315,909.

22. Traub, SD Koblenz, "Aktenvermerk . . . Besprechung mit . . . Ebert . . . am 16.7.1940," NA/ T-175/506/9370974–76; memoranda for 19. and 29.7.1940 on 9370977–78, 9370992–97.

23. Bingger to Heuser, "Bericht über die Waffen-SS," 20.4.1943, T-580/352/#9; Berger to HSSPF, 4.1.1943, T-175/131/2658205.

24. Schweizer to Heuser, 1.7.1943; Schweizer to Adam, 6.7.1943; Adam to Bingger, 9.9.1943; Bingger to Heuser, 16.9.1943; T-580/352/#13.

25. See references given in n. 24.

26. RJF, "Aufgabe, Aufbau und Einsatz der Überwachungsdienststellen," *RB* 32/43 (26.8.1943), T-81/115/134972–73; RJF, "Kriegsjugend," 221.

27. Rderl.d. RFSSuCdDtP. v. 30.1.1944, T-580/38/239.

28. König to all SRD-Gbi., 15.7.1944, T-580/352/#13. König to SSEA, 27.3.1943, T-175/131/2658045–47.

29. For spin-offs from the SRD, see *RB* 19/K (21.12.1939), T-81/113/132376; RJF, "Kriegseinsatz des HJ-Feuerwehrdienst," *RB* 29/43K (2.8.1943), T-81/105/134054; RJF, "Abstellung von Angehörigen der HJ für die Schnellkommandos der Polizei," *RB* 45/42K (3.12.1941), T-81/114/134223–24. It has been estimated that over 700,000 HJ boys were trained and used as auxiliary firefighters during the course of the war; Klose, *Generation*, 217. König to SRD Inspekteure, 17.7.1944, T-580/352/#13.

30. "Dienstbespr. d. K-Gbi. v. 10.5.–14.5.1944 in Eipel," report by Böhm, the new inspector for Schw., T-580/352/#9. Geb. Schw. to K-F, "Unterlagen zur Überweisung des Kontingentes," 25.4.1944, T-580/348/#4. König to Gbi. "Arbeitstagung in Eipel," 21.6.1944, T-580/352/#13.

31. Böhm to Nacken, "SRD," 12.12.1944, T-580/352/#13; Est. Süd, "Kriegsfreiwillige Meldescheine," 16.9.1944; Böhm to RJF, "Werbeaktion," 18.3.1944; Est. Süd, "Grosswerbeaktion 'Gerade Du,' " 27.3.1944; Böhm to Spangenberg, 14.9.1944; T-580/352/#9. HSSPF Main, order of 11.3.1945, T-580/39/339.

32. Gurr, *Rogues, Rebels, and Reformers*, 37. Radzinowicz, *Ideology and Crime*, 6. Cressey and Ward, *Delinquency*, 15–21. See also Radzinowicz, *The Growth of Crime*, and Bleuel, *Sex and Society*, first published in Germany as *Das saubere Reich* and in England as *Strength Through Joy*, some indication of the quixotic uncertainties in the minds of pub-

lishers and editors on this subject. A refreshingly different approach can be found in Huck, *Sozialgeschichte der Freizeit,* especially the chapters by Medick and D. Peukert. The latter portrays youthful proletarian rebels against the HJ as uninhibited sexual experimenters, who thus found some meaning in an otherwise unacceptable social world. In *Eidelweisspiraten* (154–56) and *Volksgenossen und Gemeinschaftsfremde* (185) Peukert views the relatively free sexual practices among youthful rebels in general as an effective form of political protest against oppressive Nazi prudery.

33. Knopp, *Kriminalität,* 49–50, 209–14. P. Werner, "Die Polizei," 243.

34. Knopp, *Kriminalität,* 209–10. Bleuel, *Sex and Society,* 322–23.

35. Knopp, *Kriminalität,* 41. For comparisons with 1939 figures, see 40, and for regional variations 42–43.

36. These statistics were derived from a list of expellees issued by the HJ Court. See *RB. Sonderdruck,* 35/41K (25.9.1941), T-81/114/133973–134024.

37. Bleuel, *Sex and Society,* 31. Wilde, *Das Schicksal der Verfemten,* 8, n. 9; 22, nn. 42–43; 123, n. 9. Cressey and Ward, *Delinquency,* 32. Knopp, *Kriminalität,* 40.

38. Knopp, *Kriminalität,* 211. F.B.I., *Uniform Crime Reports* (1933–45). Cressey and Ward, *Delinquency,* 289–93, 293–95, 295–300.

39. Randel, *Jugenddienstpflicht,* 10. Knopp, *Kriminalität,* 214. P. Werner, "Die Polizei," 243–44. On Werner, see J. Wolff, "Hitlerjugend und Jugendgerichtsbarkeit," 648; D. Peukert, "Arbeitslager und Jugend-KZ," 420.

40. Bleuel, *Sex and Society,* 325. Gruchmann, "Jugendopposition," passim. On juvenile jurisprudence in general and its subversion by HJ and SS officials, see J. Wolff, "Hitlerjugend und Jugendgerichtsbarkeit," 654–55, 658.

41. Bleuel, *Sex and Society,* 323. See Table 4.3.

42. Ibid., 323–25.

43. Maser, *Hitler,* 201–3, 352, n. 68. H. von Schirach, *Der Preis der Herrlichkeit,* 85–86. Maser says Henriette was enamored with the Führer, but her father's respect for Hitler led him politely to reject her advances. RFSS, "Schutz der weiblichen Jugend," RB 13/42K (15.6.1942), T-81/114/134400. Bleuel, *Sex and Society,* 215–17, 278–79. See Thompson, "Lebensborn and the Eugenics Policy of the Reichsführer-SS," which lays to rest many of the sensational rumors about "SS stud farms," of which Hillel and Henry, *Of Pure Blood,* is an example.

44. Rubouf, "Gebietsführertagung," T-175/123/2648490–99. Maschmann, *Account,* 148–50.

45. Knopp, *Kriminalität,* 40–41, 91, 210–11; RJF Amt Gerichtsbarkeit, *RB. Sonderdruck* 35/41K (25.9.1941), T-81/114/133973–134024.

46. Bleuel, *Sex and Society,* 129–36, 292–303. Wilde, *Das Schicksal der Verfemten,* passim. RFSS to Brustmann, Beratender Arzt im RSHA, 9.10.1942, in Heiber, *Reichsführer!,* 159. On the work of Hirschfeld as "classic . . . pseudo-scientific pornography," see Friedrich, *Before the Deluge,* 233.

47. Laqueur, *Young Germany,* 50–52. Allen, *The Infancy of Nazism,* 297–300. Fest, *The Face of the Third Reich,* 333. Stachura, *Nazi Youth,* 177, n. 62. For a sensational account of amorality in the Hitler Youth and the claim that Schirach was a homosexual, see Siemsen, *Hitler Youth.* RJF, "Die Überwachung der Gefährdung der Jugend," Arbeitsrichtl. d. HJ, 1.6.1940, in *VHB-HJ,* 938.

48. Bleuel, *Sex and Society,* 160–61.

49. These rates and percentages were calculated from statistics and tables in Knopp, *Kriminalität,* 40, 211, and *RB. Sonderdruck* 35/41K (25.9.1941), T-81/114/133973–134024.

50. *RB. Sonderdruck* 35/41K (25.9.1941), T-81/114/133973–134024. Knopp, *Kriminalität,* 214–16; Wilde, *Das Schicksal der Verfemten,* 25–31.

51. "Schreiben d. CdSHA v. 28.2.1939 an die RJF," in *VHB-HJ*, 941; RJF, "Die Aufgaben der allgemeinen Überwachung," 1939–1941, *VHB-HJ*, 938–47.

52. Klönne, *Gegen den Strom*, 110–11. Cf. Knopp, *Kriminalität*, 121. Numerous additonal examples can be found in D. Peukert, *Die Edelweisspiraten*, especially chaps. 8 and 10.

53. Brandenburg, *Die Geschichte der HJ*, 210–13. Bleuel, *Sex and Society*, 326–27. Grass, *The Tin Drum*, 360–82. RJF, "Cliquen- und Bandenbildung unter Jugendlichen," Sept. 1942, in D. Peukert, *Die Edelweisspiraten*, 160–229. The latter includes brief reports of cliques and gangs in Berlin, Bregenz, Cologne, Dortmund, Dresden, Düsseldorf, Duisburg, Erfurt, Essen, Frankfurt a.M., Halle, Hamburg, Hanover, Karlsruhe, Kiel, Landshut, Leipzig, Munich, Oberhausen, Remscheid, Saarbrücken, Troppau, Weida, Witten a.d. Ruhr, and Vienna.

54. Horn, "Youth Resistance," 34; Klönne, *Gegen den Strom*, 106–7; Muth, "Jugendopposition," 376, 388.

55. Horn, "Youth Resistance," 34–35; Boberach, *Meldungen aus dem Reich*, 403, n. 6; Muth, "Jugendopposition," 388. Cf. Hellfeld, *Edelweisspiraten*, passim; D. Peukert, *Die Edelweisspiraten*, passim.

56. Klönne, *Gegen den Strom*, 108–9. Brandenburg, *Die Geschichte der HJ*, 212–13. Hellfeld, *Edelweisspiraten*, 112–15; Muth, "Jugendopposition," 394. On the changed mood after Stalingrad, see Beck, *Under the Bombs*, 33–56; Kershaw, *Popular Opinion and Political Dissent*, 309.

57. Grass, *The Tin Drum*, 360–82. Cf. Horn, "Youth Resistance," 35, who misinterprets the significance of the Danzig "Dusters" and generally exaggerates the political importance of these juvenile delinquents by imbuing them with political intentions most of them did not have.

58. Knopp, *Kriminalität*, 132–33. Horn, "Youth Resistance," 40.

59. Knopp, *Kriminalität*, 133–34. Bleuel, *Sex and Society*, 329.

60. Knopp, *Kriminalität*, 136–38.

61. Horn, "Youth Resistance," 40–41. Bleuel, *Sex and Society*, 328.

62. Axmann to RFSS, 8.1.1942; RFSS to Axmann, 26.1.1942; RFSS to Heydrich, 26.1.1942; T-175/20/2525081–84. Brandenburg, *Die Geschichte der HJ*, 212. Bleuel, *Sex and Society*, 228–330. Horn, "Youth Resistance," 42. Muth, "Jugendopposition," 374–75. Cf. Petry, *Studenten aufs Schafott*; Jahnke, *Weisse Rose contra Hakenkreuz*.

63. Gruchmann, "Jugendopposition," 105–12; 129, n. 54; 130, n. 72. For specific resistance of KJVD and some cooperation with SAJ in underground work, see Jahnke, *Jungkommunisten im Widerstandskampf*, 31.

64. Klönne, *Gegen den Strom*, 106–8; idem, "Jugendprotest und Jugendopposition," 620; Muth, "Jugendopposition," 371–73, 407–17. Cf. Kershaw, "The Führer Image and Political Integration," 159, who is prepared to accept that 80 percent of the adult population continued to support Hitler until major defeats in Russia, reducing Haffner's figure by 10 points; see *The Meaning of Hitler*, 34.

65. D. Peukert, "Edelweisspiraten, Meuten, Swing," 322–27; idem, *Die Edelweisspiraten*, 146–58; idem, *Die KPD im Widerstand*, 388f; idem, *Volksgenossen und Gemeinschaftsfremde*, 172–207, esp. 205–7. Horn, "Youth Resistance," 32. Muth, "Jugendopposition," 407–17, esp. 411–14. D. Peukert, "Die 'Halbstarken,'" 533–48. Cf. Tenfelde, "Schwierigkeiten mit dem Alltag," 385–91; Kocka, "Zurück zur Erzählung?" 406–8; Wehler, "Geschichte von unten gesehen."

66. D. Peukert and Muth are in essential agreement on the significance of labor camps and protective custody camps for youth, although both still bring their particular perspective to the issue and both tend to ignore the pioneering work of Klönne and Meister. Muth, meanwhile, is working on a detailed study of the camp at Moringen, based on

camp records and inspection reports by judicial officials, which Peukert appears to discount in part because he feels the sources reflect merely the self-serving view of camp administrators. See D. Peukert, "Arbeitslager und Jugend-KZ," 413–34, 423, n. 30; Muth, "Jugendopposition," 381–87, 400–407, 387, n. 63. Peukert makes a valuable contribution in that he shows the relationship between the work camps and the protective custody camps, both motivated by what he calls "social racism," a term he has borrowed from Gisela Bock, who developed it in connection with her work on women in the Third Reich; see her "Frauen und ihre Arbeit im Nationalsozialismus," 113–53. Muth's important contribution consists of putting the custody camps in broad, comparative historical perspective, which might clarify outstanding issues when his study of Moringen is completed. Both approaches ought perhaps to be seen in the broader context of "social outcasts" in the Third Reich, a promising new line of inquiry which could be expanded to include more than the hitherto neglected fate of gypsies and the sterilization program: Bock, "Zum Wohle des Volkskörpers," 58–66; Meister, "Schicksale der 'Zigeunerkinder,'" 197–229; Noakes, "Social Outcasts," 83–96.

67. Thierack, "Bekämpfung jugendlicher Cliquen," 26.10.1944, in Meister, *Polizeiliches Jugendschutzlager,* 39–41. RFSS, "Bekämpfung jugendlicher Cliquen," 25.10.1944, in ibid., 41–52; D. Peukert, *Die Edelweisspiraten,* chap. 10. Cf. Muth, "Jugendopposition," 381–87, for the political background to the 1944 decision.

68. Sources as given in note 67.

69. Sources as given in note 67.

70. Meister, *Polizeiliches Jugendschutzlager,* 16–17, 31. RM d. Inneren to RM d. Justiz, "Einweisung in das Jugendschutzlager Moringen," 16.10.1941; "Führsorgeerziehung," 14.1.1942. Copies of these documents were kindly provided by Johannes Meister to whom the author hereby expresses his gratitude.

71. RJF, "Jugendschutzlager der Polizei," 19.7.1940, in *VHB-HJ,* 976. See also RJF Gbtrdschr. v. 12.5.1941; and Rderl. d. RSHA v. 12.11.1941 to Kripostellen, "Einweisung i. d. Jugendschutzlager Moringen," in *VHB-HJ,* 977–79. Meister, *Polizeiliches Jugendschutzlager,* 18–21. Geb. Schw., "HJ-Führer für Erziehungslager der Polizei," 16.5.1941, T-580/349/#5.

72. A. Müller, *Die Betreuung,* 57, n. 22.

73. Meister, *Polizeiliches Jugendschutzlager,* 22–26. RFSS, "Unterbringung im Jugendschutzlager," 26.4.1944, in Meister, *Polizeiliches Jugendschutzlager,* 28–29. J. Wolff, "Hitlerjugend und Jugendgerichtsbarkeit," 666–67.

74. Meister, *Polizeiliches Jugendschutzlager,* 32–33. RFSS, "Einweisung in die polizeilichen Jugendschutzlager," 25.4.1944, also in Meister, 50. D. Peukert, "Arbeitslager und Jugend-KZ," 432–34.

75. Meister, *Polizeiliches Jugendschutzlager,* 33–37. Cf. D. Peukert, *Die Edelweisspiraten,* chap. 10, for a report of the Landgerichtspräsident of Essen to the Justice Ministry on conditions at Moringen, dated 31.7.1944.

76. Meister to author, 7.10.1975. RMdI, "Unterbringung fremdvölkischer, insbesondere polnischer Minderjähriger," 11.12.1942; a copy supplied by Meister. Cf. D. Peukert, "Arbeitslager und Jugend-KZ," 422–25, who underestimates the number of youths involved, since he concentrates on the work camps and ignores the camp at Litzmannstadt.

77. Cf. Horn, "Youth Resistance," 37, 43; D. Peukert, *Volksgenossen und Gemeinschaftsfremde,* 205–7. Peukert's argument, that "a substantial part of the young generation rejected the educational and free-time offerings of the Nazis," hinges on the meaning of "substantial part," left undefined. It probably involved no more than 5 percent of the HJ membership, which hardly seems substantial to me (cf. n. 64). His point that the rebels

developed their "own cultural identity and alternative style," thus proving that the Nazis did not have society in their grasp despite years of domination and the use of repressive means, falls on the same crucial percentage. Whether the Nazi policies of the *Volksgemeinschaft* and chauvinism were destroyed by the "realities of class conflict" long before the military defeats, as Peukert argues, depends on the validity of Tim Mason's general line of interpretation, now repeatedly challenged by numerous scholars. Peukert's final point, that the youth rebellion prepared the way for "modern expressions of free-time behavior of youth," is an interesting argument, apparently an extension of the modernization theory of Schoenbaum and Dahrendorf.

78. Geb. Schw., "Tätigkeit der Personalabteilung Überwachung und Verbindung zur Polizei," 10.8.1939, T-81/103/120172–73. Bingger SRD report, Nov. 1941, T-81/103/119847–48. Bingger, "Untersuchung," 16.12.1941, T-81/103/119721. Bingger SRD reports, 1942–1943, BDC.

79. Geb. Schw., "Ev. Bibelzeiten," 14.8.1939, T-81/103/120176. BDM Obergau Schw., "Willkürliche Aneignung polizeilicher Befügnisse seitens Angehörigen der Hitlerjugend," 9.9.1939, T-81/98/114033. Weimann to Greiner, 12.11.1940, T-81/103/120522. Klönne, *Gegen den Strom*, 83. Stoll, "Zusammenfassender Bericht über die ev. Jugendgruppe Memmingen," (1941), T-81/103/120412–13.

80. Schmid, "Allgemeine staatsfeindliche Betätigung," 18.6.1940, T-81/103/120621. Faller, "Arbeitsbericht"; Ott, "SRD Meldung"; Holzheuer to Ott, "Meldung über Stadtkaplan Immerts u.a. Realschule Lindau, 5. Klasse," 7.5.1941; T-81/104/120544–45, 120681–83, 120756. Walk, "Arbeitsbericht," T-81/104/120781–82. Bann Nördlingen, "Monatlicher Arbeitsbericht," 30.10.1940, T-81/103/120455–59. Steinert, *Hitler's War and the Germans*, 153–54. Mayrl, "SRD Bericht Januar 1942," T-81/103/120072. Cf. RJF, "Konfessionelle Lage," 19.3.1941, T-81/97/112805–8; this document advises careful handling of the religious question and clearly indicates how surprised and disconcerted the HJ leadership was in the face of an apparent religious revival among youth.

81. Bann Wertach, "Sittliche Verwahrlosung der weiblichen Jugend," 18.6.1940, T-81/103/120620. Faller, "Bericht über die Streifen," (Spring 1940); Faller, "SRD Arbeitsbericht—Sittliche Verwahrlosung der Jugend"; Faller, "SRD Bericht . . . Sonstige Verwahrlosungserscheinungen"; Faller, "SRD Bericht . . . Homosexualität"; Walk, "Bericht über Tätigkeit des SRD"; T-81/104/120729, 120739–40, 120751–52, 120779–80.

82. Renz, "Arbeitsbericht," T-81/104/120817–18. Hilbert, "SRD-Monatsbericht," 1.11.1940; Regierungspräsidenten von Bayern to Polizeistationen, "SRD der HJ—hier Zusammenarbeit mit der Polizei," 2.9.1942; T-81/103/119688, 120523–25.

83. Ludwig, "Überwachung des Fahrtenbetriebes," 26.8.1941, T-81/103/119735–36. Klönne, *Gegen den Strom*, 107. Knopp, *Kriminalität*, 187–88. Horn, "Youth Resistance," 38. Ebeling and Hespers, *Jugend contra Nationalsozialismus*, 101.

84. Klönne, *Gegen den Strom*, 119. Horn, "Youth Resistance," 42–43. Mayrl, "SRD Bericht Bann Augsburg-Land," Jan. 1942, T-81/103/120072. Grass, *The Tin Drum*, 373–75. Granzow, *Tagebuch eines Hitlerjungen*, 85–86.

85. Geb. Schw., "Lokalkontrollen des HJ-SRD," 28.2.1942, T-580/349/#5. Bingger report, (1943), T-81/103/119682–83.

86. Stoll, "Kontrollen laut dem Gezetz zum Schutze der Jugend," 19.3.1941; Bann Wertach, "Arbeitsbericht," 18.6.1940; T-81/103/120416–18, 120619. Artelt, "SRD am Kino," 22.10.1940; Rithmeyr, "Arbeitsbericht," 1.10–3.10.1940; T-81/103/120482, 120484–85. Ott, "Kino Überwachung," 6.10.1940, T-81/104/120692–93. "Überwachung der Lichtspielhäuser," 15.10.1942, T-81/101/117187–88. RJF, "SRD-Kontrollen," *RB* 14/42K, T-81/114/134422–23. Walk, "Bericht über die Tätigkeit des SRD," T-81/104/120779–80. Bohl to Unter-

suchungsführer d. Geb. Schw., 7.4.1941, T-81/114/120804. Mayrl, "SRD Bericht," Jan. 1942, T-81/103/120172.

87. Klönne, *Gegen den Strom*, 113. Heck, *A Child of Hitler*, 91–114. For successful SRD patrolling in the Ruhr region, especially with regard to the capture of Edelweiss Pirates and their subsequent interrogation and "prosecution" by the Gestapo, see Muth, "Jugendopposition," 388–93.

88. Steinert, *Hitler's War and the Germans*, 331.

89. Klönne, *Gegen den Strom*, 83–84. Steinert, *Hitler's War and the Germans*, 16. Bleuel, *Sex and Society*, 175. "Blood and Honor," the television film produced by SWF Baden Baden and Taurus Film, Munich, which premiered on American television in November 1982, graphically and accurately portrays the suspicious and poisonous atmosphere in the family introduced by the Hitler Youth.

## Chapter 5

1. Ideologists of race believed the name came from an old Indo-Germanic or Persian term, *Artam*, which was supposed to symbolize "renewal from the antique powers of the people, from blood, soil, sun and truth." The Artamanen were thought to have been particularly adept at defending the soil. See Brandenburg, *Die Geschichte der HJ*, 77.

2. Höhne, *Death's Head*, 53–54. Kater, "Die Artamanen," 577–638, esp. 622–24. Gies, "The NSDAP and Agrarian Organizations," 45–88. Weingartner, "The SS Race and Settlement Main Office," 62–77. For Darré's important role in the "seizure of power," see Gies, "Die nationalsozialistische Machtergreifung," 210–32. Cf. Farquharson, *The Plough and the Swastika*.

3. Schoenbaum, *Hitler's Social Revolution*, 152–77. Bracher, *The German Dictatorship*, 335–36. Höhne, *Death's Head*, 50–57. Weingartner, "The SS Race and Settlement Main Office," 63. Wunderlich, *Farm Labor*, 159–60. Farquharson, *The Plough and the Swastika*, 69–70, 213–14, 247–48. For Darré's theories, see his *Das Bauerntum als Lebensquell der Nordischen Rasse* and *Neuadel aus Blut und Boden*. Cf. Bramwell, *Blood and Soil*, a radical departure from the established view of Darré, seeking to rehabilitate him as an authentic environmentalist and antiimperialist, among other things; Evans and Lee, *The German Peasantry*, which deals with the topic in broad, left-wing perspective and includes several views from GDR historians; and Moeller, *Peasants and Lords in Modern Germany*, which includes important recent studies from the revisionist perspective.

4. Kater, "Die Artamanen," 624–29. Cf. Brandenburg, *Die Geschichte der HJ*, 77–80.

5. Proksch, "Artamanen," 25–28. Kater, "Die Artamanen," 621–22. Brandenburg, *Die Geschichte der HJ*, 79.

6. Proksch, "Artamanen," 27. Kater, "Die Artamanen," 586, 621. B. von Schirach, *Die Hitlerjugend*, 51. Cf. F. Schmidt, "Bäuerliche Volksordnung," 4.

7. *DJD* (1935), 78 and *DJD* (1936), 1. Wojirsch, a machinist, was born in 1906 and joined the Party in 1927 at Halle-Merseburg. His membership number was 43,449; BDC file. Stierling, "Die agrarpolitische Jugendarbeit," 19. RJF, "Kriegsjugend," 172.

8. Wojirsch, "Winterarbeit der Artamanen," 78–80. Idem, "Kulturarbeit der Landdienstgruppen," 268–70. Idem, "Gemeinschaftssiedlungen," 9–14.

9. Hitler's slogan appears repeatedly in the literature, but it was first used as a central theme by Oldigs, "Die Landflucht und ihr Ende," 20–22. In a report prepared by the Landdienstinspektion Süd, Hitler is quoted as follows: "Youth must return to the land, to blood and soil, race and ethnicity, the eternal source of German strength; there they will once more become German peasants, the youthful foundation of the German peo-

ple; for the Germany of the future will be a land of peasants or it will cease to exist"; Landdienstinspektion Süd, *Der Landdienst ruft*, 2.

10. Oldigs, "Die Landflucht und ihr Ende," passim. Bofinger, "Überwindung der Landflucht," 18–23. Granzow, "Entvölkerter Boden ruft nach Bauern," 1–7. On the relative success of Nazi settlement policy, see Farquharson, *The Plough and the Swastika*, 145, 155. A former provincial prime minister and early supporter of Wojirsch, Granzow now served as Darré's "plenipotentiary for rebuilding of the farm community" in the National Food Estate.

11. Stierling, "Die agrarpolitische Jugendarbeit," 17–18. Klönne, *Hitlerjugend*, 30. Klose, *Generation*, 104–5. Cf. Wunderlich, *Farm Labor*, 310–19.

12. Kunzelmann, "Arbeitseinsatz von weiblichen Arbeitskräften," 15–18. Stierling, "Die agrarpolitische Jugendarbeit," 19–20.

13. Gies, "Der Reichsnährstand," 216–33. Wunderlich, *Farm Labor*, 160–62. Staebe, "Der unsterbliche Bund," 16–18. Fasold, "Das Program der Landjugendarbeit," 345–50. *VHB-HJ*, 2913–15.

14. Bofinger, "Nationalsozialistische Landjugend," 8–10. Fasold, "Das Program der Landjugendarbeit," 346. Cf. Gillingham, "The 'Deproletarianization' of German Society," 423–32.

15. Hoffmann, "Sozialprobleme der Landjugend," 20–24. Farquharson, *The Plough and the Swastika*, 189. Schoenbaum, *Hitler's Social Revolution*, 166–68. Grunberger, *The 12-Year Reich*, 168–69. Wunderlich, *Farm Labor*, 71–75. Schottky, "Zur Gesundheitsführung der Landjugend," 19–24.

16. The 11 categories: peasants, peasant girls, gardeners, female gardeners, vintagers, female vintagers, fishermen, foresters, forest workers (a lower rank), dairy farmers, female dairy farmers. See Seume, "Der RBWk," and Kater, "The Reich Vocational Contest," for other vocational categories.

17. Hoffmann, "Sozialprobleme des Landjugend," 23. RJF, "Berufsförderung der Landjugend," in *VHB-HJ*, 2914–15. "Berufserziehung im Landdienst," *DJD* (1936), 38–39. Regulations for systematic agricultural education were not issued by the Food Estate until 1938; see "Einberufung der Landarbeitslehre," *VHB-HJ*, 2915. Schoenbaum, *Hitler's Social Revolution*, 95–96. For the vocational contest, see G. Kaufmann, *Der Reichsberufswettkampf*; Axmann, *Olympia der Arbeit*. The involvement of students has been treated by Kater, "The Reich Vocational Contest." RNSt, "Reichsberufswettkampf 1936," 6.11.1935, *VHB-HJ*, 2918–19. Seume, "Der RBWk," 24–26.

18. The relevant parts of the decree are reproduced in Steindle, "Soziale Grundlagen der Landarbeitslehre," 112–15. Detailed implementation orders were issued a year later, and further changes followed; see *VHB-HJ*, 2914. For various types of agricultural workers and their miserable condition, see Wunderlich, *Farm Labor*, passim, esp. 63–67.

19. In 1937, 61 percent of the male LD groups were housed in temporary facilities, 16 percent in old houses for agricultural workers, 10 percent in farm house rooms, and only 3 percent in new LD Homes. The rest were scattered in various types of available buildings. Even HJ officials admitted that more than half of these facilities were inadequate. Steindle, "Kritik," 27–28; idem, "Soziale Grundlagen," 117. The situation for female LD groups was slightly better. It is clear that the campaign for LD Homes was part of a larger effort to build HJ Homes, which expressed itself even in the Vocational Contest, where various models of ideal dens began to emerge. See "Heime der Hitler-Jugend," *DJD* (1937), 138–39; Steindle, "Soziale Grundlagen," 116–18; Berger, "Denkschrift über den Landdienst," 2.3.1939, T-580/38/239.

20. There were actually 110,000 new entrants in agriculture in 1937, a decrease from 150,000 annual entrants since 1922. The number declined to 100,000 in 1938 and 1939; see

Wunderlich, *Farm Labor,* 307. H. Koch, "Die bisherige Entwicklung der Land-dienstlehre," 366–68. Cf. Farquharson, *The Plough and the Swastika,* 190–91; his figures are not quite accurate, and he neglects to consider the contribution of the LD to Darré's training program.

21. Steindle, "Mehr Bewegung auf dem Lande selbst," 137–38. "HJ steht in der Land-wirtschaft," *DJD* (1937), 368–69.

22. In South Germany, five Gauleiters, several government officials, numerous may-ors, heads of local labor offices, local officials of the Food Estate, and Heinrich Himmler publicly supported and promoted the Land Service in glowing terms; see Land-dienstinspektion Süd, *Der Landdienst ruft,* 4–14. Gies, "Der Reichsnährstand," 229–33. On the Four Year Plan, see Petzina, *Autarkiepolitik.* For the time being the implications of conscription were ignored by HJ officials, although its effects were soon to be felt in agriculture. More than 100,000 young farmers were drafted each year and had to be replaced by other workers; Wunderlich, *Farm Labor,* 307.

23. Stephenson, *Women in Nazi Society,* 15–16, 104–5, 162–64, 203–4. Schoenbaum, *Hitler's Social Revolution,* 178–92. Grunberger, *The 12-Year Reich,* 175–92. Bleuel, *Sex and Society,* 203–5.

24. Stierling, "Die agrarpolitische Jugendarbeit," 21. Schoenbaum, *Hitler's Social Revo-lution,* 188. Klönne, *Hitlerjugend,* 30. Axmann, "Einführung des weiblichen Pflicht-jahres," *RB. Sonderdruck* (15.3.1938), 3. Wunderlich, *Farm Labor,* 329–31.

25. Axmann, "Einführung des weiblichen Pflichtjahres," *RB. Sonderdruck* (15.3.1938), 3–4. Wunderlich, *Farm Labor,* 330, n. 193. Farquharson, *The Plough and the Swastika,* 199. Stephenson, *Women in Nazi Society,* 103–5.

26. Lauterbacher, "Landdienst-Werbeaktion," *DJD* (1938), 606–7. "Die Neuorganisa-tion des Landdienstes," *DJD* (1938), 607.

27. Koch, "Die bisherige Entwicklung der Landarbeitslehre," 367. Landdienstinspek-tion Süd, *Der Landdienst ruft,* 16–20. RFSS to Schindlmayr, 8.3.1938, in ibid., 10.

28. BDC: Two *Lebensläufe* written by Schindlmayr, one in the late 1930s and another in 1940, as part of an application for Himmler's *Wehrbauern* project, and a racial pedigree questionnaire completed in 1939 to meet one of the requirements for Himmler's permis-sion to get married. Cf. Schindlmayr to Hitler, "Gesuch um ausnahmsweise Verleihung des goldenen Parteiabzeichen"; Schön, "Dienstleistungszeugnis," 30.11.1933; Rehm and Schneider, "Empfehlung," 7.2.1934; and related documents, some of them pathetically crass in their political subservience and thirst for status.

29. Koehl, *RKFDV,* 27. Parts of Darré's speech are quoted and discussed in A. Müller, "Die neue Epoche des Landdienstes," 71–74. Idem, *Landdienst der Hitler-Jugend,* 11–13, 21. Himmler naively believed that city youths could be turned into committed farmers by resolute purpose, just as it had been possible to transform "Marxists into German National Socialists"; ibid., 12. Darré, according to Bramwell, had no such illusions; see *Blood and Soil,* 55–57.

30. Klönne, *Hitlerjugend,* 36–39. The following two paragraphs in the text are based on the wording of the agreement with appropriate considerations indicated by the notes. For the pact itself see RFSS, "Zweitschrift d. Abkommens betr. SS u. LD," 17.12.1938, T-580/38/239. See also "Landdienst—Nachwuchsorganisation der SS," *DJD* (1939), 93, and *ANBl* (10.2.1939), T-175/45/2557209–10. Cf. Grundmann, *Agrarpolitik im Dritten Reich,* 121–22, 199–200.

31. It was also a reaction to the so-called Poniatowski villages of the Polish minister of agriculture; Koehl, *RKFDV,* 44.

32. Darré to Lammers, 4.10.1939, in ibid., 44, n. 22.

33. Ibid., 74, 77. The SS-Hauptamt was still headed by August Heissmeyer, but Gottlob

Berger, who took over the SS-Ergänzungsamt in April 1938, played a key role in negotiating both agreements with the RJF. In 1940 Berger became chief of the SSHA. RuSHA after Darré's departure was headed by Otto Hofmann, who remained a relatively minor figure. See *DAL* for 1.7.43.

34. A. Müller, "Die neue Epoche des Landdienstes," 74–77. E. Schulz, "Vom Landdienstler," 484–85. "Der Landdienstgruppenführer," *DJD* (1939), 389–91.

35. A. Müller, "Die neue Epoche des Landdienstes," 78. E. Schulz, "Vom Landdienstler," 485. Koehl, *RKFDV*, 74, 133–34. Weingartner, "The SS Race and Settlement Main Office," 77.

36. Berger, "Denkschrift," 2.3.1939, T-580/38/239. The agricultural population had sustained a loss of 1.45 million people since 1933, while the number of gainfully employed had decreased by 400,000. Some 10 percent of those leaving agriculture were farmers or peasants, a fact Berger conveniently ignored; Wunderlich, *Farm Labor,* 297.

37. Berger, "Denkschrift." A. Müller, *Landdienst der Hitler-Jugend,* 20. The oath that leader candidates took held out the promise of land: "I am persuaded that I can only fulfill my educational responsibilities as Land Service Leader if I accept life on the land and the responsibilities of the agrarian community and successfully complete an agrarian career training program. I know that as a Land Service Leader I can fulfill my military obligation in the Waffen-SS and according to the agreement between the National Youth Leader and the National Leader of the SS I can be employed as a defense-peasant if I meet the requirements of the SS"; T-81/102/118885. Leue, "Heimbauten gegen Landflucht," 287–88.

38. Berger, "Denkschrift." "Der Landdienstgruppenführer." A comparison of these two documents indicates that Berger's cost estimates were not overblown.

39. Berger, "Denkschrift." Schiffer, "Das neunte Volksschuljahr als Landjahr," 1939, T-81/102/118799–802. For some interesting material originating in the Sozial- und Rechtsabteilung of Geb. Hessen-Nassau that relates to the relatively limited HJ involvement in the Land Year program, see T-81/102/118665–887. On the Zentralinstitut, where Schiffer worked and where some fairly realistic thinking about conflicting organizational functions was being done, see Samuel and Thomas, *Education and Society,* 98. Cf. Czeloth et al., "Jugendbewegung," 105–16.

40. Leue, "Heimbauten gegen Landflucht," 287. Wunderlich, *Farm Labor,* 26. See also a report on the second annual conference for *HJ-Heimbeschaffung* held in the Kroll Opera House on 23.1.1939, which emphasized LD home-building in particular; *DJD* (1939), 94–95. The future task of the LD in furthering career education was also stressed during the national conference of the RJF Social Office, 10–15.1.1939; *DJD* (1939), 95. "Der Landdienstgruppenführer," 389–91. Schulz, "Vom Landdienstler," 485.

41. RFSS in *Schulungsdienst der Hitler-Jugend, BDM Werk Glaube und Schönheit,* Folge 1, September, 1939, 15; T-81/677/4714562.

42. Pfister to Stöckl, "Werbung für die Landscharen der SS," 10.3.1939; Bann Aichbach to Stöckl, 11.3.1939; Pfister to Stöckl, 21.3.1939; T-81/103/120378–85.

43. *WuM,* 7/5 (1.3.1939).

44. Lauterbacher, Geheim Rdschr. Nr. 21/39g, 31.8.1939, T-81/96/110392–93. A. Müller, "Hitler-Jugend," 40. RJF, "Kriegsjugend," 172.

45. Kunzelmann, "Berliner Schuljahrgänge im Landdienst," *DJD* (1939), 461–62. BDM Schw., "Landdienst," 15.10.1939 and 1.12.1939; "Landdienst—Neubauern aus HJ und SS," 15.12.1939; T-81/98/113809, 113828, and 99/114687. These documents dealing with local recruiting activities make clear that they were an extension of a nationwide campaign. See also Schindlmayr to Landrat, 30.11.1939, T-580/38/239; *DJD* (1939), 95, and new organization chart, *DJD* (1939), 460.

46. A. Müller, "Hitler-Jugend," 40. *Reichsgesetzblatt* (1939), 709–10. RAM, "Vorschriften über den Landdienstgruppeneinsatz," 18.10.1939, *VHB-HJ*, 2926–49.

47. "Vereinbarung zwischen RJF u. RNSt," 8.1.1940, *VHB-HJ*, 2921. Darré signed on 8 Dec. 1939, but Lauterbacher did not do so until 8 Jan. 1940, a delay that probably reflected the uncertainty of who was to succeed Schirach. Lauterbacher may have tried to use this pact to enhance his chances against Axmann. See *DJD* (1940), 27.

48. "Anordn. d. RM f. Ernährung und Landwirtschaft," 17.1.1940, *RB* 35/K (5.4.1940), 26. RNSt, "Durchführung der Landarbeitslehre und der Landarbeitsprüfung," 22.1.1940, *VHB-HJ*, 2915–18. The training program had been determined as follows: After two years in the LD, which was considered to be "basic agrarian workers' training," and successful passing of the appropriate examination, the young volunteer of sixteen embarked on two years of agricultural training, during which he could specialize in any of a number of occupations, among them sheep farmer, hog farmer, distiller, vine grower, dairy farmer, bee keeper, furbearing animal breeder, and poultry farmer. This was followed by three years of apprenticeship, including a year-long attendance at a higher agricultural school, and the farmer's state examination. After this the individual could be installed as a "new farmer" on his own "hereditary farmstead." See A. Müller, *Landdienst der Hitler-Jugend*, 28–29.

49. Lauterbacher, "K-Anweisung für den Landdienst," *RB* 22/K (26.1.1940), 1–8; T-81/113/132709–15. R. Peukert, "Landdienst," 29. E. Schulz, "Der Landdienst," 30–33. Brandl to RJF, "Zusammenarbeit zwischen Landdienst und SRD-Inspekteuren," 7.5.1940, T-81/103/119406. RNSt, "Anrechnung der Tätigkeit als Landdienstscharführer und-scharführerin," 2.7.1940, *VHB-HJ*, 2961.

50. Steimle, "Heime für den Landdienst," 39–42.

51. Lauterbacher, "Errichtung des Amtes Bauerntum und Ostland," *RB* 32/K (27.3.1940), T-81/113/132832. See also *RB* 35/K (5.4.1940), 24. For comment on Peukert, "Rede des Reichsjugendführers" at "Landdienst—Arbeitstagung vom 7.10.–10.10.1940," T-81/98/114293. The conference took place on Peukert's home ground in Finsterbergen, Thuringia.

52. Peukert file, BDC. Kück, "HJ-Einsatz auf dem Lande," 115; "Rede des Reichsjugendführers," n. 51. On the use of forced Polish laborers in agriculture, see Homze, *Foreign Labor,* 26.

53. "Einsatz eines kommissarischen Bauerntumsbeauftragten," *RB* 35/K (5.4.1940), 23–24; "Einsetzung eines Bauerntumsbeauftragten in den Bannen," *RB* 38/K (19.4.1940); T-81/113/132888–89, 132936.

54. Stolle, "Wer verbleibt auf dem Lande?" 171–73. The thirty-two-year-old Stolle, who had joined the party in 1931, apparently was a holdover from Wojirsch's Artamanen days in Mecklenburg. He remained in the LD under Rudolf Peukert; BDC file.

55. Stolle, "Wer verbleibt auf dem Lande?" 172–73.

56. R. Peukert, "Landdienst," 28. Stephenson, *Women in Nazi Society,* 103–11. "Förderung der Landmädel," *RB* 30/K (8.3.1940), *VHB-HJ*, 2960.

57. Pranz, "Mädelarbeit auf dem Lande," 92–94. Strecke and Ost, *Jugend hinter Pflug und Werkbank,* 287.

58. "Landdienstlager im Obergau Schw.," "Landdienstwerbung," and "Landdienstscharführerin," 1.5.1940, T-81/99/114613–14. "Landjugendaustausch," 14.9.1940, T-81/99/114917; "Landdienstwerbung," 5.11.1940, T-81/98/114300–301. Danzer, "Landdienst 1940," 22–24.

59. "Rede des Reichsjugendführers," n. 51.

60. Müller, "Amt Bauerntum und Landdienst," *RB* 61/K (14.10.1940), T-81/114/133269. The new office immediately proceeded to take control over some farms and agricultural

property that had been acquired in slightly irregular ways by certain regional LD entrepreneurs. See "Ankauf, Übernahme und Schenkungen, Sowie Verwaltung und Bewirtschaftung von Landwirtschaftlichen Betrieben," *RB* 58/K (2.9.1940), *VHB-HJ*, 2958. Dietrich Orlow is mistaken in his belief that Lauterbacher was antipathetic to the SS. On the contrary, he was a protégé of Himmler's and usually could be counted on to support SS interests. See Orlow, *Nazi Party*, 2:317, 358; and Hüttenberger, *Die Gauleiter*, 206–7; RFSS to Lauterbacher, 25.5.1944, T-175/71/2587814–16. RFSS, "Aktennotiz," 14.8.1940, T-175/20/2525114–15

61. Winter, "Entscheidung für das Land," 162. Stolle, *Landdienst*, T-81/99/114964, 114967 (booklet is not paginated).

62. Obergaubefehl Schw., 28.10.1941, T-81/99/114735–41. *RB* 41/41 (15.11.1941), T-81/114/134135–40. For special emphasis on Landdienstführerinnen, who now were paid 60 to 75 RM per month in addition to free clothes, see Gbbf. Schw. (15.12.1941), T-81/98/113761; and "Führerinneneinsatz in den Ostgebieten," *RB* 41/K (1.10.1941), T-81/114/134044. Stinglwagner, "Landdiensteinsatz," 15.12.1941, T-81/98/113754–56.

63. For samples see "Aus dem Landdienst der HJ," "Aus dem Tagebuch eines Landdienstmädels" in *Schulungsdienst der HJ* (Aug. 1941), 7–11. From the same series (Sept.–Oct.) see "Landdienst der Hitler-Jugend: Eine Brücke zwischen Stadt und Land," "Ein Jahr im Landdienst der Hitler-Jugend," "Die Bauerntumsarbeit der Hitler-Jugend," "Neubildung deutschen Bauerntums," "Neue deutsche Dörfer im Osten"; T-81/677/4714939–5434.

64. Stolle, *Landdienst*. This extraordinary booklet, studded with strategic quotes, poetic flights of fancy, and high quality photographs, has undeniable rustic appeal.

65. BDC: Schindlmayr to DUTG, 9.3.1940; idem to RKFDV, "Antrag auf Vorauskunft für einer SS-Wehrbauernstelle nach dem Kriege im Osten," 24.3.1940. Schindlmayr was promoted to Obersturmführer (first lieutenant) on 20.4.1940 and Hauptsturmführer (captain) a year later, shortly after his release from the army through Himmler's intervention. From 1938 to 1940 he had been an Untersturmführer (second lieutenant); the rapid promotion was part of Himmler's patronage.

66. Schindlmayr to Brandt, 5.1.1941, T-175/35/2543726–27. BDC: idem to RKFDV, 27.3.1941; idem to Hofmann, 21.4.1941; Hofmann to Schindlmayr, 23.4. and 26.4.1941; Schindlmayr to Hofmann, 7.6.1941; Hofmann to Schindlmayr, 19.6. and 21.6.1941; Schindlmayr to Hofmann, 27.6.1941.

67. BDC: Emsters to Schulz, 7.8.1941; Schindlmayr to Hofmann, 9.7.1941; Peukert to Hofmann, 10.7.1941.

68. BDC: Peukert to RFSS, 10.7.1941; Schindlmayr to Hofmann, 14., 29.7., and 1.8.1941; Hofmann to Peukert, 5.8.1941; Hofmann to Schindlmayr, 6.8.1941.

69. Aktenvermerk on Schindlmayr-Brandt discussion of 23.8.1941 by Brandt; Brandt to Greifelt, 25.8.1941; Schindlmayr to Greifelt, "Russenjungen," 13.12.1941; BDC. Schindlmayr to Gendarmerie-Station Schönrein, "Jungenlanddienstlager Höfen—Russenjungen," 9.1.1942, T-175/35/2543826.

70. Schindlmayr to Schulz, 26.8.1941; Schindlmayr to Berger, 26.8.1941; BDC. Except for Himmler's promise of financial support given to Axmann during their meeting of the previous October, there is no other evidence to confirm Schindlmayr's charge that the RJF turned down 2 million RM. But the incident is quite plausible. HJ leaders generally were tribal puritans who jealously guarded their independent prerogatives. While they were eager to work with other party affiliates, they were not prepared to surrender the HJ to the control of any other agency. Besides, money was not a crucial matter at this time, since Schwarz had assumed the financial burdens of the Land Service.

71. Schindlmayr to RFSS, 26.8.1941; Schindlmayr to Schulz, Greifelt, and Hofmann, all on 26.8.1941; Schindlmayr to Hofmann, 15.9.1941; Hofmann to Schindlmayr, 17.9.1941; Schindlmayr to Hofmann, 28.10.1941; BDC. On Himmler's growing dissatisfaction with Hofmann due to his excessive interest in *Wehrbauern* settlement sites and obsessive empire-building, see Koehl, *The Black Corps*, 189.

72. Schindlmayr to RFSS, 28.10.1941; Schindlmayr to Hofmann, 30.10., 1.11. and 10.11.1941; BDC.

73. Schindlmayr to Brandt, 5.1.1942, T-175/35/2543890–91. Georg, *Die wirtschaftlichen Unternehmungen*, 64–65.

74. *RB 6/42K* (2.3.1942), 1. Winter file, BDC. Orlow, *Nazi Party*, 2:391–92. Wunderlich, *Farm Labor*, 210. Gies, "Der Reichsnährstand," 231–32. For the Lehrhof episode, see Berger to RFSS, "Anruf Stabsführer Möckel," 18.4.1942, T-175/139/2667519. Berger and Möckel had a close relationship and kept each other well informed. Axmann, "Errichtung der Landdienstinspektion Ost," *RB 9/42K* (1.4.1942), T-81/114/134335.

75. Schindlmayr was formally reinducted into the W-SS on 10 January, while his LD office affairs in the HJ Regional Directorate were conducted by his secretary Elfriede Rösch; T-175/35/2543895. Correspondence between Schindlmayr and Brandt, 8., 21., and 27.2.1942, T-175/35/2543800–802. Berger to Brandt, 4.3.1942, BDC. Brandt to Schindlmayr, 13.3.1942, T-175/35/2543887–88. Schindlmayr to RFSS, 17.3.1942, BDC. Schindlmayr, "Meine lieben Landdienstkameraden," T-175/35/2543885–86.

76. Winter to RFSS, 13.4.1942, T-175/35/25432543895–96. Schindlmayr to RFSS, 15.4.1942; Nordland Verlag to Brandt, 17.4.1942; BDC. Brandt to Möckel, 17.4.1942, BDC. Brandt to Nordland, T-175/35/2543890–91. Rehm to RFSS, 10.8.1942; Brandt to Schindlmayr, 11.8.1942; Schindlmayr to Bäumert, 24.10.1942; Schindlmayr to Brandt, 24.10.1942; BDC. Brandt to Schindlmayr, 4.11.1942; Schindlmayr to Vogel, 1.12.1942; Schindlmayr to Brandt, 1.12.1942; T-175/35/2543803–6. On the Nordland Verlag, see Georg, *Die wirtschaftlichen Unternehmungen*, 15–16.

77. Brandt to Schindlmayr and Berger, 15.12.1942; Greifelt to Schindlmayr, 13.12.1942; BDC. Schindlmayr to Mein, 15.6.1942; Billing to Heimschule f. Volksdeutsche Rufach, 6.7.1942; Schindlmayr to Brandt, 1.12.1942; T-175/35/2543807, 2543831–33. Schindlmayr to Schwarz, 4.5.1944; SSHA, "Veränderungsmeldung," 22.3.1945; "Gebührnis-Karte" for Schindlmayr, BDC.

78. RJF Rdschr. 30/41 (October 1941). RJF, "Kriegsjugend," 178. A. Müller, *Landdienst der Hitler-Jugend*, 30–31.

79. The monthly budget of an instructional farm of 260 acres was about 20,000 RM, less than half of which was expended for salaries and the rest for cattle, seed, fertilizer, and equipment. The entire administrative cost for the LD in a single Region, Baden-Alsace in this case, varied from 18,112 RM in October to 47,796 RM in December 1942. When this is compared with the annual costs of running an HJ Region, including all activities, which amounted to more than a million RM in Württemberg, it is clear that the cost of the Land Service, in relation to the labor performed, was not exorbitant. See a variety of financial records relating to Land Service expenditures from 1942 to 1944 on T-580/819/128.

80. Rubouf, "Gebietsführertagung," T-175/123/2648490–99. "Gemeinschaftserziehung auf dem Landdienstlehrhof," *DJD* (1942), 66–68. Stachura, *Nazi Youth*, 209. Axmann, "Parole: Osteinsatz und Landdienst," and Rüdiger, "Die Ostaufgabe der Mädel," *DJD* (15.1.1942), 1–5. Bormann, "Unterstützung des Landdienstes," 25.2.1942, T-81/114/123323.

81. Schroeder, "Soziale Förderung der Ostgebiete," *DJD* (15.1.1942), 6–9. Schroeder was the wartime chief of the RJF Social Office and also headed the Youth Office of the German Labor Front. See also his "Landdienst und Siedlung im Osten," and "Aufruf des Reichsführers SS," 10–11, 24.

82. Stein, *The Waffen-SS*, 137–96. "Germanischer Landdiensteinsatz," *DJD* (15.6.1942), 129–31. RJF, "Kriegsjugend," 179. RJF, "Anschriften d. Dienststellen," T-580/38/239.
83. "Germanischer Landdiensteinsatz," *DJD* (1942), 131. RJF, "Kriegsjugend," 179–80.
84. Gebf. Westmark, "Landdienst-Werbung," 3.9.1942, T-81/101/117219–22. Axmann, "Auslese d. Landdienstfreiwilligen," and "Sicherung d. Führung d. Landdienstlager," *RB 26/42K* (10.11.1942), 335–42. RJF, "Kriegsjugend," 174.
85. "Zurückstellung vom RAD," 19.9.1942, T-580/349/#5. Axmann, "Einsatz d. zweijährigen Landdienstfreiwilligen," *RB 31/42K* (9.12.1942). T-81/115/134631–32.
86. "Dienstwettbewerb für Landdienstscharen," *RB 24/42K* (29.10.1942), T-81/115/134556–59.
87. Winter, "Entscheidung für das Land," 163, 167, 169–70. RJF, "Kriegsjugend," 177, 179. The problem of foreign workers was acute by May 1943 when 1,750,000 rural males had been drafted and were replaced by 700,000 prisoners and 1,500,000 foreign workers. See Farquharson, *The Plough and the Swastika*, 235; Homze, *Foreign Labor*, 290–98.
88. Kostenvorschlag und Genehmigung für Landdiensttreffen in Kolmar, 26–28.2. 1944; Vierteljahresschulung der Lagerführer/führerinnen, 17–20.7.1944; Tagung der Landdienstführer und -führerinnen in Ausbach, Aug. 1944; Landdiensttreffen des Gebietes Franken, 9–10.10.1944; T-580/819/128. Landdienst-Vierteljahresschulung in Landdienstlehrhof Ellwangen, 4–8.7.1944; T-580/820/130.
89. RJF, "Kriegsjugend," 172–73. Steindle, "Kritik," 21–24. Pranz, "Mädelarbeit auf dem Lande," 93. Wunderlich, *Farm Labor*, 321. A. Müller, "Die neue Epoche des Landdienstes," 73. Winter, "Entscheidung für das Land," 162, 167–68.
90. Steindle, "Kritik," 22–23. A. Müller, "Die neue Epoche des Landdienstes," 74. Stolle, "Wer verbleibt auf dem Lande?" 172. Winter, "Entscheidung für das Land," 168. Stolle, *Landdienst: Wille und Werk*, T-81/99/114970.
91. Berger, "Denkschrift." Winter, "Entscheidung für das Land," 169. Schiffer, "Das neunte Volkschuljahr," 1–3. Geb. 13 to RJF, "Eingliederung der Landjahrpflichtigen," 23.1.1936, T-81/102/118770.
92. Steindle, "Kritik," 25–26. Stolle, "Wer verbleibt auf dem Lande?" 172–73. Winter, "Entscheidung für das Land," 166–67. Stolle, *Landdienst*, T-81/99/114971a. RJF, "Kriegsjugend," 162, 175. Farquharson, *The Plough and the Swastika*, 187, 226, 237, 253.
93. Steindle, "Kritik," 24–25.
94. Ibid., 27.
95. A. Müller, "Die neue Epoche des Landdienstes," 75–76.
96. Stolle, "Wer verbleibt auf dem Lande?" 171. See LD financial records on T-580/819–820/128, 130. For extensive negotiations relating to the acquisition of a confiscated farm in Staffelfelden (Alsace) and its transformation into an LD Lehrhof, August 1943 to October 1944, see T-580/819/128.

## Chapter 6

1. Valuable studies of Himmler's population policy and the organizational instrument he erected to implement it, in all of its extraordinary complexity, are still Koehl's *RKFDV* and Broszat's *Polenpolitik*. For activities of the RKFDV in Upper Silesia, see the manuscript by Arlt and Butschek, "Entwicklung." For Hitler Youth involvement, see RJF, "Kriegsjugend," chap. 6.
2. Friedrichs, "Notiz für den Stabsführer," 1.11.1940, T-580/38/239. This important document reveals Axmann's plans for the solution of a variety of HJ problems.
3. Orlow, *Nazi Party*, 2:309–10, 398–99.
4. For activities of the Grenzlandamt under Rudolf Schmidt (1928–1931), see HA/19–20,

T-580/353–354. For Abteilung Ausland, later Grenz- und Auslandsamt (1933–1935), see HA/19/360, T-580/540/375, T-580/597/165. The latter contains a report on the "World Conference of the HJ" in Berlin in 1935. During this period, Karl Nabersberg was a particularly strong advocate of HJ involvement in ethnic politics at home and export of HJ ideas and practices among Germanic youth abroad; see his "Arbeitsbericht für das Jahr 1934" and Smelser, *The Sudeten Problem*, 79–81, 192–93, 245. For the Grenz- und Volkspolitisches Amt (1937–1944), see T-81/97/112489–800, T-81/677/4714641–47. There is fascinating material on the "European Youth Congress," Sept. 1942, on T-81/676/5485498–547.

5. Smelser, *The Sudeten Problem*, 79–81, 192–93, 245. McKale, "Hitlerism for Export!" 239–53. Lauterbacher's report on Konrad Henlein's problems with HJ leaders in the Sudetenland, Jan. 1940, T-175/111/2635810–11. On activities of the HJ in Slovakia, 1939 to 1944, see T-175/525/9395254–404. On SS involvement in a squabble between HJ leader Prager and Henlein, see Berger to RFSS, 13.12.1939; T-175/20/2525729–31.

6. Koehl, "The Deutsche Volksliste in Poland," 359.

7. Greifelt, "Die Ostaufgabe der deutschen Jugend," 1. On Greifelt's personality, career, and role as a "social engineer," typical of several other functionaries in the RKFDV, see Koehl, "Toward an SS Typology," 115–16, and his *RKFDV*, 45, n. 24.

8. Coulon, "Grundlagen einer deutschen Ostpolitik," 83–84. Früsorge, "Grossraumplannung," 7–10, portrayed projected plans for agrarian settlements in the Warthegau, including *SS Wehrbauernhöfe*, and spoke of this new Gau as "the flowering province of the German East." Reiss, a government official in the city of Posen, saw young German settlers in the East as a "manly" new order of racially elite knights, fulfilling a medieval dream in a technocratic setting; "Deutsche im Osten," 10–12.

9. Rich, *Hitler's War Aims*, 2:68–105. Koehl, "The Deutsche Volksliste in Poland," 356. For Greiser's romantic conception of the Wartheland as a laboratory of racial purification and agricultural granary for the Greater German Reich, where young people could fulfill their high ideals of becoming farmers and soldiers, see "An die deutsche Jugend," 1–7. On the party functionaries in occupied eastern territories and their training in the NS-Ordensburgen, see Alexander, *Warthelländisches Tagebuch*.

10. For intraagency fighting, see Levine, "Local Authority and the SS State," 331–55. On the function of the HSSPF, see Buchheim, "Die Höheren SS- und Polizeiführer," and Birn, *Die Höheren SS- and Polizeiführer*. The only thorough study of the *Volksdeutsche Mittelstelle* and the takeover of the old *Verein für das Deutschtum im Ausland* by the SS is to be found in Smelser's *The Sudeten Problem*, who demonstrates the limitations of traditionalists when confronted with radical racists. On the general problem of competitive *Volkstumsarbeit*, see Ritter, *Das Deutsche Ausland-Institut*, esp. 12, 102.

11. Krausnick et al., *Anatomy of the SS State*, 275, 283. On Hildebrandt, see Koehl, "Toward an SS Typology," 118–19. On Hofmann see Hilberg, *Destruction of the European Jews*, 270, 600, 707. Hofmann became HSSPF for Alsace-Baden-Württemberg in 1943; he was later tried by a U.S. military tribunal and sentenced to twenty-five years, reduced to fifteen years by the clemency board; Koehl, *The Black Corps*, 189–90.

12. RJF, "Kriegsjugend," 42.

13. Except for limited participation in the riotous attacks on Jewish businesses in 1938 and receipt of confiscated Jewish property in Luxemburg and other places, there is little evidence that the HJ as an organization was *directly* involved in the persecution and liquidation of Jews; see Hilberg, *Destruction of the European Jews*, 27, 392.

14. Koehl, "The Politics of Resettlement," 234–37. Cf. Döring, "Ein Jahr Ansiedlung," 76–81.

15. Koehl, "The Deutsche Volksliste in Poland," 359–61. On the invasion of German

officialdom, see Gerber, *Staatliche Wirtschaftslenkung*, and Herzog, *Besatzungsverwaltungen*. Cf. Broszat, *Polenpolitik*, 19–28.

16. On Lorenz, see Koehl, "Toward an SS Typology," 117–18, and *RKFDV*, 37–39; Jacobsen, *Nationalsozialistische Aussenpolitik*, 236–37. For insight into Menzel's character, see exchange between Menzel and Bicker, former leader of German youth in Alsace-Lorraine, 20.1.–9.2.1941, T-81/96/110388–90. For KLV activity: B. von Schirach, *Ich glaubte an Hitler*, 270–71; Klose, *Generation*, 254–55; Brandenburg, *Die Geschichte der HJ*, 231; RJF, "Kriegsjugend," 63–80. For negative recollection of a KLV experience, see "Interview mit Günter O.," in D. Peukert, *Die Edelweisspiraten*, 14–27.

17. "Einsatz . . . Umsiedlungsaktion," *RB* 10/41K (22.2.1941), 1–12; RJF, "Rahmenplan f. d. Schulung," Jan. 1941; Menzel, "Umsiedlungsaktion Zwischenbericht," 15.1.–15.3.1941, T-81/95/110302–55. RJF, "Bearbeitung der Volkstumsfragen," 21.3.1941, *VHB-HJ*, 2356.

18. RJF, "Zusammenarbeit . . . VOMI," 4.7.1941, *VHB-HJ*, 621. "Einsatz . . . Umsiedlungsaktion," *RB* 10/41K. Menzel, "Umsiedlungsaktion," 1–3, Anlage, 1. On SS recruitment, see Herzog, *Die Volksdeutschen*.

19. RJF, "Rahmenplan f. d. Schulung," Jan. 1941, T-81/95/110314–29.

20. Ibid.

21. Menzel, "Umsiedlungsaktion," 3–4, Anlage, 4–6. Cf. Schulz, "Hitler-Jugend in den Umsiedlungslager," 89–90.

22. RJF, "Einsatz . . . Umsiedlungsaktion," *RB* 28/41K (18.6.1941), T-81/114/133830–39.

23. Vohdin, "Bewährung des BDM," 183–85. A. Müller, "Neue Heimat," 232–33. How vulnerable the ethnic German minority groups were to the appeals of high German culture is illustrated in Rimland, *The Wanderers*.

24. VoMi, "Umsiedlermädel," 29.4.1941, T-81/95/110300. RJF, "Einsatz . . . Umsiedleraktion," *RB* 28/41K, T-81/114/133830–39.

25. Reichskassenverwalter der HJ, "Einsatz von Mitarbeitern," 4.7.1941, *VHB-HJ*, 2357. VoMi, "HJ-Lehrgänge," 8.7.1941, *VHB-HJ*, 624. For Himmler's pressure on his VoMi and RKFDV subordinates, see KLV Umsiedlung, "Jugendarbeit in den Umsiedlerlager," 26.8.1941, *VHB-HJ*, 626; and Geb. Schw. Rdschr. (30.8.41), T-580/349/#5. "Abrechnung verauslagter Fahrgelder," 24.11.1941, *VHB-HJ*, 620–22.

26. Menzel, "Umsiedlerjugend in sicherer Obhut," 274–78. Kohte, "Arbeit im Osten," 9–15.

27. RJF, "Stand der Umsiedlung," 1.6.1942, T-81/95/110330–35. Geb. Schw. "Osteinsatz in der sozialen Jugendarbeit," (1942), T-580/349/#5. RJF, "BDM-Osteinsatz im Generalgouvernement," *RB* 13/42K (15.6.1942), T-81/114/134398–99.

28. Axmann, "Errichtung der Hauptabteilung 'Festigung deutschen Volkstums,' " *RB* 9/42 (1.4.1942), T-81/114/134335. RJF, "Kriegsjugend," 44.

29. RJF, "Kriegsjugend," 51. BDM Schw., "Meldung für das Generalgouvernement," 15.6.1940, T-81/98/113866. Vohdin, "Bewährung des BDM," 183–85. A. Müller, "Neue Heimat," 232–33.

30. Menzel, "Einsatz . . . Umsiedlungsaktion," section on "Führernachwuchs Landdienst," 4–5, and Anlage listing LD camps, T-81/95/110342–43, 110355. RJF, "Kriegsjugend," 173.

31. Rüdiger, "Die Ostaufgabe der Mädel," 3–5. RJF, "Kriegsjugend," 51.

32. BDM Schw., "Hauptamtliche BDM Führerinnen . . . Wartheland," and "BDM Führerinnen als Schulhelferinnen," 3.4.1941, T-81/99/114831–33. Sprenger, "Wir brauchen Junglehrer," 84–86.

33. Albrecht, "Hauswirtschaftliche Ertüchtigungspflicht," 178–81. The *Landjahr* already had twenty-six camps in the East, containing 700 youngsters from the old Reich,

and was highly regarded as a potential source of teachers; see Sprenger, "Wir brauchen Junglehrer," 85.

34. KLV, "Mädeleinsatz im Osten," (1941), T-81/95/110336–38.

35. Freimann, "Osteinsatz des BDM," T-81/95/110356–62.

36. Freimann, "Arbeitsbericht v. d. Umsiedlerlagern," (1941), T-81/95/110371, 110376–79.

37. A. Müller, "Hitler-Jugend," 49f. RJF, "Kriegsjugend," 51. Further details can be extracted from the following sources. For Alsace-Lorraine: T-81, rolls 99–100, 102, 118, 121, 178; T-175, roll 227; and T-580, rolls 819–820. For Eupen-Malmédy-Luxemburg and Belgium: T-81, rolls 101–102, 135–36; and T-175, roll 272. For Austria and Styria: T-81, rolls 101, 676; T-580, rolls 60–61, 66; and T-84, roll 6.

38. "Vierwöchige Einsatzlager," RB 7/42 (16.3.1942), 69–70; "Einstellung v. Beauftragten," ibid., 70; T-81/114/134317–18.

39. RAM, "Einsatz i. d. eingegliederten Ostgebieten," RB 8/42 (24.3.1942), 72–74; "Gesundheitssicherung," ibid., 75–79; T-81/114/134323–29. Pax, "Lehrkräfte für den Osten," 119–21.

40. Schadow, "Die Ausrichtung der Berufsnachwuchslenkung," 299–302. Geb. Schw., "Osteinsatz in der sozialen Jugendarbeit," (June 1942), T-580/349/#5. "BDM-Osteinsatz," RB 22/42K (10.10.1942), T-81/115/134536–37.

41. Greiser and Forster, "BDM-Schuldienst im Osten," 21–23; Wolpert, "Die BDM-Schulhelferin," 23–25.

42. Wolpert, "Die BDM-Schulhelferin," 24–25.

43. Schramm, "Die politische Aufgabe," 25–27. Schramm was deputy chief of the School Section of Forster's Reichsstaathalter office in Danzig.

44. Axmann, "Hitler-Jugend-Führer-Osteinsatz," RB 13/43K (18.4.1943), T-81/115/134750–51, 134761–63. Cf. "Jugendführer nach dem Osten," DJD (1943), 152–53.

45. Greiser and Forster, "BDM-Schuldienst im Osten," 21. RJF, "Kriegsjugend," 51–52, 173, 179. Menzel, "Umsiedlungsaktion Zwischenbericht," 15.1.–15.3.1941, T-81/95/110302–55.

46. Düppe file, BDC.

47. Ibid.

48. RJF, "Kriegsjugend," 42.

49. Koehl, "The Deutsche Volksliste in Poland," 358.

50. RJF, "Kriegsjugend," 42–43.

51. Ibid., 43–44; Krausnick et al., Anatomy of the SS State, 286–88.

52. RJF, "Kriegsjugend," 44–45.

53. Ibid.

54. Ibid., 52–53.

55. Ibid., 50–51.

56. Ibid., 45–46. For Himmler's order, see RB 18/43 (13.5.1943), T-81/115/134803. Cf. "Volkstumseinsatz im Grenzraum," DJD (1943), 150–52. Still another type of camp was the premilitary training camp for resettled youth at Bistritz, organized in 1943; see VoMi, "Wehrertüchtigungslager für Umsiedlerjugend," 8.7.1943, T-81/277/2398329.

57. RJF, "Kriegsjugend," 46–47. Düppe to DAI, "Umsiedlerdokumentation," 1.1.1943, T-81/277/2398304. Hehn to DAI, "Die HJ-Reichsführerschule für Umsiedler," 28.8.1943, T-81/277/2398307.

58. Schmidt to DAI, "Umsiedlerdokumentation," 1.1.1943, T-81/277/2398179–81. On the SS-sponsored project of the DAI designed to document the population and demographic changes in Eastern Europe, see Ritter, Das Deutsche Ausland-Institut, 136–45. The DAI was subordinated to the VoMi in 1943 and thus became an SS appendage, although strong SS influence prevailed earlier.

59. RJF, "Kriegsjugend," 48–49.

60. RJF, "Die Jugendarbeit in den besetzten Ostgebieten," *DJD* (15.4.1943), 89–91. Rich, *Hitler's War Aims*, 2:361. Koehl, *The Black Corps*, 183. On the history of Ethnic Germans in general, see Komjathy and Stockwell, *German Minorities*; Stumpp, *The German-Russians*.

61. "Bearbeitung von Jugendangelegenheiten," and "Errichtung der Befehlsstelle Osten," *DJD* (15.4.1943), 112. *RB* 18/42 (2.9.1942). A lode of material originating in the *Befehlstelle Osten* and the youth department of Rosenberg's office has survived: T-459/1/ 977–1201, T-459/2/1–811, and T-459, rolls 5–9.

62. Nickel file, BDC.

63. On the organization of the "Memeldeutsche Jugend" in 1939, see T-580/74/344. See also "Die Deutsche Jungenschaft Litauens," et al., T-81/293/2417544–86. Lüer file, BDC. Nickel, "Volksdeutsche Jugend," 91–96. "Osteuropas Jugend gegen den Bolshevismus," *DJD* (15.4.1943), 96–98.

64. E. Krüger, "Der Jugendaustausch," 99–102. Curiously, the RJF used the same term as the SS used for the mobile killing squads organized by the RSHA.

65. Arrangements were made also by the VoMi and the VDA to bring ethnic German youngsters from Rumania, who were being resettled, to Germany for professional training under RJF auspices. See Lübke, "Volksdeutsche Jugend," 275–76. Krüger, "Der Jugendaustausch," 101. "Program zur Verkündigung des Weissruthenischen Jugendwerkes," 22.6.1943, T-454/3/4909330–757. "Die Jugendarbeit in den besetzten Ostgebieten," 1943, T-454/16/405–10. Davidson, *The Trial of the Germans*, 303–4. Herzog, *Besatzungsverwaltung*, 46–47. IMT 14:501–6; 18:450; 22:566.

66. Wright, *The Ordeal of Total War*, 116. On Himmler's plans to kidnap Polish children for Germanization as early as 1941, see Kamenetsky, *Secret Nazi Plans*, 98–100, 208–9.

67. Maschmann, *Account*, 76, 108. Abban, "Osteinsatz des Bann 424, Hamburg," 21.12.1942, T-81/330/2463950–63. Lumpp, "Erlebnisbericht über die fünfte BDM-Einsatzfahrt in den Warthegau," Nov. 1940, T-81/96/110382–86. Lumpp sent her report to the DAI, but it ended up in the files of the RJF, where some sensitive soul had noted in the margin that it "should be destroyed," apparently because it candidly pictured the unflattering conditions in the Warthegau, which might have discouraged future volunteers. Cf. Finckh, *Mit uns zieht die neue Zeit*, 144–48.

68. Abban, "Osteinsatz des Bann 424, Hamburg," n. 67.

69. Maschmann, *Account*, 89, 111–12. Melita Maschmann, whose perceptive and sensitive memoir is by far the best written by any former BDM leader, spent several years working in the Warthegau with the HJ and BDM administration and with the settlers themselves in BDM and Labor Service camps. Her detailed recollections and judicious judgments provide the leaven for the more sententious and prejudicial contemporary accounts of other participants whose reports are used in this final assessment.

70. Ibid., 71–73, 120, 127–29. Finckh, *Mit uns zieht die neue Zeit*, 147–48.

71. Maschmann, *Account*, 113–14. Abban, "Osteinsatz des Bann 424, Hamburg." Friese, "Über die Siedler im Kreis Welun," 27.9.1944, 22–25; (T-81/288/2412013–53).

72. Friese, "Über die Siedler im Kreis Welun," 20–21; Abban, "Osteinsatz des Bann 424, Hamburg"; Maschmann, *Account*, 114–15.

73. Lumpp, "Erlebnisbericht über die fünfte BDM-Einsatzfahrt in den Warthegau"; Friese, "Über die Siedler im Kreis Welun," 6–7, 20–21, 25–32; Maschmann, *Account*, 105–8.

74. Maschmann, *Account*, 94. Friese, "Über die Siedler im Kreis Welun," 22–25. Dr. Friese, whose substantial report to the DAI reveals her firm commitment to the "ideals" of Nazi population policy without ignoring the negative details and uncertain long-

range effects, was a long-term member of the Institute. She had worked for the Institute among the German minority in the South Tyrol in 1934 and 1935. Born in Stuttgart, Friese was forty-three years old and had a teaching career behind her. Before becoming the Beauftragte für den BDM-Osteinsatz in the District of Welun she had been active in the BDM, the NSV, and the Nazi Shop Cell Organization. She had been a member of the Nazi Teachers' Association since 1933, although she did not join the party until 1937. Party officials characterized her as "a good National Socialist and exemplary educator." After returning from the East in 1944 she worked with the *HJ-Flakhelfer* project near Munich. See BDC file.

75. Friese, "Über die Siedler im Kreis Welun," 27.9.1944, 25–32.

76. Ibid., 6–7. On previous settlement activity under the Royal Prussian Colonization Commission, see Koehl, "Colonialism Inside Germany."

77. Maschmann, *Account*, 64, 68–70.

78. Friese, "Über die Siedler im Kreis Welun," 27.9.1944, 7–12; Maschmann, *Account*, 64, 70, 118.

79. Friese, "Über die Siedler im Kreis Welun," 27.9.1944, 14.

80. Abban, "Osteinsatz des Bann 424, Hamburg"; from her picture in the account it appears Miss Abban was about 20 years old. Her report was prepared with meticulous care and convincingly conveys the excitement and adventure that the Osteinsatz frequently generated. Because it was so innocuous, music was a particularly effective Germanizing tool. See Stürtz, Musikreferentin des Geb. Köln-Aachen, "Bericht," Nov. 1942, T-81/99/115052–53; Maschmann, *Account*, 55; Nickel, "Volksdeutsche Jugend," 95.

81. Abban, "Osteinsatz." Cf. Maschmann, *Account*, 130. On the peculiarity of Danzig-West Prussia, see Levine, "Local Authority and the SS State."

82. Friese, "Über die Siedler im Kreis Welun," 2–4, 7–12.

83. Ibid., 1–2, 20–21.

84. Ibid., 32. Cf. Maschmann, *Account*, 102, who thought the German element in the East was like a "thin net," which if stretched too far would certainly break. She argued with a Food Estate official about this in a public meeting, causing a minor scandal.

85. Friese, "Über die Siedler im Kreis Welun," 35–37. Cf. Maschmann, *Account*, 97–100, whose characterization of settlers was much the same, even if tempered by self-conscious embarrassment in recalling her old attitude of superiority.

## Chapter 7

1. Simpson, *Why Hitler?*, 97. Klose, *Generation*, 108. Bleuel, *Sex and Society*, 137. G. Kaufmann, *Kommende*, 126.

2. Rauschning, *The Voice of Destruction*, 251–52.

3. Bernett, *Nationalsozialistische Leibeserziehung*, 19–20, 54. Bernett's valuable book consists of key excerpts from many sources interwoven with interpretive summaries. Cf. Klönne, "Die Hitlerjugendgeneration," 97–98, for discussion of "boxer ethos."

4. E. Weber, "Gymnastics and Sports," 95, 98.

5. Weiss, *Sport*, 9, 14, 17, 243. Slusher, *Man, Sport and Existence*, 3.

6. Bäumler quoted in Hoffmann and Breitmeyer, *Sport und Staat*, 19, 21, 33. RJF, *HJ im Dienst*, 18. Malitz, *Die Leibesübungen*.

7. E. Weber, "Gymnastics and Sports," 71, 72, 77, 90. Bernett, *Nationalsozialistische Leibeserziehung*, 45. Hagen, "Hitlerjugend und Leibesübungen," 413.

8. E. Weber, "Gymnastics and Sports," 91. Wetzel, *Politische Leibeserziehung*, 26. Cf. Wetzel quoted in Bernett, *Nationalsozialistische Leibeserziehung*, 60. Surén, *Kraftgymnastik*, 32.

9. *Richtlinien für die Leibeserziehung* in Mosse, *Nazi Culture*, 281–82. Hagen, "Hitlerjugend und Leibesübungen," 409.

10. Hagen, "Hitlerjugend und Leibesübungen," 409–11, 414. Cf. O. C. Mitchell, *Common Man*.

11. Darré quoted in Bernett, *Nationalsozialistische Leibeserziehung*, 35. Bode quoted ibid., 36, and his *Leib und Seele*, 11–12. Groh and Schneemann quoted in Bernett, *Nationalsozialistische Leibeserziehung*, 69 and 40, respectively.

12. Huizinga, *Homo Ludens*, 102. For a critique of Huizinga's popular book, see Caillois, *Man, Play, and Games*, 3. E. Weber, "Gymnastics and Sports," 90.

13. *Meyers Lexikon*, 621. Schlünder quoted in *WuM* (1936), 17. Cf. Lidtke, "Songs and Nazis," 167–200.

14. Stellrecht, *Die Wehrerziehung*, 101. Reinecker, "Soldaten," 190.

15. Wichmann, *Vormilitärische Ausbildung*, 103. Hagen, "Hitlerjugend und Leibesübungen," 410. L. Wolff, "Die Wehrmacht," 186. Mierke, "Jugendführer," 196–97.

16. G. Kaufmann, *Kommende*, 104–7, 109.

17. RJF, "Sommerplan für die körperliche Schulung der HJ," *RB* 14/I (18.4.1936), 291–99. "KK-Schiessen," *VHB-HJ*, 1301. RJF, "Vereinbarung zw. d. DRfL u. d. NSDAP," *RB* 27/I (1936), 616–17.

18. RJF, "Sommerplan," n. 17.

19. Ibid. Mandell, *The Nazi Olympics*, 285. Cf. Ueberhorst, *Edmund Neuendorff*; idem, *Frisch, frei, stark und treu*; idem, *Modern Olympics*.

20. G. Kaufmann, *Kommende*, 108. Stachura, *Nazi Youth*, 252–53.

21. "KK-Schiessen," *VHB-HJ*, 1303. CdSSHA, "SS-Befehl," 26.3.1936, T-175/152/2681129. Hausser to SSOab, et al., 15.6.1936, T-175/96/2616442.

22. G. Kaufmann, *Kommende*, 115. RJF, "Verwendung von Reservisten," *RB* 34/II (8.10.1937), 927; "HJ-Schiesswartelehrgänge," *RB* 4/II (4.2.1938), 109. Cf. *RB* 12/II (1.4.1938), 360. "Vorträge des Herrn Oberleutnant Rommel," *RB* 10/II (1937), 222; B. von Schirach, *Ich glaubte an Hitler*, 232–34; Brandenburg, *Die Geschichte der HJ*, 171.

23. RJF, "Propaganda-Aktion für das Bau von KK-Schiessständen," *RB* 4/III (4.2.1938), *VHB-HJ*, 1316; "Reichsschiesswettkampf," *RB* 23/III (2.7.1938), 613f. G. Kaufmann, *Kommende*, 115–16.

24. G. Kaufmann, *Kommende*, 115–16. RJF, "Verwendung von Schreckschuss- und Scheintodpistolen," *RB* 34/III (8.10.1937), 928.

25. "Vereinbarung zwischen dem OKW und der RJF," *RB* 4/IV (3.2.1939), T-175/45/2557235–38. "Zusammenarbeit Wehrmacht-HJ"; "Vormilitärische Ausbildung"; "Vereinbarung . . . Reichskriegerbund"; *DJD* (1939), 438–39, 486, 509.

26. Bann Pforzheim to Gff., 14.9.1939, T-81/100/116171. RJF, "Ausbildungsleiter," *RB* 13/K (24.11.1939); "K-Übungsleiterlehrgänge," *RB* 19/K (12.12.1939); "HJ-Schiesswärte/K-Übungsleiter," *RB* 25/K (3.2.1940); RJF, "K-Übungsleitern," 15.7.1941; *VHB-HJ*, 1287–1300.

27. RJF, "Die Leibeserziehung," *VHB-HJ*, 1282–86.

28. Schlünder, "Erziehung zur Wehrfreudigkeit," 195–96. Greiser, "Erfahrungen eines Lagerführers," 73. Schlünder quoted in RJF, *Olympiade 1936*, 368. Ebersbach, "Die Jugend nach vier Jahren Krieg," 202–3.

29. Halter to Schlünder, 3.5.1941; RJF to Peschke, "Einberufungsbefehl," 3.5.1941; Memo of Bav. Min. of Economics, 11.6.1941; Halter to Peschke, 27.6. and 1.7.1941; Halter to Schlünder, 31.10.1941; Peschke to RJF, 1.11.1941; RJF to Geb. Schw., 19.1.1942; T-580/348/#4. Cf. RJF, "Kriegsjugend," 11.

30. Schlünder file, BDC. G. Kaufmann, *Kommende*, 118–26. Voigtländer, "Sondereinheiten," 200–207.

31. *VHB-HJ,* 1273. Schlünder, "Erziehung zur Wehrfreudigkeit," 196. Schlünder's dissatisfaction with army trainers was revealed during a conference of regional HJ leaders; see T-175/123/2648490–99.

32. See n. 21. SD Koblenz, "Turnen in der HJ," 14.2.1938, T-81/101/117665; RJF, "Unterstützung d. HJ-Schiessdienstes," *RB* 31/K (15.3.1940), T-81/113/132823; Berger to RFSS, "SD-Bericht über WEL Oberdonau," 26.11.1942, T-175/21/2526114–18; Halter to Schlünder, "Meldung über Führerschulung," 4.6.1941, T-580/348/#4.

33. RJF, "Kriegsjugend," 11.

34. Schlünder, "Erziehung zur Wehrfreudigkeit," 193–94.

35. "Wehrertüchtigung (lager)," 29.3.1942, *VHB-HJ,* 1331–32. RJF, "WEL der HJ," *RB* 9/42K (1.4.1942), T-81/114/134334–35.

36. Axmann, "WEL der HJ," *ANBl* 8/42, 75; "Erfassung u. Einberufung," GRS 11/42 (28.4.1942); RAM, "Leistungswochen u. WEL," 22.4.1942; Rderl. d. RMdI, 15.5.1942; Rderl. d. RMfWEV, 26.5.1942; Erl. d. JfdDR v. 27.5.1942; Erl. d. RWM v. 11.6.1942; and Erl. d. Beauftr. f. d. Vierjahresplan v. 24.6.1942; *VHB-HJ,* 1323–36. Cf. Erl. d. JfdDR v. 21.4.1943, "Lehrgänge," T-580/350/#6/1.

37. RJF, "Kriegsjugend," 13–14. G. Kaufmann, *Kommende,* 330. Hein, "Was leisten die WEL," 70.

38. On appointment of inspectors and personnel changes, see *RB* 15/42, 27/42K, and 31/42K, T-81/114/-115/134443, 134591, 134633. Cf. "Inspekteure für WEL." WELR 1/44 and 2/44, T-580/350/#6/1.

39. Hein file, BDC. Brandenburg, *Die Geschichte der HJ,* 230.

40. Hein, "Was leisten die Wehrertüchtigungslager?" *DJD* (15.3.1943), 68–73. Berger, "SD-Bericht über WEL Oberdonau," 26.11.1942, T-175/21/2526114–15.

41. Berger to RFSS, "SD-Bericht über WEL Oberdonau," n. 40. For Daniels and Ehlert, see *DAL,* 1934–1943, T-175/204–5.

42. Jüttner to RFSS, "Verhältnis der HJ zur W-SS," 12.11.1942, T-175/21/2526123–25. Jüttner made these arguments by way of replying to the critical SD report about SS behavior in WEL Oberdonau.

43. Berger to RFSS, "SD-Bericht über WEL Oberdonau," n. 40. For the report itself, see Kaltenbrunner to RFSS, "Verhältnis der HJ zur W-SS," 30.10.1942, and Gahrmann to Kaltenbrunner, (October 1942), T-175/21/2526136–43.

44. RFSS to Berger and Jüttner, 18.11.1942, T-175/21/2526127–28. RFSS Memo, 3.12.1942, T-175/21/2526114. RJF, "Dienstbesprechung d. HA II v. 17.-24.10.1943 in Luxemburg," WELR 12/43 (n.d.), T-580/350/#6/1.

45. Berger to RFSS, "Germanische Jugend," 29.1.1943, T-175/124/2599403. Brandt to Berger, "Germanische Jugend," 5.2.1943, T-175/124/2599402. "Stärke d. männlichen Jugend," 27.2.1943, T-580/88/436. RJF, "Lager f. d. Germanische Jugend," WELR 11/43 (16.9.1943), T-580/350/#6/1. *Mitt. d. CdSSHA,* 1 (15.10.1943), 8.

46. "Geschäftsverteilungsplan d. SSHA, 1.7.1944," T-175/153/2683823. Berger's organizational achievement and successful recruitment, despite opposition, become evident when the following documents are examined: "Kommandierung u. Verwendung v. Ausbildern," 16.9.1943; "Jahres-Tagung d. Lagerführer," 21.9.1943; T-580/351/#7. "Dienstbespr. d. HA II," WELR 12/43, T-580/350/#6/1. "Auswechslung d. Ausbilderstabes," 28.10.1943; "Auswechslung d. Ausbilderstabes—Tagung in Luxemburg," 10.11.1943, T-580/351/#7. "Reorganisation d. WEL," 7.1.1944; "Beschickung d. WEL m. Ausbildern," 1.3.1944, T-580/350/#6/1.

47. The untitled and undated SD report, found on T-175/21/2526136–43, appears to have been prepared by SS-Sturmbannführer Theo Gahrmann, chief of SD Sector Linz, sometime in October 1942, and sent on to Ernst Kaltenbrunner, who at that time was

HSSPF in Austria but soon to become Reinhard Heydrich's successor as chief of RSHA. Gahrmann, who followed Kaltenbrunner to a post in central police headquarters in 1944, seems to have gotten his information from several disgruntled HJ leaders who spoke freely to SD informers. Kaltenbrunner passed the report on to Heydrich, who in turn sent it to Himmler.

48. Gahrmann SD Report; see n. 47.

49. Brandl to Grosser, "Errichtung eines 3. WEL," 23.2.1943; Ziegler to RJF, 5.5.1943; T-580/351/#7. Bohl to RJF, "Lagerführer," 10.10.1943; T-580/350/#6/1. Ziegler to RJF, "Jahres-Tagungen," 21.9.1943; Ziegler to Brandl, 9.6.1943, T-580/351/#7.

50. Halter to Schlünder, "Abschlussbericht," 1.7. and 26.7.1942; Ziegler to K-Stabsl., 28.11.1942; Ziegler, "Beurteilung v. SS-Ausbildern," 14.12.1942; Ziegler to RJF, "Beginn-meldung," 2.6.1943; T-580/351/#7.

51. Schlünder telegr. 6308, "dienstbesprechungen wel," 7.12.1942; Brandl to RJF, 8.3.1943; Voigtländer to Brandl, 26.3.1943; K-Leiter d. Stabes to Hptabt. II, "Lagerführer Unterjoch," 24.4.1944; Brandl to Kreunzer, "Lagerführer Posch," 27.4.1944. Cf. RJF to Geb. Schw., "Lagerführer," 8. and 10.9.1943; T-580/350/#6/1. Ziegler to Est. Süd, "Aus-bilderstab," 5.4. and 13.8.1943; Ziegler to RJF, "Beförderung von SS-Ausbildern," 16.9.1943; Ziegler to RJF, "Kommandierung u. Verwendung v. Ausbildern," 16.9.1943; Ziegler to Ehlert, 5.5.1943, T-580/351/#7.

52. Ziegler to Est. Süd, "Beurteilung . . . Gartner," 8.12.1942; Ziegler to RJF, "SS-Hptschaf. Gartner," 3.8.1943; Ziegler to RJF, "Gebirgs-WEL Rautz," 12.8.1943; Ziegler to RJF, "Gebirgs-WEL Rautz," 6.9.1943; T-580/350/#6/1.

53. Ziegler to Hptabt. II, "Abwechslung des Ausbilderstabes," 10.11.1943; Brandl to StGkm. VII, "Ablösung der SS-Ausbilder," 18.11.1943; Ziegler to Est. Süd, "Ablösung der SS-Ausbilder," 23.11.1943; T-580/351/#7. Brandl to Büchl and to the Oberbürgermeister of Augsburg re "Weinzuteilung," 7. and 12.12.1943, T-580/350/#6/1.

54. RJF, "Reorganisation der WEL," 7.1.1944; RJF, "Sportausbilder," WELR 1/44 (11.1.1944); RJF, "Beschickung der WEL," WELR 3/44 (1.3.1944); T-580/350/#6/1.

55. RJF, "Sommerausbildungsplan 1943," T-580/348/#3.

56. "Weltanschauliche Schulung," GRS 16/42 (1.7.1942), VHB-HJ, 1341. RJF, "Weltan-schauliche Schulung," Anlage 1, T-580/348/#3.

57. "Weltanschauliche Schulung," GRS 16/42 (1.7.1942), VHB-HJ, 1341. RJF, "Weltan-schauliche Schulung," Anlage 1, T-580/348/#3.

58. "Sommerausbildungsplan 1943," n. 55. Hein, "Was leisten die WEL," 69.

59. "Sommerausbildungsplan 1943," n. 55. Stünke, quoted in Benze and Gräfer, Erziehungsmächte, 88.

60. Strobel, "Beurteilung," 3.11.1942; Brandl to Strobel, 17.11.1942; Ziegler to Brandl, "HJL-Silber, KU-Ausweise," 17.11.1942; Strobel to Brandl, "Verleihung des HJL," 2.12.1942; T-580/351/#7.

61. See report of Wehrmacht Major Commes, attached to the WBK Mönchen-Glad-bach and serving as Verbindungsoffizier zur HJ for Geb. Düsseldorf, 18.8.1942, T-81/101/117736. Gahrmann SD Report. Granzow, Tagebuch eines Hitlerjungen, 28–33. WELR 2/44 (1.2.1944), T-580/350/#6/1.

62. Granzow, Tagebuch eines Hitlerjungen, 29–30. Schlünder, "Auftreten . . . in d. Öf-fentlichkeit," and "Mitnahme von Frauen und Kinder," WELR 3/44 (1.3.1944); Schlün-der, "Briefe von Lagerteilnehmer," WELR 1/43 (8.2.1943); Schlünder, "Postkontrollen," WELR 9/43 (11.8.1943); T-580/350/#6/1. Commes report, n. 61.

63. Ziegler Stinglwagner, 16.11.1942, T-580/351/#7. Cf. "Arbeitsbummelei," 21.1.1944, T-580/350/#5/2.

64. Liebenow's lengthy lecture was distributed to all people who had anything to do

with premilitary training and may have been stimulated by fairly widespread, excessive exertions demanded of teenage trainees; "Grundsätzliches über das Leistungsvermögen Jugendlicher," WELR 3/44 (1.3.1944), T-580/350/#6/1.

65. Stinglwagner, "Ärztliche Untersuchung," Schw. Rdschr. 20/42 (2.10.1942), T-580/349/#5. Ziegler to Bahl, 25.11.1942, T-580/350/#6/1. RJF, "Ausleseuntersuchungen," RB 22/43K (7.6.1943), T-81/115/134888. Ziegler to Korpsartzt d. StGkm. VII, 8.12.1944, T-580/351/#7. Greiser, "Erfahrungen eines Lagerführers," 72. Ebersbach, "Die Jugend nach vier Jahren Krieg," 199.

66. Böhler, "Lehrgangsteilnehmer Karl Jochem u. Peter Ledermann," 19.4.1943, T-81/100/115971. Ziegler to Est. Süd, "HJ-Angehöriger Jacob Geri," 25.5.1943, T-580/347/#2. See several documents, including "Strafbescheid" against Edighoffer and Kaap by the HJ Court of Baden, 5.6.1943, T-81/100/115871–72, 115959–63.

67. Anonymous letter addressed to "SS-Oberscharführer Lanninger," (1942), T-175/159/2691428. Marginal scribbles indicate that SS trainers surmised the dissident was a "teacher-trainee from Düren," although the letter had been mailed in Cologne.

68. Steeg to Alberts, 1.10.1942; Hudgen to Kopp, 28.9.1942;T-175/159/2691431–34. Granzow, *Tagebuch eines Hitlerjungen,* 33.

69. Est. West to Lanninger, 9.9.1942; Lanninger to Est. West, 1.10.1942; "Prüfungsurlaub" and "Beurteilung"; T-175/159/2691436–39, 2691824, 2691839, 2691843–44.

70. Ziegler, "Jahres-Abschluss-Übersicht, Harburg," 15.12.1943; "Abschluss-Bericht, 1942," T-580/351/#7.

71. "Werbung in d. WEL f. d. W-SS," GRS 14/42 (11.6.1942), VHB-HJ, 1338–39. RJF, "Kriegsfreiwillige," and "Führer u. Unterführernachwuchs," WELR 2/44 (1.2.1944), T-580/350/#6/1. Lanninger to Est. West, 1.10.1942, T-175/159/2691436–39.

72. Granzow, *Tagebuch eines Hitlerjungen,* 32.

73. RJF, "Werbung d. W-SS in den WEL," T-81/96/110424. Cf. WELR 9/43 (11.8.1943), T-580/350/#6/1. Ziegler to StGkm. VII, "Unterführer Nachwuchs," 21.9.1943, T-580/351/#7.

74. Reinbacher, "Erfahrungsvorschläge in der Kriegsfreiwilligenwerbung," 4.4.1944, T-580/352/#9.

75. Ibid. Waiblinger to Miller, "Werber d. W-SS," 6.7.1944, T-580/352/#9.

76. Sydnor, *Soldiers of Destruction,* 195.

77. SSEA to Est. Süd, "Werbung für die W-SS/Besuch des Ritterkreuzträgers SS-Oschaf. Christen," 8.8.1944, T-580/352/#9.

78. Mierke, "Jugendführer," 192. Hein, "Was leisten die WEL," 71. Schlünder, "Erziehung zur Wehrfreudigkeit," 194.

79. StGkm. VII to OKH, "Vormilitärische Wehrertüchtigung der HJ WEL—Erfahrungsbericht," 22.2.1943, T-580/351/#7. Liddell Hart, *The German Generals Talk,* 256. Hirschfeld in DJD (15.8.1943), 189.

80. L. Wolff, "Die Wehrmacht," 186. Greiser, "Erfahrungen eines Lagerführers." Hein, "Was leisten die WEL?" 71, 68–69. Schlünder, "Fortschritte," 188; idem, "Erziehung zur Wehrfreudigkeit," 194. The RJF was so proud of its achievements that Axmann arranged a national "Day of Premilitary Training" in the fall of 1943 and 1944 to show off these accomplishments. In hundreds of cities and towns the HJ special formations and regular HJ boys were organized in competitive matches to demonstrate their shooting abilities, their knowledge of maneuvering in various types of terrain, and other military skills. Hitler sent a congratulatory telegram to Axmann. In most places the NSFK and NSKK participated in the events. High army officers and party officials lent importance to the festivals. See "Tag der Wehrertüchtigung," RB 27/43K, (7.7.1943), T-81/115/134926–27; OKH, "Tag der Wehrertüchtigung," 25.8.1943, T-81/96/110492–94;

Hitler to Axmann, 4.9.1943, T-81/96/110486; Axmann speech, T-81/96/110487; "Tag der Wehrertüchtigung am 8.10.1944," Schw. GRS 18/44, (20.9.1944), T-580/350/#5/2.
81. Hein, "Was leisten die WEL?" 70. Ebersbach, "Die Jugend nach vier Jahren Krieg," 202.

## Chapter 8

1. Koehl, *The Black Corps*, 157–59. H. W. Koch, *Hitler Youth*, 228. Stachura, *German Youth Movement*, 159. Maschmann, *Account*, 57. Heck, *A Child of Hitler*, 35. Shelton, *To Lose a War*, 32. Finckh, *Mit uns zieht die neue Zeit*, 101. B. von Schirach, *Ich glaubte an Hitler*, 251. Griesmayr and Würschinger, *Idee und Gestalt*, 266. Blohm, *Hitler-Jugend*, 296.
2. CdSSEA to Est., 1.2.1940, T-175/104/2626688–90.
3. "Ergänzungsbestimmungen d. W-SS," (1940), T-354/552/4320001–13. Berger to RFSS, "Werbung für . . . 'Grossdeutschland,'" 18.10.1940, T-175/71/2587817. RFSS, "Erfassungs u. Meldewesen," 16.1.1940, T-580/87/436.
4. "Grundriss zum Werbevortrag," (1940–41), T-354/552/4319625. Est. Main, "Rdschr. Nr. 1," (1940), T-175/191/2729204–6. Halder, *Kriegstagebuch* 1:186. Stein, *The Waffen-SS*, 45.
5. For details of the SS struggle with OKW over volunteers, see Rempel, "Gottlob Berger," 107–122; Schickel, "Wehrmacht und SS," 581–606.
6. Stein, *The Waffen-SS*, 29–34, 40–48. Est. Nordost, "Bericht über . . . Musterung," 11.1.1940, T-175/70/2586854–59.
7. RFSS, "HJ-Führer in d. W-SS," 14.3.1940, T-175/36/2545693. Cf. *VHB-HJ*, 1167–68. Geb. Schw., "Führerbewerber," Rdschr. 17/42, 28.8.1942, T-580/349/#5. "Merkblatt f. d. Eintritt," (1940s), T-175/191/2729217–19. "SA-, SS-, HJ-Führer u. Politischer Leiter," *VOWSS* 5 (1.8.1940) in *VHB-HJ*, 1168. SSFHA, memo Az. 17/2.12.40, T-354/552/4319825–26. Wegner, *Hitlers Politische Soldaten*, 149–71.
8. Stein, *The Waffen-SS*, 96–97. Wegner, *Hitlers Politische Soldaten*, 273–75. Rempel, "Gottlob Berger," 111–14.
9. "Überführung d. Jg. 1921 in die SS," *RB* 58/K (21.9.1940), T-81/113/133225–26. CdSSHA, "Überweisung von HJ-Angehörigen zur A-SS," 19.10.1940, T-175/27/2534209.
10. Est. Süd, "HJ-Untersuchungen d. Jg. 1923," 7.11.1940, T-354/552/4319543. For reports of individual HJ Banne see 4319545–48. "Einberufungen bei d. W-SS, 1940," T-175/110/2635114. Cf. "Übersicht ü. Stärke d. Gebjg. 1916–1939," 1.4.1940, T-175/127/2652410–12. Höhne, *Death's Head*, xii.
11. Berger to SSFHA, "OKW, Anforderung des Altersaufbau," 14.1.1941, T-175/110/2635126–27. RFSS to Oberabschnittsführer, 31.1.1941, T-175/110/2635109–10.
12. "Freistellung von HJ-Führern," Rdschr. d. RJF 2/41 (1.3.1941), T-81/101/117366. RJF, "Zusammenarbeit m. d. SS," Geb. Rdschr. 32/41 (24.9.1941), *VHB-HJ*, 1168. CdSSHA, "Einstellungsvorgänge," 9.6.1942, T-175/60/2576488. SSEA processed 154,495 papers 1.1.1940–30.4.1942.
13. CdSSHA to OKW, "Einstellung," 19.2.1941, T-175/110/2635071. Geb. Schw., "Einstellung," Sammelbrief 7/41 (16.4.1941), T-580/349/#5. Geb. Westmark, "Wehrmachtslehrgänge," 3.4.1941, T-81/101/117463. OKW, "Ergänzung d. W-SS," 15.7.1941, T-354/470/4212049–52. OKW to SSEA, "Ersatzbedarf," 3.9.1941, T-175/131/2658038. CdSSHA, "Statistik d. Ergänzungswesen," 9.6.1942, T-175/60/2576487–89.
14. Rubouf, "Gebietsführertagung der HJ in München von 5. bis 7.12.1941," T-175/123/2648490–99. Friessner, "Jugendgemässe Wehrertüchtigung," 197–200. L. Wolff, "Die Wehrmacht," 186–87.
15. Berger to RFSS, "Abkommen mit der HJ," 22.1.1942, T-175/20/2525075–76. "Abstellung v. Ausbildern," Rdschr. d. RJF 7/42 (1.3.1942), *VHB-HJ*, 1169.

16. Berger to RFSS, "Anruf, Stabsführer Möckel," 18.4.1942, T-175/139/2667519-20. "Grussverhältnis," *VOWSS* 11 (11.6.1942), T-580/349/#5.

17. Schmundt to Herff, "Werbung für die W-SS," 20.11.1942, T-175/131/2658039-40. RJF, "Einstellung v. minderjährigen Freiwilligen," *RB* 9/42 (1.4.1942), T-81/114/134337. Goerlitz, *History of the German General Staff*, 322.

18. K-F. d. Bann Memmingen to Gef. 22/312, 30.4.1942, T-580/348/#2/2. Shortly after this, Ernst Bingger became SRD inspector for Schwaben.

19. "Ausführungsbestimmungen f. d. Offiziernachwuchs," 30.7.1941, *RB* 27/41K (16.6.1941), T-81/100/116128-29. Schlünder to Geb., "Nachwuchs f. d. Nachrichtenverbände," 6.11.1942, T-580/348/#2/2. Reports of Banne in same folder. RJF, "Nachwuchs," *RB* 32/42K (22.12.1942), T-81/115/134653.

20. OKW, "Aushebungen f. d. W-SS in RAD-Lagern," 11.2.1943, T-175/131/2658036-37. Wolff to Berger, 24.2.1943, T-175/70/2586826. Bormann to RFSS, 24.2.1943, T-175/70/2586828-31. RFSS to Bormann, 13.3.1943, T-175/70/2586813-14.

21. Kallmeyer to Simon, "Werbeaktion d. SS . . . Halle/Saale," 26.2.1943, T-175/70/2586825-26.

22. Hierl to RFSS, 9.4.1943, T-175/70/2586820-22. RFSS to Hierl, 20.3.1943, T-175/70/2586799. Berger to RFSS, "Beschwerden d. Gauleitung Magdeburg-Anhalt," Mar. 1943, T-175/70/2586795-96.

23. Lammers to RFSS, "Werbung," 28.3.1943, T-175/70/2586798. RFSS to Lammers, "Werbung," 11.4.1943, T-175/70/2586792. Berger to RFSS, 6.4.1943, T-175/70/2586793-94.

24. See T-175/131/2658042.

25. SSFHA, "Zusammenfassung d. Berichte . . . RAD-Aktion," Feb. 1943, T-175/131/2658012-25.

26. Ibid.

27. RFSS to Bormann, 14.5.1943, T-175/131/2658026. Lang, *The Secretary*, 125-37.

28. König to "Sturmbannführer," 27.3.1943, T-175/131/2658045.

29. Wehrkreis I, "Bestimmungswidrige Werbung," 2.4.1943, T-175/131/2658041. Berger to RFSS, "Vortrag Gen. Schmundt," 18.4.1943, T-175/131/2658031-35.

30. Brandt to Bender, Apr. 1943, T-175/70/2686701. For a typical hearing result, see 2586740. Cf. Weingartner, "Law and Justice in the Nazi SS."

31. NSDAP, Gau Baden, "Werbeaktion," 16.3.1943, T-81/124/1459947.

32. Est. Süd to Geb. Schw., "Grosswerbeaktion," 19.2.1943, T-580/348/#22.

33. Geb. Schw., "Werbeaktion," Rdschr. 5/43 (26.2.1943), T-580/349/#5. Bann Augsburg to Ludwig, 8.3.1943, T-580/348/#2/2. Est. Süd to K-Stabsleiter, Geb. Schw., "Werbeaktion," 16.3.1943, T-580/347/#2. Jürgens to Ludwig, "Werbung," 25.3.1943, T-580/348/#2/2. Reports of Banne, T-580/347/#2. Geb. Schw. to RJF, "Werbung . . . laut *RB* 7/43K," 16.4.1943, T-580/347/#2. Berger to RFSS, "Vortrag Gen. Schmundt," 18.4.1943, T-175/131/2658031-35.

34. OKH, "Nachwuchswerbung . . . 'Grossdeutschland,'" 5.4.1943, T-84/241/6599900-901. Schlünder circular, 11.6.1943, T-84/241/6399900-901. Insp. d. Pz. Tr., "Allgemeine Nachwuchswerbung," 14.7.1943, T-84/242/6600829-32. OKW, "Übernahme eines Amtes in d. HJ d. Wehrmachtsbeamte," 2.4.1943, T-580/349/#5. Geb. Schw., "Kommandierung von Soldaten als Hauptstellenleiter II," Rdschr. 25/43 (1.11.1943), T-580/349/#5/1. OKH to Wehrkreise, 9.12.1943, T-81/102/119077. OKW, "Freiwillige d. W-SS," 15.6.1943, T-84/241/6599899.

35. Berger to RFSS, "Untersuchung d. Jg. 1927 (später 1928-1929)," 17.8.1943, T-175/18/2522485-86.

36. Schlünder to Stinglwagner, "Werbeaktion," 22.1.1944, T-580/38/239.

37. Ibid.; Geb. Schw. to Banne, "Werbung," 9.2.1944, T-580/352/#9.

38. Lauterbacher to RFSS, 17.5.1944; RFSS to Lauterbacher, 25.5.1944; T-175/71/ 2587814–16. Wortmann, *Baldur von Schirach*, 184, 248. *IMT*, 14:538–62.

39. Böhm to Est. Süd, "Werbeaktion," 18.2.1944; Geb. Schw. to Bann, "SS-Werbung," 17.3.1944; T-580/352/#9. Axmann to Stinglwagner, "SS-Werbung 'Gerade Du,'" 19.4.1944; Geb. Schw. to Bann, "'Gerade Du,'" 19.4.1944; T-580/38/239. Stinglwagner to RJF, "Nachmeldung zum Zwischenbericht," 22.3.1944; idem, "'Gerade Du,'" 30.4.1944; idem, "Fernschr. v. 21.5.44," 24.5.1944; RJF/SRD, "Abschlussbericht Grosswerbeaktion," 26.7.1944; T-580/352/#9.

40. Geb. Schw., "Kriegsfreiwillige d. Jahrgangs 1928," 4.10.1944; Geb. Schw., "Kriegsfreiwilligenwerbung," 18.4.1944; T-580/350/#5/2.

41. Geb. Schw., "Mitt. d. StGkm," 17.3.1944, T-580/350/#5/2. Bremme, "Erfassung v. Hitlerjungen," 6.1.1944, T-84/242/6600814–15. Geb. Schw., "Feldkameradschaften der Banne," 20.7.1944, T-580/350/#5/2. Geb. Westmark, "Freiwillige für PK-Einheiten," 26.6.1944, T-81/100/116935.

42. CdSSHA to Naumann, 16.8.1944, T-175/71/2588282. Brandt to Berger, 27.8.1944, T-175/71/2588280. Berger to RFSS, "Ersatzwesen," 27.1.1945, T-580/88/436.

43. For minor projects not discussed in the text, see OKH, "Scharfschützen," 21.2.1945; OKW, "Hilfsausbilder," 3.3.1945; T-84/241/6599865–66. HSSPF Main, "Gemäss Rdschr.," 11.3.1945, T-580/39/239. Bann Siegerland, "SS-Einsatz," 22.2.1945, T-81/101/ 117872.

44. RFSS/Befh. d. Ersatzheeres, "Führernachwuchs," (Dec. 1944 or Jan. 1945), T-175/28/2535398. Est. VII to Gauleitung, "Führernachwuchs Jhrg. 1930," 2.1.1945, T-580/39/239. Geb. 36 to Banne, "Führernachwuchs," 5.1.1945, T-580/38/239. Berger to RFSS, 5.2.1945, T-175/28/2535397, 2535403.

45. DAL, 9.11.44, T-175/129/2655468. The regular German army seems not to have gotten its plans for a *Helferinnenkorps* off the ground. Keitel issued orders to create a female auxiliary in November 1944, but implementation orders were not issued by OKH until 16 April 1945, when it was too late to have any effect. See Rose, *Werwolf*, 107–8. Cf. Willmot, "Women in the Third Reich," 10–20.

46. "Meldung von Verstössen gegen den Reichsführerbefehl zum Schutze der weiblichen Jugend vom 6.4.1942," *VOWSS*, (15.6.1943), T-175/179/2714075.

47. SSFHA, "SS-Nachtrichtenmaiden," 27.3.1943, T-580/43/252.

48. CdFMW to RFSS, "Dienstordnung," 26.8.1943, T-580/43/252. Stephenson, *The Nazi Organisation of Women*, 97–129.

49. For this voluminous, tedious, yet illuminating correspondence, see T-175/61/ 22577219–356. On the involvement of the BDM in the war effort, see Klaus, *Mädchen in der Hitlerjugend*, 120–25. On the conception of women in the ideological world of national socialism, see ibid., passim; Koonz, *Mothers in the Fatherland*, 175–219.

50. RFSS, "Ausdehnung der Richtlinien für die Unterbringung und Führsorge der im Bereich der SS und Polizei eingesetzten deutschen Frauen . . . auf weibliche Jugendliche unter 21 Jahren," 18.10.1943, NA/175/61/2577295; for text of the "Richtlinien von 30.11.1942," see 2577296–98. For Dr. Jutta Rüdiger, who was head of the BDM from 1939 to 1945, see Maschmann, *Account*; Klaus, *Mädchen in der Hitlerjugend*; Rüdiger, "Das Bund Deutscher Mädel."

51. CdFMW, "Vorläufige Einsatzordnung für SS-Helferinnen," 2.2.1944, T-580/43/252.

52. Schuster to Brandt, 7.4.1944; Brandt to Schuster, 15.4.1944; RFSS to Sachs, June 1944; RFSS to Klumm, 15.9.1944; T-580/43/252.

53. "Besprechung . . . mit dem Chef des Schulungsamtes," 18.3.1943, T-175/192/2731696.

54. Mutschler, "Neugestaltung des Grundlehrgangs," 16.11.1944, T-580/43/252.

55. SS-Helferinnenschule, "Monatsbericht der Abt. I WE," 2.10.1944, T-175/192/

2731697–700. The princess was shortly promoted to leadership of the school when it was transferred to Heidenheim because of the approaching front line. See her extremely personal and subservient letter to Himmler, 30.11.1944, in Heiber, *Reichsführer!*, 296–97. For the role of her husband, see Goebbels, *Diaries*, 406; Bracher, *The German Dictatorship*, 136; Kater, *The Nazi Party*, 162–63.

56. Grill, *The Nazi Movement in Baden*, 224–25, 311–13, 368; Stephenson, *The Nazi Organisation of Women*, 112–13.

57. CdFMW-WNK, "SS-HK," 25.10.1943, T-580/43/252.

58. Ibid. For rumors about BDM, see Klaus, *Mädchen in der Hitlerjugend*, 110; Bleuel, *Sex and Society*, passim.

59. Schäfer to Renkel, "Werbung . . . SS-Helferinnen," 19.1.1944, T-81/98/113286.

60. RFSS, "SS-HK," 20.2.1944; SSFHA, "SS-HK," 14.3.1944, T-580/43/252.

61. CdRuHA, "Auslese von Nachrichtenhelferinnen," 18.5.1944, T-580/43/252.

62. Oab. Südost, "Werbung für das SS-HK," 6.6.1944, T-580/43/252.

63. Gauleiter, "SS-HK," 22.6.1944, T-580/43/252.

64. Schäffer to Renkel, "Abstellung von BDM-Mädels," 4.7.1944, T-81/98/113287. While there is no evidence to tell us when the BDM Signals Units were organized, it must have occurred about this time, and in response to SS demands for SSHK recruits. The communications office of the SS Main Sector Southeast in Breslau requested teaching materials, course objectives, and curricula, as well as experienced teaching assistants and such teaching instruments as Morse code machines and *Zehn-finger Blindschreiber* from Oberehnheim. These were to be used in preparing the BDM signals girls for the SSHK. See "Bereitstellung von Ausbildungsstätten der N-HJ," 19.8.1944, T-175/192/2731111.

65. Berger, "Nachwuchswerbung," 2.8.1944; RFSS, 12.8.1944; T-580/43/252.

66. Oberehnheim, "Der Weg in das SS-HK," 17.11.1944, T-580/43/252. Dambach to Berger, 21.12.1944, T-175/61/2577225. "Beförderung zur Führerin im SS-HK," (1944), T-175/23/2528471–72. Bann Siegerland, "SS-Einsatz," 22.2.1944, T-81/101/117872.

67. "Nachwuchs für das SS-HK aus dem BDM," 7.11.1944, T-580/43/252.

68. SSHA to Dambach, "SS-Helferinnen," 23.11.1944, T-580/43/252. *IMT*, 20:337–56.

69. Kdr. So/Ls. to Amt B 1, "Werbung für den SS-HK"; Staiger, "Werbung für das SS-HK," 18.1.1945, T-580/43/252. Staiger seems to have been operating out of the RJF in Berlin-Grünewald at this time. The school was evacuated to Heidenheim/Brenz near Stuttgart in early 1945.

70. CdORPO to HSSPF, "Übernahme d. Helferinnen," 6.1.1945, T-580/43/252.

71. SS-Helferinnenschule, "E-Stellenleiter-Besprechung am 19.1.45 in Eipel," T-580/43/252.

72. Berger to Brandt, "Parteikanzlei-Reichsjugendführung," 27.5.1944, T-175/155/2685701–2. Est. Ulm to Bann 438, "Erhöhte Zusammenarbeit," 1.3.1944, T-175/159/2690602. Geb. Schw., "Freistellung v. RAD d. Jg. 1927," 19.2.1944, T-580/350/#5/2. OKW to Wkk., 16.12.1944, T-175/18/2522483. Berger to RFSS, 18.12.1944, T-175/18/2522482. Berger, "Zum Aufbau der Waffen-SS," 55–56. Krausnick et al., *Anatomy of the SS State*, 600. Höhne, *Death's Head*, 520. The 150,000 figure is arrived at by taking 20 percent of the combined numbers of militarily fit youngsters from the 1927 and 1928 classes (185,600) and allowing for eliminations due to youthfulness and recruiting complications at the end of the war. See "Übersicht über Stärke der Geburtsjahrgänge 1916–1939," T-175/127/2652410.

## Chapter 9

1. Bartov, *The Eastern Front*, 1–6, 142–56.

2. The untapped manuscript found in the NSDAP Hauptarchiv, RJF, "Kriegsjugend Adolf Hitlers," is a rich source for scholars who might want to explore the exploitation of children on the home front. The author plans to publish a critically annotated edition of the manuscript.

3. The HJD exposed the relationship between HJ and SS in a fatal way. The connection between two Nazi generations, the process of socialization under the Nazis, and the ultimate implications of the HJ-SS alliance, revealed in numerous small ways, was compressed within the confines of a single combat division, deliberately patterned to take advantage of a decade of association. Peter Paret's review of Gwynne Dyer's *War* suggests that a departure from the popular version of military history is overdue. Similar suggestions have been made by Ian Kershaw, *The Nazi Dictatorship*, 149, n. 2, and Richard Bessel, "Living with the Nazis," 213. The author plans to explore a new approach in a future study of the Hitler Youth Division.

4. Kissel, "Der Deutsche Volkssturm," 214.

5. Stuckart to RFSS, 2.10.1944, T-175/20/2525062–64. The worried defense commissars were Josef Bürckel (Westmark), Alfred Meyer (Westfalen-Nord), Friedrich Rainer (Kärnten), and Siegfried Uiberreitther (Steiermark). If Speer is to be believed, there was no danger from his side, but Sauckel may have given Bormann and Möckel reason for suspician; Speer, *Inside the Third Reich*, 469, 585; Homze, *Foreign Labor*, 311. To be sure, Speer, Sauckel, and Bormann were locked in constant rivalry at the end.

6. NSDAP Strassburg, 20.9.1944, T-81/99/115669. Axmann to RFSS, Jan. 1945; RFSS to Axmann, 19.1.1945, T-580/88/436.

7. Berger to RFSS, "Ersatzwesen," 27.1.1945; RFSS to Berger, "Ersatzwesen," 22.2.1945; T-580/88/436. Speer, *Inside the Third Reich*, 524.

8. OKH, "Scharfschützen," 21.2.1945, T-84/241/6599866.

9. Bormann, "Verstärkung d. kämpfenden Truppe," 28.2.1945, T-580/79/368.

10. OKW, "Hilfsausbilder der HJ-Geb. Jg. 1927," 3.3.1945, T-84/241/6599865. Hechler, *Bridge at Remagen*, 52–53.

11. HSSPF Main, 11.3.1945; Panzer, "Plan für Postbeförderung," 4.4.1945; T-580/39/239.

12. Metzner, "Panzernähbekämpfungstruppe der HJ," 3.4.1945, T-580/78/367. Rose, *Werwolf*, 114–16.

13. Geb. Hochland, "Panzervernichtungs-Bataillons," Apr. 1945, T-81/642/54447222–23.

14. Geb. Hochland, "A-Fall," Apr. 1945, T-81/642/5444726–33.

15. Hofmeister, "Mob-Plan d. Banndienststelle Wasserberg," 1.4.1945, T-81/642/5444820–23. Merk, Bann Bergtesgaden, "Die Aufstellung d. Mob.-Planes," 1.4.1945, T-81/642/5455794–96.

16. Ryan, *The Last Battle*, 39. Rose, *Werwolf*, 115.

17. Ryan, *The Last Battle*, 378–79.

18. Ibid., 367–69 (quotation on 368).

19. Trevor-Roper, *The Last Days*, 173. Toland, *The Last 100 Days*, 457. Thorwald, *Flight*, 220–22. Weingartner, *Hitler's Guard*, 138.

20. Ryan, *The Last Battle*, 451–52. Flower and Reeves, *The Taste of Courage*, 1011, 1012, 1014.

21. Maschmann, *Account*, 157–61.

22. Trevor-Roper, *The Last Days*, 206, n. 1, 222, 249, 276. Toland, *The Last 100 Days*, 485. Maschmann, *Account*, 158. Thorwald, *Flight*, 248. Griesmayr and Würschinger, *Idee und Gestalt*, 270. Sorge, *The Other Price*, 48.

23. B. von Schirach, *Ich glaubte an Hitler*, 312–13; Toland, *The Last 100 Days*, 375.

24. Toland, *The Last 100 Days*, 390–91. B. von Schirach, *Ich glaubte an Hitler*, 313. Cf. Gosztony, *Endkampf an der Donau*.

25. Kissel, *Der Deutsche Volkssturm*, 222. Fraschka, *Das Letzte Aufgebot*, 7, 11, 223. Tauber, *Beyond Eagle and Swastika*, 1:539–40.

26. Whiting, *Hitler's Werewolves*, 82–85, 105–8. Rose, *Werwolf*, 13–22.

27. Rose, *Werwolf*, 22. Auerbach, "Die Organisation des Werwolf," 354–55. Minott, *The Fortress*, 29–30.

28. Minott, *The Fortress*, 29.

29. Kahn, *Werewolves*.

30. Whiting, *Hitler's Werewolves*, 68–70. Auerbach, "Die Organisation des Werwolf," 354. Rose, *Werwolf*, 15–16, 32–36.

31. Whiting, *Hitler's Werewolves*, 72–73.

32. Ibid., 74.

33. Ibid., 148.

34. Stöckl, "A-Fall," 6.4.1945, T-81/642/5444717–19. Tauber, *Beyond Eagle and Swastika*, 1:23; 2:1004.

35. Rose, *Werwolf*, 116–21.

36. Whiting, *Hitler's Werewolves*, 189.

37. Flower and Reeves, *The Taste of Courage*, 1011. Thorwald, *Flight*, 253.

38. Maschmann, *Account*, 168–69.

39. Whiting, *Hitler's Werewolves*, 190. Auerbach, "Die Organisation des Werwolf," 355. Schachtman, *Postwar Population Transfers*, 65. Tauber, *Beyond Eagle and Swastika*, 1:23; 2:1004–5.

40. Maschmann, *Account*, 169–70, 179.

41. B. von Schirach, *Ich glaubte an Hitler*, 315–18. Wortmann, *Baldur von Schirach*, 193–94. Stachura, *Nazi Youth*, 245–46.

42. Tauber, *Beyond Eagle and Swastika*, 1:123, 239–40; 2:1036. Stachura, *Nazi Youth*, 210. Tetens, *The New Germany*, 60, 112. Cf. *Frankfurter Rundschau*, 1.10.1952.

43. Tauber, *Beyond Eagle and Swastika*, 1:405; 2:1005, 1040–41.

44. Ibid., 1:171–72.

45. Ibid., 1:126–27, 192–93, 385, 423, 426–27, 613, 897; 2:1345.

46. Hass, *Jugend unterm Schicksal*, 13, 20–21, 26–27, 30, 57–59, 228–29.

47. Ibid., 79–80, 100, 126, 132, 228–29.

48. Ibid., 137–38, 157. Nicolaisen, *Die Flakhelfer*, 9–15. Cf. H.-A. Koch, *Flak*; Schätz, *Schüler-Soldaten*.

49. Hass, *Jugend unterm Schicksal*, 214–15, 222–24. Friedländer, *Kurt Gerstein*. Frei, "German Theology," 98–112. Craig, *The Germans*, 98–103. The despair of the HJ generation has not been expressed with more gripping realism than Borchert's *The Man Outside*.

50. Klönne, "Die Hitlerjugendgeneration," 99; Jaide, "Die Jugend und der Nationalsozialismus," 723–31; Schoenbaum, "What German Boys Say about Hitler"; Klose, "Hitler in der Schule." Craig, *The Germans*, 184–89. Tenfelde, "Schwierigkeiten mit dem Alltag," 380–81. On Bitburg, see *New York Times*, 28.4.–9.5.1985; Hartman, *Bitburg*. Cf. L. G. Feldman, *The Special Relationship*, xi–xv, 273–76; Miller, "Erasing the Past."

## Chapter 10

1. Hamerow, "Guilt, Redemption, and Writing German History," 71; Craig, *The Germans*, 11. Cf. Hamerow, *Reflections on History*.

2. See works by Beck, Bessel, Childers, Deist, Haffner, Hamilton, Jäckel, Kater, Kershaw, Koonz, and D. Peukert.

3. H. Krüger, *A Crack in the Wall*, 39–41.

4. Haffner, *The Meaning of Hitler,* 34; Kershaw, "The Führer Image and Political Integration," 159.

5. See chap. 4, n. 64.

6. In this connection Bramwell's view of Darré is interesting, provided one accepts the partisan promotion of the peasantry as a separate and indispensable social class; see *Blood and Soil,* 201–8.

7. The double meaning of Krüger's German title is lost in the translation. *Das zerbrochene Haus* becomes merely *A Crack in the Wall.* He says in the afterword of the American editon: "National Socialist fanaticism was certainly not to be found in the teenager from a petit-bourgeois Berlin family. On the contrary, within the limits of his modest opportunities, he always disengaged himself and was even able to place into evidence a few undeniable though fruitless acts of political resistance. But was that enough? Were there not, beyond guilt and atonement, universal erroneous attitudes that furnished the preconditions for Hitler's dictatorship in Germany?" (236–37).

# Bibliography

## Archival Materials

Berlin Document Center, West Berlin
  Correspondence
  Personnel Files
The Hoover Institution, Stanford, Calif.
  Hauptarchiv der NSDAP (Microfilm)
The Library of Congress, Washington, D.C.
  *Amtliches Nachrichtenblatt des Jugendführers des Deutschen Reiches*
  *Reichsbefehl der Reichsjugendführung der NSDAP: Befehle und Mitteilungen für*
  *die Führer und Führerinnen der Hitler-Jugend*
  *Rundschreiben der Reichsjugendführung*
  *Verordnungsblatt der Reichsjugendführung der NSDAP (Hitler-Jugend)*
  Note: All four of the above semiconfidential periodic publications can also
  be found in various microfilm collections.
The National Archives, Washington, D.C. (Microfilm)
  Arlt, Fritz, and Butschek, Hans. "Entwicklung, Organisation, Arbeits-
  leitung der Dienststelle des Gauleiters und Oberpräsidenten als Beauftrag-
  ter des Reichsführers SS, Reichskommissars für die Festigung deutschen
  Volkstums in Oberschlesien von September 1939 bis Januar 1943." (T-81/280/
  2402158f.)
  *Miscellaneous German Records Collection* (T-84)
  *Miscellaneous SS Records: Einwandererzentralstelle, Waffen-SS, and SS-*
  *Oberabschnitte* (T-354)
  *Records of the National Socialist German Labor Party (Nationalsozialistische*
  *Deutsche Arbeiterpartei)* (T-81)
  *Records of the National Socialist German Labor Party and Affiliates, "Schumacher*
  *Material"* (T-580 and T-611)
  *Records of the Reich Leader of the SS and Chief of the German Police (Reichsführer*
  *SS und Chef der Deutschen Polizei)* (T-175)
  *Records of the Reich Ministry for the Occupied Eastern Territories, 1941–45*
  (T-454)
  *Records of the Reich Office of the Reich Commissioner for the Baltic States,*
  *1941–45* (T-459)
  Reichsjugendführung, Presse und Propaganda Amt. "Kriegsjugend
  Adolf Hitlers." Unpublished manuscript. (HA/roll 19/folder 358.)

322   ▪   **Bibliography**

The University of Wisconsin Library, Madison, Wis.
Nabersberg, Karl. "Arbeitsbericht für das Jahr 1934 der Abteilung Ausland in der Reichsjugendführung. N.d. (Berlin, 1934).

**Published Documentary Material, Handbooks, Yearbooks, and Reports**

Absolon, Rudolf. *Wehrgesetz und Wehrdienst, 1935–1945: Das Personalwesen in der Wehrmacht.* Boppard am Rhein, 1960.
Aley, Peter. *Jugendliteratur im Dritten Reich: Dokumente und Kommentare.* Gütersloh, 1967.
Benze, Rudolf, and Gräfer, Gustav. *Erziehungsmächte und Erziehungshoheit im Grossdeutschen Reich.* Leipzig, 1940.
Boberach, Heinz, ed. *Meldungen aus dem Reich: Auswahl aus den geheimen Lageberichten des Sicherheitsdienstes der SS, 1939–1944.* Neuwied, 1965.
Brennecke, Fritz. *The Nazi Primer: Official Handbook for Schooling the Hitler Youth.* New York, 1938.
Bundesarchiv. *Aufstellung zur Filmreihe "Jugend im NS-Staat"—Katalog.* Koblenz: Kulturamt der Stadt Koblenz, 1978.
*Dienstalterliste der Schutzstaffel der NSDAP.* Berlin: Personalkanzlei des Reichsführers-SS und SS Personalhauptamt, 1934–44. (T-175/204–205.)
Ebeling, Hans, and Hespers, Dieter, eds. *Jugend contra Nationalsozialismus: "Rundbriefe" und "Sonderinformationen deutscher Jugend."* Frechen, 1966.
Federal Bureau of Investigation. *Uniform Crime Reports.* Washington, D.C., 1933–45.
Halder, Franz. *Kriegstagebuch.* Edited by Hans-Adolf Jacobsen. 3 vols. Stuttgart, 1962–64.
Hauner, Milan. *Hitler: A Chronology of His Life and Time.* New York, 1983.
Heiber, Helmut, ed. *Reichsführer!. . . Briefe an und von Himmler.* Stuttgart, 1968.
Kahn, Siegbert, ed. *Werewolves: German Imperialism—Some Facts.* London: Free German Movement in Great Britain, 1945.
Kaufmann, Günter, and Burmann, Hans, eds. *Handbuch des gesamten Jugendrechts.* 2 vols. Berlin, n.d. (T-81/679–680.)
Klietmann, Kurt G. *Die Waffen-SS: Eine Dokumentation.* Osnabrück, 1965.
Knopp, W. *Kriminalität und Gefährdung der Jugend: Lagebericht bis zum Stande vom 1. Januar 1941.* Berlin, 1941.
Kohlrausch, Eduard, and Lange, Richard, eds. *Strafgesetzbuch mit Nebengesetzen und Erläuterungen.* Berlin, 1944.
Landdienstinspektion Süd. *Der Landdienst ruft.* Munich, 1938. (T-580/38/239.)
Meister, Johannes. *Polizeiliches Jugendschutzlager (1940–1945), Vorbeugungshaft.* Kiesberg, 1969.
*Meyers Lexikon.* 6th ed. Leipzig, 1939.
Mitchell, Brian. *European Historical Statistics, 1750–1970.* New York, 1975.
Mosse, George L., ed. *Nazi Culture: Intellectual, Cultural and Social Life in the Third Reich.* New York, 1966.
*Nazi Conspiracy and Aggression.* 10 vols. Washington, D.C., 1946–1948.
*Organisationsbuch der NSDAP.* Munich, 1938.

Peukert, Detlev. *Die Edelweisspiraten: Protestbewegung jugendlicher Arbeiter im Dritten Reich: Eine Dokumentation.* Cologne, 1980.

Picker, Henry. *Hitlers Tischgespräche im Führerhauptquartier 1941–1942.* Stuttgart, 1963.

*Reichsgesetzblatt.* Berlin, 1935–1944.

Reichsjugendführung. *HJ im Dienst: Ausbildungsvorschrift für die Ertüchtigung der deutschen Jugend.* Berlin, 1935.

————. *Olympiade 1936 und die Leibesübungen im nationalsozialistischen Staat.* Berlin, 1936.

————. *Die Organisation der Hitler-Jugend.* Berlin, n.d.

————. *Vorschriftenhandbuch der Hitler-Jugend.* Berlin, 1942–43. (T-81/678–679.)

Roth, Heinrich. *Katholische Jugend in der NS-Zeit unter besonderer Berücksichtigung des Katholischen Jungmännerverbandes: Daten und Dokumente.* Düsseldorf, 1959.

Schirach, Baldur von. *Revolution der Erziehung: Reden aus den Jahren des Aufbaus.* Munich, 1939.

Seuffert, Josef. *Franz muss in den Krieg: Ein Junge in Hitlers Armee.* Düsseldorf, 1964.

Siemering, Hertha, ed. *Die Deutsche Jugendverbände: Ihre Ziele, Ihre Organisation sowie Ihre neuere Entwicklung und Tätigkeit.* Berlin, 1931.

————, ed. *Deutschlands Jugend in Bevölkerung und Wirtschaft: Eine statistische Untersuchung.* Berlin, 1937.

*Statistisches Jahrbuch für das Deutsche Reich.* Berlin, 1935/1941/42.

Stockhorst, Erich. *Fünftausend Köpfe: Wer war was im Dritten Reich.* N.p., 1967.

*Trial of the Major War Criminals before the International Military Tribunal.* 42 vols. Nuremberg, 1946–49.

Ueberhorst, Horst, ed. *Elite für die Diktatur: Die Nationalpolitischen Erziehungsanstalten 1933–1945: Ein Dokumentarbericht.* Düsseldorf, 1969.

Vollmer, Bernhard. *Volksopposition im Polizeistaat, Gestapo- und Regierungsberichte, 1934–1936.* Stuttgart, 1957.

Volz, Hans. *Daten der Geschichte der NSDAP.* Berlin, 1938.

## Diaries, Memoirs, Novels, and Similar Materials

Alexander, S. [pseud. Hohenstein]. *Wartheländisches Tagebuch aus den Jahren 1941/42.* Stuttgart, 1961.

Allen, William, ed. *The Infancy of Nazism: The Memoirs of Ex-Gauleiter Albert Krebs, 1923–1933.* New York, 1976.

Angress, Werner T. *Generation zwischen Furcht und Hoffnung: Jüdische Jugend im Dritten Reich.* Hamburg, 1985.

Blohm, Erich. *Hitler-Jugend: Soziale Tatgemeinschaft.* 2d ed. Vlotho/Weser, 1979.

Borchert, Wolfang. *The Man Outside.* Translated by David Porter. New York, 1971.

Finckh, Renate. *Mit uns zieht die neue Zeit.* Baden-Baden, 1979.

Fraschka, Günter. *Das Letzte Aufgebot: Vom Sterben der deutschen Jugend.* Rastatt, 1960.

Goebbels, Joseph. *The Goebbels Diaries*. Edited and translated by Louis P. Lochner. New York, 1948.

———. *Final Entries 1945: The Diaries of Joseph Goebbels*. Edited by Hugh Trevor-Roper and translated by Richard Barry. New York, 1978.

Goethe, Johann Wolfgang von. *Faust*. Part I with Part II, Act V. Translated by Bayard Quincy Morgan. Indianapolis, 1957.

Gosztony, Peter. *Endkampf an der Donau 1944/45*. Düsseldorf, 1969.

———, ed. *Der Kampf um Berlin 1945 in Augenzeugenberichten*. Düsseldorf, 1970.

Granzow, Klaus. *Tagebuch eines Hitlerjungen, 1943–1945*. Bremen, 1965.

Grass, Günter. *The Tin Drum*. Translated by Ralph Manheim. New York, 1964.

Griesmayr, Gottfried, and Würschinger, Otto. *Idee und Gestalt der Hitlerjugend*. 2d ed. Leoni am Starnberger See, 1979.

Hass, Kurt, ed. *Jugend unterm Schicksal: Lebensberichte junger Deutschen, 1946–1949*. Bern, 1950.

Hausser, Paul. *Soldaten wie andere auch: Der Weg der Waffen-SS*. Osnabrück, 1967.

Heck, Alfons. *A Child of Hitler: Germany in the Days When God Wore a Swastika*. Frederick, Colo., 1985.

Krüger, Horst. *A Crack in the Wall: Growing Up under Hitler*. Translated by Ruth Hein. New York, 1986. Originally published as *Das zerbrochene Haus* (Hamburg, 1966).

Maschmann, Melita. *Account Rendered: A Dossier on My Former Self*. Translated by Geoffrey Strahan. London, 1965. Originally published as *Fazit: Kein Rechtfertigungsversuch* (Stuttgart, 1963).

Rimland, Ingrid. *The Wanderers: The Saga of Three Women Who Survived*. St. Louis, Mo., 1977.

Schirach, Baldur von. *Ich glaubte an Hitler*. Hamburg, 1968.

Schirach, Henriette von. *The Price of Glory*. Translated by Willi Frischauer. London, 1960.

Shelton, Regina Maria. *To Lose a War: Memories of a German Girl*. Carbondale, Ill., 1982.

Siemsen, Hans. *Hitler Youth*. Translated by Trevor Blewitt and Phylis Blewitt. London, 1940.

Speer, Albert. *Inside the Third Reich*. Translated by Richard Winston and Clara Winston. New York, 1971.

## Contemporary and Party Publications

*Das Junge Deutschland (DJD)*
*Deutsche Turn-Zeitung (DTZ)*
*Nationalsozialistische Monatshefte (NSM)*
*Süddeutsche Monatshefte (SDM)*
*Wille und Macht (WuM)*

Albrecht, Gertrud. "Hauswirtschaftliche Ertüchtigungspflicht in den neuen Gebieten." *DJD* 35 (1941): 178–81.

Axmann, Artur. "Das modernste nationalsozialistische Erziehungsmittel." *DJD* 36 (1940): 277–79.

_____. *Olympia der Arbeit: Der Reichsberufswettkampf.* Berlin, 1939.

_____. "Parole: Osteinsatz und Landdienst." *DJD* 36 (1942): 1–3.

"Berufserziehung im Landdienst." *DJD* 30 (1936): 38–39.

Bode, Rudolf. "Die geistigen Grundlagen für Körperbildung und Tanz im Nationalsozialistischen Staat." *DTZ* (1933).

_____. *Leib und Seele in der Leibeserziehung.* Berlin, 1938.

Bofinger, Hans. "Nationalsozialistiche Landjugend." *WuM* 3 (1935): 8–10.

_____. "Überwindung der Landflucht." *WuM* 3 (1935): 18–23.

Coulon, Dr. "Grundlagen einer deutschen Ostpolitik: Die Volksliste im Wartheland." *DJD* 35 (1941): 81–84.

Danzer, Klaus. "Landdienst 1940." *WuM* 8 (1940): 22–24.

Darré, R. Walther. *Das Bauerntum als Lebensquell der Nordischen Rasse.* Munich, 1929.

_____. *Neuadel aus Blut und Boden.* Munich, 1930.

Döring, Hans. "Ein Jahr Ansiedlung im deutschen Osten: Das grösste Siedlungswerk aller Zeiten." *DJD* 35 (1941): 76–81.

Ebersbach, Georg. "Die Jugend nach vier Jahren Krieg." *DJD* 37 (1943): 202–3.

Fasold, Sepp. "Das Program der Landjugendarbeit." *DJD* 29 (1935): 345–50.

Friessner, Hans. "Jugendgemässe Wehrertüchtigung." *DJD* 35 (1941): 197–200.

Früsorge, Erich. "Grossraumplannung und bäuerliche Siedlung im Warthegau." *WuM* 9 (1941): 7–10.

"Germanischer Landdiensteinsatz." *DJD* 36 (1942): 129–31.

Granzow, Walter. "Entvölkerter Boden ruft nach Bauern: Der Weg zur Neubildung deutschen Bauerntums." *DJD* 30 (1936): 1–8.

Greifelt, Ulrich. "Die Ostaufgabe der deutschen Jugend." *DJD* 35 (1941): 73–76.

Greiser, Arthur. "Erfahrungen eines Lagerführers." *DJD* 37 (1943): 72–73.

Greiser, Arthur, and Forster, Albert. "BDM-Schuldienst im Osten." *DJD* 38 (1944): 21–23.

Hagen, Harro. "Die Erziehung in der Hitlerjugend." *SDM* 32 (March 1935): 355–62.

_____. "Hitlerjugend und Leibesübungen." *NSM* 5 (1934): 408–14.

"Heime der Hitler-Jugend." *DJD* 31 (1937): 138–39.

Hein, Gerhard. "Was leisten die Wehrertüchtigungslager? Bericht des Inspekteurs." *DJD* 37 (1943): 68–71.

Hemm, Ludwig. *Die Unteren Führer in der HJ: Versuch Ihrer Psychologischen Typengliederung.* Leipzig, 1940.

"HJ steht in der Landwirtschaft." *DJD* 31 (1937): 368–69.

Hoffmann, Paul. "Sozialprobleme der Landjugend." *DJD* 30 (1936): 20–24.

Hoffmann, P. G., und Breitmeyer, A. *Sport und Staat: Im Auftrag des Reichssportführers.* Berlin, 1936.

Kaufmann, Günter. *Das Kommende Deutschland: Die Erziehung der Jugend im Reich Adolf Hitlers.* 3d ed. Berlin, 1943.

_____. *Der Reichsberufswettkampf.* Berlin, 1935.

Koch, Hermann. "Die bisherige Entwicklung der Landdienstlehre." *DJD* 30 (1937): 366–68.

Kohte, Wolfgang. "Arbeit im Osten—Heimat im Osten: Gedanken nach der Umsiedlung." *WuM* 9 (1941): 9–15.

Krüger, Eduard. "Der Jugendaustausch mit dem Osten." *DJD* 37 (1943): 99–102.

Kück, Karl. "HJ-Einsatz auf dem Lande." *DJD* 34 (1940): 115.

Kunzelmann, Gertrud. "Arbeitseinsatz von weiblichen Arbeitskräften auf dem Lande." *DJD* 29 (1936): 15–18.

————. "Berliner Schuljahrgänge im Landdienst." *DJD* 33 (1939): 461–62.

"Landdienst—Nachwuchsorganisation der SS." *DJD* 33 (1939): 93–95.

"Der Landdienstgruppenführer der HJ." *DJD* 33 (1939): 389–91.

Lauterbacher, Hartmann. "Landdienst—Werbeaktion." *DJD* 32 (1938): 606–7.

Leue, H-L. "Heimbauten gegen Landflucht: Pläne des Landdienstes der HJ." *DJD* 32 (1939): 287–88.

Lingg, Anton. *Die Verwaltung der Nationalsozialistischen Deutschen Arbeiterpartei.* Munich, 1939.

Lübke, Heinz. "Volksdeutsche Jugend im Reich." *DJD* 37 (1943): 275–76.

Lüer, Heinrich. "Der Jugenddienstarrest." *DJD* 33 (1940): 250–54.

Malitz, Bruno. *Die Leibesübungen in der Nationalsozialistischen Idee.* Munich, 1933.

Menzel, Hans. "Umsiedlerjugend in sicherer Obhut: Ein Leistungsbericht." *DJD* 35 (1941): 274–78.

Mierke, Karl. "Jugendführer als Offiziernachwuchs." *DJD* 37 (1943): 196–97.

Müller, Albert. *Die Betreuung der Jugend: Überblick über eine Aufgabe der Volksgemeinschaft.* Munich, 1943.

————, ed. "Hitler-Jugend 1933–1943." *DJD* 37 (1943): 1–64.

————, ed. *Landdienst der Hitler-Jugend.* Berlin, 1942. (T-580/38/239.)

————, ed. "Die neue Epoche des Landdienstes." *DJD* 33 (1939): 71–78.

————. "Neue Heimat im Osten: Von der Bewährung des BDM." *DJD* 34 (1940): 232–33.

Neesse, Gottfried. "Die Einigung der deutschen Jugend im nationalsozialistischen Reich." *WuM* 4 (1936): 10–16.

————. *Die Nationalsozialistische Deutsche Arbeiterpartei: Versuch einer Rechtsdeutung.* Stuttgart, 1935.

"Die Neuorganisation des Landdienstes." *DJD* 32 (1938): 606–7.

Nickel, Siegfried. "Volksdeutsche Jugend im Aufbau." *DJD* 37 (1943): 91–96.

Oldigs, Lühr. "Die Landflucht und ihr Ende." *WuM* 2 (1934): 20–22.

Pax, E. "Lehrkräfte für den Osten." *DJD* 36 (1942): 119–21.

Peukert, Rudi. "Landdienst—Weg zum Bauern." *DJD* 34 (1940): 28–30.

Pranz, Erna. "Mädelarbeit auf dem Lande: Bewährung im Kriege." *DJD* 34 (1940): 92–94.

Proksch, Rudolf. "Artamanen, Der Beginn einer Bewegung zur Heimkehr der Jugend aufs Land." *WuM* 7 (1939): 25–28.

Randel, Edgar. *Die Jugenddienstpflicht.* Berlin, 1942.

Rauschning, Hermann. *The Revolution of Nihilism: Warning to the West.* New York, 1939.

————. *The Voice of Destruction.* New York, 1940.

Reinecker, Herbert. "Soldaten der nächsten Stunde." *DJD* 37 (1943): 190–200.

Reiss, Arthur. "Deutsche im Osten." *WuM* 9 (1941): 10–12.

Rüdiger, Jutta. "Das Bund Deutscher Mädel in der Hitler-Jugend." In *Das Dritte*

*Reich im Aufbau,* edited by Paul Meier-Benneckenstein. Vol. 1. *Übersichte und Leistungsberichte.* Berlin, 1939.

―――. "Die Ostaufgabe der Mädel." *DJD* 36 (1942): 3–5.

Sautter, Reinhold. *Hitlerjugend, das Erlebnis einer grossen Kameradschaft.* Munich, 1941.

Schadow, Georg. "Die Ausrichtung der Berufsnachwuchslenkung auf die Bedürfnisse des Ostens." *DJD* 36 (1942): 299–303.

Schirach, Baldur von. *Die Hitlerjugend: Idee und Gestalt.* Berlin, 1934.

Schirach, Max von. *Geschichte der Familie von Schirach.* Berlin, 1939.

Schlünder, Ernst. "Erziehung zur Wehrfreudigkeit." *DJD* 35 (1941): 195–96.

―――. "Fortschritte der vormilitärischen Ausbildung." *DJD* 37 (1943): 187–89.

Schmidt, Friedrich. "Bäuerliche Volksordnung—oder? Die Partei und ihre Jugend im Kampf gegen die Landflucht." *WuM* 7 (1939): 1–9.

Schottky, Dr. "Zur Gesundheitsführung der Landjugend." *DJD* (1936): 19–24.

Schramm, Franz. "Die politische Aufgabe." *DJD* 38 (1944): 25–27.

Schroeder, Otto. "Aufruf des Reichsführers SS." *DJD* 36 (1942): 24.

―――. "Landdienst und Siedlung im Osten." *DJD* 36 (1942): 10–11.

―――. "Soziale Förderung der Ostgebiete." *DJD* 36 (1942): 6–9.

Schulz, Ernst. "Der Landdienst der HJ im Kriegsjahr 1940." *DJD* 34 (1940): 30–33.

―――. "Vom Landdienstler zum Wehrbauern." *DJD* 33 (1939): 484–85.

Schulz, Heinrich. "Die Durchführung der Jugenddienstpflicht: Massnahmen gegen Zuwiderhandlungen." *DJD* 34 (1940): 198–201.

―――. "Hitler-Jugend in den Umsiedlungslager." *DJD* 35 (1941): 89–90.

Seume, Reinhold. "Der RBWk. im Dienste der Nährungsfreiheit." *DJD* 30 (1936): 24–26.

Spranger, Eduard. *Psychologie des Jugendalters.* 18th ed. Leipzig, 1945.

Sprenger, Gauamtsleiter Dr. "Wir brauchen Junglehrer für den Osten." *DJD* 35 (1941): 84–86.

Staebe, Gustav. "Der unsterbliche Bund: Zur Eingliederung der Landjugend in die HJ." *DJD* 28 (1934): 16–18.

Steimle, Theodor. "Heime für den Landdienst kriegswirtschaftlich wichtig." *DJD* 34 (1940): 39–42.

Steindle, Hans. "Kritik des Landdienstes: Die Struktur des Einsatzes— Erfolgsaussichten der Arbeit." *DJD* 32 (1938): 20–28.

―――. "Mehr Bewegung auf dem Lande selbst: Anerkennung des Landdienstes." *DJD* 31 (1937): 137–38.

―――. "Soziale Grundlagen der Landarbeitslehre: Anregungen aus der Landdienstarbeit der HJ." *DJD* 31 (1937): 112–19.

Stellrecht, Helmut. *Die Wehrerziehung der Deutschen Jugend.* Berlin, 1937.

Stierling, Griffion. "Die agrarpolitische Jugendarbeit im neuen Reich." *WuM* 3 (1935): 17–22.

Stolle, Otto, ed. *Landdienst der Hitler-Jugend: Wille und Werk.* Berlin, 1941.

―――. "Wer verbleibt auf dem Lande? Kritik des Landdienstes." *DJD* 35 (1941): 171–73.

Strecke, Erich, and Ost, Leopold. *Jugend hinter Pflug und Werkbank.* Munich, 1941.

# 328 ■ Bibliography

Surén, Hans. *Kraftgymnastik.* Stuttgart, 1935.

Tetzlaff, Walter. *Das Disziplinarrecht der Hitler-Jugend: Entwicklung, gegenwärtiger Stand, Ausgestaltung.* Berlin, 1944.

Usadel, Georg F. H. *Zucht und Ordnung: Grundlagen einer NS Ethik.* Hamburg, 1942.

Vohdin, Liselotte. "Bewährung des BDM." *DJD* 35 (1941): 183–85.

Voigtländer, Heinz; Loewer, Hans; Borchert, Walter; and Mathes, Erich. "Sondereinheiten der Hitler-Jugend." *DJD* 35 (1941): 200–207.

Vornefeld, Herbert. "Gebote und Verbote." *DJD* 34 (1940): 19–22.

Werner, Paul. "Die Polizei in Ihrem Kampf gegen die Gefährdung der Jugend." *DJD* 35 (1941): 243–45.

Wetzel, Heinz, ed. *Politische Leibeserziehung,* 2d ed. Berlin, 1938.

Wichmann, Hans. *Vormilitärische Ausbildung in Frankreich, Italien und der Sowjet Union.* Hamburg, 1938.

Winter, Simon. "Entscheidung für das Land: Ein Rechenschaftsbericht über dem Landdienst der Hitler-Jugend." *DJD* 37 (1943): 161–72.

Wojirsch, Albert. "Gemeinschaftssiedlungen des Landienstes der HJ: Eine Förderung an die Zukunft." *DJD* 30 (1936): 9–14.

———. "Kulturarbeit der Landdienstgruppen." *DJD* 29 (1935): 268–70.

———. "Winterarbeit der Artamanen." *DJD* 29 (1935): 78–80.

Wolff, Ludwig. "Die Wehrmacht zur Wehrertüchtigung der Hitler-Jugend." *DJD* 37 (1943): 186–87.

Wolpert, Elly. "Die BDM-Schulhelferin." *DJD* 38 (1944): 23–25.

## Secondary Sources

Ackermann, Josef. *Heinrich Himmler als Ideologe.* Göttingen, 1970.

Allen, William S. "Farewell to Class Analysis in the Rise of Nazism: Comment." *Central European History* 17 (1984): 54–62.

———. *The Nazi Seizure of Power: The Experience of a Single German Town, 1930–1935.* Chicago, 1965.

Andrews, Herbert D. "The Social Composition of the NSDAP: Problems and Possible Solutions." *German Studies Review* 9 (1986): 293–318.

Arendt, Hans-Jürgen. "Mädchenerziehung im faschistischen Deutschland, unter besonderer Berücksichtigung des BDM." *Jahrbuch der Erziehungs- und Schulgeschichte* 23 (1983): 107–27.

Auerbach, Hellmuth. "Die Organisation des Werwolf." In *Gutachten des Instituts für Zeitgeschichte.* Edited by the Institut für Zeitgeschichte. Munich, 1958.

Aycoberry, Pierre. *The Nazi Question: An Essay on the Interpretations of National Socialism (1922–1975).* New York, 1981.

Baird, Jay W. *The Mythical World of Nazi War Propaganda, 1939–1944.* Minneapolis, Minn., 1974.

Barrett, Michael B., ed. *Proceedings of the Citadel Symposium on Hitler and the National Socialist Era, 24–25 April 1980.* Charleston, S.C., 1982.

Bartov, Omer. *The Eastern Front, 1941–1945: German Troops and the Barbarisation of Warfare.* New York, 1986.

Beck, Earl R. "The Anti-Nazi 'Swing Youth' 1942–1945." *Journal of Popular Culture* 19 (Winter 1985).
————. *Under the Bombs: The German Home Front, 1942–1945.* Lexington, Ky., 1986.
Benz, Wolfgang, ed. *Miscellanea: Festschrift für Helmut Krausnick zum 75. Geburtstag.* Stuttgart, 1980.
Berger, Gottlob. "Zum Aufbau der Waffen-SS." *Nation Europa* 3 (1953): 55–56.
Berghahn, Volker R., and Kitchen, Martin, eds. *Germany in the Age of Total War.* London, 1981.
Bernett, Hajo, ed. *Nationalsozialistische Leibeserziehung.* Schorndorf bei Stuttgart, 1966.
Bessel, Richard. "Living with the Nazis: Some Recent Writing on the Social History of the Third Reich." *European History Quarterly* 14 (1984): 211–20.
————. *Political Violence and the Rise of Nazism: The Storm Troopers in Eastern Germany 1925–1934.* New Haven, 1984.
Bessel, Richard, ed. *Life in the Third Reich.* Oxford, 1987.
Bessel, Richard, and Feuchtwanger, E. J., eds. *Social Change and Political Development in Weimar Germany.* London, 1981.
Beyer, Günther, ed. "Alltag im Nationalsozialismus: Krefelder Jugend in den Jahren 1933–1937." *Heimat (Krefeld)* 54 (1983): 40–51.
Birn, Ruth Bettina. *Die Höheren SS- und Polizeiführer: Himmlers Vertreter im Reich und in den besetzten Gebieten.* Düsseldorf, 1987.
Black, Peter R. *Ernst Kaltenbrunner: Ideological Soldier of the Third Reich.* Princeton, N.J., 1984.
Blackburn, Gilmer W. *Education in the Third Reich: A Study of Race and History in Nazi Textbooks.* Albany, N.Y., 1985.
Bleuel, Hans Peter. *Sex and Society in Nazi Germany.* New York, 1974.
Bock, Gisela. "Frauen und ihre Arbeit im Nationalsozialismus." In *Frauen in der Geschichte,* edited by Annette Kuhn and Gerhard Schneider.
————. "Zum Wohle des Volkskörpers . . . : Abtreibung und Sterilisation im Nationalsozialismus." *Journal für Geschichte* 2 (1980): 58–66.
Boehnert, Gunnar C. "The Jurists in the SS Führerkorps, 1925–1939." In *Der 'Führerstaat,'* edited by Gerhard Hirschfeld and Lothar Kettenacker.
————. "The Third Reich and the Problem of 'Social Revolution': German Officers and the SS." In *Germany in the Age of Total War,* edited by Volker Berghahn and Martin Kitchen.
Bollmus, Reinhard. *Das Amt Rosenberg und seine Gegner: Studien zum Machtkampf im nationalsozialistischen Herrschaftssystem.* Stuttgart, 1970.
Bowlby, Chris. "Blutmai 1929: Police, Parties and Proletarians in a Berlin Confrontation." *Historical Journal* 29 (1986): 137–58.
Bracher, Karl Dietrich. *The German Dictatorship: The Origins, Structure, and Effects of National Socialism.* New York, 1970.
————. *Zeitgeschichtliche Kontroversen: Um Faschismus, Totalitarismus, Demokratie.* Munich, 1976.
Bramwell, Anna. *Blood and Soil: Walther Darré and Hitler's Green Party.* Abbotsbrook, 1985.

_____. "Was this Man Walter Darré 'Father of the Greens'?" *History Today* 34 (September 1984): 7–13.

Brandenburg, Hans-Christian. *Die Geschichte der HJ: Wege und Irrwege einer Generation.* Cologne, 1968.

Bridenthal, Renate. "Beyond Kinder, Küche, Kirche: Weimar Women at Work." *Central European History* 6 (1973):148–66.

Broszat, Martin. *Hitler and the Collapse of Weimar Germany.* Leamington Spa, 1987.

_____. *The Hitler State: The Foundation and Development of the Internal Structure of the Third Reich.* New York, 1981.

_____. *Nationalsozialistische Polenpolitik, 1939–1945.* Stuttgart, 1961.

_____. "National Socialism, Its Social Basis and Psychological Impact." In *Upheaval and Continuity,* edited by E. J. Feuchtwanger.

_____. "Soziale Motivation und Führer-Bindung des Nationalsozialismus." *Vierteljahrshefte für Zeitgeschichte* 18 (1970): 392–409.

_____. "Zur Struktur der NS-Massenbewegung." *Vierteljahrshefte für Zeitgeschichte* 31 (1983): 52–76.

Broszat, Martin; Fröhlich, Elke; and Grossman, Anton, eds. *Bayern in der NS-Zeit.* 6 vols. Munich, 1977–84.

Browder, George C. "The SD: The Significance of Organization and Image." In *Police Forces in History,* vol. 2, edited by George L. Mosse.

Buchheim, Hans. "Die Höheren SS- und Polizeiführer." *Vierteljahrshefte für Zeitgeschichte* 11 (1963): 362–91.

_____. "Die SS in der Verfassung des Dritten Reiches." *Vierteljahrshefte für Zeitgeschichte* 3 (1955): 127–57.

_____. *SS und Polizei im NS-Staat.* Bonn, 1964.

_____. *Totalitarian Rule: Its Nature and Characteristics.* Middletown, Conn., 1968.

Caillois, Roger. *Man, Play, and Games.* Glencoe, Ill., 1961.

Caplan, Jane. "Civil Service Support for National Socialism." In *Der Führerstaat,* edited by Gerhard Hirschfeld and Lothar Kettenacker.

Cecil, Robert. *The Myth of the Master Race: Alfred Rosenberg and Nazi Ideology.* New York, 1972.

Childers, Thomas. *The Nazi Voter: The Social Foundations of Fascism in Germany, 1919–1933.* Chapel Hill, N.C., 1983.

_____. "The Social Bases of the National Socialist Vote." *Journal of Contemporary History* 11 (1976): 17–31.

Craig, Gordon A. *The Germans.* New York, 1982.

_____. *Germany, 1866–1945.* Oxford, 1978.

Cressey, Donald R., and Ward, David A. *Delinquency, Crime, and Social Process.* New York, 1969.

Czeloth, Hans, ed. "Jugendbewegung: Reservat oder nationalsozialistische Kaderschule? Das 'Landjahr' in der Diskussion." *Jahrbuch des Archivs der deutschen Jugendbewegung* 14 (1982–83): 105–16.

Dahrendorf, Ralf. *Society and Democracy in Germany.* Garden City, N.Y., 1967.

Davidson, Eugene. *Trial of the Germans: An Account of Twenty-two Defendants before the International Military Tribunal at Nürnberg.* New York, 1966.

Dawidowicz, Lucy S. *The War against the Jews, 1933–1945*. New York, 1976.

Deist, Wilhelm, ed. *The German Military in the Age of Total War*. Leamington Spa, 1985.

Deschner, Günther. *Reinhard Heydrich: A Biography*. New York, 1981.

De Witt, Thomas E. J. "The Economics and Politics of Welfare in the Third Reich." *Central European History* 11 (1978): 256–78.

_____. " 'The Struggle against Hunger and Cold': Winter Relief in Nazi Germany, 1933–1939." *Canadian Journal of History* 12 (1978): 361–81.

Dicks, Henry V. *Licensed Mass Murder: A Socio-Psychological Study of Some SS Killers*. New York, 1972.

Diehl, James M. *Paramilitary Politics in Weimar Germany*. Bloomington, Ind., 1977.

Diehl-Thiele, Peter. *Partei und Staat im Dritten Reich: Untersuchungen zum Verhältnis von NSDAP und allgemeiner inneren Staatsverwaltung, 1933–1945*. 2d ed. Munich, 1971.

Douthit, Nathan. "Police Professionalism and the War against Crime in the United States, 1920–1930s." In *Police Forces in History*, edited by George L. Mosse.

Dyer, Gwynne. *War*. Homewood, Ill., 1985.

Eberts, Erich. *Arbeiterjugend 1904–1945: Sozialistische Erziehungsgemeinschaft— Politische Organisation*. 2d ed. Frankfurt/Main, 1981.

Erikson, Erik H. *Identity: Youth and Crisis*. New York, 1968.

_____. "Youth: Fidelity and Diversity." *Daedalus* 91 (1962): 5–27.

Esler, Anthony, ed. *The Youth Revolution: The Conflict of Generations in Modern History*. Lexington, Mass., 1974.

Evans, Richard J., ed. *The German Working Class 1888–1933: The Politics of Everyday Life*. London, 1982.

Evans, Richard J., and Lee, W. R., eds. *The German Peasantry: Conflict and Community in Rural Society from the Eighteenth to the Twentieth Centuries*. New York, 1986.

Farquharson, J. E. *The Plough and the Swastika: The NSDAP and Agriculture in Germany 1928–45*. London and Beverly Hills, 1976.

Feldman, Gerald D. "German Economic History." *Central European History* 19 (1986): 174–85.

Feldman, Lily Gardner. *The Special Relationship between West Germany and Israel*. Boston, 1984.

Fest, Joachim C. *The Face of the Third Reich: Portraits of the Nazi Leadership*. New York, 1970.

Feuchtwanger, E. J., ed. *Upheaval and Continuity*. Pittsburgh, Pa., 1974.

Fischer, Conan. "Class Enemies or Class Brothers? Communist-Nazi Relations in Germany 1929–33." *European History Quarterly* 15 (1985): 259–79.

_____. "The Occupational Background of the SA's Rank and File Membership during the Depression Years, 1929 to Mid-1934." In *The Shaping of the Nazi State*, edited by Peter D. Stachura.

_____. "The SA of the NSDAP: Social Background and Ideology of the Rank and File in the Early 1930s." *Journal of Contemporary History* 17 (1982): 651–70.

_____. *Stormtroopers: A Social, Economic and Ideological Analysis, 1929–35.* London, 1983.

Flower, Desmond, and Reeves, James, eds. *The Taste of Courage: The War, 1939–1945.* New York, 1960.

Frei, Hans W. "German Theology: Transcendence and Secularity." In *Postwar German Culture,* edited by Charles E. McClelland and Steven P. Scher.

Friedländer, Saul. *Kurt Gerstein: The Ambiguity of Good.* New York, 1969.

_____. *Reflections of Nazism: An Essay on Kitsch and Death.* New York, 1986.

Friedrich, Otto. *Before the Deluge: A Portrait of Berlin in the 1920's.* New York, 1972.

"Generations in Conflict." *Journal of Contemporary History* 5 (1970). [Special issue.]

Georg, Enno. *Die wirtschaftlichen Unternehmungen der SS.* Stuttgart, 1963.

Gerber, Berthold. *Staatliche Wirtschaftslenkung in den besetzten und annektierten Ostgebieten.* Tübingen, 1960.

Geyer, Michael. "The Nazi State Reconsidered." In *Life in the Third Reich,* edited by Richard Bessel.

_____. "Professionals and Junkers: German Rearmament and Politics." In *Social Change and Political Development,* edited by Richard Bessel and E. J. Feuchtwanger.

Gies, Horst. "Die nationalsozialistische Machtergreifung auf dem agrarpolitischen Sektor." *Zeitschrift für Agrargeschichte und Agrarsoziologie* 16 (1968): 210–32.

_____. "The NSDAP and Agrarian Organizations in the Final Phase of the Weimar Republic." In *Nazism and the Third Reich,* edited by Henry A. Turner, Jr.

_____. "Der Reichsnährstand—Organ berufsständischer Selbstverwaltung oder Instrument staatlicher Wirtschaftslenkung." *Zeitschrift für Agrargeschichte und Agrarsoziologie* 21 (1973): 216–33.

Giles, Geoffrey J. "German Students and Higher Education Policy in the Second World War." *Central European History* 17 (1984): 330–54.

_____. *Students and National Socialism in Germany.* Princeton, N.J., 1985.

Gillingham, John. "The 'Deproletarianization' of German Society: Vocational Training in the Third Reich." *Journal of Social History* 19 (1986): 423–32.

Gillis, John. *Youth and History: Tradition and Change in European Age Relations, 1770–Present.* New York, 1974.

Goerlitz, Walter. *History of the German General Staff, 1657–1945.* New York, 1953.

Götz von Olenhusen, Irmtraud. "Die Krise der jungen Generation und der Aufstieg des Nationalsozialismus." *Jahrbuch des Archivs der deutschen Jugendbewegung* 12 (1980): 53–82.

Gordon, Harold J., Jr. *Hitler and the Beer Hall Putsch.* Princeton, N.J., 1972.

Grill, Johnpeter Horst. *The Nazi Movement in Baden, 1920–1945.* Chapel Hill, N.C., 1983.

_____. "The Nazi Party's Rural Propaganda Before 1928." *Central European History* 15 (1982): 149–85.

Gruchmann, Lothar. "Jugendopposition und Justiz im Dritten Reich: Die Probleme bei der Verfolgung der 'Leipziger Meuten' durch die Gerichte."

In *Miscellanea: Festschrift für Helmut Krausnick zum 75. Geburtstag,* edited by Wolfgang Benz.

Grunberger, Richard. *The 12-Year Reich: A Social History of Nazi Germany, 1933–1945.* New York, 1971.

Grundmann, Friedrich. *Agrarpolitik im "Dritten Reich": Anspruch und Wirklichkeit des Reichserbhofgesetzes.* Hamburg, 1979.

Gurr, Ted R. *Rogues, Rebels, and Reformers: A Political History of Urban Crime and Conflict.* Beverly Hills, Calif., 1976.

*Gutachten des Instituts für Zeitgeschichte.* Munich, 1958.

Habermas, Jürgen, ed. *Observations on 'The Spiritual Situation of the Age': Contemporary German Perspectives.* Cambridge, Mass., 1984.

Haffner, Sebastian. *The Meaning of Hitler.* Translated by Ewald Osers. Cambridge, Mass., 1983.

Hamerow, Theodore S. "Guilt, Redemption, and Writing German History." *The American Historical Review* 88 (1983): 53–72.

————. *Reflections on History and Historians.* Madison, Wis., 1987.

Hamilton, Richard F. *Who Voted for Hitler?* Princeton, N.J., 1982.

Hartman, Geoffrey H., ed. *Bitburg in Moral and Political Perspective.* Bloomington, Ind., 1986.

Hechler, Kenneth W. *The Bridge at Remagen.* New York, 1957.

Heer, Friedrich. *Challenge of Youth.* University, Ala., 1974.

Hehr, Dieter, and Hippe, Wolfgang. *Navajos und Edelweisspiraten: Berichte vom Jugendwiderstand im Dritten Reich.* Frankfurt/Main, 1981.

Heiduk, Franz. "Beiträge zur Geschichte der Jugendopposition in Schlesien 1933–1945." *Archiven der schlesischen Kirchengeschichte* 42 (1984): 17–49.

Heller, Karl H. "The Remodeled Praetorians: The German Ordnungspolizei as Guardians of the 'New Order.'" In *Nazism and the Common Man,* edited by Otis C. Mitchell.

Hellfeld, Matthias von. *Edelweisspiraten in Köln: Jugendrebellion gegen das 3. Reich: Das Beispiel Köln-Ehrenfeld.* Cologne, 1981.

Herzog, Robert. *Besatzungsverwaltungen in den besetzten Ostgebieten.* Tübingen, 1960.

————. *Die Volksdeutschen in der Waffen-SS.* Tübingen, 1955.

Herzstein, Robert Edwin. Review of Kershaw's *Popular Opinion and Political Dissent. The American Historical Review* 89 (1984): 793–95.

————. *The War That Hitler Won.* New York, 1986.

Hiden, John, and Farquharson, John. *Explaining Hitler's Germany: Historians and the Third Reich.* London, 1983.

Hilberg, Raul. *The Destruction of the European Jews.* Chicago, 1967.

Hildebrand, Klaus. "Monokratie oder Polykratie? Hitlers Herrschaft und das Dritte Reich." In *Der "Führerstaat,"* edited by Gerhard Hirschfeld and Lothar Kettenacker.

————. *The Third Reich.* London, 1984.

Hillel, Marc, and Henry, Clarissa. *Of Pure Blood.* New York, 1978.

Hirschfeld, Gerhard, and Kettenacker, Lothar, eds. *Der "Führerstaat": Mythos und Realität, Studien zur Struktur und Politik des Dritten Reiches.* Stuttgart, 1981.

Hitler, Adolf. *Mein Kampf.* Translated by Ralph Manheim. Boston, 1973.

Hoffmann, Peter. *The History of the German Resistance, 1933–1945.* Cambridge, Mass., 1977.

Höhne, Heinz. *The Order of the Death's Head: The Story of Hitler's SS.* New York, 1971.

Homze, Edward L. *Foreign Labor in Nazi Germany.* Princeton, N.J., 1967.

Horn, Daniel. "Coercion and Compulsion in the Hitler Youth, 1933–1945." *The Historian* 43 (1980): 639–63.

―――. "The National Socialist Schülerbund and the Hitler Youth, 1919–1933." *Central European History* 11 (1978): 355–75.

―――. "The Struggle for Catholic Youth in Hitler's Germany: An Assessment." *Catholic Historical Review* 65 (1979): 561–82.

―――. "Youth Resistance in the Third Reich: A Social Portrait." *Journal of Social History* 7 (1973): 26–50.

Horn, Wolfgang. *Führerideologie und Parteiorganisation in der NSDAP (1919–1933).* Düsseldorf, 1972.

Huck, Gerhard, ed. *Sozialgeschichte der Freizeit: Untersuchungen zum Wandel der Alltagskultur in Deutschland.* 2d ed. Wuppertal, 1982.

Huizinga, Johan. *Homo Ludens: A Study of the Play-Element in Culture.* Boston, 1955.

Hüttenberger, Peter. *Die Gauleiter: Studie zum Wandel des Machtgefüges in der NSDAP.* Stuttgart, 1969.

Iggers, Georg. *The Social History of Politics: Critical Perspectives in West German Historical Writing Since 1945.* New York, 1986.

Institut für Zeitgeschichte. *Totalitarismus und Faschismus.* [Colloquium.] Munich, 1980.

Jacob, Herbert. *German Administration since Bismarck: Central Authority Versus Local Autonomy.* New Haven, Conn., 1963.

Jacobsen, Hans-Adolf. *Nationalsozialistische Aussenpolitik, 1933–1938.* Frankfurt/Main, 1968.

Jahnke, Karl-Heinz. *Entscheidungen: Jugend im Widerstand 1933–1945.* Frankfurt/Main, 1976.

―――. *Jungkommunisten im Widerstandskampf gegen den Hitlerfaschismus.* East Berlin, 1977.

―――. *Weisse Rose contra Hakenkreuz.* Frankfurt/Main, 1969.

Jaide, Walter. "Die Jugend und der Nationalsozialismus." *Die Neue Gesellschaft* 12 (1965): 723–31.

Jarausch, Konrad H. "German Social History—American Style." *Journal of Social History* 19 (1985): 349–59.

―――. "The Perils of Professionalism: Lawyers, Teachers, and Engineers in Nazi Germany." *German Studies Review* 9 (1986): 107–37.

―――. "Promises and Problems of Quantitative Research in Central European History." *Central European History* 11 (1978): 279–89.

―――. "Removing the Nazi Stain?: The Quarrel of the German Historians." *German Studies Review* 11 (1988): 285–301.

―――. "Restoring Youth to Its Own History." *History of Education Quarterly* 15 (1975): 445–56.

Kamenetsky, Ihor. *Secret Nazi Plans for Eastern Europe: A Study in Lebensraum Policies.* New York, 1961.

Kater, Michael H. *Das "Ahnenerbe" der SS 1935–1945: Ein Beitrag zur Kulturpolitik des Dritten Reiches.* Stuttgart, 1974.

————. "Die Artamanen—Völkische Jugend in der Weimarer Republik." *Historische Zeitschrift* 213 (1971): 577–638.

————. "Bürgerliche Jugendbewegung und Hitlerjugend in Deutschland von 1926 bis 1939." *Archiv für Sozialgeschichte* 17 (1977): 27–74.

————. "Die deutsche Elternschaft im nationalsozialistischen Erziehungssystem." *Vierteljahrschrift für Sozial- und Wirtschaftsgeschichte* 67 (1980): 484–512.

————. "Generationskonflikt als Entwicklungsfaktor in der NS-Bewegung vor 1933." *Geschichte und Gesellschaft* 11 (1985): 217–43.

————. "Hitler in a Social Context." *Central European History* 14 (1981): 243–72.

————. "Hitlerjugend und Schule im Dritten Reich." *Historische Zeitschrift* 228 (1979): 572–623.

————. *The Nazi Party: A Social Profile of Members and Leaders, 1919–1945.* Cambridge, Mass., 1983.

————. "Nazism and the Third Reich in Recent Historiography." *Canadian Journal of History* 20 (1985): 85–101.

————. "The Reich Vocational Contest and Students of Higher Learning in Nazi Germany." *Central European History* 7 (1974): 225–61.

————. *Studentenschaft und Rechtsradikalismus in Deutschland, 1918–1933: Eine sozialgeschichtliche Studie zur Bildungskrise in der Weimar Republik.* Hamburg, 1975.

————. "Zum gegenseitigen Verhältnis von SA und SS in der Sozialgeschichte des Nationalsozialismus von 1925 bis 1939." *Vierteljahrschrift für Sozial- und Wirtschaftsgeschichte* 62 (1975): 339–79.

Kaufmann, Erich, ed. *Der Polizeiliche Eingriff in Freiheiten und Rechte.* Frankfurt/Main, 1951.

Kele, Max H. *Nazis and Workers: National Socialist Appeals to German Labor, 1919–1933.* Chapel Hill, N.C., 1972.

Kershaw, Ian. "Alltägliches und Ausseralltägliches: Ihre Bedeutung für die Volksmeinung." In *Die Reihen fast geschlossen,* edited by Detlev J. K. Peukert and Jürgen Reulecke.

————. "The Führer Image and Political Integration: The Popular Conception of Hitler in Bavaria during the Third Reich." In *Der "Führerstaat": Mythos und Realität. Studien zur Struktur und Politik des Dritten Reiches,* edited by Gerhard Hirschfeld and Lothar Kettenacker.

————. "Hitler and the Germans." In *Life in the Third Reich,* edited by Richard Bessel.

————. *Der Hitler-Mythos: Volksmeinung und Propaganda im Dritten Reich.* Stuttgart, 1980.

————. *The Nazi Dictatorship: Problems and Perspectives of Interpretation.* London, 1985.

————. *Popular Opinion and Political Dissent in the Third Reich: Bavaria 1933–1945.* Oxford, 1983.

Kettenacker, Lothar. "Sozialpsychologische Aspekte der Führer-Herrschaft." In *Der "Führerstaat,"* edited by Gerhard Hirschfeld and Lothar Kettenacker.

Kissel, Hans. "Der Deutsche Volkssturm, 1944–1945." *Wehrwissentschaftliche Rundschau* 10 (1960).

Klaus, Martin. *Mädchen in der Hitlerjugend: Die Erziehung zur "deutschen Frau."* Cologne, 1980.

Kleinöder, Evi. "Verfolgung und Widerstand der katholischen Jugendvereine: Eine Fallstudie über Eichstätt." In *Bayern in der NS-Zeit,* vol. 2, edited by Martin Broszat and Elke Fröhlich.

Klönne, Arno. *Gegen den Strom: Bericht über den Jugendwiderstand im Dritten Reich.* Hanover, 1957.

———. *Hitlerjugend: Die Jugend und Ihre Organisation im Dritten Reich.* Hanover, 1960.

———. "Die Hitlerjugendgeneration." *Politische Studien* 10 (1959): 93–99.

———. "Jugendprotest und Jugendopposition: Von der HJ-Erziehung zum Cliquenwesen der Kriegszeit." In *Bayern in der NS-Zeit,* vol. 4, edited by Martin Broszat and Anton Grossman.

———. "Jugendwiderstand, Jugendopposition und Jugendprotest im Dritten Reich." *Jahrbuch des Archivs der deutschen Jugendbewegung* 14 (1982–83): 65–76.

Klose, Werner. *Generation im Gleichschritt: Ein Dokumentarbericht.* Oldenburg, 1964.

———. "Hitler in der Schule." *Die Zeit,* July 7, 1978.

———. *Lebensformen Deutscher Jugend: Vom Wandervogel zur Popgeneration.* Munich, 1970.

Knoop-Graf, Anneliese. " 'Im Namen der deutschen Jugend . . .': Willi Graf und 'Die Weisse Rose.' " *Jahrbuch des Archivs der deutschen Jugendbewegung* 14 (1982–83): 77–98.

Koch, Hansjoachim W., ed. *Aspects of the Third Reich.* New York, 1986.

———. *The Hitler Youth: Origins and Development 1922–45.* New York, 1976.

Koch, Horst-Adalbert. *Flak: die Geschichte der Deutschen Flakartillerie und der Einsatz der Luftwaffenhelfer.* Bad Nauheim, 1965.

Kocka, Jürgen. "Zurück zur Erzählung? Pläyoder für historische Argumentation." *Geschichte und Gesellschaft* 10 (1984): 395–408.

Koehl, Robert Lewis. *The Black Corps: The Structure and Power Struggles of the Nazi SS.* Madison, Wis., 1983.

———. "The Character of the Nazi SS." *Journal of Modern History* 34 (1962): 275–83.

———. "Colonialism Inside Germany, 1886–1918." *Journal of Modern History* 25 (1953): 255–72.

———. "The Deutsche Volksliste in Poland, 1939–1945." *Journal of Central European Affairs* 15 (1956): 354–66.

———. "Feudal Aspects of National Socialism." *American Political Science Review* 54 (1960): 921–33.

———. "The Politics of Resettlement." *The Western Political Quarterly* 6 (1953): 231–42.

———. *RKFDV: German Resettlement and Population Policy, 1939–1945: A History of the Reich Commission for the Strengthening of Germandom.* Cambridge, Mass., 1957.

————. "Toward an SS Typology: Social Engineers." *American Journal of Economics and Sociology* 18 (1959): 113–26.

Kohler, Eric D. "The Crisis in the Prussian Schutzpolizei, 1930–32." In *Police Forces in History,* edited by George L. Mosse.

Komjathy, Anthony, and Stockwell, Rebecca. *German Minorities and the Third Reich: Ethnic Germans of East Central Europe between the Wars.* New York, 1980.

Koon, Tracy H. *Believe, Obey, Fight: Political Socialization of Youth in Fascist Italy, 1922–1943.* Chapel Hill, N.C., 1985.

Koonz, Claudia. *Mothers in the Fatherland: Women, the Family, and Nazi Politics.* New York, 1987.

Krausnick, Helmut; Buchheim, Hans; Broszat, Martin; and Jacobson, Hans-Adolf. *Anatomy of the SS State.* New York, 1968.

Krausnick, Helmut, and Wilhelm, Hans-Heinrich. *Die Truppe des Weltanschauungskrieges: Die Einsatzgruppen der Sicherheitspolizei und des SD, 1938–1942.* Stuttgart, 1981.

Kuhn, Annette, and Schneider, Gerhard, eds. *Frauen in der Geschichte.* Düsseldorf, 1979.

Lane, Barbara Miller. "Nazi Ideology: Some Unfinished Business." *Central European History* 7 (1974): 3–30.

Lang, Jochen von. *The Secretary: Martin Bormann, The Man Who Manipulated Hitler.* Athens, Ohio, 1981.

Laqueur, Walter Z. *Young Germany: A History of the German Youth Movement.* New York, 1962.

Lersner, Dieter Freiherr von. *Die Evangelischen Jugendverbände Württembergs und die Hitler-Jugend: 1933–1934.* Göttingen, 1958.

Levine, Herbert S. "Local Authority and the SS State: The Conflict over Population Policy in Danzig-West Prussia, 1939–1945." *Central European History* 2 (1969): 331–55.

Liang, Hsi-huey. *The Berlin Police Force in the Weimar Republic.* Berkeley and Los Angeles, Calif., 1970.

Liddell Hart, B. H. *The German Generals Talk.* New York, 1964.

Lidtke, Vernon L. "Songs and Nazis: Political Music and Social Change in Twentieth-Century Germany." In *Essays on Culture and Society in Modern Germany,* edited by Gary D. Stark and Bede Karl Lackner.

Loewenberg, Peter. "The Psychohistorical Origins of the Nazi Youth Cohort." *The American Historical Review* 76 (1971): 1457–1502.

————. "The Unsuccessful Adolescence of Heinrich Himmler." *The American Historical Review* 76 (1971): 612–41.

Luža, Radomir. *Austro-German Relations in the Anschluss Era.* Princeton, N.J., 1975.

McClelland, Charles E., and Scher, Steven P. *Postwar German Culture: An Anthology.* New York, 1974.

McKale, Donald M. "Hitlerism for Export! The Nazi Attempt to Control

Schools and Youth Clubs Outside Germany." *Journal of European Studies* 5 (1975): 239–53.

Mandell, Richard D. *The Nazi Olympics.* New York, 1971.

Maser, Werner. *Hitler: Legend, Myth & Reality.* New York, 1974.

Mason, Timothy W. *Sozialpolitik im Dritten Reich: Arbeiterklasse und Volksgemeinschaft.* 2d ed. Opladen, 1978.

———. "Intention and Explanation: A Current Controversy about the Interpretation of National Socialism." In *Der "Führerstaat,"* edited by Gerhard Hirschfeld and Lothar Kettenacker.

Meisler, Yoash. "Himmler's Doctrine of the SS Leadership." *Jahrbuch des Instituts für Deutsche Geschichte* 8 (1979): 389–432.

Meister, Johannes. "Schicksale der 'Zigeunerkinder' aus der St. Josefspflege in Mulfingen." *Württembergisches Franken* 68 (1983): 197–229.

Merkl, Peter H. *The Making of a Stormtrooper.* Princeton, N.J., 1980.

———. *Political Violence under the Swastika: 481 Early Nazis.* Princeton, N.J., 1975.

Messerschmidt, Manfred. "The Wehrmacht and the Volksgemeinschaft." *Journal of Contemporary History* 18 (1983): 719–44.

Miller, Judith. "Erasing the Past: Europe's Amnesia about the Holocaust." *The New York Times Magazine,* November 16, 1986.

Minott, Rodney G. *The Fortress that Never Was: The Myth of Hitler's Bavarian Stronghold.* New York, 1964.

Mistele, Karl H. "Zur Geschichte des deutschen Volkssturms in Oberfranken." *Geschichte am Obermain* 12 (1979–80): 110–23.

Mitchell, Otis C., ed. *Nazism and the Common Man: Essays in German History (1929–1939).* 2d ed. Washington, 1981.

Moeller, Robert G., ed. *Peasants and Lords in Modern Germany: Recent Studies in Agricultural History.* Boston, 1986

Moller, Herbert. "Rebellious Youth as a Force for Change." In *The Youth Revolution,* edited by Anthony Esler.

———. "Youth as a Force in the Modern World." *Comparative Studies in Society and History* 10 (1967–68): 237–60.

Mommsen, Hans. *Beamtentum in Dritten Reich.* Stuttgart, 1966.

Mommsen, W. J., and Hirschfeld, Gerhard, eds. *Social Protest, Violence and Terror in Nineteenth and Twentieth Century Europe.* New York, 1982.

Mosse, George L., ed. *Police Forces in History: Sage Readers in 20th Century History.* 2 vols. London, 1975.

Mühlberger, Detlef. "The Sociology of the NSDAP: The Question of Working-Class Membership." *Journal of Contemporary History* 15 (1980): 493–511.

Müller, K. J., and Opitz, E., eds. *Militär und Militarismus in der Weimarer Republik.* Düsseldorf, 1978.

Müller, Norbert. "Zum Character und Kriegseinsatz der faschistischen Ordnungspolizei." *Militärgeschichte* 23 (1984): 515–20.

Muth, Heinrich. "Jugendopposition im Dritten Reich." *Vierteljahrshefte für Zeitgeschichte* 30 (1982): 369–417.

Neufeldt, Hans-Joachim; Huck, Jürgen; and Tessin, Georg. *Zur Geschichte der Ordnungspolizei, 1936–1945.* Koblenz, 1957.

Neusüss-Hunkel, Ermenhild. *Die SS.* Hanover, 1956.

Nicolaisen, Hans-Dietrich. *Die Flakhelfer: Luftwaffenhelfer und Marinehelfer im Zweiten Weltkrieg.* Berlin, 1981.

Niethammer, Lutz, ed. *"Die Jahre weiss man nicht, wo man die heute hinsetzen sol": Faschismuserfahrungen im Ruhrgebiet.* Berlin, 1983.

_____, ed. *Wohnen im Wandel: Beiträge zur Geschichte des Alltags in der bürgerlichen Gesellschaft.* Wuppertal, 1979.

Noakes, Jeremy. *The Nazi Party in Lower Saxony, 1921–1933.* London, 1971.

_____. "Social Outcasts in the Third Reich." In *Life in the Third Reich,* edited by Richard Bessel.

Nyomarkay, Joseph. *Charisma and Factionalism in the Nazi Party.* Minneapolis, Minn., 1967.

O'Neill, Robert J. *The German Army and the Nazi Party, 1933–1939.* London, 1966.

Orlow, Dietrich. "Die Adolf-Hitler-Schulen." *Vierteljahrshefte für Zeitgeschichte* 12 (1965): 272–84.

_____. *The History of the Nazi Party.* 2 vols. Pittsburgh, Pa., 1969–73.

Paetel, Karl O. *Jugendbewegung und Politik.* Bad Godesberg, 1961.

_____. *Jugend in der Entscheidung: 1913–1933–1945.* Bad Godesberg, 1963.

_____. "Die SS: Ein Beitrag zur Soziologie des Nationalsozialismus." *Vierteljahrshefte für Zeitgeschichte* 2 (1954): 1–33.

Paret, Peter. "Gwynne Dyer's War." [Review.] *The American Historical Review* 91 (1986): 882–83.

Pauley, Bruce F. *Hitler and the Forgotten Nazis: A History of Austrian National Socialism.* Chapel Hill, N.C., 1981.

Peterson, Edward N. "The Bureaucracy and the Nazi Party." *Review of Politics* (1966): 172–92.

_____. *The Limits of Hitler's Power.* Princeton, N.J., 1969.

Petrick, Fritz. *Zur sozialen Lage der Arbeiterjugend in Deutschland 1933–1939.* East Berlin, 1974.

Petry, Christian. *Studenten aufs Schafott: Die Weisse Rose und ihr scheitern.* Munich, 1968.

Petzina, Dieter. *Autarkiepolitik im Dritten Reich: Der nationalsozialistische Vierjahresplan.* Stuttgart, 1968.

Peukert, Detlev J. K. "Arbeitslager und Jugend-KZ: die 'Behandlung Gemeinschaftsfremder' im Dritten Reich." In *Die Reihen fast geschlossen,* edited by Detlev J. K. Peukert and Jürgen Reulecke.

_____. "Edelweisspiraten, Meuten, Swing: Jugendsubkulturen im Dritten Reich." In *Sozialgeschichte der Freizeit,* edited by Gerhard Huck.

_____. "Die Erwerblosigkeit junger Arbeiter in der Weltwirtschaftskrise in Deutschland 1929–1933." *Vierteljahrschrift für Sozial- und Wirtschaftsgeschichte* 72 (1985): 305–28.

_____. "Die 'Halbstarken.'" *Zeitschrift für Pädogogik* 30 (1984): 533–48.

_____. *Inside Nazi Germany: Conformity, Opposition, and Racism in Everyday Life.* New Haven, Conn., 1987.

_____. *Die KPD im Widerstand: Verfolgung und Untergrundarbeit an Rhein und Ruhr 1933–1945.* Wuppertal, 1980.

_____. *Volksgenossen und Gemeinschaftsfremde: Anpassung, Ausmerze und Aufbegehren unter dem Nationalsozialismus.* Cologne, 1982.

Peukert, Detlev J. K., and Reulecke, Jürgen, eds. *Die Reihen fast geschlossen: Beiträge zur Geschichte des Alltags unterm Nationalsozialismus*. Wuppertal, 1981.

Pietschmann, Horst. "Der KJVD 1927/28 im Ringen für die Verteidigung der sozialen Tagesinteressen der werktätigen Jugend." *Wissenschaftliche Zeitschrift der Universität Rostock* 34 (1985): 11–17.

Plant, Richard. *The Pink Triangle: The Nazi War against Homosexuals*. New York, 1986.

Pridham, Geoffrey. *Hitler's Rise to Power: The Nazi Movement in Bavaria, 1923–1933*. New York, 1974.

Priepke, Manfred. *Die evangelische Jugend im Widerstand gegen das Dritte Reich von 1933–1936*. Hanover, 1960.

Pronay, Nicholas, and Wilson, Keith, eds. *The Political Re-Education of Germany and Her Allies After World War II*. Totowa, N.J., 1985.

Pross, Harry. *Jugend-Eros-Politik: Die Geschichte der deutschen Jugendverbände*. Bern, 1964.

Radzinowicz, Leon. *The Growth of Crime: The International Experience*. New York, 1977.

—————. *Ideology and Crime*. New York, 1966.

Reitlinger, Gerald. *The SS: Alibi of a Nation, 1922–1945*. New York, 1957.

Rempel, Gerhard. "Gottlob Berger and Waffen-SS Recruitment: 1939–1945." *Militärgeschichtliche Mitteilungen* 27 (1980): 107–22.

—————. "Training Teenage Spies and Policeboys: The Hitler-Jugend Streifendienst." In *Proceedings of the Citadel Symposium on Hitler and the National Socialist Era. 24–25 April 1980*, edited by Michael B. Barrett.

Reulecke, Jürgen, and Weber, Wolfhard, eds., *Fabrik Familie Feierabend*. Wuppertal, 1978.

Rich, Norman. *Hitler's War Aims*. 2 vols. New York, 1973–74.

Richardson, James F. "Berlin Police in the Weimar Republic: A Comparison with Police Forces in the United States." In *Police Forces in History*, edited by George L. Mosse.

Riedel, Heinrich. *Kampf um die Jugend: Evangelische Jugendarbeit 1933–1945*. Munich, 1976.

Ritter, Ernst. *Das Deutsche Ausland-Institut in Stuttgart 1917–1945: Ein Beispiel deutscher Volkstumsarbeit zwischen den Weltkriegen*. Wiesbaden, 1976.

Rose, Arno. *Werwolf 1944–1945: Eine Dokumentation*. Stuttgart, 1980.

Rosenhaft, Eve. *Beating the Fascists? The German Communists and Political Violence, 1929–1933*. New York, 1983.

—————. "Gewalt in der Politik: Zum Problem des 'Sozialen Militarismus.'" In *Militär und Militarismus in der Weimarer Republik*, edited by K. J. Müller and E. Opitz.

—————. "Organising the 'Lumpenproletariat': Cliques and Communists in Berlin during the Weimar Republic." In *The German Working Class 1888–1933: The Politics of Everyday Life*, edited by Richard J. Evans.

—————. "Working-class Life and Working-class Politics: Communists, Nazis and the State in the Battle for the Streets, Berlin 1928–1932." In *Social Change and Political Development in Weimar Germany,* edited by Richard Bessel and E. J. Feuchtwanger.

Ryan, Cornelius. *The Last Battle.* New York, 1966.

Samuel, R. H., and Thomas, R. Hinton. *Education and Society in Modern Germany.* Westport, Conn., 1971.

Sauer, Wolfgang. "National Socialism: Totalitarianism or Fascism?" *The American Historical Review* 73 (1967): 404–24.

Schachtman, Joseph B. *Postwar Population Transfers in Europe, 1945–1955.* Philadelphia, Pa., 1962.

Schäfer, Wolfgang. *NSDAP: Entwicklung und Struktur der Staatspartei des Dritten Reiches.* Hanover, 1956.

Schätz, Ludwig. *Schüler-Soldaten: Die Geschichte der Luftwaffenhelfer im zweiten Weltkrieg.* Frankfurt/Main, 1972.

Schellenberg, Barbara. *Katholische Jugend und Drittes Reich.* Mainz, 1975.

Schickel, Alfred. "Wehrmacht und SS: Eine Untersuchung über ihre Stellung und Rolle in den Plannungen der nationalsozialistischen Führer." *Geschichte in Wissenschaft und Unterricht* 21 (1970): 581–606.

Schieder, Wolfgang, ed. *Faschismus als soziale Bewegung: Deutschland und Italien im Vergleich.* Hamburg, 1976.

Schmidt, Matthias. *Albert Speer: The End of a Myth.* New York, 1984.

Schoenbaum, David. *Hitler's Social Revolution: Class and Status in Nazi Germany, 1933–1939.* Garden City, N.Y., 1967.

_____. "What German Boys Say about Hitler." *The New York Times Magazine,* January 9, 1966.

Scholl, Inge. *Students against Tyranny: The Resistance of the White Rose, Munich, 1942–1943.* Middletown, Conn., 1970.

Scholtz, Harald. "Die NS-Ordensburgen." *Vierteljahrshefte für Zeitgeschichte* 15 (1967): 269–98.

Schultz, Jürgen. *Die Akademie für Jugendführung der Hitlerjugend in Braunschweig.* Braunschweig, 1978.

Schulz, Gerhard. *Faschismus-Nationalsozialismus: Versionen und theoretische Kontroversen, 1922–1972.* Frankfurt, 1974.

Schulze, Harry [Harry Wilde, pseud.]. *Das Schicksal der Verfemten: Die Verfolgung der Homosexuellen im 'Dritten Reich' und ihre Stellung in der heutigen Gesellschaft.* Tübingen, 1969.

Schwersenz, Jizchak, and Wolff, Edith. "Jüdische Jugend im Untergrund: Eine zionistische Gruppe in Berlin während des Zweiten Weltkrieges." *Das Parlament* 31 (1981): B16–B38.

Seidler, Franz W. "Das Nationalsozialistische Kraftfahrkorps und die Organisation Todt im Zweiten Weltkrieg." *Vierteljahrshefte für Zeitgeschichte* 32 (1984): 625–28.

Seraphim, Hans-Günter. "SS-Verfügungstruppe und Wehrmacht." *Wehrwissentschaftliche Rundschau* 5 (1955): 569–85.

Simpson, Amos E., ed. *Why Hitler?* Boston, 1971.

Sinkwitz, Peter, ed. "Historische Agrarliteratur." *Zeitschrift für Agrargeschichte und Agrarsoziologie* 33 (1985): 125–63.

Slusher, Howard S. *Man, Sport and Existence: A Critical Analysis.* Philadelphia, Pa., 1967.

Smelser, Ronald M. *Robert Ley: Hitler's Labor Front Leader.* Leamington Spa, 1988.

―――. *The Sudeten Problem, 1933–1938: Volkstumspolitik and the Formulation of Nazi Foreign Policy.* Middletown, Conn., 1975.

Smith, Bradley F. *Adolf Hitler: His Family, Childhood and Youth.* Stanford, Calif., 1967.

―――. *Heinrich Himmler: A Nazi in the Making, 1900–1926.* Stanford, Calif., 1971.

Sorge, Martin K. *The Other Price of Hitler's War: German Military and Civilian Losses Resulting From World War II.* Westport, Conn., 1986.

Spitzer, Alan B. "The Historical Problem of Generations." *The American Historical Review* 78 (1973): 1353–85.

Stachura, Peter D. "Deutsche Jugendbewegung und Nationalsozialismus." *Jahrbuch des Archivs der deutschen Jugendbewegung* 12 (1980): 35–53.

―――. *The German Youth Movement 1900–1945: An Interpretation and Documentary History.* New York, 1981.

―――. "The Hitler Youth in Crisis: The Case of Reichsführer Kurt Gruber, October 1931." *European Studies Review* 6 (1976): 331–56.

―――. "The Ideology of the Hitler Youth in the Kampfzeit." *Journal of Contemporary History* 8 (1973): 155–67.

―――. "The National Socialist Machtergreifung and the German Youth Movement: Co-ordination and Reorganization, 1933–34." *Journal of European Studies* 5 (1975): 255–72.

―――. *Nazi Youth in the Weimar Republic.* Santa Barbara, Calif., 1975.

―――. "Who Were the Nazis? A Socio-Political Analysis of the National Socialist Machtübernahme." *European Studies Review* 11 (1981): 293–321.

―――, ed. *The Nazi Machtergreifung.* London, 1983.

―――, ed. *The Shaping of the Nazi State.* London, 1978.

―――, ed. *Unemployment and the Great Depression in Weimar Germany.* New York, 1986.

Stark, Gary D., and Lackner, Bede Karl, eds. *Essays on Culture and Society in Modern Germany.* College Station, Tex., 1982.

Stein, George H. *The Waffen-SS: Hitler's Elite Guard at War, 1939–1945.* Ithaca, N.Y., 1966.

Steinberg, Michael S. *Sabers and Brownshirts: The German Students' Path to National Socialism, 1918–1935.* Chicago, 1977.

Steinert, Marlis G. *Hitler's War and the Germans: Public Mood and Attitude during the Second World War.* Athens, Ohio, 1977.

Stephenson, Jill. *The Nazi Organisation of Women.* London, 1981.

―――. *Women in Nazi Society.* London, 1975.

―――. "Women's Labor Service in Nazi Germany." *Central European History* 15 (1982): 241–65.

Stokes, Lawrence D. "The Social Composition of the Nazi Party in Eutin 1925–32." *International Review of Social History* 23 (1978): 1–32.

———. "Otto Ohlendorf, the Sicherheitsdienst and Public Opinion in Nazi Germany." In *Police Forces in History,* edited by George L. Mosse.

Stolleis, M. "Gemeinschaft und Volksgemeinschaft: Zur juristischen Terminologie im Nationalsozialismus." *Vierteljahrshefte für Zeitgeschichte* 20 (1972): 16–38.

Stumpp, Karl. *The German-Russians: Two Centuries of Pioneering.* New York, 1967.

Sydnor, Charles W., Jr. "The History of the SS Totenkopfdivision and the Postwar Mythology of the Waffen SS." *Central European History* 6 (1973): 339–62.

———. *Soldiers of Destruction: The SS Death's Head Division, 1933–1945.* Princeton, N.J., 1977.

Tauber, Kurt. *Beyond Eagle and Swastika: German Nationalism since 1945.* 2 vols. Middletown, Conn., 1967.

Tenfelde, Klaus. "Schwierigkeiten mit dem Alltag." *Geschichte und Gesellschaft* 10 (1984): 376–94.

Tetens, T. H. *The New Germany and the Old Nazis.* New York, 1961.

Thompson, Larry V. "Lebensborn and the Eugenics Policy of the Reichsführer-SS." *Central European History* 4 (1971): 54–77.

Thorwald, Juergen. *Flight in the Winter.* New York, 1951.

Tiemann, Dieter. "Die deutsch-französischen Jugendbeziehungen der Zwischenkriegszeit." *Jahrbuch des Archivs der deutschen Jugendbewegung* 14 (1982–83): 47–64.

Toland, John. *The Last 100 Days.* New York, 1967.

Trevor-Roper, H. R. *The Last Days of Hitler.* 3d ed. New York, 1962.

Tuchel, Johannes. "Jugend, Alltag und Gewaltverbrechen im Dritten Reich: Zu neueren Arbeiten und Wiederauflagen über den Nationalsozialismus." *Internationale wissenschaftliche Korrespondenz zur Geschichte deutscher Arbeiterbewegung* 20 (1984): 44–49.

Turner, Henry A., Jr., ed. *Nazism and the Third Reich.* New York, 1972.

Ueberhorst, Horst. *Edmund Neuendorff: Turnführer ins Dritte Reich.* Frankfurt, 1970.

———. *Frisch, frei, stark und treu: Die Arbeitersportbewegung in Deutschland, 1893–1933.* Düsseldorf, 1973.

———. *Modern Olympics.* Cornwell, N.Y., 1977.

Walker, Lawrence D. "Le Concordat avec le Reich et les organisations de jeunesse." *Revue d'histoire de la deuxième guerre mondiale* 93 (1974): 3–16.

———. *Hitler Youth and Catholic Youth, 1933–1936: A Study in Totalitarian Conquest.* Washington, D.C., 1970.

———. "'Young Priests' as Opponents: Factors Associated with Clerical Opposition to the Nazis in Bavaria, 1933." *Catholic Historical Review* 65 (1979): 402–13.

Warlimont, Walter. *Inside Hitler's Headquarters, 1939–45.* Translated by R. H. Barry. New York, 1964.

Weber, Eugen. "Gymnastics and Sports in Fin-de-Siècle France: Opium of the Classes?" *The American Historical Review* 76 (1971): 70–98.

Weber, R. G. S. *The German Student Corps in the Third Reich.* New York, 1986.

Wegner, Bernd. "Die Garde des 'Führers' und die 'Feuerwehr' der Ostfront: Zur neueren Literatur über die Waffen-SS." *Militärgeschichtliche Mitteilungen* 23 (1978): 210–36.

―――. *Hitlers Politische Soldaten: Die Waffen-SS 1933–1945: Studien zu Leitbild, Struktur und Funktion einer nationalsozialistischen Elite*. 2d ed. Paderborn, 1983.

Wehler, H.-U. "Geschichte von unten gesehen." *Die Zeit*, May 10, 1985.

Weingartner, James J. *Crossroads of Death: The Story of the Malmédy Massacre and Trial*. Berkeley and Los Angeles, 1979.

―――. *Hitler's Guard: The Story of the Leibstandarte SS Adolf Hitler, 1933–1945*. Carbondale, Ill., 1974.

―――. "Law and Justice in the Nazi SS: The Case of Konrad Morgen." *Central European History* 16 (1983): 276–94.

―――. "Sepp Dietrich, Heinrich Himmler and the Leibstandarte SS Adolf Hitler, 1933–1938." *Central European History* 1 (1968): 264–84.

―――. "The SS Race and Settlement Office: Towards an *Orden* of Blood and Soil." *The Historian* 34 (1971): 62–77.

Weiss, Paul. *Sport: A Philosophic Inquiry*. Carbondale, Ill., 1969.

Werner, Karl Ferdinand. "On Some Examples of the National-Socialist View of History." *Journal of Contemporary History* 3 (1968): 193–206.

Wheeler-Bennett, J. W. *The Nemesis of Power: The German Army in Politics, 1918–1945*. New York, 1964.

White, Dan S. "Outpropagandizing the Nazis: The SPD's 'Front Generation' and the Politics of Mass Persuasion, 1930–1933." In *Proceedings of the Citadel Symposium on Hitler and the National Socialist Era. 24–25 April 1980*, edited by Michael B. Barrett.

Whiting, Charles. *Hitler's Werewolves: The Story of the Nazi Resistance Movement 1944–1945*. New York, 1972.

Willmot, Louise. "Women in the Third Reich: The Auxiliary Military Service Law of 1944." *German History* 2 (Summer 1985): 10–20.

Winkler, Heinrich August. "Der entbehrliche Stand: Zur Mittelstandspolitik im 'Dritten Reich.'" *Archiv für Sozialgeschichte* 17 (1977): 1–40.

―――. "Vom Mythos der Volksgemeinschaft." *Archiv für Sozialgeschichte* 17 (1977): 484–90.

Wolff, Jörg. "Hitlerjugend und Jugendgerichtsbarkeit 1933–1945." *Vierteljahrshefte für Zeitgeschichte* 33 (1985): 640–67.

Wolfson, Manfred. "Constraint and Choice in the SS Leadership." *The Western Political Quarterly* 18 (1965): 551–68.

Wortmann, Michael. *Baldur von Schirach: Hitlers Jugendführer*. Cologne, 1982.

Wright, Gordon. *The Ordeal of Total War 1939–1945*. New York, 1968.

Wunderlich, Frieda. *Farm Labor in Germany 1810–1945*. Princeton, N.J., 1961.

Ziegler, Herbert F. "The Demographic and Social Structure of the SS-Officer Corps in 1938—Some Preliminary Findings." In *Proceedings of the Citadel Symposium on Hitler and the National Socialist Era. 24–25 April 1980*, edited by Michael B. Barrett.

Zitelmann, Rainer. *Hitler: Selbstverständnis eines Revolutionärs*. Leamington Spa, 1986.

## Dissertations

Browder, George C. "Sipo and SD, 1931–1940: Formation of an Instrument of Power." Ph.D. diss., University of Wisconsin, 1968.

Gelwick, Robert A. "Personnel Policies and Procedures of the Waffen-SS." Ph.D. diss., University of Nebraska, 1971.

Lükemann, Ulf. "Der Reichsschatzmeister der NSDAP: Ein Beitrag zur inneren Parteistruktur." Ph.D. diss., Berlin, 1963.

Rempel, Gerhard. "The Misguided Generation: Hitler Youth and SS, 1933–1945." Ph.D. diss., University of Wisconsin, 1971.

Schmier, Louis. "Martin Bormann and the Nazi Party, 1941–1945." Ph.D. diss., University of North Carolina, 1968.

Schroeder, Richard. "The Hitler Youth as a Paramilitary Organization." Ph.D. diss., University of Chicago, 1975.

Shalka, Robert John. "The General-SS in Central Germany 1937–1939: A Social and Institutional Study of SS Main Sector Fulda-Werra." Ph.D. diss., University of Wisconsin, 1972. .

Taylor, John W. "Youth Welfare in Germany." Ph.D. diss., Columbia University, 1936.

Toboll, Dieter-Horst. "Evangelische Jugendbewegung 1919–1933, dargestellt an dem Bund deutscher Jugendvereine und dem Christdeutschen Bund." Ph.D. diss., Bonn University, 1971.

White, David O. "Hitler's Youth Leader: A Study of the Heroic Imagery in the Major Public Statements of Baldur von Schirach." Ph.D. diss., University of Oregon, 1970.

# Index

## 350 ▪ Index